Classroom Management

Classroom Management

CREATING A SUCCESSFUL K-12
LEARNING COMMUNITY

Sixth Edition

Paul R. Burden
Kansas State University

WILEY

SENIOR ACQUISITIONS EDITOR	Kate Bradford
PROJECT MANAGER	Gladys Soto
PROJECT SPECIALIST	Nichole Urban
CONTENT MANAGEMENT DIRECTOR	Lisa Wojcik
SENIOR CONTENT SPECIALIST	Nicole Repasky
PRODUCTION EDITOR	Padmapriya Soundararajan
PHOTO RESEARCHER	Billy Ray
COVER PHOTO CREDIT	© iofoto/Getty Images, Inc.

This book was set in 10/12 Times LT Std Roman by SPi Global and printed and bound by LSC Communications.

This book is printed on acid free paper.∞

Founded in 1807, John Wiley & Sons, Inc. has been a valued source of knowledge and understanding for more than 200 years, helping people around the world meet their needs and fulfill their aspirations. Our company is built on a foundation of principles that include responsibility to the communities we serve and where we live and work. In 2008, we launched a Corporate Citizenship Initiative, a global effort to address the environmental, social, economic, and ethical challenges we face in our business. Among the issues we are addressing are carbon impact, paper specifications and procurement, ethical conduct within our business and among our vendors, and community and charitable support. For more information, please visit our website: www.wiley.com/go/citizenship.

Evaluation copies are provided to qualified academics and professionals for review purposes only, for use in their courses during the next academic year. These copies are licensed and may not be sold or transferred to a third party. Upon completion of the review period, please return the evaluation copy to Wiley. Return instructions and a free of charge return shipping label are available at: www.wiley.com/go/returnlabel. If you have chosen to adopt this textbook for use in your course, please accept this book as your complimentary desk copy. Outside of the United States, please contact your local sales representative.

ISBN: 9781119352891 (PBK)

Library of Congress Cataloging in Publication Data:

Names: Burden, Paul R.
Title: Classroom management : creating a successful k-12 learning community / Paul R. Burden.
Description: Sixth edition. | Hoboken, NJ : John Wiley, [2017] | Includes
    bibliographical references and index.
Identifiers: LCCN 2016036074 | ISBN 9781119352891 (pbk.)
Subjects: LCSH: Classroom management—United States. | School
    discipline—United States.
Classification: LCC LB3013 .B873 2016 | DDC 371.102/4—dc23 LC record available at https://lccn.loc.gov/2016036074

The inside back cover will contain printing identification and country of origin if omitted from this page. In addition, if the ISBN on the back cover differs from the ISBN on this page, the one on the back cover is correct.

10 9 8 7 6 5 4 3 2 1

Contents

About the Author

Paul R. Burden is an assistant dean and professor in the College of Education at Kansas State University, Manhattan, where he has supervised student teachers and taught courses on teaching methods, classroom management and discipline, foundations of education, and instructional leadership. Previously, he was a middle-level science teacher in Buffalo, New York, and later earned his doctoral degree at the Ohio State University. He received the College of Education's Outstanding Undergraduate Teaching Award at Kansas State University and the Distinguished Service award from the National Staff Development Council.

His publications include *Methods for Effective Teaching* (Pearson, 2016), *Countdown to the First Day of School* (2006, National Education Association), *Powerful Classroom Management Strategies: Motivating Students to Learn* (2000, Corwin Press), as well as *Establishing Career Ladders in Teaching* (1987, Charles C Thomas Publishers). He served for 11 years as the editor of the *Journal of Staff Development*, a quarterly journal sponsored by the National Staff Development Council, and has presented over 70 papers at regional and national educational conferences in addition to authoring 15 articles and 4 book chapters.

Married with three children, Dr. Burden enjoys traveling with his family and working on genealogy. He can be contacted at Kansas State University, 7 Bluemont Hall, Manhattan, Kansas 66506; (785) 532-5595; burden@ksu.edu.

Preface

This sixth edition of *Classroom Management* has been written to guide teachers and prospective teachers as they create a positive classroom community, with the involvement and cooperation of the students. Fundamental principles of classroom management and discipline are presented, along with ways to involve students in the creation of their learning environment.

The book is a scholarly synthesis of the research base on classroom management and discipline, yet is written and formatted in a way that is easy to read, understand, and apply. It carries a practical, realistic view of teaching with the content being organized in a logical, sequential order. The content is applicable for teachers at all levels—elementary, middle level, and high school.

Intended Audience

This book is especially appropriate as the sole book for an undergraduate course on classroom management and discipline or for a seminar on student teaching or professional development. It may be used as a supplementary book to another textbook in educational psychology or teaching methods courses. Additionally, the book may be used in graduate classes, seminars, and staff development programs for in-service teachers. The book may be seen as a handbook for future reference due to its comprehensive coverage of the issues and its use of lists, tables, and figures for recommended practice. The information provides a foundation for decision making.

New to This Edition

- A number of significant changes were made in this new edition, including the following:

  - Added a new feature—Classroom Case Study—in each chapter to engage the reader in decision making about the chapter content

  - Updated content in sections in several chapters:

    - Management and Instructional Variables (in Chapter 1)

    - Student and Teacher Perceptions of Classroom Management (in Chapter 1)

    - Building Caring Relationships (in Chapter 1)

    - Communicating Caring and Support (in Chapter 5)

    - Provide Assistance with the Response to Intervention (RTI) (in Chapter 7)

    - Getting to Know Your Students (in Chapter 7)

    - Bullying (in Chapter 9)

    - Working with Colleagues (in Chapter 11)

    - Collaboration Skills and Dispositions (in Chapter 11)

- Consolidated content on students with challenging circumstances and moved it to Chapter 7

- Consolidated content on planning for motivation and moved it to Chapter 8

- Restructured the sections on discipline interventions and the three-step response plan (in Chapter 9)

- Updated the "Voices from the Classroom" features, which include teacher quotes, many of them from urban districts, with a balance of elementary and middle/high school teachers

- Updated the "What Would You Decide?" features with content to engage the reader in classroom-related scenarios about the chapter content

- Added 45 new and current references, updated 58 existing references, and removed old references

Special Features

Classroom Management: Creating a Successful K–12 Learning Community has several important features that make it both instructor and reader friendly.

- *Standards Tables.* Three tables of professional standards can be found on the pages after the preface.

- *Objectives.* Each chapter begins with a list of objectives to identify expected reader outcomes.

- *Chapter Outline.* Each chapter begins with an outline of headings and subheadings to serve as an advance organizer for the chapter content.

- *Voices from the Classroom.* Several of these features are included in each chapter to provide descriptions by real elementary, middle school, and high school teachers about ways they deal with particular topics addressed in the chapter. These teachers come from all parts of the country and all different community sizes. There are over 50 Voices from the Classroom features, evenly balanced among elementary and middle/high school levels, including many from urban districts.

- *Classroom Case Studies.* Each chapter includes a case study describing a situation that a teacher might encounter. Two or three questions following each case study require the reader to reflect on and apply chapter concepts.

- *What Would You Decide?* Several of these features are placed in each chapter to engage the reader in the content. Each one includes several sentences describing a classroom situation concerning an issue in the chapter, followed by a few questions asking the reader to make decisions about the application of the concepts.

- *Major Concepts.* At the end of each chapter, a list of major concepts serves as a summary of the significant chapter ideas.

- *Discussion/Reflective Questions.* Questions at the end of each chapter promote discussion and reflection in a classroom or seminar in which a number of people are considering the chapter's content.

- *Suggested Activities.* Supplemental activities are suggested at the end of each chapter to enable the reader to investigate and apply issues addressed in the chapter.

- *Further Reading.* An annotated list of recommended readings at the end of each chapter suggests readings for further enrichment.

- *References.* All citations made in the book are included in a reference section at the end of the book to show the source of the research base.

Relating This Book to Standards

Content in this book relates to the professional standards of many agencies. Standards are used to guide the development of new teachers, help in-service teachers improve their performance, and assess both teacher preparation and teacher performance. Many teacher education programs are designed around the Interstate New Teacher Assessment and Support Consortium (InTASC) standards. Those standards were updated in 2011, so states using those standards will likely adjust their teaching standards accordingly. Many states require a passing score on the Principles of Learning and Teaching test (Praxis II) before granting a teaching license. The Praxis III standards (which are consistent with Danielson's Framework for Teaching domains) are used to assess and improve the teaching of in-service teachers. A brief description of the standards is provided here, and tables of those standards follow the preface.

InTASC Standards

The Interstate New Teacher Assessment and Support Consortium (INTASC) was created in 1987 as a consortium of state education agencies and national educational organizations dedicated to the reform of the preparation, licensing, and ongoing professional development of teachers. Its primary constituency is state education agencies responsible for teacher licensing, program approval, and professional development. Its work is guided by one basic premise: *An effective teacher must be able to integrate content knowledge with the specific strengths and needs of students to assure that all students learn and perform at high levels.* With the 2011 updating of the standards, the Interstate Teacher Assessment and Support Consortium removed the word *new* from its name and made the *n* in its acronym lowercase (now it is InTASC). More information can be found at this website: http://www.ccsso.org/Resources/Programs/Interstate_Teacher_Assessment_Consortium_%28InTASC%29.html.

Praxis Series

The Praxis Series is a set of tests developed and disseminated by the Educational Testing Service (ETS) for assessing skills and knowledge of each stage of a beginning teacher's career, from entry into teacher education to actual classroom performance. More information about the Praxis Series can be found at this website: http://www.ets.org/praxis. There are three parts of the Praxis Series:

- **Praxis I:** Preprofessional Skills Tests (PPST). These academic skills tests are designed to be taken early in a student's college career to measure reading, writing, and mathematics skills.

- **Praxis II:** Subject Assessments. There are several assessments available in the Praxis II series, and they measure a teacher candidate's knowledge of the subjects they will teach, as well as general and subject-specific pedagogical skills and knowledge. One of these assessments is the Principles of Learning and Teaching (PLT) test, which many states require teachers to pass for their licensure.

- **Praxis III:** Classroom Performance Assessments. These assessments are conducted for beginning teachers in classroom settings. Assessment of teaching practice is through direct observation of classroom practice, a review of documentation prepared by the teacher, and semistructured interviews. The framework for knowledge and skills for these assessments consists of 19 assessment criteria organized within four categories: planning and preparation, the classroom environment, instruction, and professional responsibilities. Charlotte Danielson's (2007) *Enhancing Professional Practice: A Framework for Teaching* is based on the categories of the Praxis III Classroom Performance Assessments.

This *Classroom Management* book is not intended to address the preprofessional skills of reading, writing, and mathematics in Praxis I. However, it is designed to address the Praxis II test on Principles of Learning and Teaching and the Praxis III classroom performance criteria areas.

Acknowledgments

Many people provided support and guidance as I prepared this book. A very special acknowledgment goes to my wife Jennie who was understanding during the times I was hidden away at my office working on the revised manuscript. The editors and staff at Wiley facilitated the preparation and refinement of this book. A number of classroom teachers provided descriptions of their professional practice, which are included in the Voices from the Classroom features in each chapter. The experiences that these teachers share help illustrate the issues and bring life to the content. In addition, Sandi Faulconer provided valuable assistance at Kansas State University in preparing several tables and helping coordinate a number of activities.

Paul Burden

Standards

InTASC Model Core Teaching Standards

The following table indicates how the 2011 Interstate Teacher Assessment and Support Consortium (InTASC) model core teaching standards are addressed in this book.

THE LEARNER AND LEARNING	Chapter Coverage
1. **Learner Development** Understands how learners grow and develop, recognizing that patterns of learning and development vary individually within and across the cognitive, linguistic, social, emotional, and physical areas, and designs and implements developmentally appropriate and challenging learning experiences.	1, 2, 3, 7, 8
2. **Learning Differences** Uses understanding of individual differences and diverse cultures and communities to ensure inclusive learning environments that enable each learner to meet high standards.	7
3. **Learning Environments** Works with others to create environments that support individual and collaborative learning, and that encourage positive social interaction, active engagement in learning, and self-motivation.	5, 6, 7, 8, 9, 10

CONTENT KNOWLEDGE	
4. **Content Knowledge** Understands the central concepts, tools of inquiry, and structures of the discipline(s) he or she teaches and creates learning experiences that make these aspects of the discipline accessible and meaningful for learners to assure mastery of the content.	3, 8
5. **Application of Content** Understands how to connect concepts and use differing perspectives to engage learners in critical thinking, creativity, and collaborative problem solving related to authentic local and global issues.	3, 8

INSTRUCTIONAL PRACTICE	
6. **Assessment** Understands and uses multiple methods of assessment to engage learners in their own growth, to monitor learner progress, and to guide the teacher's and learner's decision making.	3, 7, 8
7. **Planning for Instruction** Plans instruction that supports every student in meeting rigorous learning goals by drawing upon knowledge of content areas, curriculum, cross-disciplinary skills, and pedagogy, as well as knowledge of learners and the community context.	3, 5, 7, 8
8. **Instructional Strategies** Understands and uses a variety of instructional strategies to encourage learners to develop deep understanding of content areas and their connections, and to build skills to apply knowledge in meaningful ways.	2, 8

(continued)

PROFESSIONAL RESPONSIBILITY

9. Professional Learning and Ethical Practice Engages in ongoing professional learning and uses evidence to continually evaluate his/her practice, particularly the effects of his/her choices and actions on others (learners, families, other professionals, and the community), and adapts practice to meet the needs of each learner.	1, 2
10. Leadership and Collaboration Seeks appropriate leadership roles and opportunities to take responsibility for student learning, to collaborate with learners, families, colleagues, other school professionals, and community members to ensure learner growth, and to advance the profession.	11

Praxis II: Standards for Principles of Learning and Teaching

The following table indicates how the Praxis II standards for the Principles of Learning and Teaching are addressed in this book.

PRAXIS II Standard	Chapter Coverage
1. Students as Learners Student development and the learning process Students as diverse learners Student motivation and the learning environment	1–8
2. Instruction and Assessment Instructional strategies Planning instruction Assessment strategies	2, 3, 7, 8
3. Communication Techniques Basic, effective verbal and nonverbal communication techniques Effect of cultural and gender differences on communications in the classroom Types of communications and interactions that can stimulate discussion in different ways for particular purposes	2, 5, 6, 7, 8, 9, 10
4. Profession and Community The reflective practitioner The larger community	1, 2, 11

Praxis III: Standards for Classroom Performance Assessments

The following table indicates how the Praxis III standards are addressed in this book. Charlotte Danielson's (2007) *Enhancing Professional Practice: A Framework for Teaching* is based on the categories of the Praxis III Classroom Performance Assessments.

PRAXIS III Standard	Chapter Coverage
1. **Planning and Preparation** Demonstrating knowledge of content and pedagogy Demonstrating knowledge of students Selecting instructional goals Demonstrating knowledge of resources Designing coherent instruction Designing student assessments	1, 2, 3, 7, 8
2. **The Classroom Environment** Creating an environment of respect and rapport Establishing a culture for learning Managing classroom procedures Managing student behavior Organizing physical space	1–6, 8–11
3. **Instruction** Communicating with students Using questioning and discussion techniques Engaging students in learning Using assessment in instruction Demonstrating flexibility and responsiveness	5, 6, 7, 8
4. **Professional Responsibilities** Reflecting on teaching Maintaining accurate records Communicating with families Participating in a professional community Growing and developing professionally Showing professionalism	1, 2, 3, 4, 8, 11

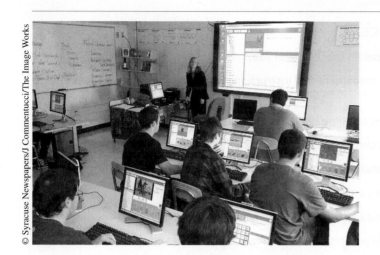

Understanding Management and Discipline in the Classroom

CHAPTER OBJECTIVES

This chapter provides information that will help you:

- Describe and apply the management and instructional variables for effective classroom management.

- Develop and nurture caring relationships in the classroom.

- Describe the role of classroom management in creating a learning community.

- Identify the areas of responsibility in classroom management and discipline.

- Determine what constitutes order in the classroom.

- Describe the types and causes of student misbehavior.

- Apply principles for working with students to create a positive learning environment.

What do award-winning teachers do that make them so popular and successful? Do they jazz up the curriculum in some way? Do they use especially creative instructional approaches? Do they warm up to the students as if they were their own children? Do they add some magic or sparkle to the classroom experience? The answer is probably a little of each of those things. But it likely goes deeper than that.

Successful teachers are often very effective managers of the classroom environment. They create a positive learning community where students are actively involved in their own learning and in the management of the classroom. They organize the physical environment, manage student behavior, create a respectful environment, facilitate instruction, promote safety and wellness, and interact with others when needed. All of these actions relate to classroom management. The main objective is to create a positive learning community and then to take steps to maintain that positive environment by guiding and correcting student behavior.

What Is Classroom Management?

Classroom management involves teacher actions to create a learning environment that encourages positive social interaction, active engagement in learning, and self-motivation.

Several key questions come to mind regarding classroom management.

- How can the physical environment be organized?

- How can the school year begin effectively? What rules and procedures are appropriate?

- How can students be held academically accountable?

- How can appropriate behavior be encouraged and supported?

- How might order be restored if there are disruptions?

- How can class time and instruction be managed effectively?

- How can the safety of students be assured?

All of these issues are part of classroom management.

Before discussing these areas of responsibility in classroom management, this section explores management and instructional variables, student and teacher perceptions of classroom management, and caring relationships.

Management and Instructional Variables

In their review of the process-outcome research on classroom management, Gettinger and Kohler (2006) reported that effective teaching is related to a teacher's ability to use appropriate management strategies while simultaneously providing high-quality instruction. These teacher behaviors contribute to achievement gains as well as other benefits such as task engagement, active learning, motivation, and positive attitudes that prevent misbehavior. According to Gettinger and Kohler, the following classroom management and instructional variables are designed to promote positive behavior and academic gains:

Classroom Management Variables:

- Classroom rules
- Smooth transitions between activities
- Beginning-of-the-year management activities
- Efficient use of learning time
- Monitoring student performance
- Communicating awareness of the classroom behavior

Instructional Variables:

- Teacher-directed learning
- High level of active student involvement or responding
- Guided student practice to promote success
- Flexible instruction to match student needs
- Cooperative learning strategies
- Humor and enthusiasm incorporated into teaching
- Use of motivational strategies that foster goal orientation

Elements of effective teaching and classroom management derived from the process-outcome research serve as the foundation for many teacher professional development programs and preservice training programs. In fact, that research served as the basis for many of the professional teaching standards outlined on the standards tables displayed in this book just after the Preface. This process-outcome research attests to the important role of the teacher in creating and maintaining a positive classroom environment that promotes academic and social competence.

Student and Teacher Perceptions of Classroom Management

Hoy and Weinstein (2006) reviewed the research concerning student and teacher perceptions of classroom management, and they found these perceptions differed.

Student Perceptions

The research demonstrated that students who like their teachers and perceive them to be supportive are more likely to engage in prosocial, responsible behavior; to adhere to classroom rules and norms; and to engage in academic activities. Thus, students perceive "good" teachers as worthy of respect, cooperation, and participation. Three factors were central to student perceptions of "good" teachers:

1. Ability to establish caring relationships with students

2. Ability to exercise authority without being rigid, threatening, or punitive

3. Ability to make learning fun

For students, good classroom management requires a fair and reasonable system of classroom rules and procedures that protect and respect students. Teachers are expected to care for the students, their learning, and their personal lives before the students will respect and cooperate with the teachers. Students want teachers to maintain order without being mean or punitive. As they mature, students value choices and chances for responsibilities; they do not want to feel coerced or controlled.

Teacher Perceptions

In contrast to student perceptions, teachers are more focused on order and on academic concerns; they want students to cooperate in class activities and perform well on assessments. Compliance is a common teacher goal for disciplinary interventions. Teachers seem to believe that students need to earn their respect, relationship, concern, and interest. Choices and autonomy support come with successful self-regulation and not before. Some teachers believe that being "mean" or firm may be necessary, in the beginning at least, to establish authority (bringing to mind the adage of "Don't smile until Christmas").

Practical Implications

The differences in student and teacher perceptions concerning classroom management have implications for practice. First, teachers must recognize that to teach well, they must also put effort into creating positive relationships with students. The research demonstrates the link between positive student–teacher relationships and students' motivation to become engaged with academic activities. Second, teachers should exercise their authority in fair, respectful ways, and not through the use of punitive techniques that cause public humiliation. Students cite the importance of setting limits and enforcing expectations, but in reasonable ways. Third, teachers need to acknowledge the inseparable relationship between classroom management and instruction. Lessons that encourage active student participation and address student interests, needs, and backgrounds will foster academic achievement as well as the goodwill, respect, and cooperation that are needed for a productive learning environment.

Building Caring Relationships

Elias and Schwab (2006) reviewed the research on social and emotional learning and its relationship to classroom management. Their findings confirm the importance of developing caring relationships in the classroom to support instruction and classroom management.

Developing a supportive community in the classroom helps to impart a sense of each student's belonging, to alleviate students' social anxieties and frustrations, to motivate students to comply with teacher requests, and to act prosocially with peers. Consequently, the level of respect for teachers and students increases, negative and aggressive social behaviors are reduced, and students are more likely to comply with the rules. Because of this, building caring relationships

VOICES FROM THE CLASSROOM   What Is Classroom Management?

Claudia Arguello Coca, fifth-grade teacher, Las Cruces, New Mexico

When I began teaching 10 years ago, I thought classroom management meant being the one in control of my class. Control was the number one objective for me, because then I knew that my students would be safe, would receive the best instruction, and would be well behaved (thus making me look good). But every approach I used to control the environment did not work.

Gradually, I learned that children will follow you if you encourage them and take the time to catch them doing great things. Some flexibility is also needed. Students want to impress you and will do anything you ask if you manage your class by focusing on hardworking students and positive behaviors. These lessons have allowed me to have great success with my students.

I always keep in mind that my students are little children. I make a huge effort to treat them like little children, offer them kind words, create a safe and predictable environment, and provide a fun learning stage. I have one rule for myself—always talk to my students as if their parents were standing behind them. When I work with my students, I want us to work together cooperatively. This only happens when my students feel safe and comfortable with me.

is the first step in the promotion of responsible behavior and the prevention of misbehavior (Davis, Summers, & Miller, 2012).

Relationships in the classroom fall into three types: teacher–student, student–student, and the classroom community.

Teacher-Student Relationships

When students sense that a teacher cares for them, they see the teacher as more credible and as an ally. This increases motivation to follow directions, to adhere to rules, and to put in effort for classroom activities. Teachers can express caring and respect for students by being welcoming, learning about students' lives, being sensitive to students' concerns, establishing and enforcing clear expectations for behavior, being fair, welcoming students' input, being like a real person (as well as a teacher), being aware of the student culture, promoting autonomy, being inclusive, searching for students' strengths, and developing communication skills (Jones, 2011; Weinstein & Novodvorsky, 2015).

Student-Student Relationships and the Classroom Community

Teachers can establish the conditions for social interaction and can intervene to help these relationships develop positively in several ways. First, teachers can begin the year by helping students feel comfortable with each other in the classroom. This can be done with group-building activities, opportunities to share personal experiences and interests, and establishing an ethic of teamwork and helping one another with everyday tasks and problems. Second, teachers can involve students in deciding what rules should govern the classroom. Third, teachers can discuss, teach, and model a problem-solving approach to understanding and resolving personal mistakes and dilemmas (Garrett, 2014).

Areas of Responsibility

An effective classroom manager handles the following seven areas of responsibility in classroom management and discipline (see Table 1.1):

1. **Select a philosophical model of classroom management and discipline.** A number of educators have proposed certain models of classroom management and discipline, such as teaching with love and logic, cooperative discipline, discipline with dignity, and assertive

■ TABLE 1.1 **Areas of Responsibility in Classroom Management and Discipline**

Classroom management involves teacher actions to create a learning environment that encourages positive social interaction, active engagement in learning, and self-motivation. An effective classroom manager handles these areas of responsibility:

1. Select a philosophical model of classroom management and discipline.
2. Organize the physical environment.
3. Manage student behavior.
4. Create a respectful, supportive learning environment.
5. Manage and facilitate instruction.
6. Promote classroom safety and wellness.
7. Interact with colleagues, families, and others to achieve classroom management objectives.

discipline (see Chapter 2). These models reflect various philosophical views of student development, teaching and learning, and classroom management. Viewing these proposed models on a continuum, they range from low teacher control to high teacher control.

These theoretical models are useful to teachers because they offer a basis for analyzing, understanding, and managing student and teacher behavior. With an understanding of these varied theoretical approaches, you can assess your position on these issues and then select a philosophical model that is consistent with your beliefs. The techniques you use to manage student behavior should be consistent with your beliefs about how students learn and develop.

2. **Organize the physical environment.** The way the desks, tables, and other classroom materials are arranged affects instruction and influences order in the classroom (see Chapter 3). To create an effective learning environment, you will need to organize several aspects of the physical space. First, you will need to arrange the floor space by the placement of student desks, the teacher's desk, bookcases, filing cabinets, tables, and activity centers. Second, you will need to decide how to store a number of materials, including textbooks and resource books, frequently used instructional materials, teacher supplies and instructional materials, equipment, and infrequently used materials. Finally, you will need to decide how to use bulletin boards and wall space. Decisions in all of these areas will determine how you will organize the physical environment for teaching and learning.

3. **Manage student behavior.** Guidelines are needed to promote order in the classroom and to provide a conducive learning environment (see Chapter 4). Rules and procedures support teaching and learning and provide students with clear expectations and well-defined norms. This, in turn, helps create a safe, secure atmosphere for learning.

Rules are general codes of conduct that are intended to guide individual student behavior in an attempt to promote positive interaction and avoid disruptive behavior. *Procedures* are approved ways to achieve specific tasks in the classroom, such as handing in completed work or sharpening a pencil.

When misbehavior occurs, teachers need to respond in an effort to get the student back on task and to maintain order in the classroom. A three-step response plan is discussed in Chapter 9, including providing assistance to get the student back on task as the first step, followed by the use of mild responses such as nonverbal and verbal signals, and then ending with moderate responses such as withdrawing privileges or changing the seat assignment. Special approaches are often needed to deal with challenging students (see Chapter 10).

To establish order, you must teach, demonstrate, establish, and enforce classroom procedures and routines at the start of the year. Successful classroom managers hover over activities at the beginning of the year and usher them along until students have learned the work system.

4. **Create a respectful, supportive learning environment.** There are many facets to creating a favorable learning environment, but it is vital for a positive learning community. First, teachers can take a number of actions to establish a cooperative, responsible classroom by developing positive teacher–student relationships, promoting students' self-esteem, and building group cohesiveness (see Chapter 5). These actions will help create an environment where students feel valued and comfortable, thus setting the stage for teaching and learning. Second, teachers can focus student attention on appropriate classroom behavior by helping students assume responsibility for their behavior, by maintaining student attention and involvement, and by reinforcing desired behaviors (see Chapter 5).

    Third, a comprehensive plan can be developed to motivate students to learn, involving decisions about instructional tasks, feedback and evaluation, and academic and behavioral expectations (see Chapter 8). Finally, teachers can be most effective in creating a respectful, supportive learning environment when they have an understanding of the diverse learners in their classroom and of students with special needs (see Chapter 7).

5. **Manage and facilitate instruction.** Certain factors in a lesson have a bearing on classroom order, and teachers need to take these factors into account when planning lessons (see Chapter 8). These include decisions about the degree of structure of the lesson, the type of instructional groups to use, and the means of holding the students academically accountable.

    There are also certain actions that teachers often take at the beginning, middle, and end of a lesson that affect the order of the classroom. These include actions such as taking attendance, giving directions, distributing materials, handling transitions, summarizing the lesson, and preparing to leave. Collectively, these instructional management skills help manage and facilitate instruction while also influencing classroom order.

6. **Promote classroom safety and wellness.** Students need to feel physically and emotionally safe before they can give their full attention to the instructional tasks. Strategies used to manage student behavior, create a supportive classroom, and manage and facilitate instruction all contribute to classroom safety and wellness. In addition, teachers sometimes need to take actions to solve problems and conflicts that threaten classroom order and the learning environment. For that reason, it is helpful to have a set of tools such as dealing with conflict resolution and anger management to solve problems (see Chapter 10).

    Students who are considered difficult or challenging may threaten the sense of safety and wellness in the classroom. Their actions may cause other students to take guarded or even confrontational actions in response to difficult students. For that reason, teachers need to be prepared to deal with challenging students in constructive ways (Chapter 10).

7. **Interact with colleagues, families, and others to achieve classroom management objectives.** Working with families is another means to help maintain order in the classroom (see Chapter 11). When families and teachers communicate and get along together, students are more likely to receive the needed guidance and support and will probably have more self-control in the classroom. In addition, teachers may need to consult and interact with colleagues and others when difficulties occur with classroom management and student behavior.

A Community of Learners

Over the years, the way teachers have gone about instruction has changed as more is known about the nature of teaching and learning. In recent years, more emphasis has been placed on building learning communities in the classroom because students appear to be most successful in that environment. Problems with student misbehavior are also minimized in an environment where students are actively involved in their classroom and their instruction.

A learning community is designed to help all students feel safe, respected, and valued in order to learn new skills. Anxiety, discomfort, and fear are incompatible with the learning process and make teaching and learning difficult. Successful classrooms are those in which students feel supported in their learning, are willing to take risks, are challenged to become fully human with one another, and are open to new possibilities.

With the increasing diversity in classrooms, the need to create supportive classroom communities becomes even more important. Teachers must identify community building as a high priority if we are to have classrooms that include diverse students and make them welcome, appreciated, and valued members of the classroom environment. Actions can be taken to build an inclusive classroom learning community.

In *Because We Can Change the World*, Sapon-Shevin (2010) identified five characteristics of learning communities:

1. **Security.** A safe, secure community allows for growth and exploration. A nurturing community is a place where it is safe to be yourself, take risks, ask for help and support, and delight in accomplishments. A safe environment helps protect students from distractions and disruptions that interfere with the learning process.

2. **Open communication.** In a cohesive environment, there is open communication. All forms of communication—oral, written, artistic, and nonverbal—are encouraged. In safe, accepting environments, students' individual differences and needs are openly acknowledged. Students share freely what is happening, what they need, and what they are worried about. Since all students have the right to feel safe, for example, open communication should be encouraged to address the concerns.

3. **Mutual liking.** In supportive classroom communities, students are encouraged to know and like their classmates. Opportunities are provided for students to interact with one another, and students are given many chances and strategies for learning to see and say nice things about classmates.

4. **Shared goals or objectives.** Cooperative communities are those in which students work together to reach a shared goal or objective. This can be achieved with whole-class projects where students work toward a goal while interacting and supporting one another.

5. **Connectedness and trust.** In learning communities, students feel a part of the whole. They know that they are needed, valued members of the group. They know that others are depending on them to put forth their best effort. Trust and connectedness mean sharing the good things as well as any concerns or problems.

VOICES FROM THE CLASSROOM   Creating a Peaceful Classroom Community

Sheila Shelby, fifth-grade teacher, Columbia, South Carolina

Determining rules and procedures for the classroom is essential for effective classroom management to be sustained throughout the school year. At the beginning of school, I spend a great deal of time working with students to create an accepting and supportive learning community.

During this time, I read *Peace Begins with You* by Katherine Scholes. As I read the book, students are asked to listen for ways that we can be peacemakers. Afterward, we discuss these ideas and generate a list of four or five ways that we can be peacemakers in our own classroom community. This list has included items such as helping our classmates and teachers, listening and following directions, having and showing good manners, sharing, and resolving conflicts.

To create a learning community, teachers often plan lessons designed to involve students in cooperative learning activities. These activities seem to have three elements that are critical to their success: face-to-face interactions, a feeling of positive interdependence, and a feeling of individual accountability. In addition, it is necessary to teach students social skills and to process group functioning for these learning activities to be successful.

Teachers also need to arrange the physical environment for instruction, guide and correct behavior, and create a supportive classroom. All of these responsibilities for creating a learning community relate to classroom management. In *Widening the Circle*, Sapon-Shevin (2007) describes ways to build inclusive classroom communities.

Understanding Misbehavior

Even with an effective management system in place, students may lose interest in the lesson and get off task. You must be prepared to respond with appropriate strategies to restore order. To provide a context for your decision making in this area, you should first understand order in the classroom, misbehavior in context, the types and causes of misbehavior, and the degree of severity that is exhibited.

It is important first to recognize that the best way to deal with discipline problems is to avoid them in the first place. You should develop challenging, interesting, and exciting lessons and treat students with dignity and respect. If misbehavior then occurs, you can consider the guidelines and principles presented in Chapter 9 for dealing with inappropriate behavior.

Order in the Classroom

A learning community needs to have order for students to be successful. *Order* means that students are following the actions necessary for a particular classroom event to be successful; students are focused on the instructional tasks and are not misbehaving. Establishing and maintaining order is an important part of classroom management.

It is useful to distinguish the difference between off-task behavior and misbehavior. *Off-task behavior* includes student actions that are not focused on the instructional activities, yet would not be considered to be disruptive or be defined as misbehavior. Off-task behavior includes daydreaming, writing notes or doodling, or not paying attention.

Misbehavior includes behavior that interferes with your teaching, interferes with the rights of others to learn, is psychologically or physically unsafe, or destroys property (Levin & Nolan, 2014). Classroom order is threatened by misbehavior. *Discipline* is the act of responding to misbehaving students in an effort to restore order.

There are several important issues concerning order.

1. **A minimal level of order is necessary for instruction to occur.** Order can be established for instruction by actions such as selecting rules and procedures, encouraging and reinforcing appropriate behavior, reacting to misbehavior, and managing instructional tasks. With many students off task, instruction cannot occur.

2. **Student involvement in learning tasks is affected by order in the classroom.** An effective classroom manager places emphasis on managing the group rather than managing individual students. When there is order in the classroom, then individual students can become engaged in the instructional tasks.

3. **Student cooperation is necessary to establish order.** Order in classrooms is achieved *with* students and depends on their willingness to be part of the sequence of events. Students in a learning community want to cooperate because they see the benefits for them.

4. **Expectations for order are affected by a number of classroom variables.** Teacher expectations for order may vary depending on factors such as the type of instructional activities, the maturity level of the students, the time of day, the time in the lesson, and the particular students involved. For example, a teacher might not enforce a certain rule at the end of a class period when students are gathering their books and materials in the same way as when a discussion is underway in the middle of the class period.

Misbehavior in Context

Students who are off task are not performing the planned instructional activity. They may be pausing to think about an issue, daydreaming, or doing other things that are nondisruptive but prohibit them from being engaged in the instructional activities. Students who are off task need to be addressed differently than students who are purposely misbehaving and interfering with the academic activities. In such cases, you may need to intervene to stop the misbehavior.

Recognize that your decisions about interventions are complex judgments about the act, the student, and the circumstances at a particular moment in classroom time. Some student actions are clearly misbehavior and require teacher intervention. In many cases, however, the situation is not quite so simple. The key to understanding misbehavior is to view what students do in the context of the classroom structure. Not every infraction of a rule is necessarily misbehavior. For instance, inattention in the last few minutes of a class session will often be tolerated because the lesson is coming to an end. However, you would most likely intervene when inattention is evident earlier in the class.

Misbehavior, then, needs to be seen as "action in context" and requires interpretation based on what the teacher knows about the likely configuration of events. You need to make reliable judgments about the probable consequences of students' actions in different situations. Consistency in your response does not mean that you need to behave in the same way every time, but rather, that your judgments are reliable and consistent.

Types of Misbehavior

Misbehavior includes behavior that interferes with your teaching, interferes with the rights of others to learn, is psychologically or physically unsafe, or destroys property. This misbehavior may show up in the classroom in a number of ways, as indicated in the following categories:

- **Needless talk.** Student talks during instructional time about topics unrelated to the lesson or talks when should be silent.

- **Annoying others.** Student teases, calls names, or bothers others.

- **Moving around the room.** Student moves around the room without permission or goes to areas where not permitted.

- **Noncompliance.** Student does not do what is requested, breaks rules, argues, makes excuses, delays, does the opposite of what is asked.

- **Disruption.** Student talks or laughs inappropriately, hums or makes noises, gets into things, causes "accidents."

- **Aggressive actions.** Student shows hostility toward others, pushes or fights, verbally abuses, is cruel to others, damages property, steals others' property.

- **Defiance of authority.** Student talks back to the teacher, is hostile to comply with the teacher's requests.

Causes of Misbehavior

One way to understand classroom control is to determine why students misbehave. In some cases, the reasons are complex and personal and perhaps beyond your comprehension or control. However, a number of causes of misbehavior can be addressed directly by the teacher.

1. **Health factors.** Student behavior problems may be related to health factors. Lack of sleep, an allergy, illness, or an inadequate diet may greatly affect the student's ability to complete assignments or interact with others. For some children, sugar has an effect on their behavior and may result in hyperactivity. Physical impairments such as a vision or hearing loss, paralysis, or a severe physiological disorder may also contribute to behavior problems.

2. **Neurological conditions.** Some students may have a mental disorder that affects their behavior in some way. For example, attention deficit disorder is a mental disorder in which the area of the brain that controls motor activity doesn't work as it should. This is among the most common childhood mental disorders and affects 9 percent of American children age 13 to 18 years, according to the National Institute of Mental Health (2013). Such students may be inattentive (are easily distracted, don't follow directions well, shift from one unfinished task to another, and seem not to be listening), hyperactive (are talkative or fidgety), and impulsive (don't wait their turn, blurt out answers, and engage in dangerous activities without considering the consequences). Children born with fetal alcohol syndrome may be hyperactive or impulsive, and crack babies (children born to women who were using crack cocaine during pregnancy) may exhibit similar behaviors.

3. **Medication or drugs.** Medication or drugs, whether legal or illegal, may also be a factor. Over-the-counter medicine for nasal congestion, for example, may cause a student to be less alert than usual. Alcohol or drug abuse also may contribute to unusual behavior at school.

4. **Influences from the home or society.** Conditions in the student's home may be related to behavior problems. Student behavior problems may be associated with a lack of adequate clothing or housing, parental supervision and types of discipline, home routines, or significant events such as divorce or the death of a friend or relative. Factors in the community or in society also may contribute to student behavior problems. There has been considerable

---

VOICES FROM THE CLASSROOM   Hidden Causes of Misbehavior

Kurt Graber, high school science teacher, Dallas, Texas

Some of our students have challenging and even turbulent lives. It can be both emotionally and physiologically difficult for them to achieve a state of readiness to learn when they arrive in our classrooms. We may see the negative classroom behaviors, but we sometimes do not see the causes of their misbehavior. When we are able to identify the cause of the misbehavior, we are sometimes more able to help them.

For example, Johnny was provoking a fight with nearly everyone in class one morning. We didn't know until later that, once again, Johnny had been slapped around in the school parking lot by his stepfather. In class, we only saw his fighting and didn't realize he was in pain and distress.

Sharona came to class nearly every day with a wide array of new and highly fashionable cosmetics—lip gloss, foundation, makeup, eyeliner, and even some lotion for the boys. She had it all. Her show-and-tell in the opening minutes of each day led to some disruption. We later learned that she hails from a small Latin American country and that she is somewhat insecure about herself. She used the cosmetics as a way to gain approval from her peers. For our science fair, I fortunately was able to guide her to do a project about making lipstick, and this earned her quite a bit of admiration and popularity in a constructive way.

concern and debate over the effects of television on the beliefs and conduct of children. Violence on television is seen by some to influence students to be more aggressive.

5. **The physical environment.** The physical arrangement of the classroom, temperature, noise, and lighting may affect student behavior. Student crowding may also be involved. These factors may contribute to a student's lack of commitment to a lesson and may lead to inattention and misbehavior.

6. **Poor behavior decisions by students.** The classroom is a complex environment for students as well as for teachers. Students are confronted with challenges, temptations, and circumstances that will cause them to make decisions about their own behavior. Their own personalities and habits come into play here. Given all of these factors, students will sometimes make poor decisions that lead to misbehavior.

7. **Other students in the classroom.** Some misbehavior results from students being provoked by other students in the classroom. A student may be drawn into an incident of misbehavior when another student does something inappropriate. In addition, peer pressure from other students may cause individual students to misbehave in ways they would not consider by themselves.

8. **Teacher factors when managing the class.** Teachers sometimes needlessly create disciplinary problems by the way they manage and conduct their classes. Inappropriate teacher behaviors include being overly negative, maintaining an authoritarian climate, overreacting to situations, using mass punishment for all students, blaming students, lacking a clear instructional goal, repeating or reviewing already learned material, pausing too long during instruction, dealing with one student at length, and lacking recognition of student ability levels. Although few teachers can avoid all of these behaviors all of the time, effective teachers recognize the potentially damaging effects of classroom order and discipline. Being aware of these characteristics is the first step to avoiding them. It is useful periodically to reflect on your own teaching behavior to determine if you are taking actions that are contributing to inattention or misbehavior.

9. **Teacher factors concerning instruction.** Teachers make many decisions about the content and delivery of instruction. Students may lose interest in a lesson if the teacher presents uninteresting lessons, does not plan meaningful activities or engage students in the lessons, is ineffective in instructional delivery, or does not deliberately plan to incorporate motivational elements into the instruction. When students lose interest in a lesson, they are more likely to get off task and misbehave.

Degrees of Severity

Misbehavior ranges from mildly to severely disruptive behavior. Severely disruptive behavior and crime in schools may involve violence, vandalism, coercion, robbery, theft, and drug use. These behaviors typically occur outside the classroom in places such as the lunchroom, corridors, or outside the building. Moderate levels of misbehavior involve tardiness, cutting class, talking, calling out answers in class, mild forms of verbal and physical aggression, inattentiveness, and

■ WHAT WOULD YOU DECIDE?   Dealing with a Sleepy Student

You have a student in your classroom who has difficulty paying attention in class and appears to be sleepy much of the time. Once during a classroom film, the student fell asleep. Many days she does not complete her class work or homework.

1. What might be some reasons for the student's sleepiness and lack of attention in class?

2. What might you do to identify the actual cause of the sleepiness and inattention?

■ CLASSROOM CASE STUDY   Analyzing a Teacher's Classroom Management

Jasmine Nichols is an experienced third-grade teacher in an urban school district. Misbehavior is rare in her classroom because she creates a secure environment that fosters mutual respect. Ms. Nichols and her students generate the classroom rules and their consequences during the first class session of the school year. Each student is asked to sign a copy of the rules and consequences, verifying his or her commitment to them and assuming responsibility for his or her own behavior. The rules and expectations are then posted in the classroom.

Ms. Nichols also gives thought to the classroom arrangement to eliminate distractions for her students. Students' desks are located at a reasonable distance from pencil sharpeners, trash cans, and other such distractions. Infrequently used items are out of the way in a nearby supply closet. Ms. Nichols often moves around the room and monitors her students to be sure they are on task.

At the start of the year, Ms. Nichols plans for activities to help students get to know each other. She becomes aware of the students' interests and needs and takes that information into consideration when planning lessons. She also uses a variety of instructional approaches and always tries to promote active student involvement. She takes steps to monitor student conduct and reinforce appropriate behavior consistent with academic goals. When any student gets off task or misbehaves, however, Ms. Nichols responds promptly with actions that are part of her predetermined discipline plan. Furthermore, she communicates with families regularly about academic and behavioral issues.

Focus Questions

1. Identify the *classroom management* variables that Ms. Nichols addresses to promote and maintain appropriate behavior.

2. Identify the *instructional* variables that Ms. Nichols addresses to promote and academic achievement.

3. What steps did she take to develop a positive classroom community and to promote a caring classroom?

---

failure to bring supplies and books. Most misbehavior is comparatively mild and is related to attention, crowd control, and getting work accomplished in the classroom.

When selecting an appropriate response to misbehavior, it is important that you take into account the degree of severity of the misbehavior. You can evaluate severity by factors such as appropriateness, magnitude, intent, and extent to which a behavior differs from what is expected in a particular setting. The degree of your response should match the degree of severity of the misbehavior. Teachers often ignore certain minor misbehaviors because their intervention may be more disruptive than the misbehavior.

Principles for Working with Students and Preventing Misbehavior

Problem behaviors have a variety of causes, and evidence suggests that some factors are within the school and classroom environment (Charles, 2014). To promote classrooms that are conducive to learning and to help prevent problem behaviors, teachers must address certain contextual factors within the classroom. The *Handbook of Classroom Management* (Evertson & Weinstein, 2006) reviews research, practice, and contemporary issues and provides considerable guidance for classroom practice. Here are some basic principles for working with students in a manner that establishes a positive, productive classroom in which students learn and have a satisfying educational experience:

1. **Maintain focus on your major task in teaching.** Your major task is to help students be successful in achieving educational objectives, to promote student learning, and to help students develop the knowledge and skills to be successful in your classroom and beyond.

2. **Understand your students' needs and how to meet them.** Know your students' likes and dislikes, what motivates them, their needs and desires, and what influences their lives. Use that information to create an appropriate learning environment.

3. **Understand and respect ethnic or cultural differences.** Teachers are more prepared to facilitate learning and guide behavior when they understand the ethnic or cultural background of their students.

4. **Know what causes misbehavior and how to deal with those causes.** Take steps to reduce or remove the causes of misbehavior.

5. **Provide clear rules and procedures to guide student conduct.** Rules and procedures need to be clearly identified and taught so students understand the behavioral expectations.

6. **Have a specific plan for responding to misbehavior with a hierarchy of interventions.** Have a specific set of strategies to stop the misbehavior, keep students positively on track, and preserve good relations.

7. **Reduce the use of punitive methods of control.** Coercive or punitive environments may promote antisocial behavior. Other techniques that involve the students in creating a positive learning environment are more desirable.

8. **Take actions to establish a cooperative, responsible classroom.** Use techniques to maintain attention and involvement, reinforce desired behaviors, promote student accountability and responsibility, and create a positive learning community.

9. **Involve students meaningfully in making decisions.** Decisions can involve things such as the selection of classroom rules and procedures, instructional activities and assessments, and curriculum materials. Student involvement generates commitment to the learning process and to the classroom environment.

10. **Teach critical social skills.** Many students lack the social skills necessary to relate positively to peers and to do well academically. Teachers who help students develop these social skills help promote learning and successful classroom discipline.

11. **Involve parents and guardians to a reasonable degree.** Communicate with the parents regularly about what you are doing in the classroom and about the progress of their children. Make it clear that you want and need their support.

MAJOR CONCEPTS

1. Classroom management involves teacher actions to create a learning environment that encourages positive social interaction, active engagement in learning, and self-motivation.

2. Effective teaching is related to a teacher's ability to use appropriate management strategies while simultaneously providing high-quality instruction.

3. Classroom management variables and instructional variables promote positive behavior and academic gains.

4. Students and teachers have different perceptions about classroom management. Implications for teachers include the need to put effort into creating positive relationships with students, developing reasonable rules and procedures, and recognizing the relationship between classroom management and instruction.

5. Caring relationships in the classroom help support instruction and classroom management.

6. There are several areas of responsibility in classroom management and discipline (see Table 1.1).

7. A learning community is designed to help all students feel safe, respected, and valued in order to learn new skills. Characteristics of a learning community include security, open communication, mutual liking, shared goals or objectives, and connectedness and trust.

8. Order means that students are following the actions necessary for a particular classroom event to be successful; students are focused on the instructional tasks and are not misbehaving.

9. Misbehavior includes behaviors that interfere with the act of teaching, interfere with the rights of others to learn, are psychologically or physically unsafe, or destroy property.

10. Off-task behavior includes student actions that are not focused on the instructional activities, yet are not considered disruptive or defined as misbehavior.

11. Misbehavior ranges from mildly to severely disruptive behavior.

DISCUSSION/REFLECTIVE QUESTIONS

1. Recall your schooling experiences and describe examples where your teacher created caring relationships in the classroom. What did the teacher do to create the caring relationships between the teacher and student, and between students? Also recall negative examples.

2. When considering student perceptions of what constitutes good teaching, what are the classroom management and instructional implications for teachers?

3. Of the seven areas of responsibility in classroom management (see Table 1.1), which are the three most important from your perspective? Why?

4. How would you describe a positive learning community? Identify some examples from your own schooling experience.

5. Give some examples of off-task behaviors and misbehaviors. Clarify the difference.

6. Why is it important to know the cause of the student's misbehavior?

7. What are some benefits and disadvantages of involving students in making decisions about issues such as the selection of rules and procedures, instructional activities and assessments, and curriculum materials?

SUGGESTED ACTIVITIES

1. Make a plan of specific activities and other actions that you would take at the start of the school year to help your students feel comfortable with each other in the classroom (e.g., group-building activities, opportunities to share personal experiences and interests, and promoting teamwork).

2. One aspect of a learning community is having shared goals or objectives. Think of a unit you might teach and identify five ways that you could build shared goals into your plans.

3. Talk to several teachers to see what they consider to be mild, moderate, and severe misbehavior. Ask how they respond to the misbehavior at each level. Ask if they have a systematic plan to address misbehavior.

FURTHER READING

Charney, R. S. (2002). *Teaching children to care: Classroom management for ethical and academic growth, K–8* (Rev. ed.). Turners Falls, MA: Center for Responsive Schools.
Provides substantial ideas for building a learning community, making the community work, using teachers' voices to promote and maintain community, and addressing difficult classroom behaviors.

Levine, D. A. (2003). *Building classroom communities: Strategies for developing a culture of caring.* Bloomington, IN: Solution Tree.
Describes ways to create a classroom where students feel a sense of belonging. Includes creating emotionally safe classrooms, encouraging honor and respect, facilitating interdependence and generosity, and teaching empathy.

Lundy, K. G., & Swartz, L. (2011). *Creating caring classrooms: How to encourage students to communicate, create, and be compassionate of others.* Markham, Ontario, Canada: Pembroke Publishers. (Distributed in the U.S. by Stenhouse Publishers.)

Describes ways to build community, communication, collaboration, and compassion in the classroom.

Sapon-Shevin, M. (2007). *Widening the circle: The power of inclusive classrooms.* Boston: Beacon Press.
Ten lessons from inclusive classrooms are identified, and ways to build inclusive classrooms are described to promote social justice and promote student learning.

Sapon-Shevin, M. (2010). *Because we can change the world: A practical guide to building cooperative, inclusive classroom communities* (2nd ed.). Thousand Oaks, CA: Corwin Press.
Discusses techniques to develop a cohesive classroom community in pre-K through middle-school classrooms. Emphasizes creating a caring, supportive classroom.

The Degree of Control

When deciding how to handle classroom management and discipline, you probably will take into account your views of child development, your educational philosophies, and other factors. These views can be categorized in various ways, but perhaps the most useful organizer is by the degree of control that you exert on the students and the classroom. A continuum showing a range of low to high teacher control can be used to illustrate the various educational views, and the various discipline models can be placed on the continuum. This continuum is based on the organizer that Wolfgang (2009) used when examining models of discipline.

A *model of discipline* is a set of cohesive approaches to deal with establishing, maintaining, and restoring order in the classroom that represent a certain philosophical perspective on a continuum of low to high teacher control. Table 2.1 provides a summary of the characteristics of various discipline models, ranging from low to high teacher control. Table 2.2 identifies representative authors for each of the three discipline models.

Your approach to freedom and control may fall into one particular part of the continuum, but this does not mean that you will follow this approach in every situation. You may branch out and use other strategies as the situation warrants. Now, let's look at the models at each point on the continuum.

■ TABLE 2.1 **Characteristics of Various Discipline Models**

Descriptors	The Guiding Model	The Interacting Model	The Intervening Model
Degree of teacher control	Low	Medium	High
Degree of student control	High	Medium	Low
Degree of concern for the students' thoughts, feelings, and preferences	High	Medium	Low
Theoretical basis	Humanistic and Psychoanalytic Thought	Developmental and Social Psychology	Behaviorism
View of children	• Children develop primarily from inner forces • Decision making enables personal growth • Students are masters of their destiny	• Children develop from both internal and external forces	• Children develop primarily from external forces and conditions • Children are molded and shaped by influences from their environment
Main processes used	• Develop caring, self-directed students • Build teacher–student relationships	• Confront and contract with students when solving problems • Counsel students	• Establish the rules, and deliver the rewards and punishments
Approaches used by teachers	• Structure the environment to facilitate students' control over their own behavior • Help students see the problem and guide them into an appropriate decision to solve the problem • Be an empathic listener • Allow students to express their feelings	• Interact with children to clarify and establish boundaries • Enforce the boundaries • Formulate mutually acceptable solutions to problems	• Control the environment • Select and use appropriate reinforcers and punishments

■ TABLE 2.2   Proponents of Various Discipline Models

The Guiding Model	The Interacting Model	The Intervening Model
Low-Control Approaches	Medium-Control Approaches	High-Control Approaches
Congruent Communication *Haim Ginott* • Use sane messages • Invite student cooperation • Express helpfulness and acceptance	**Logical Consequences** *Rudolf Dreikurs* • Teach in a democratic manner • Identify and confront students' mistaken goals • Use logical consequences	**Behavior Modification** *B. F. Skinner* • Identify desired behaviors • Shape behavior through reinforcement • Use behavior modification systematically
Discipline as Self-Control **(Teacher Effectiveness Training)** *Thomas Gordon* • Identify problem ownership • Maximize communication • Use the power of influence	**Cooperative Discipline** *Linda Albert* • Establish a sense of belonging • Build student self-esteem • Promote cooperative relationships	**Assertive Discipline** *Lee and Marlene Canter* • Recognize classroom rights • Teach desired behavior • Establish consequences
Teaching with Love and Logic *Jim Fay and David Funk* • Share control with students • Maintain student self-concepts • Balance consequences with empathy	**Positive Classroom Discipline** *Jane Nelsen, Lynn Lott, and H. Stephen Glenn* • Use classroom meetings • Exhibit caring attitudes and behaviors • Use management skills	**Positive Discipline** *Fredric Jones* • Structure classrooms • Set limits and promote cooperation • Have backup systems
Inner Discipline *Barbara Coloroso* • Enable students to solve problems • Provide support and structure • Treat students with dignity and respect	**Noncoercive Discipline** **(Reality Therapy and Control Theory)** *William Glasser* • Provide quality education • Help students make good decisions • Provide support and encouragement	**Discipline Without Stress** *Marvin Marshall* • Promote responsibility rather than obedience • Guide and monitor behavior • Teach the social development and management system
From Discipline to Community *Alfie Kohn* • Provide an engaging curriculum • Develop a caring community • Allow students to make choices	**Discipline with Dignity** *Richard Curwin, Allen Mendler, and Brian Mendler* • Create a three-dimensional plan • Establish a social contract • Teach students to make responsible choices	
	Win–Win Discipline *Spencer Kagan* • Work with students to solve problems • Focus on short- and long-term solutions • Help students make responsible choices	

Low Teacher Control Approaches

Low-control approaches are based on the philosophical belief that students have primary responsibility for controlling their own behavior and that they have the capability to make these decisions. Children are seen to have an inner potential, and opportunities to make decisions enable personal growth. The child's thoughts, feelings, ideas, and preferences are taken into account when dealing with instruction, classroom management, and discipline.

The teacher has the responsibility for structuring the classroom environment to facilitate the students' control over their own behavior. When determining classroom rules, for example, teachers guide the discussion and help students recognize appropriate behavior and select related rules and consequences. When misbehavior occurs, the teacher helps students see the problem and guides students in making an appropriate decision to resolve the problem. With these nondirective teacher actions, low teacher control approaches fall into the guiding model of discipline.

With this philosophical belief, students have a high degree of autonomy while the teacher exerts a low degree of control. This does not mean that the classroom is a chaotic place for learning. There are standards that the students will help develop, and the teacher is ultimately responsible for enforcing the standards to enable learning to take place in an orderly environment.

Low-control educators might use several types of nondirective approaches to <u>create a supportive learning environment and to guide behavior.</u> To illustrate these nondirective, low teacher control approaches, the discipline models from five representative authors are discussed in the following sections.

[handwritten margin note: Stds have a primary responsibility for controlling themselves.]

[handwritten margin note: Teacher creates structure to facilitate stds controlling themselves.]

Congruent Communication: Haim Ginott

Haim Ginott (1922–1973) was a professor of psychology at New York University and at Adelphi University. Among educators, he is most known for his books that address relationships between adults and children. *Between Parent and Child* (2003) and *Between Parent and Teenager* (1988) offered ideas on how to communicate effectively with children. Ginott focused on how adults can build the self-concepts of children, especially emphasizing that adults should avoid attacks on the child's character and instead focus on the situation or actions. Later, Ginott carried these principles to educators in *Teacher and Child* (1972), proposing that teachers maintain a secure, humanitarian, and productive classroom through the use of congruent communication and appropriate use of praise.

Congruent communication is a harmonious and authentic way of talking in which teacher messages to students match the students' feelings about the situations and about themselves. In this way, teachers can avoid insulting and intimidating their students and instead express an attitude of helpfulness and acceptance while showing increased sensitivity to their needs and desires.

There are several ways that teachers can express congruent communication, all directed at protecting or building students' self-esteem:

- **Deliver sane messages.** Sane messages address situations rather than the students' characters. They acknowledge and accept student feelings. Too often, teachers may use language that blames, orders, admonishes, accuses, ridicules, belittles, or threatens children. This language does not promote children's self-esteem. Instead, Ginott proposes that teachers use language that focuses on the situation and the facts, not threatening that child's self-esteem.

- **Express anger appropriately.** Ginott points out that students can irritate and annoy teachers, making them angry. Anger is a genuine feeling, and teachers should express their anger in reasonable and appropriate ways that do not jeopardize the self-esteem of their students. An effective way is simply to say, "It makes me angry when . . . ," or "I am appalled when . . . ." In this way, the students hear what is upsetting the teacher without hearing put-down statements such as "You are so irresponsible when you . . . ."

[handwritten margin note: not promote children's self-esteem.]

[handwritten margin note: me statements]

- **Invite cooperation.** Provide opportunities for students to experience independence, thus accepting their capabilities. Give students a choice in matters that affect life in the classroom, including things such as seating arrangements and certain classroom procedures. Avoid long, drawn-out directions, and instead give a brief statement and allow students to decide what their specific course of action should be. By inviting cooperation, you begin to break down students' dependency on yourself.

- **Accept and acknowledge student feelings.** When a problem occurs, listen to students and accept the feelings they are expressing as real. Serve as a sounding board to help students clarify their feelings and let them know that such feelings are common.

- **Avoid labeling the student.** Ginott maintains there is no place for statements such as "You are so irresponsible, unreliable." "You are such a disgrace to this class, this school, your family." When students hear these statements, they begin to believe them, and then they may start to develop a negative self-image. Avoid labeling, while striving to be helpful and encouraging.

- **Use direction as a means of correction.** Instead of criticizing students when a problem occurs, Ginott proposes that teachers describe the situation to the students and offer guidance about what they should be doing. For example, when a student spills some supplies on the floor, offer some suggestions about ways to do the cleanup rather than criticize the student.

- **Avoid harmful questions.** Ginott points out that an enlightened teacher avoids asking questions and making comments that are likely to incite resentment and invite resistance. For example, don't ask "Why" questions such as "Why can't you be good for a change?" and "Why do you forget everything I tell you?" Instead, point out that there is a problem and invite the student to discuss ways to solve the problem.

- **Accept students' comments.** Students may ask questions or make statements that seem unrelated to the topic under discussion. Show respect and give the student credit for the question or comment because it may be important to the student in some way.

- **Do not use sarcasm.** While you may use sarcasm as a way to be witty, it may sound clever only to yourself and not to the students receiving the comments. Students may end up with hurt feelings and damaged self-esteem.

- **Avoid hurried help.** When a problem arises, listen to the problem, rephrase it, clarify it, give the students credit for formulating it, and then ask, "What options are open to you?" In this way, you provide students with an opportunity to acquire competence in problem solving and confidence in themselves. Hurried responses to problems are less likely to achieve these purposes.

- **Be brief when dealing with minor mishaps.** Long, logical explanations are not needed when there is a lost paper, a broken pencil, or a forgotten assignment. Brief statements should be solution oriented.

■ WHAT WOULD YOU DECIDE?   Applying Ginott's Low Teacher Control

In your class, you have students working in small groups on a project. Then one of the students begins to talk in an angry way to another group member, stands up, and tosses some papers aside.

1. How would you communicate with that student using Ginott's principles of congruent communication (e.g., to

express sane messages, express anger appropriately, and invite cooperation)?

2. How might your actions be affected if the student was of a different ethnic group from you?

Discipline as Self-Control: Thomas Gordon

Book

Thomas Gordon, a clinical psychologist, is known for his pioneering method of teaching communication skills and conflict resolution to teachers, parents, youth, and business leaders. In education, he is most known for T.E.T.: *Teacher Effectiveness Training* (2003) and *Discipline That Works: Promoting Self-Discipline in Children* (1991). Gordon maintains that effective discipline cannot be achieved through rewards and punishments, but rather, through techniques to promote students' own self-control. He proposed approaches to help students make positive decisions, become more self-reliant, and control their own behavior. To help students make positive decisions, however, teachers must give up their controlling power.

Teachers guide and influence students and also take actions to create an environment where students can make decisions about their behavior. Several principles incorporate the essence of Gordon's concepts.

1. **Identify who owns the problem.** Gordon used a device called a behavior window to determine who owns the problem. The student's behavior may cause a problem for the teacher or for the student, or there may be no problem. The person feeling the negative consequences of the behavior is said to own the problem, and this person is the one to take steps to solve the problem.

Behavior window

2. **Use confrontive skills when teachers own the problem.** Teachers can modify the environment, recognize and respond to student feelings, word statements so they do not trigger the student's coping mechanism, shift gears, and use a no-lose method of conflict resolution. All of these approaches are intended to help guide and influence the students into effective interactions in the classroom.

3. **Use helping skills when the student owns the problem.** When a student owns the problem, the student needs to take steps to solve it. Teachers can provide assistance through the use of helping skills. This can be done by using listening skills and by avoiding communication roadblocks.

4. **Use preventive skills when neither the student nor teacher has a problem with the behavior.** As a means to prevent problems from occurring, teachers can use techniques such as collaboratively setting rules and using participative problem solving and decision making.

Teaching with Love and Logic: Jim Fay and David Funk

Book

In *Teaching with Love and Logic* (1995), Jim Fay and David Funk describe how to create a classroom environment in which students can develop their own self-discipline and independent problem-solving skills. *Love and logic* is an approach to working with students that teaches students to think for themselves, raises the level of student responsibility, and prepares students to function effectively in society.

There are four basic principles of love and logic: (1) maintain the student's self-concept; (2) share control with the students; (3) balance the consequences with empathy; and (4) share the thinking by asking questions and modeling. With those principles as the foundation for the discipline plan, Fay and Funk selected three basic rules for their love and logic program: (1) use enforceable limits; (2) provide choices within the limits; and (3) apply consequences with empathy.

In describing various types of teaching styles, Fay and Funk (1995, pp. 197–198) describe teachers using the love and logic approach to discipline as *consultants*. Consultant teachers do the following:

1. Set enforceable limits through enforceable statements.

2. Provide messages of personal worth, dignity, and strength through choices.

3. Provide consequences with empathy rather than punishment.

4. Demonstrate how to take good care of themselves and be responsible.

5. Share feelings about their personal performance and responsibilities.

6. Help people solve problems by exploring alternatives while allowing them to make their own decisions.

7. Provide latitude, within reasonable limits, for students to complete responsibilities.

8. Induce thinking through questions.

9. Use more actions than words to convey values.

10. Allow students to experience life's natural consequences, allow time to think through a problem, encourage shared thinking and shared control, and let them be teachers as well as students.

The love and logic approach gives students considerable credit for having the ability to solve their own problems, and teachers create an environment where students have the opportunity to make such decisions.

Inner Discipline: Barbara Coloroso

In *Kids Are Worth It! Giving Your Child the Gift of Inner Discipline* (2002), Barbara Coloroso emphasizes guiding students to make their own decisions and to take responsibility for their choices. To have good discipline, teachers must do three things: (1) treat students with respect and dignity; (2) give them a sense of power in their lives; and (3) give them opportunities to make decisions, take responsibility for their actions, and learn from their successes and mistakes. She believes that dealing with problems and accepting the consequences help students take charge of their lives.

Through these approaches, Coloroso believes that students will develop inner discipline. Her beliefs are humanistic and focused on promoting students' self-worth and dignity. She believes that with guidance from adults, students can grow to like themselves and think for themselves. To enable students to develop inner discipline, teachers need to provide the appropriate degree of structure and support for students.

As a starting point, Coloroso says that teachers need to ask themselves, "What is my goal in teaching?" and "What is my teaching philosophy?" The first question deals with what teachers hope to achieve, and the second with how they will approach the tasks. Because teachers act in accordance with their beliefs, it is important for them to clarify these beliefs concerning the degree of freedom and control they apply to their classrooms. Teachers who want to control students use rewards and punishments, but teachers who want to empower students to make decisions and to resolve their own problems will give students opportunities to think, act, and take responsibility.

■ WHAT WOULD YOU DECIDE?   Applying Low Teacher Control Approaches

Teachers adopting the low teacher control approach—the guiding model—to discipline intentionally exhibit a low degree of control when structuring the classroom environment and responding to misbehavior. They structure the environment to facilitate students' control over their environment and behavior.

1. If you adopted the guiding model, how would you approach the selection of rules and procedures at the start of the school year?

2. If you adopted the guiding model, how might you react to a student who is talking in class, disturbing others, and not getting her work done?

The best way to teach students how to make good decisions is to put them in situations that call for decisions; ask them to make the decision, possibly with guidance from the teacher; and let them experience the results of their decision. Coloroso believes that teachers should not rescue students from bad decisions, but rather guide the student to new decisions that will solve the problem. When students are given ownership of problems and situations, this allows students to take responsibility for their decisions. She describes a six-step problem-solving strategy that students can use to identify and define the problem, list and evaluate possible solutions, and select, implement, and evaluate the preferred option.

From Discipline to Community: Alfie Kohn

Alfie Kohn is recognized as one of the most original thinkers in education today. A former teacher, he is now a full-time writer and lecturer. He has written five influential books, two of them linking to discipline models: *Punished by Rewards* (1999) and *Beyond Discipline: From Compliance to Community* (2006).

Kohn challenges traditional thinking by suggesting that our first question about children should not be "How can we make them do what we want?" but rather "What do they require in order to flourish, and how can we provide those things?" After reviewing a number of popular discipline programs, Kohn concludes that all are based on threat, reward, and punishment as the means to obtain student compliance. Kohn even views "consequences" as being punishments. Nothing useful comes from rewards and punishments because they cause students to mistrust their own judgment and stunt their becoming caring and self-reliant.

Instead, Kohn says that teachers should focus on developing caring, supportive classrooms where students participate fully in solving problems, including problems with behavior. He advises teachers to develop a sense of community in their classrooms, where students feel safe and are continually brought into making decisions, expressing their opinions, and working cooperatively toward solutions that benefit the class.

When starting the school year, Kohn doesn't think rules are a good idea. When rules are used, Kohn is critical that students look for loopholes, teachers function as police officers, and punishment is used as a consequence. He maintains that students learn best when they have the opportunity to reflect on the proper way to conduct themselves. In this way, the teacher and students work together to identify how they want their classroom to be and how that can be made to happen. Students help create their own learning environment.

Kohn does not dismiss the value of structure and limits on student behavior. He presents criteria for determining how defensible a structure or limit is. Some of his criteria include purpose, restrictiveness, flexibility, developmental appropriateness, presentation style, and student involvement.

Classroom meetings are seen by Kohn as valuable tools to create a community and to address classroom problems and issues. Classroom meetings bring social and ethical benefits, foster intellectual development, motivate students to be more effective leaders, and greatly cut down on the need to deal with discipline problems. Kohn sees four focal points in these meetings:

1. Share—talk about interesting events.

2. Decide about issues that affect the class, such as procedures for working on projects.

3. Plan for various curricular or instructional issues.

4. Reflect about issues such as what has been learned, what might have worked better, or what changes might improve the class.

All of these strategies will help create a community, which Kohn defines as a place in which students feel cared about and are encouraged to care about each other. Students then feel valued and respected, and the students matter to one another and the teacher. When students come to think in the plural, they feel connected to each other and feel physically and emotionally safe.

Medium Teacher Control Approaches

Medium-control approaches are based on the philosophical belief that development comes from a combination of innate and outer forces. Thus, the control of student behavior is a joint responsibility of the student and teacher. Medium-control teachers accept the student-centered psychology that is reflected in the low-control philosophy, but they also recognize that learning takes place in a group context. Therefore, the teacher promotes individual student control over behavior whenever possible, but places the needs of the group as a whole over the needs of individual students. The child's thoughts, feelings, ideas, and preferences are taken into account when dealing with instruction, classroom management, and discipline, but ultimately, the teacher's primary focus is on behavior and meeting the academic needs of the group.

Students are given opportunities to control their behavior in an effort to develop the ability to make appropriate decisions, yet they may not initially recognize that some of their behavior might be a hindrance to their own growth and development. Students need to recognize the consequences of their behavior and make adjustments to reach more favorable results.

The teacher and students often develop rules and procedures jointly. Teachers may begin the discussion of rules by presenting one or two rules that must be followed, or the teacher may hold veto power over the rules that the students select. This represents a higher degree of control than is used by low-control teachers. Medium-control teachers, then, would be responsible for enforcing the rules and helping students recognize the consequences of their decisions and actions. Medium-control educators might use logical consequences, cooperative discipline, noncoercive approaches, or other interactive approaches. These strategies fall into the interacting model of discipline.

Several educators have described cohesive approaches to deal with students that represent the medium-control approach when creating a supportive learning environment and guiding student behavior. The discipline models from several representative authors are discussed in the following sections.

Logical Consequences: Rudolf Dreikurs

Rudolf Dreikurs (Dreikurs, Grunwald, & Pepper, 1998) based his strategies on the belief that students are motivated to get recognition and to belong with others. Students seek social acceptance from conforming to the group and making useful contributions to it. Dreikurs views his

■ WHAT WOULD YOU DECIDE?   Applying Medium Teacher Control Approaches

Teachers adopting the medium teacher control approach—the interacting model—to discipline want to involve students to some degree in establishing guidelines in the classroom and in dealing with misbehavior. The teachers may enforce the boundaries and work with the students to determine suitable solutions.

1. How might your selection of rules and consequences be influenced by this philosophical approach?

2. How might this philosophical approach to control also affect your decision making about aspects of curriculum and instruction, such as your choice of instructional activities and assessment techniques?

3. If two students had a loud verbal disagreement in your classroom, how would you deal with the incident with the use of medium-control approaches?

approaches as democratic in that teachers and students together decide on the rules and consequences, and they have joint responsibility for maintaining a positive classroom climate. This encourages students to become more responsibly self-governing.

To Dreikurs, discipline is not punishment; it is teaching students to impose limits on themselves. With his approaches, students are responsible for their own actions, have respect for themselves and others, have the responsibility to influence others to behave appropriately, and are responsible for knowing the classroom rules and consequences. Based on Dreikurs's ideas, there are several techniques that you can use to help misbehaving students behave appropriately without reliance on punishment.

First, identify the goal of the misbehavior. Examine the key signs of the misbehavior and also consider your feelings and reactions as a means to tentatively identify the goal of the student's misbehavior. The student's goal may be to gain attention, to seek power, to seek revenge, or to display inadequacy. Then disclose this goal to the student in a private session as a means to confirm the goal. This is a positive means of confronting a misbehaving student. Its purpose is to heighten the student's awareness of the motives for the misbehavior.

Second, alter your reactions to the misbehavior. Once the goal of misbehavior has been identified, first control your immediate reaction to misbehavior so that your response does not reinforce the misbehavior. For example, if the student's goal is to seek attention, never give immediate attention, but try to ignore the behavior whenever possible. Then, have a discussion with the student to identify a number of alternatives for changing the behavior.

Third, provide encouragement statements to students. Encouragement consists of words or actions that acknowledge student work and express confidence in the students (Dreikurs, Cassel, & Ferguson, 2004). Encouragement statements help students see what they did to lead to a positive result and also help students feel confident about their own abilities. For example, you might say, "I see that your extra studying for the test paid off, because you did so well." The focus is on what the student did that led to the result obtained.

Most important, use logical consequences. Instead of using punishment, Dreikurs prefers to let students experience the consequences that flow from misbehavior. A *logical consequence* is an event that is arranged by the teacher that is directly and logically related to the misbehavior. For instance, if a student leaves paper on the classroom floor, the student must pick the paper off the floor. If a student breaks the rule of speaking out without raising his or her hand, the teacher ignores the response and calls on a student whose hand is up. If a student makes marks on the desk, the student is required to remove them.

Cooperative Discipline: Linda Albert

Based largely on the philosophy and psychology of Alfred Adler and Rudolf Dreikurs, Linda Albert (2003) developed a classroom management and discipline plan called *cooperative discipline*. Similar to Dreikurs's ideas, cooperative discipline is founded on three concepts of behavior: (1) students choose their behavior; (2) the ultimate goal of student behavior is to fulfill the need to belong; and (3) students misbehave to achieve one of four immediate goals (attention, power, revenge, and avoidance of failure).

Albert's main focus is on helping teachers meet student needs so that students choose to cooperate with the teacher and with each other. Her cooperative discipline includes five action steps:

1. Pinpoint and describe the student's behavior.

2. Identify the goal of the misbehavior.

3. Choose intervention techniques for the moment of misbehavior.

4. Select encouragement techniques to build self-esteem.

5. Involve parents as partners.

Albert's cooperative discipline program, therefore, is designed to establish positive classroom control through appropriate interventions and to build self-esteem through encouragement.

The building blocks of self-esteem are helping students feel capable, helping students connect (become involved and engaged in the classroom), and helping students contribute (discussed more fully in Chapter 6). To achieve the goals of cooperative discipline intervention and encouragement strategies, use democratic procedures and policies, implement cooperative learning strategies, conduct classroom guidance activities, and choose appropriate curriculum methods and materials.

Albert offers a number of strategies to implement her cooperative discipline plan. She presents intervention techniques when misbehavior occurs, ways to reinforce desirable behavior, approaches to create a cooperative classroom climate, and ways to avoid and defuse confrontations. Albert also proposes that teachers and students collaboratively develop a classroom code of conduct to involve students and foster their sense of responsibility to the group.

Positive Discipline: Jane Nelsen, Lynn Lott, and Stephen Glenn

Jane Nelsen has also adapted Rudolf Dreikurs's concepts into a program called positive discipline. In *Positive Discipline*, Nelsen (2006) identified kindness, respect, firmness, and encouragement as the main ingredients of this program for parents and teachers. There are several key elements to Nelsen's approach:

- Use natural and logical consequences as a means to inspire a positive atmosphere for winning children over rather than winning over children.

- Understand that children have four goals of misbehavior (attention, power, revenge, and assumed inadequacy).

- Use kindness and firmness at the same time when addressing misbehavior.

- Allow adults and children mutual respect.

VOICES FROM THE CLASSROOM   Nonpunitive Responses

Janet Kulbiski, Kindergarten Teacher, Manhattan, Kansas

After reading Jane Nelsen's book *Positive Discipline in the Classroom* (2013), I changed my attitude about misbehavior and tried some different behavior management strategies in my classroom. I now see misbehavior as an opportunity for teaching appropriate action.

Several of Nelsen's techniques have been very helpful in my classroom. I use natural and logical consequences, allow students choices, and redirect misbehavior. Natural consequences occur without intervention from anyone, such as when a child does not wear his coat and then gets cold. Logical consequences, by contrast, require intervention connected in some logical way to what the child did. If a child draws a picture on the table, a logical consequence would be that the child cleans it up.

It is important to give students choices whenever possible. This gives them a sense of control and worth, but all choices must be acceptable to you. For example, "Please, put the toy on my desk or in your backpack." Redirecting student behavior involves reminding them of the expected behavior. For example, instead of saying, "Don't run," I say, "We always walk." Eliminating "don't" from my vocabulary has helped a lot.

When I deal with misbehavior, I try to always use the situation as an opportunity for the child to learn the expected behavior. My goal is to leave the child feeling good about himself or herself and equipped to handle the situation appropriately next time.

- Provide family and class meetings, which can be effectively used to address misbehavior.

- Use encouragement as a means of inspiring self-evaluation and focusing on the actions of the child.

Nelsen has described how positive discipline principles can be applied to the classroom through the use of classroom meetings. In *Positive Discipline in the Classroom*, Nelsen, Lott, and Glenn (2013) provide detailed descriptions for ways to conduct effective classroom meetings. In addition to eliminating discipline problems, classroom meetings help students develop social, academic, and life skills, and they help students feel that they are personally capable and significant, and that they can influence their own lives.

With positive discipline, teachers demonstrate caring by showing personal interest, talking with the students, offering encouragement, and providing opportunities to nurture important life skills. Nelsen and colleagues caution that it is easy to misuse logical consequences because they are often simply punishments. Instead, they maintain that teachers think in terms of solutions rather than consequences. To do so, Nelsen suggests strategies such as involving students in solutions to problems, focusing on the future rather than the present, planning solutions carefully in advance, and making connections between opportunity, responsibility, and consequence.

Noncoercive Discipline: William Glasser

William Glasser, a psychiatrist, received national attention with the publication of *Reality Therapy* (1965), in which he proposed that treating behavioral problems should focus on present circumstances rather than antecedents of the inappropriate behavior. Glasser took his reality therapy message to educators in *Schools Without Failure* (1969). He noted that successful social relationships are basic human needs. Glasser maintained that students have a responsibility for making good choices about their behavior and that they must live with their choices.

When using reality therapy, teachers and students need to jointly establish classroom rules, and the teacher is to enforce the rules consistently without accepting excuses. When misbehavior occurs, the teacher should ask the student, "What are you doing? Is it helping you or the class? What could you do that would help?" The student is asked to make some value judgments about the behavior, and the teacher can suggest suitable alternatives. Together, they create a plan to eliminate the problem behavior. When necessary, the teacher needs to invoke appropriate consequences.

Over time, Glasser expanded his reality therapy concepts. With the development of control theory (1985, 1986), he added the needs of belonging and love, control, freedom, and fun. Without attention to those needs, students are bound to fail. Glasser maintained that discipline problems should be viewed as total behaviors, meaning that the entire context of the situation needs to be examined in an effort to seek a solution. For example, physical inactivity may contribute to student misbehavior, whereas this element might be overlooked if the situation were examined in a more confined way.

With control theory, you must recognize that students want to have their needs met. Students feel pleasure when these needs are met and frustration when they are not. You must create the conditions in which students feel a sense of belonging, have some power and control, have some freedom in the learning and schooling process, and have fun. Thus, students will not be frustrated and discipline problems should be limited.

More recently in *The Quality School* (1998a), Glasser described how to manage students without coercion. Glasser asserts that the nature of school management must be changed in order to meet students' needs and promote effective learning. In fact, he criticizes current school managers for accepting low-quality work. In *The Quality School Teacher* (1998b) and *Every Student Can Succeed* (2000), Glasser offers specific strategies for teachers to move to quality schools.

Discipline with Dignity: Richard Curwin, Allen Mendler, and Brian Mendler

Causes of misbehavior (handwritten annotation)

In *Discipline with Dignity* (2008), Richard Curwin, Allen Mendler, and Brian Mendler point out that discipline problems may be caused by student boredom, feelings of powerlessness, unclear limits, a lack of acceptable outlets for feelings, and attacks on dignity. To deal with these causes and to create an effective learning environment, Curwin and colleagues have developed a three-dimensional discipline plan: (1) the *prevention dimension* focuses on what the teacher can do to actively prevent discipline problems and how to deal with the stress associated with classroom disruptions; (2) the *action dimension* deals with actions the teacher can take when misbehavior occurs; and (3) the *resolution dimension* addresses ways teachers can resolve problems with chronic rule breakers and more extreme, out-of-control students.

Their model of discipline involves working with the students to develop the discipline plan; they label this the "responsibility model." This model requires teachers to give up some of their power to involve students in decision making, which Curwin and colleagues maintain is far more consistent with current classroom emphasis on critical thinking and decision making. The main goal of the responsibility model is to teach students to make responsible choices, and students are expected to learn from the outcomes of these decisions. This model fosters critical thinking and promotes shared decision making. Students feel affirmed even though they don't always get their way. They understand that they have some control of the events that happen to them, and they get a chance to learn that teachers also have rights, power, knowledge, and leadership (B. D. Mendler, R. L. Curwin, & A. N. Mendler, 2008).

This discipline plan uses discipline as a learning process rather than a system of retribution. It has four principles:

1. Dealing with student behavior is part of the job.

2. Always treat students with dignity.

3. Discipline works best when integrated with effective teaching practices.

4. Acting out is sometimes an act of sanity.

A social contract is a basic tool for discipline planning in the responsibility model. The *social contract* is an agreement between the teacher and students about the rules and consequences for classroom behavior. Curwin and colleagues identify the following as important aspects of designing the contract: involve students in the process; ensure that rules are clear; develop consequences, not punishments; develop predictable consequences; allow the contract to change with class needs; have safeguards to protect the dignity of all students; increase communication among teachers, students, administrators, and parents; and integrate discipline methodology with the teaching of content.

Curwin and colleagues identify nine principles when delivering consequences: (1) always implement a consequence when needed; (2) simply state the rule and consequence; (3) be physically close to the student when implementing a consequence; (4) make direct eye contact when delivering a consequence; (5) use a soft voice; (6) catch a student being good; (7) don't embarrass a student in front of his peers; (8) be firm and anger-free when giving the consequence; (9) do not accept excuses, bargaining, or whining.

Curwin and colleagues also recognize the relationship between discipline and the process of teaching. In doing so, they discuss motivation, learning styles, enthusiasm in instructional delivery, evaluation and grading, and competition. They further discuss the unique challenges in dealing with out-of-control students and students with special problems.

Win–Win Discipline: Spencer Kagan

Spencer Kagan is an educational consultant who specializes in researching and developing discipline strategies and life skills training. Along with Patricia Kyle and Sally Scott, Kagan developed a model of discipline called *Win–Win Discipline* (Kagan, Kyle, & Scott, 2004). The two purposes of this model are to help students meet their needs through responsible, nondisruptive behavior and to develop long-term life skills. To be on the same side in establishing good discipline, teachers and students treat discipline as a joint responsibility.

There are three pillars to win–win discipline: (1) Same side: The teacher, students, and parents work together rather than at odds with each other toward building responsible behavior; (2) Collaboration: Teachers and students cocreate immediate and long-term solutions to behavior problems; and (3) Learned responsibility: Teachers help students make responsible choices in how they conduct themselves. Any disruptive behavior that interrupts the learning process can become an important learning opportunity.

Kagan and colleagues identified four types of disruptive behavior—aggression, breaking rules, confrontation, and disengagement. Further, they proposed that disruptive behavior springs from students seeking attention, avoiding failure, being angry, seeking control, and being energetic, bored, or uninformed. Teacher responses are identified for each of these causes. Interventions are designed to help students meet their needs through responsible choices, and the interventions are tailored in accordance to the type of disruption and the reason for the misbehavior.

Heavy emphasis is placed on preventing disruptive behavior through attention to curriculum, instruction, and management. Win–win discipline enables teachers to work with students so that needs that might otherwise prompt disruptive behavior can be identified and satisfied in nondisruptive ways. Students do not often disrupt when engaged in a curriculum that is interesting and adequately challenging.

High Teacher Control Approaches

High-control approaches are based on the philosophical belief that students' growth and development are the result of external conditions. Children are seen as being molded and shaped by influences from the environment; they are not seen as having an innate potential. Therefore, teachers and adults need to select desired student behaviors, reinforce appropriate behaviors, and take actions to extinguish inappropriate behaviors. Little attention is given to the thoughts, feelings, and preferences of the students since adults are more experienced in instructional matters and have the responsibility for choosing what is best for student development and behavior control.

Teachers using high-control approaches believe that student behavior must be controlled because the students themselves are not able to effectively monitor and control their own behavior. The teachers select the rules and procedures for the classroom, commonly without student input. Teachers then reinforce desired behavior and take actions to have students stop inappropriate, undesired behavior. When misbehavior occurs, teachers take steps to stop the disruption quickly and redirect the student to more positive behavior. Behavior modification, behavioral contracting, and reinforcers are characteristic of high-control approaches. Compared to the previous models, there is more emphasis on managing the behavior of the individuals than the group.

Several educators have described cohesive approaches to deal with students that represent the high teacher control approach to classroom control and order. These approaches are discussed in the following sections.

■ WHAT WOULD YOU DECIDE?   Your Philosophical Perspective

Some teachers are very teacher centered and prefer to make most of the decisions and direct what goes on in the classroom. Other teachers are student centered and prefer to give some decision-making responsibility to the students and have more student–student interaction. There is a range of these perspectives, from low teacher control to high teacher control.

1. Where do you fall on that continuum of teacher-centered to student-centered perspectives? Why do you place yourself at that point?

2. What are the implications of your philosophical perspective on the selection of rules and procedures, course content, instructional approaches, and assessments?

Behavior Modification: B. F. Skinner

B. F. Skinner (1902–1990) spent most of his academic career at Harvard University, where he conducted experimental studies in learning. In *Beyond Freedom and Dignity* (1971), Skinner challenged traditional views of freedom and dignity and instead claimed that our choices are determined by the environmental conditions under which we live and what has happened to us. The application of these ideas to classroom practice has been called *behavior modification*, a technique that uses reinforcement and punishment to shape behavior.

Behavior modification, as proposed by Skinner and others, has several distinguishing features. Behavior is shaped by its consequences and by what happens to the individual immediately afterward. The systematic use of reinforcers, or rewards, can shape behavior in desired directions. Behavior becomes weaker if it is not followed by reinforcement. Behavior is also weakened by punishment.

Behavior modification is applied in the classroom primarily in two ways: (1) when the teacher rewards the student after a desired act, the student tends to repeat the act and (2) when the student performs an undesired act, the teacher either ignores the act or punishes the student; the misbehaving student then becomes less likely to repeat the act.

Several types of reinforcers can be used:

- Edible reinforcers, such as candy, cookies, gum, drinks, nuts, or various other snacks.

- Social reinforcers, such as words, gestures, stickers, certificates, and facial and bodily expressions of approval by the teacher.

- Material or tangible reinforcers, which are real objects that students can earn as rewards for desired behavior.

- Token reinforcers, including stars, points, buttons, or other items that can be accumulated by students for desired behavior and then "cashed in" for other material or tangible reinforcers.

- Activity reinforcers, which include those activities that students prefer in school.

Reinforcers are further discussed in Chapter 5. Behavior modification works best when used in an organized, systematic, and consistent way. The various types of behavior modification systems seem to fit into five categories (Miltenberger, 2016):

1. The "catch them being good" approach involves making positive statements to students who are doing what is expected of them. For example, a teacher might thank a student for getting out class materials and being ready to start the class.

2. The rules–ignore–praise approach involves establishing a set of classroom rules, ignoring inappropriate behavior, and praising appropriate behavior. This approach works best in elementary grades and is less effective in secondary grades.

3. The rules–reward–punishment approach involves establishing classroom rules, rewarding appropriate behavior, and punishing inappropriate behavior. This system is quite appropriate for older students.

4. The contingency management approach is a system of tangible reinforcers where students earn tokens for appropriate behavior that can be exchanged at a later time for material rewards.

5. Contracting involves preparing a contract for an individual student who has chronic problems or is hard to manage.

Assertive Discipline: Lee and Marlene Canter

Lee Canter is an educator who first came into prominence in 1976 with the publication of *Assertive Discipline* (Canter, 2010), a take-charge approach for teachers to control their classrooms in a firm and positive manner. Since that time, he has created an organization called Canter and Associates that prepares a variety of materials concerning classroom discipline and conducts workshops and training programs for teachers, administrators, parents, and other educators.

Over the years, Canter has expanded and built on the basic behavior management principles from the assertive discipline book. Since today's teachers face even more complex situations, a more comprehensive model was developed. The revised edition of *Assertive Discipline* (2010) goes beyond the initial take-charge approach and includes additional classroom management procedures. In the revised *Assertive Discipline*, Canter discusses the assertive attitude necessary to deal with classroom management and discipline, the parts of a classroom discipline plan, aspects of teaching responsible behavior, and ways to deal with difficult students. The goal of assertive discipline is to teach students to choose responsible behavior, and in doing so, to raise their self-esteem and increase their academic success.

Canter maintains that teachers have the right and responsibility to (1) establish rules and directions that clearly define the limits of acceptable and unacceptable student behavior; (2) teach these rules and directions; and (3) ask for assistance from parents and administrators when support is needed in handling the behavior of students. The manner in which teachers respond to student behavior affects students' self-esteem and success in school. Therefore, teachers must use an assertive response style to state expectations clearly and confidently to students and reinforce these words with actions.

■ **CLASSROOM CASE STUDY**   A Cooperative Learning Unit Turns Sour

Pedro Ramirez was excited about a new unit he had planned for his high school science students on global climate change. He wanted his students to explore several key aspects: the research evidence, political agreements or disagreements about climate change, the ecological changes, and the influences on people throughout the world. Mr. Ramirez split his class into cooperative learning groups, with each group having responsibility for a separate major aspect. He provided many resources for each group and asked the groups to be ready to report their findings after the groups worked on their topic for several class periods.

Students were on task in their groups at first, but gradually students in each group got off task. There was talking, tex-ting, tossing papers, and walking around the room. By the third class session, only a few students in each group were working on the tasks. Mr. Ramirez was very disappointed and reached a breaking point soon after the start of the fourth class session of group work.

Focus Questions

1. If you were in his shoes, what would you do at that moment?

2. At that moment, what would a teacher with a low teacher control approach do? With a medium-control approach? With a high-control approach? (See Tables 2.1 and 2.2.)

3. What could Mr. Ramirez have done in his planning and preparation to minimize this off-task behavior?

A classroom discipline plan has three parts: (1) rules that students must follow at all times; (2) positive recognition that students will receive for following the rules; and (3) consequences that result when students choose not to follow the rules. Sample rules may be to follow directions, keep hands and feet to oneself, or be in the classroom and seated when the bell rings. Positive recognition may include various forms of praise, positive notes sent home to parents, positive notes to students, or special activities or privileges.

Consequences are delivered systematically with each occurrence of misbehavior. The first time a student breaks a rule, the student receives a warning. The second time, the student may lose a privilege, such as being last in line for lunch or staying in class one minute after the bell. The third time, the student loses additional privileges. The fourth time, the teacher calls the parents. The fifth time, the student is sent to the principal. In cases of severe misbehavior, these preliminary steps may be skipped and the student is sent to the principal.

Another part of Canter's assertive discipline plan is to teach responsible behavior. This includes determining and teaching specific directions (classroom procedures), using positive recognition to motivate students to behave, redirecting nondisruptive off-task behavior, and implementing consequences. Canter further emphasizes that successful teachers need to blend academic and behavior management efforts into a cohesive whole so that classroom management actions are not apparent.

Canter gives special attention to dealing with difficult students, who represent perhaps 5–10 percent of the students you may encounter. In *Assertive Discipline,* Canter provides recommendations for conducting a one-to-one problem-solving conference with the teacher and the difficult student. The goal of the conference is to help the student gain insight into the problem and ultimately choose more responsible behavior. Guidelines are offered to provide positive support to build positive relationships with difficult students, and recommendations are made for developing an individualized behavior plan. Parents and administrators can offer additional support when dealing with difficult students. Lee and Marlene Canter have a separate book on this subject: *Succeeding with Difficult Students* (2008). Lee Canter further expanded his concepts in *Classroom Management for Academic Success* (2014).

Positive Discipline: Fredric Jones

Fredric Jones is a psychologist who conducted research on classroom practices and developed training programs for improving teacher effectiveness in behavior management and instruction. In *Positive Classroom Discipline* (1987), Jones emphasized that teachers can help students support their own self-control. Jones' *Tools for Teaching* (2013) extends the discussion of these issues. Jones recommends that teachers use the following five strategies to enact positive discipline.

1. **Structure the classroom.** Teachers need to consider various rules, routines, and standards; seating arrangements; and student–teacher relationships when structuring the classroom. Rules, procedures, routines, and classroom standards need to be taught to students so they understand the standards and expectations in the classroom. Jones points out that the arrangement of the classroom furniture can maximize teacher mobility and allow greater physical proximity to students on a moment-to-moment basis. While presenting several ways to arrange student desks in a classroom, Jones indicates that any arrangement that provides quick and easy access to all students is likely to be successful. Jones also prefers to have assigned seats for students to disperse the good students between the chronic disrupters.

2. **Maintain control by using appropriate instructional strategies.** Jones maintains that teachers lose control of their classes when they spend too much time with each student, such as during seatwork. Teachers commonly spend time to find out where a student is having difficulty, to explain further the part the student doesn't understand, and to supply students

VOICES FROM THE CLASSROOM   Positive Recognition in Assertive Discipline

Cammie Fulk, Fifth-Grade Teacher, Fulks Run, Virginia

To provide positive recognition in my assertive discipline plan, I post a personal calendar for each student each month. If a student has behaved well and completed all of the work for the day, a stamp is placed on that date. If not, then the reason for not receiving the stamp is written on that date. When a student receives five stamps in a row, a reward is given. For ten stamps in a row, a free homework pass is provided. At the end of each month, the calendar is sent home to be signed by the parents and then returned to me. This personal calendar has become a strong motivator in my fifth-grade classroom.

In addition to the personal calendars, I have a gem jar on my desk as a reward for the entire class. It is simply a clear coffee cup with three permanent levels marked on the side to indicate 5, 10, and 15 minutes of free time earned. As I observe the entire class on task, I place several gems in the jar. Gems may be marbles, bubble gum, candy corn, jelly beans, or other small items. Gems can be earned for a variety of behaviors such as good hall behavior, the entire class on task, the entire class completing homework, or other valued actions. The sound of the gems hitting the glass cup brings smiles to my fifth graders.

with additional explanations and examples. Instead, Jones recommends that teachers use the three-step sequence of praise, prompt, and leave. In this sequence, teachers first praise students for what they have done correctly so far. Second, prompt students by telling them exactly what to do next and encourage them to do it. The teacher then leaves to let the student take the needed action and also to be available to help other students.

3. **Maintain control with limit-setting techniques.** Jones proposed a series of specific actions that can be taken when a student is *getting off task*. These techniques primarily involve the use of body language to convince the students that the teacher is in control. These steps involve being aware of and monitoring the behavior of all students; terminating instruction when necessary to deal with a student; turning, looking, and saying the student's name; moving to the edge of the student's desk; moving away from the student's desk when the student gets back to work; placing your palms on the desk and giving a short, direct verbal prompt if the student does not get back to work; moving closer over the desk; and finally moving next to the student behind the student's desk.

4. **Build patterns of cooperation.** Jones proposed an incentive system called preferred activity time (PAT) that can be used so students can earn certain benefits if they behave and cooperate. The PAT may be a variety of activities and privileges that are given to the class as a whole at the start of a predetermined time (a week's worth). On the one hand, when an individual student misbehaves, the teacher uses a stopwatch or timer to record the length of time of the infraction, and this amount of time is subtracted from the class's total time. On the other hand, students can earn bonus time for the class by cleaning up the classroom in a hurry, being in their seats in time, or some other desired behavior.

5. **Develop appropriate backup systems in the event of misbehavior.** Backups are to be used systematically from lesser sanctions to more serious ones. Low-level sanctions involve issuing a warning; pulling a card with the student's name, address, and telephone number; and then sending a letter to the parents. (But first the student is given an opportunity to correct the behavior; if so, then the letter is not sent.) Mid-level sanctions include time-out, detention, loss of privileges, and a parent conference. High-level sanctions include in-school suspension, Saturday school, delivering the student to a parent at work, asking a parent to accompany the student in school, suspension, police intervention, and expulsion.

Discipline Without Stress: Marvin Marshall

Discipline Without Stress promotes responsibility and learning using an approach that is totally noncoercive, but not permissive. Prior to becoming a staff developer and international speaker, Marvin Marshall was a classroom teacher, guidance counselor, principal, and college instructor. In *Discipline Without Stress, Punishments, or Rewards*, Marshall (2012) described a comprehensive system to guide and monitor student behavior and to promote responsibility and learning.

The following principles are incorporated into the Discipline Without Stress model (pp. 275–276):

- Being positive is a more constructive teacher than being negative.

- Choice empowers.

- Self-evaluation is essential for lasting improvement.

- People choose their own behaviors.

- Self-correction is the most effective approach to change behavior.

- Acting responsibly is the most satisfying of rewards.

- Growth is greater when authority is used without punishment.

Although many of the program features blend into the interacting model of discipline, Marshall places his system into the intervening model of discipline, since there is a high degree of teacher control in directing the environment.

As a starting point in his Discipline Without Stress teaching model, Marshall stresses the importance of teaching and practicing procedures and not assuming that students automatically know how to do what the teacher desires students to do. Next, Marshall identifies three principles to practice with students in a classroom: (1) *positivity*—practice changing negatives into positives ("No running" becomes "We walk in the hallways."); (2) *choice*—permit students to choose their responses to a situation so they become more self-controlled, responsible, and empowered; and (3) *reflection*—ask questions that guide students to reflect and self-evaluate.

Another important aspect of Marshall's program is the Raise Responsibility System (RRS), which has three components: (1) teaching—teaching the hierarchy of social development to students; (2) asking—checking for understanding when students are irresponsible; and (3) eliciting—guiding choices when students continue to misbehave.

In the first part of the RRS, students are taught the hierarchy of social development to students; this is proactive. A hierarchy is employed because of the natural tendency to reach the highest level. Teaching at the outset is in contrast to a reactive approach after misbehaviors occur. The four levels of social development in this hierarchy are labeled with letters, with "A" being the lowest level and "D" being the highest level. The four levels, in descending order from most developed, are as follows:

D: *Democracy* (motivation is internal)

- Develops self-discipline

- Demonstrates initiative

- Demonstrates responsibility

- Does good because it is the right thing to do

C: *Cooperation/conformity* (motivation is external)

- Considerate

- Complies

- Conforms

- Cooperates when someone else is present

B: *Bossing/bullying* (needs to be bossed to behave)

- Bothers others

- Bosses or bullies others

- Breaks classroom standards

A: Anarchy

- Absence of order

- Aimless and chaotic

Only levels C and D are acceptable. The difference in these two levels is in the motivation rather than the behavior.

In the second part of the RRS, disruptions are handled by checking for understanding. This involves asking reflective questions pertaining to the levels of the hierarchy of social development, rather than framing the questions about the student's action. Consistently asking the students to reflect is the key to enacting change.

The third part of the RRS involves guiding students in the choices they make. This step is used for students who have already acknowledged irresponsible behavior and yet continue to misbehave on an unacceptable level. Guided choices stop the disruption by using authority, without being coercive or punitive. A consequence is elicited to help the student prevent repetition of the behaviors that he or she exhibited from level A or B. This step is in contrast to the usual approach of imposing a punishment or consequence in which the student has no ownership.

Overall, this program is designed to influence students into making responsible decisions about their classroom behavior. Discipline Without Stress focuses on promoting responsibility rather than on obedience. Obedience does not create desire. When responsibility is promoted, however, obedience becomes a natural byproduct.

Determining Your Management Plan

How do you develop a philosophy of classroom management and a management plan for your classroom? Bosch (2007) maintains that classroom management must reflect the personality and teaching style of the individual teacher and is a skill that must be learned, practiced, and evaluated,

☰ Developing Your Management Plan Examining Your Philosophical Beliefs

To help form your philosophy of classroom management, answer the following questions to reflect your current beliefs. You may modify your responses over time as you explore more information about classroom management and discipline.

- What is the purpose of education?

- What is a good teacher, and what is good teaching?

- What should be the goals of a classroom management plan?

- What degree of control do I want to maintain in the classroom? Do I see myself as an autocratic or a democratic teacher, or somewhere in between?

- How do I want my degree of control to be evident in my instructional, management, and disciplinary practices in the classroom?

- Which model of discipline (shown in Table 2.1 and Table 2.2) appeals to me? Why?

and modified to fit the changing situations in classrooms. Further, teachers must be able to modify and adjust their management strategies as conditions warrant, just as they modify their teaching strategies to match students' needs and learning styles.

Your goals, values, and beliefs about classroom management, discipline, instruction, and child development will affect your management philosophy, and your philosophy, in turn, will affect how you select and enact the particular aspects of your management plan.

Your Management Philosophy

Before you determine your management plan, you must select a philosophical model for classroom management and discipline. This chapter provided a brief orientation to various models of discipline, which went from low to high teacher control, representing a continuum of philosophical perspectives for control in the classroom. This discussion on control is a useful starting point as you consider your philosophical perspective on classroom management and discipline. Adapted from Manning and Bucher (2013), the chapter feature on "Developing Your Management Plan" lists several questions about additional educational issues to prompt your consideration of education, teaching and learning, management, and discipline to help you clarify your philosophical beliefs.

To what degree do you want to exercise control in your classroom? That is the fundamental question when deciding on your approach to classroom management and discipline. To answer that question, you will likely consider a number of factors, such as your views of educational philosophy, psychology, and child development. For example, when determining your approach to control, you will likely take into account your beliefs about what is the dominant influence on a child's development—inner forces, outer forces, or a combination of the two. You may want to review Table 2.1 on the characteristics of the discipline models and Table 2.2 on the proponents of various discipline models.

Your Management Plan

Your analysis of the philosophical views of classroom management and discipline will probably reveal whether you are inclined to use low-, medium-, or high-control approaches, each representing a different philosophical perspective. After determining your relative placement on the teacher control continuum, decide whether you want to use a particular discipline model shown in Table 2.2, synthesize two or more models, or create your own approach. Even if you choose one model, you may find that the context of the classroom and the actual events cause you to shift from that model and use elements of other approaches. You don't have to accept the entire set of actions proposed by a certain model. When determining the relative merits of the different discipline models, it may be useful to establish criteria to compare the relative characteristics, strengths, and weaknesses of each model.

There is more to developing your management plan than selecting a particular discipline model. To enact your philosophical view of classroom management and discipline, you will need to make decisions about the seven domains of responsibility in classroom management and discipline outlined in Chapter 1. Those domains can serve as organizers for your decision making to create an effective learning community.

To facilitate your thinking and decisions concerning the seven domains, Table 2.3 lists categories that could be included in your classroom management plan. Each category is discussed in this book, with some categories being addressed in an entire chapter.

■ TABLE 2.3　Clarifying Your Classroom Management Plan

The following categories provide a framework for you to clarify and write your classroom management plan

Philosophy on Classroom Management and Discipline
➤ First provide background information about your personality, teaching style, and philosophy of education to reveal the origins and foundation of your classroom management philosophy
➤ Next, describe your philosophy on classroom management and discipline for your own classroom. What are your purposes forz an effective classroom management plan? To what degree do you plan to control the decision making and actions in the classroom? To what degree will you involve students?

The Classroom Arrangement
➤ How will you arrange student seating, the teacher's desk, furniture arrangement, bulletin boards, technology placement, storage of materials, and the use of wall space? This could include a diagram to show the placement of these features

Rules
➤ What behavior will you expect of your students?
➤ What rules will you display and use in your classroom?
➤ Describe how you determined the rules. Would you involve students in identifying the rules? If so, to what degree? How will you communicate the rules to the students, parents, and administrators?

Responses to Misbehavior
➤ What will you do when a student misbehaves and breaks a rule? Will you have a hierarchy of consequences to deal with mild, moderate, and severe misbehavior? Specifically, what is your plan?

Procedures
➤ What procedures will you use in your classroom (e.g., distributing materials, collecting homework, transitions in and out of the room, and providing students assistance)? How will you teach the procedures to the students?

Creating a Respectful, Supportive Learning Environment
➤ What type of classroom atmosphere would you like to create? What specifically will you do to create that atmosphere? How can you maintain and reinforce appropriate student behavior? How can you promote cooperation?

Managing and Facilitating Instruction
➤ How will your lessons be structured? How will you begin and end your lessons? How will you group your students for instruction? How will you manage lesson delivery? How will you make modifications for diverse learners? How will you integrate technology in instruction?

Motivating Students to Learn
➤ How will you include motivational strategies in your instruction, evaluation, and feedback? How will you incorporate these motivational issues into all levels of your instructional planning?

Promoting Safety and Wellness
➤ How will you provide a physically and emotionally safe environment for students in your classroom? How will you respond to disruptive or violent behavior in the classroom? How might you prevent it?

Interacting with Parents, Colleagues, and Others
➤ What are the reasons for communicating and interacting with parents, colleagues, and others? How will you communicate with them? How frequently?

MAJOR CONCEPTS

1. A continuum showing a range of low to high teacher control can be used to illustrate the various educational views expressed by educators about classroom management and discipline.

2. Low-control approaches are based on the philosophical belief that students have primary responsibility for controlling their own behavior and that they have the capability to make these decisions.

3. Educators representative of the low-control approach are Haim Ginott, Thomas Gordon, Jim Fay, David Funk, Barbara Coloroso, and Alfie Kohn.

4. Medium-control approaches are based on the philosophical belief that students develop from a combination of natural forces within the child and outer forces of the child's environment. Thus, the control of student behavior is a joint responsibility of the student and the teacher.

5. Educators representative of the medium-control approach are Rudolf Dreikurs, Linda Albert, Jane Nelsen, William Glasser, Richard Curwin, Allen Mendler, and Spencer Kagan.

6. High-control approaches are based on the philosophical belief that students' growth and development are the result of external

conditions. Children are seen as molded and shaped by influences from the environment where they live.

7. Educators representative of the high-control approach are B. F. Skinner, Lee Canter, Fredric Jones, and Marvin Marshall.

8. When deciding on your approach to control, you will likely consider your views of educational philosophy, psychology, and child development. It may also be useful to identify whether you are inclined to use low-, medium-, or high-control approaches on the teacher behavior continuum.

DISCUSSION/REFLECTIVE QUESTIONS

1. What are the merits and problems that might be associated with each of the three levels of teacher control?

2. Recall a favorite teacher you had. What level of control did that teacher use? What are the indicators of that level of control?

3. What are the possible benefits and problems of conducting classroom meetings, as proposed by Alfie Kohn?

4. How would you define a logical consequence (see Dreikurs)? Identify some examples of student misbehavior and the logical consequence that could be linked to each behavior.

5. Why is the Fredric Jones model included in the high-control category?

SUGGESTED ACTIVITIES

1. Think about your schooling experiences and identify teachers you had who fell in the low-, medium-, and high-control approaches. How positive were your experiences in those classes?

2. Talk with several teachers to learn about the degree of control they use when selecting rules and dealing with misbehavior. Identify which discipline model each teacher seems to reflect.

3. From one or more schools, examine any documents about discipline expectations or plans for teachers or the entire school. Also see if there are any committees or formal procedures in the school to address discipline problems. Do these policies or committees represent any particular approach to discipline?

FURTHER READING

Charles, C. M. (2014). *Building classroom discipline* (11th ed.). Boston: Pearson.

In separate chapters, the book provides an overview of the discipline models of several educators. Also includes chapters examining the nature of misbehavior, working effectively with all students, and formalizing your personal system of discipline.

Hardin, C. J. (2012). *Effective classroom management: Models and strategies for today's classroom* (3rd ed.). Boston: Pearson.

In separate chapters, the book provides descriptions of many models of discipline ranging from low to high teacher control. Also includes a chapter on creating your own system.

Manning, M. L., & Bucher, K. T. (2013). *Classroom management: Models, applications, and cases* (3rd ed.). Boston: Pearson.

In separate chapters, the book provides descriptions of the classroom management and discipline plans of several leading educators. Also includes chapters on understanding the need for classroom management and on building your own management plan.

© Michelle D. Bridwell/PhotoEdit

chapter

3

Preparing for the School Year

CHAPTER OUTLINE

CHAPTER OBJECTIVES

This chapter provides information that will help you:

- Make instructional and management decisions and preparations before school starts.

- Determine your processes for assessment, record keeping, and recording.

- Establish a plan to deal with misbehavior.
- Plan how to conduct the first days of the school year.
- Determine how to organize your classroom and materials.

Imagine that you are going to take a two-week vacation to see the numerous state and national parks in southern Utah and northern Arizona. You gather information about the parks and attractions from a variety of sources, and then you start to plan your itinerary. Next, you make motel reservations and list all of the things you need to take with you, such as hiking shoes, water bottles, sunscreen, sunglasses, camera, and clothing. Soon before you leave on the trip, you stop your newspaper and mail delivery and make arrangements for your pets for the days you are gone. All of these arrangements, and probably more, are needed to have a fun, trouble-free vacation.

Starting the school year also requires this type of planning. Even before school starts, you can make a number of decisions about instructional and management preparations, plans to promote a positive learning climate, arrangements for assessments and record keeping, plans for the first day of school, and arrangements for floor space, storage, and other aspects of classroom space. Early planning and decision making on these issues will help ensure a positive start to the school year. These classroom management issues are explored in this chapter.

Preparing for the School Year

If you surveyed experienced teachers about the role of management at the beginning of the school year, you would undoubtedly hear comments about management and instructional preparations before school starts and about ways to plan for the first days of the school year. Studies on classroom management have verified that the first few days of the school year set the tone for the entire year (Emmer & Evertson, 2017; Evertson & Emmer, 2017; R. J. Marzano, J. S. Marzano, & D. J. Pickering, 2003; R. J. Marzano, B. B. Gaddy, M. C. Foseid, M. P. Foseid, & J. S. Marzano, 2009).

To begin, you can make management preparations, make instructional preparations, plan to manage assessments and record keeping, establish a plan for misbehavior, and also prepare for the first day of school. When the school year finally begins, there are certain actions that are appropriate during the first day and over the following few days. A number of these issues are addressed in this section. There are a number of resources that provide more details than can be discussed in this chapter. Resources are available for the elementary grades (K. A. Bosch & M. E. Bosch, 2015; Jonson, 2010; Kelly, 2010; Moran, Stobbe, Baron, Miller, & Moir, 2009), secondary grades (Bongalan, Moir, & Baron, 2010; Sprick, 2013; Thompson, 2011; Wyatt & White, 2007), and grades K–12 (Bluestein, 2010; Guillaume, 2016; Kronowitz, 2012; Marzano et al., 2009; McEwan, 2006; Partin, 2009; Thompson, 2013; H. K. Wong & R. T. Wong, 2009, 2014).

Making Management Preparations

It is important to carefully consider management issues such as your school environment, room and seating arrangements, materials, rules and procedures, and communication with parents. Based on a study of experienced teachers (Schell & Burden, 2006), you could direct your attention to the following classroom management issues.

1. **The school environment.** The first step is to become thoroughly familiar with the total environment before school starts: the room, school, facilities, personnel, services, resources, policies and procedures, other teachers, children, and the community. You will then have more information on which to base decisions, will probably feel more confident about your job, and will not need to devote time in the first few weeks to gather this information.

2. **Support materials.** After examining the curriculum guide and the textbooks, you might have ideas about activities for a certain unit or lesson. Supplementary materials may be needed when the time comes to teach that lesson. This is the time to gather any additional support materials such as games and devices, pictures, DVDs, ideas for activities, charts, maps, and graphs. The school may have discretionary funds for the purchase of these types of resources. They may be obtained from school supply catalogs, a local teacher store, or even at garage sales.

3. **Filing system.** It is useful to set up a filing system for storing district and school communications and other important documents. Papers that should be kept in a filing cabinet include the district's policy handbook; correspondence from the principal, superintendent, or other supervisors; correspondence from professional organizations; lesson plans; and items on curricular content. Some teachers use file folders. A separate file folder may be created for each course unit to hold pertinent notes and resource materials. Similarly, digital files of important material should be stored in an orderly manner on your computer. Textbooks, resource books, manipulative materials, and other types of instructional supplies and materials also need to be organized and stored.

4. **Classroom procedures.** You can follow various procedures to accomplish specific tasks. Procedures may be identified regarding handing in completed work, sharpening a pencil, using the restroom, or putting away supplies. Before school starts, identify actions or activities requiring procedures that will contribute to a smoothly running classroom, and then decide what those procedures should be.

5. **Classroom helpers.** Teachers call on students at all grade levels as helpers to perform various classroom tasks. Make a list of tasks that need to be done and then decide which ones students can perform. Give attention to how task assignment will be rotated to give every student an opportunity to help. Roles are often held for one or two weeks before being reassigned. Depending on the grade level and circumstances, some tasks may include students as line leader, light switcher, pencil sharpener, paper collector, plant waterer, Whiteboard eraser, window and blind opener, and supply manager.

6. **Class lists and rosters.** It is useful to plan a means to record whether students have returned their book orders, picture money, field trip permission forms, and so on. You can prepare a generic class roster listing the students' names in alphabetical order in the left column, with blank columns on the right to check off the action. It is helpful to create the list on a computer so that an updated sheet can be easily generated when the roster changes.

7. **School/home communication.** Open communication with families is vital. Before school starts, many teachers prepare an introductory letter to families to welcome them and to inform them about the teacher, the curriculum, grading practices and standards, the homework policy, rules and procedures, and so on (discussed more fully in Chapter 11). This letter can be sent home with the students on the first day of school. Teachers can also make plans for other types of communication with families such as emails, phone calls, progress reports, or a back-to-school night.

8. **Birthdays and other celebrations.** Depending on your grade level, you may want to recognize student birthdays. Most schools have very specific policies for celebrating major holidays, such as Halloween, Christmas, Hanukkah, Martin Luther King Day, and Easter. Inquire about these policies so you will understand what is expected.

VOICES FROM THE CLASSROOM Using a Class List for Various Purposes

Marge McClintock, fifth-grade science and social studies teacher, New Providence, New Jersey

As soon as I am given my class list of students for the year, I assign the students numbers in alphabetical order for each class. The students are told their numbers and are required to put their numbers on all of their work. This has several benefits. When homework or seatwork is handed in, I ask a student to put the papers in numerical order for me. I can see in an instant which numbers are missing and take whatever action is needed.

Another benefit is managing the students on class trips. Although I always carry a class list with me on the trips, it is much faster to have the students call out their numbers in order when they're back on the bus or whenever roll needs to be taken.

A third benefit is in dividing the class into groups. It can be as easy as evens and odds. Or I can require the students to use higher order math skills by saying, "All the students whose number can be factored by 3, please come to the front of the class. All students whose number can be factored by 2 and who aren't in the '3' group, please go to the back of the room. All the rest, stay where you are."

9. **Distributing textbooks.** Sometime in the first few days of school, you will need to distribute textbooks. You need to obtain the textbooks and prepare an inventory form on which to record each book number, with a space in which to write the student's name. Think about when and how the textbooks will be distributed. Since the first day of school often necessitates many announcements and activities, you might want to wait until the second or third day before distributing textbooks or distribute them just before they are needed for the first time. Attention might be given to the specific means of distribution. One way is to have students line up one row at a time and go to the table where the books are stacked. When giving the book to the student, you can record the student's name on the inventory form.

10. **Room identification.** On the first day of school, students need to locate your classroom. Especially for students new to the building, it is important to have the room clearly labeled. A poster on the outside doorway should include the room number, the teacher's name, and the grade level and/or subject (e.g., Room 211, Mr. Wagner, and World History). This information should be written on the chalkboard so students see that they are in the correct classroom. Some type of welcoming statement should also be placed on the chalkboard, such as, "Welcome, I'm glad you're here."

11. **Room arrangement.** Room arrangement is an issue that can be decided before school starts. Take into account the fixed features in the room, instructional materials and supplies, traffic areas, work areas, boundaries for activity areas, visibility to see all students, and the purposes of various seating arrangements. Determine the arrangement in the classroom for your desk, the students' desks, tables, bookshelves, filing cabinets, and other furniture. The room arrangement you select should be consistent with your instructional goals and activities. Teacher-led instructional approaches such as presentations and demonstrations will require one type of room arrangement, whereas small-group work would require a different type of arrangement.

12. **Seat selections and arrangements.** One teacher may prefer to assign each student's seat, while another may let the students select their seats. This decision should be made before school starts. In either case, be sure that there are enough seats for the number of students you expect. You might take the age level and maturity of the students into account as you select the manner of assigning seats. You might change the seating arrangements during the school year to accommodate work groups, to move students who need close supervision to more accessible seats, or simply to provide a change.

13. **Room decoration.** It is important to make your classroom an attractive, comfortable place. Consider having some plants in the classroom, or even an aquarium. Displays of pictures, posters, charts, and maps also help cover the walls with informative and appealing materials. Attractive bulletin boards add color. You might prepare one bulletin board listing classroom information and use another one to display seasonal items. After school starts, you can have students prepare bulletin boards.

Making Instructional Preparations

Prior to the start of the school year, carefully consider a variety of instructional issues such as long-range plans, supplementary materials, student assessment, a folder for substitute teachers, a syllabus, and so on. Based on a study of experienced teachers (Schell & Burden, 2006), you would direct your attention to the following instructional issues.

1. **Long-range plans.** It is helpful to peruse the curriculum guides and other related materials so you can appreciate what should be covered by the end of the school year. Some tentative decisions need to be made on the amount of time to spend on each particular unit. Some curriculum guides include recommendations for the number of weeks to spend on each unit.

   You may want to solicit advice from other teachers, particularly from those who teach your same subject or grade level. To the extent possible, make your rough schedules conform to the school calendar by taking into account grading periods and holidays. Be careful not to overschedule yourself. Leave some time for review near the end of each unit or chapter, for reteaching as the situation warrants, and for unexpected occurrences such as school closings due to inclement weather.

2. **Supplementary materials.** For each major curricular topic in your rough long-range plans, start an ongoing list of related supplementary materials or activities. It may include field trip locations, resource people, media, games, assignments, bulletin boards, and additional books. Inquire about library or media center resources, such as audio discs or DVDs, and order and reserve them. Determine what online resources you might use and make sure you have the appropriate passwords. You might prepare other supplementary materials to use during the first few weeks of school.

3. **Skeleton plans.** A *skeleton plan* is a brief overview of intended accomplishments. It often includes a weekly list of expected accomplishments. Skeleton plans include more details than the long-range yearly plans but not the detail needed for daily lesson plans. Skeleton plans for the first three or four weeks serve as a guide for preparing the more detailed lesson plans.

4. **Weekly time schedules.** You should establish your weekly schedule before school starts and include a copy in a handy place such as in your lesson plan book. The weekly schedule is often displayed in a chart, with the weekdays listed at the top and the hours listed on the left-hand column. The principal or others probably will determine the class schedule for middle and secondary teachers in the school building, and the schedule will show what grade level and subject is taught during each class period.

5. **Daily lesson plans.** After you have completed the skeleton plans for the first three or four weeks, it is time to prepare the daily lesson plans for the first week of school. Lesson plan formats vary; one that is often used includes boxes for the days of the week and the subjects taught. In these boxes, you might include notes about objectives, a list of topics to be covered or activities to be conducted, materials, and means of assessment. Beginning and probationary teachers are often required to show the principal or assistant principal their weekly lesson plans for the coming week. See Figure 3.1 for an illustration of plans of different durations.

FIGURE 3.1   Plans of Different Durations

6. **Syllabus.** You need to give students information about each course at the start of the year. You could plan and prepare this information as well as any related materials before school starts. The *course syllabus* includes the course title, the title of the textbook and any other primary resource materials, a brief course description, a list of course objectives, a content outline, course requirements (e.g., tests, homework, and projects), how grades will be calculated (e.g., the points for each requirement and the point total needed for certain grades), a description of the homework policy, the attendance and tardiness policy, and a listing of classroom rules and procedures.

7. **Policy sheets.** The syllabus might include all related classroom policies and procedures, although some teachers do not include these items. Depending on the grade level and circumstances, some teachers do not provide a course syllabus. As a result, a teacher might prepare a separate policy sheet for the students stating the classroom rules and procedures, the policy for attendance and tardiness, and the like. If a course syllabus is not used, this policy sheet might also state the grading policy.

8. **Tentative student assessment.** It is useful to make an initial assessment of the students' understanding and skills at the start of the school year so you can better recognize the abilities and differences within the class. These assessments could be conducted sometime during the first week of school, but you should think about how to plan for the assessment and

■ WHAT WOULD YOU DECIDE?   Starting with Long-Range Plans

Prior to the school year, you will need to make some long-range plans that will provide a framework for your daily and weekly plans. These general plans may be for the entire year, and then be broken down into semesters, grading periods, and units.

1. What curriculum guides and other materials will you need to gather to provide a basis for your long-range planning decisions?

2. How will you determine the amount of time to be spent on each unit for each course?

3. How will you keep of a record of your long-range plans?

4. What information would you put into your plans for the first marking term? How will this help in your unit and lesson planning?

---

then make any necessary arrangements before school starts. Assessment procedures might include worksheets, oral activities, observation checklists, pretests, or review lessons. After conducting these early assessments, you should then record the results on a class roster that was drawn up earlier.

9. **Homework.** Give careful consideration to how you will evaluate students and determine report card grades. One element of student evaluation often involves homework, and preparation for developing a homework policy can be done before school starts. Prepare a homework policy in the form of a letter that is sent home to families at the start of the school year (see Chapter 11). The homework policy should explain why homework is assigned, explain the types of homework you will assign, inform parents of the amount and frequency of homework, provide guidelines for when and how students are to complete homework, let parents know you will positively reinforce students who complete homework, explain what you will do when students do not complete homework, and clarify what is expected of the parent.

10. **Backup materials.** It is useful to have some backup materials available when instruction takes less time than anticipated, when a change of plans is necessary, or when students finish their activities early. These backup materials may be related to the particular topics being covered at the time. Many teachers have a collection of puzzles, educational games, discussion questions, brainteasers, creative writing, word searches, and riddles. You can gather these materials before school starts.

11. **Opening class routine.** Students often perform better when they know that a particular routine will be regularly followed at the start of class. You can decide on the particular actions to be taken. You may need to take attendance, make announcements, and attend to other tasks at the start of the class period. The purpose of having a routine is to provide an orderly transition as students enter the room and get ready for instruction. Some teachers have students review vocabulary words or other problems related to the curriculum while other tasks are performed.

12. **Folder for substitute teachers.** A substitute teacher will take your place when you are absent. It is important to prepare materials for substitute teachers to help support what they do, maximize the learning, and minimize any off-task behavior. Many teachers keep a folder for substitute teachers that includes important information. It can be kept on your desk with the plan book.

   The type of material in a folder for substitute teachers varies, but the following information would be useful to include: a copy of the daily schedule, times of recess and lunch, a list of the classroom rules, a list of classroom procedures (e.g., morning opening, taking attendance, lunch count, lunch, dismissal, and fire drills), a list of reliable students in each class period, hall pass procedures (to go to the restroom, library, or office), information on where to find certain items (e.g., lesson plans, audiovisual equipment, and supplies), names of others to contact for information or help (e.g., a nearby teacher with room number), and a list and description of students with special needs. Much of this information can be collected before school starts, and additional information can be added as needed.

13. **Paraprofessionals.** Paraprofessionals, paraeducators, and teacher aides are among the various titles used for noncertified paid assistants in the classroom. Paraprofessionals can provide considerable assistance in the classroom under the guidance of the teacher. If you have a paraprofessional available, identify ways that you might use this person to facilitate instruction. Resources are available to give you guidance in your decisions (e.g., Ashbaker & Morgan, 2013; Doyle, 2008; Nevin, Villa, & Thousand, 2008). Guidelines are also available for paraprofessionals concerning behavioral interventions (Ashbaker & Morgan, 2015) and effective support in inclusive classrooms (Causton-Theoharis & Kluth, 2009; Hammeken, 2008).

Managing Assessment, Record Keeping, and Reporting

It is vital to give advance thought concerning how you will assess student achievement, record student progress and scores, and report the assessment information. Assessment always has been important in teaching, but the No Child Left Behind (2002) act and additional state and local accountability demands for ensuring student learning have placed a higher level of attention on assessment and reporting. Even before the school year starts, you should decide how you will assess student learning, keep records of student performance, and report the assessment data.

Electronic gradebooks are provided in many districts, or you can purchase one you like (assuming your district does not require the same electronic gradebook for all teachers). These have a spreadsheet design in which scores for each type of assessment can be entered for each student. Electronic gradebooks facilitate record keeping and reporting of grades.

- **Assessment.** Although there are many aspects to assessment, you will need to select the means of assessment. Teacher-made tests and quizzes are common. In addition, you may choose to have students demonstrate their learning through the use of performance-based measures with (1) *products* (e.g., portfolios, work samples, projects, and lab reports) or (2) *performances* (e.g., oral presentations, presentations with media, demonstrations, debates, and athletic demonstrations). For each of these assessment approaches, you will also need to determine how you will assess the level of student proficiency. This could be done through an answer key for a test, or with the use of rubrics or other rating forms for performance-based measures.

- **Record Keeping.** Once students have been assessed and you have scored their work, you must keep records in a gradebook. Gradebooks typically have a section for the daily attendance log, achievement scores, and conduct scores. All student assessment scores are placed in the gradebook, so prior thinking about your overall assessment plan will help you design the columns and labels in a useful manner. In addition to scores for performance on test items, portfolios, or other measuring techniques, some teachers have separate charts to record student proficiency for particular knowledge and skills related to the curriculum standards.

Entering the assessment scores in the gradebook is only part of your task. Then you must have a plan to translate all of the performance measures into a grade at the end of the report card period. For example, in a given subject, will you have a weight of 20 percent for homework, 40 percent for tests, 20 percent for a portfolio, and 20 percent for

VOICES FROM THE CLASSROOM   Planning for a Substitute Teacher

Mary Pat Whiteside, middle school teacher, Palm Coast, Florida

Establishing procedures for times when you are absent helps avoid stress for you, your students, and your substitute teacher. The first step is to discuss with your students your expectations for their behavior when a substitute teacher is there. I start by having my students discuss their worst experiences with a substitute. Then I ask if they want substitutes to leave our school and go out to the community bearing tales of horror. Next, I tell students that my rule for them is to treat substitutes better than they treat me. Inappropriate behavior by them leads to punishment by me and a phone call home.

The second step is to plan for the substitute teacher. I have a folder labeled "Substitute," which includes seating charts, class attendance lists, clear plans designed for easy understanding, a folder of extra work, the location of my emergency lesson plans, and a substitute feedback sheet.

At the top of the feedback sheet, I ask that the classroom rules be enforced, and I ask for short notes from the substitute about each class's general behavior. I also ask the substitute to list any students who were uncooperative, disruptive, or tardy. I ask that the substitute not discipline my students, but leave me the information and I will handle any problems that arose when I return. This system works well for me, and I now look forward to returning to order instead of chaos.

cooperative group projects? Furthermore, what performance level constitutes an A or a B? You need to think about your grading system before the start of the school year and establish your plan.

- **Reporting.** Your school district will likely determine a number of aspects of what will be recorded on report cards and how the information will be reported. First, the district determines what achievement and nonachievement (e.g., conduct) progress will be reported. Also, it determines what grading system will be used (e.g., letter grades, pass/fail, and checklists). There may be additional ways the district determines how grades are reported.

  In addition to report cards, you can communicate students' progress to their families in many ways, such as through parent–teacher conferences, newsletters, and open houses. During a parent–teacher conference, you may want to have a portfolio for each student ready to show representative work. For a newsletter, you may want to share information about the activities and the performance of the entire class. Give advance thought about what information you will be reporting and develop a plan for the kinds of data and materials you need to gather and report.

Establishing a Plan to Deal with Misbehavior

With an understanding of classroom management and discipline, you will need to develop a plan for dealing with misbehavior in the classroom. A seven-step plan is presented here that begins with the establishment of a system of rules and procedures. You need to provide a supportive environment during instruction and also provide situational assistance when students get off task. If the student does not get back on task, you need to move through advancing levels of consequences. If none of these actions work, you may need to involve other personnel.

You should deal with misbehavior in a way that is effective while also avoiding unnecessary disruptions. Researchers and educators have proposed movement from low to high intervention when developing a plan to address misbehavior (e.g., Charles, 2014; Levin & Nolan, 2014;

Wolfgang, 2009). Once the rules and procedures and a supportive classroom environment are in place, the teacher moves from low to high interventions, as described:

1. **Establish your system of rules and procedures.** Establish an appropriate system of rules and procedures as a foundation for dealing with discipline (discussed more fully in Chapter 4). It is vital that you select a system of rules and procedures appropriate to the situation. This system should incorporate reward or reinforcement for desirable behavior and the consequences of misbehavior. No single approach is best for all teachers and all teaching situations. For instance, rules and procedures for a 10th-grade English class would not be appropriate for a 3rd-grade class. Furthermore, the system needs to be consistent with established school and district policies and with your own educational philosophy, personality, and preferences.

2. **Provide a supportive environment during class sessions.** Once the system of rules and procedures has been established at the start of the school year, you need to maintain a supportive environment. Actions taken in the normal course of instruction are for the purpose of guiding and reinforcing students for positive behavior (discussed more fully in Chapter 5).

   Providing a supportive environment is accomplished primarily through cueing and reinforcing appropriate behavior and getting and holding attention. Cueing and reinforcing involve stressing positive, desirable behaviors; recognizing and reinforcing desired behaviors; and praising effectively. Getting and holding attention necessitate focusing attention at the start of lessons; keeping lessons moving at a good pace; monitoring attention during lessons; stimulating attention periodically; maintaining accountability; and terminating lessons that have gone on too long. Treat students with dignity and respect and offer challenging, interesting, and exciting classes.

3. **Provide situational assistance during class sessions.** Students may get off task during a lesson. This off-task behavior may be in the form of misbehavior or may simply be a lapse in attention. Either way, you need to promptly provide situational assistance. *Situational assistance* denotes actions that you take to get the student back on task with the least amount of intervention and disruption possible. Situational assistance can be provided by removing distracting objects, reinforcing appropriate behaviors, boosting student interest, providing cues, helping students over hurdles, redirecting the behavior, altering the lesson, and other approaches (discussed more fully in Chapter 9).

4. **Use mild responses.** If a student continues to be off task after situational assistance is provided, then you need to use mild responses to correct the student's behavior. These are not intended to be punitive. Mild responses may be nonverbal or verbal (see Chapter 9). Nonverbal responses include ignoring the behavior, using signal interference, using proximity control, or using touch control. Verbal responses include reinforcing peers, calling on the student during the lesson, using humor, giving a direct appeal or command, reminding the student of the rule, and several other approaches.

5. **Use moderate responses.** If students do not respond favorably to mild responses and continue to exhibit off-task behavior, you need to deliver moderate responses (see Chapter 9). These punitive responses deal with misbehavior by removing the desired stimulus so as to minimize the inappropriate behavior. Moderate responses include the use of logical consequences and various behavior modification techniques such as time-out and loss of privileges.

6. **Use stronger responses.** If moderate responses are insufficient, then you need to move to a more intrusive type of intervention (see Chapter 10). These stronger responses are intended to be punitive, by adding aversive stimuli such as reprimands and overcorrection. The purpose of aversive stimuli is to decrease unwanted behavior.

7. **Involve others when necessary.** If all efforts have failed to get the student to behave properly, then you need to involve other persons in the process. This occurs most commonly with chronic or severe behaviors. You may consult or involve counselors, psychologists, principals and assistant principals, teaching colleagues, college personnel, mental health centers, school social workers, school nurses, supervisors and department heads, and families (see Chapter 10). Their assistance and involvement will vary, depending on their expertise.

Planning for the First Day

Starting the school year effectively is vitally important when implementing a system of classroom management. Marzano and colleagues report that a strong first day and an emphasis on classroom management in the first few days make a big difference in getting off to a good start. Several principles should guide your decisions about planning the start of the school year and your actions in the first few days (Emmer & Evertson, 2017; Evertson & Emmer, 2017; Good & Brophy, 2008; H. K. Wong & R. T. Wong, 2009, 2014).

1. **Plan to clearly state your rules, procedures, and academic expectations.** When students arrive in your class for the first time, they may have uncertainties. They will want to know your expectations for behavior and for academic work. They will want to know what the rules are for general behavior and also the consequences for adhering to or breaking them (discussed more fully in Chapter 4). They want to know what the procedures are for going to the restroom, turning in homework, sharpening their pencils, talking during seatwork, and other specific activities. They will be interested in finding out about course requirements, grading policies, standards for work, and other aspects of the academic program.

   Your philosophical perspective about classroom management will likely affect your decisions. As discussed in Chapter 2 on the models of discipline, you need to consider the degree you want to involve students in identifying the rules and procedures. Some teachers like to determine the rules before school starts, while other teachers prefer to involve students in the discussion of the rules to develop a sense of ownership. Still other teachers let the students discuss and determine the rules themselves. You need to decide on your approach to the selection of rules and procedures prior to the start of school.

   It is especially important to take the necessary time during the first few days of school to describe your expectations in detail about behavior and work. Emphasize and be explicit about desirable behavior. Combine learning about procedures, rules, and course requirements with your initial content activities to build a good foundation for the year.

2. **Plan uncomplicated lessons to help students be successful.** Content activities and assignments during the first week should be designed to ensure maximum student success. Select relatively uncomplicated lessons at the start of the school year so that few students will likely need individual help. This allows you to focus on monitoring behavior and to respond to students in ways that shape and reinforce appropriate behavior. It provides you with opportunities to reinforce students for their academic work and to begin to develop positive relationships with students.

3. **Keep a whole-class focus.** Plan activities for the first week that have a whole-class focus, rather than small-group activities. Whole-class activities make it easier to monitor student behavior and performance. In this way, you can focus on reinforcing appropriate behavior and preventing inappropriate behavior.

4. **Be available, visible, and in charge.** You must be in charge of students at all times. Move around and be physically near the students and maintain a good field of vision to see all students wherever you stand. Move around during seatwork to check on student progress.

■ WHAT WOULD YOU DECIDE?   Dealing with Late Students on the First Day

It's the first day of school. You've just gone over many instructional and management topics for your sixth-grade class and had some introductory, get-acquainted activities. Then two students arrive an hour late. They've missed all of that information and the introductory activities. You don't want to disadvantage the two students, but you also think you should move ahead with the rest of the class.

1. What would you do at that moment? How do you move the rest of the class ahead while still making provision for the two late students to obtain the needed introductory information and also to get to know the other students?

2. What other problems might you anticipate on the first day? How might you address those problems?

5. **Plan strategies to deal with potential problems.** Unexpected events can develop when you meet your students for the first time. These might include interruptions by parents, office staff, custodians, or others; late arrivals on the first day; one or more students being assigned to your class after the first day; and an insufficient number of textbooks or necessary materials. You can give advance thought to how you would deal with common, unplanned events should they occur. Treat each unexpected situation in a calm, professional manner. This will serve as a good model for your students when they confront unexpected or challenging events. Treat students respectfully and deal with some of the needed details later. For example, you can ask a late enrolling student to take a seat and begin work, and then you could handle the particular enrollment procedures later.

6. **Closely monitor student compliance with rules and procedures.** By closely monitoring students, you can provide cues and reinforcement for appropriate behavior. Better classroom managers monitor their students' compliance with rules consistently, intervene to correct inappropriate behavior whenever necessary, and mention rules or describe desirable behavior when giving feedback. Effective managers stress specific corrective feedback rather than criticism or threat of punishment when students fail to comply with rules and procedures.

7. **Stop inappropriate behavior quickly.** Inappropriate or disruptive behavior should be handled quickly and consistently. Minor misbehavior that is not corrected often increases in intensity or is taken up by other students. Quickly respond to inappropriate behavior to maximize on-task behavior. Act in a professional manner to settle the difficulty and preserve the student's dignity in front of the other students.

8. **Organize instruction on the basis of ability levels.** The cumulative record folders will indicate students' prior academic performance in reading, math, and other subjects. Select instructional content and activities to meet the ability levels of your students.

9. **Hold students academically accountable.** Develop procedures that keep students accountable for their academic work. This may include papers to be turned in at the end of class, homework, in-class activities, or other means. Return the completed papers promptly and with feedback. Some teachers give a weekly assignment sheet to each student. This sheet is completed by the student, checked by the parent, and returned to the teacher daily.

10. **Be clear when communicating information.** Effective teachers clearly and explicitly present information, give directions, and state objectives. When discussing complex tasks, break them down into step-by-step procedures.

11. **Maintain students' attention.** Arrange seating so all students can easily face the area where their main attention needs to be held. Get everyone's focused attention before starting a lesson. Monitor students for signs of confusion or inattention and be sensitive to student concerns.

12. **Organize the flow of lesson activities.** Effective classroom managers waste little time getting the students organized for the lesson. They maximize student attention and task engagement during activities by maintaining momentum and providing signals and cues. They successfully deal with more than one thing at a time (e.g., talking with one student but also keeping an eye on the rest of the class).

Conducting the First Day

The first day of school is often a time of nervousness for teachers and students. Fortunately, you can do a number of things on the first day to address student concerns:

1. **Greet the students.** Stand by the classroom door before class begins. When students are about to enter your classroom, greet them with a smile and a handshake. As you do this, tell them your name, your room number, the subject or period, if needed; the grade level and anything else appropriate, such as the student's seating assignment (H. K. Wong & R. T. Wong, 2009). Your name, room number, section or period, and grade level or subject should be posted outside your door and on the chalkboard.

2. **Tell students about their seat assignment.** There are various ways to handle seat assignments for students. Some teachers prefer to let students select their seats, while other teachers prefer to assign seats. Either way, students should be told what to do as they enter the classroom for the first time. If you determine the seating assignment, there are several possible ways to inform students of their seat assignment as they enter the room. You might have the seating arrangement displayed on a projection screen for each class when they enter the room. Also have a copy of the seating chart in hand as the students are greeted at the door.

■ **CLASSROOM CASE STUDY**   A Poor Start on the Opening Day

Cheryl Templeton wanted to have an interesting opening day for her middle school language arts students. In the first class session with her fourth-period class, she briefly introduced herself, described the rules, and provided an overview of the content they would cover in the course. She then split the class of 28 students into five groups and asked each group to go to a designated area of the room where they could cluster their desks for their small-group work.

She gave directions for the groups to address some new course content and then told them to proceed with their group work. While the groups were discussing the material, Ms. Templeton was at her desk assembling some materials for her fifth-period class. Soon, it became apparent that all was not going well. The students weren't exactly sure what they were supposed to do since the directions were so long and complicated.

Since it was the first day and they didn't know each other, some group members felt uncomfortable interacting with the other students and did not participate. The content they were asked to address also seemed to be too advanced for many of the students. As a result, an increasing number of students got off task and some started to misbehave. For those actually doing the work, they weren't sure if the group was to have a single report or if each student was to turn in his/her report. They also didn't know where to turn in the report at the end of the activity.

Ms. Templeton noticed some of these actions, yet stayed at her desk and had little interaction with the students during this activity. At the end of the class, students felt frustrated and apprehensive about what type of year they would have in this class.

Focus Questions

1. What were the errors that Ms. Templeton made in planning and conducting this class session?

2. What could she have done to avoid the problems and to have a successful class session?

3. Concerning only one dimension, what could she have done to help the students get to know each other?

3. **Correct improper room entry.** Observe students as they enter the room and take their seats. Some students may not go directly to their seats or may behave inappropriately. It is important to ask a student who enters the room inappropriately to return to the door and enter properly. Be calm, but firm; tell the student why this is being done, give specific directions, check for understanding, and acknowledge the understanding (H. K. Wong & R. T. Wong, 2009). The communication might be something like this:

Todd, please come back to the door.
I am sorry, but that is not the way you enter our classroom every day. You were noisy, you did not go to your seat, and you pushed Ann.
When you enter this classroom, you walk in quietly, go directly to your seat, and get to work immediately on the assignment that is posted.
Are there any questions?
Thank you, Todd. Now show me that you can go to your seat properly.

During the interaction, be sure to use the student's name and be polite with a "please" and "thank you."

4. **Handle administrative tasks.** Taking attendance is one of the first administrative tasks to be done at the start of the class period. Have the students raise their hands when called to indicate that they are present and to give you an opportunity to see the face that goes with the name. As you call each name, ask the student whether you pronounced it correctly. After the first day of school, some teachers prefer not to take attendance at the start of class. Instead, they give an assignment that the students are to begin as soon as they enter the classroom. After the students are underway, the teacher can take attendance by visually scanning the room; the names do not need to be called. This approach, or one similar to it, takes very little time and allows students to move quickly into the academic work.

5. **Make introductions.** Students appreciate knowing something about the teacher. At the start of the class period, tell the students your name and some personal information, such as the number of years you have been teaching, professional development activities, family, personal interests and activities, hobbies, and other background information. This helps the students know you as a person and may be informative and comforting to them. This is also the time to let the students know that you are enthusiastic about working with them and that you will be reasonable and fair with them. Some teachers like to use this opening time to have the students briefly introduce themselves. Some get-acquainted activities for students could be included on the first day to help promote good feelings.

6. **Discuss classroom rules and procedures.** All classrooms need rules and procedures if they are to run smoothly and efficiently. Rules should be taught on the first day of class to establish the general code of conduct (discussed more fully in Chapter 4). Post the rules in a conspicuous place in the classroom. If a letter has been prepared for parents that describes the rules and procedures, this should be given to the students so they can take it home.

Some classroom procedures may be taught on the first day of school, but many teachers prefer to teach procedures (e.g., distributing materials, getting ready to leave the classroom, and handing in papers) over the next several school days instead. Procedures can be taught when the need for them first occurs. For example, when it is time to collect papers at the end of an activity, you could teach students the appropriate procedure.

7. **Present course requirements.** Before school started, you would have prepared the course requirements and syllabus. On the first day, students want to know what content will be

■ WHAT WOULD YOU DECIDE?   Planning an Initial Activity in Your Classroom

On one of the first days of the new school year, you want to have an activity that provides some content review concerning what the students learned in the previous year. You also want to provide a preview for the content that will be addressed during the coming year in your class:

1. What are some ways this content review might be conducted in interesting ways to the students yet meaningful enough so that you get a picture of their current knowledge?

2. How might you provide a preview for the content that will be addressed this year? How might you use a graphic organizer for this purpose? How might you use other creative strategies for this purpose?

3. How might you relate the content to various cultural backgrounds of your students?

---

covered and what is expected of them concerning grading. Take time to discuss the course content and some of the activities planned for the year. If you have prepared a syllabus, hand it out. Discuss the grading requirements concerning tests, homework, projects, and the like and indicate what levels are needed for the various letter grades.

8. **Conduct an initial activity.** Depending on the amount of time available on the first day, many teachers plan an initial activity related to the curriculum. It should provide a review of some material that students had in the previous year or may be a preview of content to be covered. Either way, the activity should be designed so that the students can complete it without much assistance and with much success. This leaves you free to monitor the students during the activity, to provide assistance when necessary, and to take corrective action on off-task behavior.

9. **End the class period.** A routine to end the class period is needed, and this must be taught to students. Procedures need to be established and time saved for actions such as returning books and supplies, disposing of scrap paper and cleaning up the classroom, and putting away books and other materials in preparation for leaving the classroom.

Organizing Your Classroom and Materials

Decisions about room arrangement must be made before students arrive on the first day of school. Before arranging the classroom, consider (1) the movement patterns of students throughout the classroom; (2) the need for students to obtain a variety of materials, texts, reference books, equipment, and supplies; and (3) the need for students to see the instructional presentations and display materials.

Arrange and decorate your room in a manner that supports effective classroom management. Teachers organize their use of space by creating sets of procedures and expectations and by monitoring, directing, and responding to students and classroom (Emmer & Gerwels, 2006). How you arrange your classroom will influence your selection of procedures, expectations, and ways of monitoring and interacting with your students. How you deal with these issues will influence the degree that students stay on task or get off task and misbehave. Thus, careful attention must be given to arranging the classroom and materials.

Good room arrangement can help teachers cope with the complex demands of teaching by minimizing interruptions, delays, and dead times. Based on studies of effective classroom managers, there are five keys to good room arrangement (Emmer & Evertson, 2017; Evertson & Emmer, 2017).

1. **Use a room arrangement consistent with your instructional goals and activities.** You will need to think about the main types of instructional activities that will be used in your classes and then organize the seating, materials, and equipment compatibly. Teacher-led presentations, demonstrations, or recitations will require students to be seated so they can see the instructional area. In contrast, small-group work will require very different room arrangements.

2. **Keep high-traffic areas free of congestion.** High-traffic areas include the space around doorways, the pencil sharpener and trash can, group work areas, certain bookshelves and supply areas, the teacher's desk, and student desks. High-traffic areas should be separated from each other, have plenty of space, and be easily accessible. For example, try not to seat a student next to the pencil sharpener because of the heavy traffic and the possibility of inappropriate behavior.

3. **Be sure students can be seen easily by the teacher.** It is important that teachers easily see students to identify when a student needs assistance or to prevent task avoidance or disruption. Clear lines of sight must be maintained between student work areas and areas of the room that the teacher will frequent.

4. **Keep frequently used teaching materials and student supplies readily accessible.** By having easy access and efficient storage of these materials, activities are more likely to begin and end promptly, and time spent on getting ready and cleaning up will be minimized. Establishing regulated storage areas can help reduce the occurrence of students leaving materials in their desks or taking them out of the room.

5. **Be certain students can easily see instructional presentations and displays.** The seating arrangement should allow all students to see the chalkboard or the multimedia screen without moving their chairs, turning their desks around, or craning their necks. Place the primary instructional area in a prominent location to help students pay attention and to facilitate note taking.

Floor Space

A classroom typically contains many items that take up floor space such as student desks, the teacher's desk, bookcases, tables, and activity centers. When determining how to arrange the classroom, you need to consider the functions of the space and the various factors mentioned earlier in an effort to facilitate learning and to minimize interruptions and delays.

VOICES FROM THE CLASSROOM   Creating a Center for Make-Up Work

Susan Lovelace, high school teacher, Sebastian, Florida

I realized that I was spending much time with students before and after class who wanted to know what they missed when they were absent. As a result, I organized an area for make-up work information in the back of the classroom. I purchased a dry-erase board and six pocket folders, each with a different color for each of the classes I teach. Above that board, I put a sign that reads, "What Did I Miss?"

At the end of the day, I write the assignment or activities that we covered in class that day on the dry-erase board. For each folder under the dry-erase board, I put any handouts, worksheets, or returned work in the labeled pocket folder for each class. For example, my first-period class knows they have the blue folder, so students know where to look.

Now my students know to go directly to the make-up work center to find out what they missed, and I am not using valuable time repeating make-up work information several times a day.

   A good starting point in creating the floor plan is to decide where you will conduct whole-group instruction. Examine the room and identify where you will stand or work when you address the entire class to conduct lessons or give directions. This area should have a whiteboard, projector screen, a table on which to place the projector, a small table to hold items needed during instruction, and an electrical outlet. Consider the following items:

- **Student desks.** Even if other arrangements are to be used later in the year, you might start the year with student desks in rows facing the major instructional area, since it is easier to manage students with this pattern. Be sure all students can see the major instructional area without having their backs to it and without having to get out of their seats. It is important to keep student desks away from high-traffic areas. Avoid placing their desks near the door, pencil sharpener, trash can, and supply areas. Leave ample aisles between the desks to enable easy movement of students and yourself when monitoring seatwork. Figure 3.2 shows a number of possible seating arrangements.

A. Rows

B. Rows

C. Rows

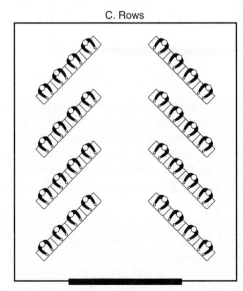

D. Clusters of 4 desks

FIGURE 3.2   Possible Seating Arrangements

FIGURE 3.2 *(continued)*

- **The teacher's desk.** Your desk should be situated so that you can see the students, but it is not essential that the desk be at the front of the room. Placement of your desk at the rear of the room, in fact, may help when monitoring students during independent work. Students facing away from you cannot discern when you are looking at them unless they turn around. This tends to encourage students to stay at their assigned tasks. Instead of sitting at their desk during independent work, many teachers prefer to move around the room to monitor and assist students.

- **Bookcases and filing cabinets.** Other items should be placed so students' visibility of whiteboards or relevant displays is not obstructed. These items should also not interfere with your monitoring of students. If a bookcase contains frequently used items such as resource books, dictionaries, or supplies, then it should be conveniently located and monitored. Seldom-used items should be stored in an out-of-the-way place. If there is only one bookcase, it is helpful to use it for frequently used items.

- **Activity centers or work areas.** An *activity center* is an area where one or more students come to work on a special activity. It may be in the form of a learning center or a computer work area. One or more tables commonly serve as the work surfaces. When you select the placement of tables for this area, be sure that you can see all students in the work area, keep traffic lanes clear, and avoid congested areas. A center often will have special equipment such as a computer or other materials and supplies. Enough table and work space must be provided for students to work efficiently. It is useful to place the work area at the side or the back of the room and to the backs of other students.

- **Computer workstations.** Placement of the computers will be affected by electrical outlets and Internet connections. Position the computers so that you can easily view them to be sure students are on task. Some schools have computers on rolling carts to be shared among several classrooms. In that case, you will need to select a place for the rolling cart and arrange for a clear pathway to the selected location. You also may need to arrange for space for paper, printing cartridges, and other supplies.

It might be necessary to establish special procedures for electronic devices, including computers. Some schools allow students to bring in their own devices, whether laptops, iPads, or smartphones; in which case, a strong wireless network will be important. As more computer-related technology is used in the classroom, attention needs to be given to space for student work along with guidance and support for these activities.

Storage Space

Teachers and students use a wide variety of instructional materials. All of these materials are not used every day and must be stored when not in use. Therefore, storage space must be provided for textbooks and resource books, frequently used instructional materials, teacher's supplies and instructional materials, equipment, and infrequently used materials. Here are some guidelines:

1. **Textbooks and resource books.** Some textbooks are not retained by students and thus must be stored in the classroom for easy access. Resource books obtained from the school library, public library, or other sources may be available for student use. All of these books should be stored in a bookcase that enables easy access.

2. **Instructional materials.** Instructional materials that students need will vary with the subject area that you teach. These may include rulers, scissors, special paper, pencils, staplers, tape, glue, and other supplies. As with textbooks and resource books, a storage location should be selected to enable easy access to the materials. Clearly labeled containers for each of the supply items are often very helpful in maintaining an orderly supply area. These materials may be stored on shelves of a bookcase or cabinet, or on a counter.

3. **Teacher supplies.** Supplies that only you would use should be kept in your desk or in storage areas used only by you. These supplies include items such as hall passes, attendance and lunch count forms, lesson plan books, tablets, file folders, flash drives, and whiteboard markers. These items should be placed in secure places so students do not have access to them.

4. **Equipment.** The type of equipment needing to be stored will vary considerably, depending on a teacher's grade level and subject area. A physical education teacher, for example, may need to store many types of equipment and supplies when not needed for a class session. Art teachers might need to store special presses that are not used every day.

5. **Infrequently used items.** Some instructional materials are used only once a year. These include seasonal decorations (e.g., Halloween and Thanksgiving), bulletin board displays, or special project materials. Certain instructional materials may be used for only one unit, as in the case of a model of the human eye for a science class. Some teachers prefer to keep seasonal decorations or other infrequently used materials at their homes.

VOICES FROM THE CLASSROOM   Organizing Your Materials and Space

Leila Post, fourth-grade teacher, Reno, Nevada

I find that good organization makes me a better teacher. I organize my daily lessons and activities in five plastic trays lined across a counter, and they are labeled by the day of the week. On top of each tray is another tray for a second week. This allows me to plan and collect related materials for two weeks at a time. This organization also makes it easier for a substitute teacher to locate all the needed materials.

I have student supplies easily accessible on shelves, and I have labeled trays for turning in daily seatwork, homework, and center work. At each cluster of student desks, I have a plastic basket containing glue, erasers, pencils, and crayons. Each student is assigned a number at the start of the school year, and this number is used to identify all folders, mailboxes, scissors, and other items. I find classroom organization of teacher and student materials reduces wasted time, increases productivity, and teaches organizational skills to the students.

Bulletin Boards and Wall Space

Constructive use of bulletin boards and wall space can contribute to a positive classroom environment. This can be achieved by displaying relevant instructional material, assignments, rules, schedules, student work, and other items of interest. Many teachers involve students in the selection of content and the preparation of bulletin boards and the use of wall space. One approach is to select a different group of students to plan and prepare a bulletin board each month.

Some teachers prefer to dedicate each bulletin board to a certain purpose. For example, one bulletin board can be used to post classroom rules, a daily or weekly schedule, classroom helpers, lunch menus, a school map, emergency information, or any other procedural information. Another bulletin board can be used to display student work. A third type of bulletin board can be simply for decoration, with seasonal, motivational, or artistic items. Other bulletin boards can be used to post information and news articles about school or community events. In addition, bulletin boards can also be used to post content-related news articles, posters, or information.

Some of the material commonly placed on bulletin boards, such a listing of classroom rules, can be placed on posters and displayed on the walls of the classroom if the content will not likely change during the school year. Designated areas of the chalkboard or whiteboard can also be used to display student assignments or special announcements because this information is likely to change daily.

MAJOR CONCEPTS

1. Many management and instructional preparations can be completed prior to the start of the school year.

2. Plans for dealing with misbehavior, assessment, record keeping, and reporting should be made prior to the start of the school year.

3. Early planning and decision making about classroom management issues will help ensure a positive beginning to the school year.

4. Organizing your classroom and materials includes attention to seating, floor space, storage space, bulletin boards, and wall space.

5. Room arrangements can enhance the learning environment and also help reduce traffic congestion.

DISCUSSION/REFLECTIVE QUESTIONS

1. In what ways might you use students as classroom helpers? How might this affect the learning environment?

2. What are the benefits of planning uncomplicated lessons at the start of the school year? What might happen if the lessons are too challenging?

3. What are the merits of having a plan for systematically dealing with misbehavior?

4. What are the merits and disadvantages for placing students' seats in rows?

5. When planning to organize your classroom and materials, what are important issues that you would take into account as you make your decisions?

SUGGESTED ACTIVITIES

1. Think about how you will record your instructional plans (lesson plans, weekly plans, and long-range plans). Will this information be on forms or on the computer? How will you plan to store and retrieve these plans for future use?

2. Talk with several teachers to find out how they do long-range planning for the school year, each semester, each marking period, and each unit.

3. Select several ways to organize students' seats and evaluate the merits and the problems associated with each seating pattern.

4. Consider how you would like your students to work in your classroom computer workstation. What procedures and guidelines would you establish to enhance productive work and minimize disruption?

FURTHER READING

K–12

Guillaume, A. M. (2016). *K–12 classroom teaching: A primer for new professionals* (5th ed.). Boston: Pearson.
Provides a very practical ad comprehensive overview to many aspects of teaching, including issues needing attention at the start of the school year.

Kronowitz, E. L. (2012). *The teacher's guide to success* (2nd ed.). Boston: Pearson.
Provides thorough descriptions of the first day, organization and management, discipline, planning, engaging learners, assessing, and professional life in balance.

Partin, R. L. (2009). *The classroom teacher's survival guide* (3rd ed.). San Francisco: Jossey-Bass.
Provides practical strategies, management techniques on creating a supportive learning environment, nurturing positive student behavior, organizational strategies, planning, instructional strategies, assessment, and building a learning community.

Thompson, J. G. (2013). *First-year teacher's survival guide* (3rd ed.). San Francisco: Jossey-Bass.
Provides an excellent, thorough, yet practical guide to all aspects of starting your school year. Many useful charts and specific guides. Covers planning for behavior, curriculum, and instruction.

Wong, H. K., & Wong, R. T. (2009). *The first days of school: How to be an effective teacher* (4th ed.). Mountain View, CA: Harry Wong Publications.
A highly popular guide for beginning teachers. Loaded with very practical guidelines on positive expectations, classroom management, lesson mastery, and other vital topics.

Elementary

Jonson, K. F. (2010). *The new elementary teacher's handbook: Flourishing in your first year* (3rd ed.). Thousand Oaks, CA: Corwin Press.
Provides thorough, practical advice on topics such as organizing the classroom, managing the classroom, preparing instructional plans, dealing with discipline, assessing student work, and working with parents.

Lindberg, J. A., & Swick, A. M. (2006). *Common-sense classroom management for elementary school teachers* (2nd ed.). Thousand Oaks, CA: Corwin Press.
Includes many specific suggestions on organization, planning, classroom atmosphere, discipline, and instruction.

Moran, C., Stobbe, J., Baron, W., Miller, J., & Moir, E. (2009). *Keys to the elementary classroom: A new teacher's guide to the first month of school* (3rd ed.). Thousand Oaks, CA: Corwin Press.
Addresses planning, creating the environment, assessments, routines and procedures, activities in the opening days and weeks, and communication.

Rominger, L., Hesisinger, K., & Elkin, N. (2001). *Your first year as an elementary school teacher*. New York: Three Rivers Press.

Middle and Secondary

Bongalan, R., Moir, E., & Baron, W. (2010). *Keys to the secondary classroom: A new teacher's guide to the first months of school* (3rd ed.). Thousand Oaks, CA: Corwin Press.
Addresses the adolescent learner, starting the school year, rules and procedures, community and team building, standards-based curriculum, planning, assessment, and communicating.

Thompson, J. G. (2011). *Discipline survival guide for the secondary teacher* (2nd ed.). San Francisco: Jossey-Bass.
Provides comprehensive guidelines for creating a successful discipline climate and addresses issues such as promoting self-discipline, man-

Describes preparing for the start of the year, setting up your classroom, planning lessons, classroom management, assessment, homework, and communication.

agement systems, motivating students, instructional strategies, discipline prevention strategies, and response systems.

Wyatt, R. L., & White, J. E. (2007). *Making your first year a success: A classroom survival guide for middle and high school teachers* (2nd ed.). Thousand Oaks, CA: Corwin Press.
A brief guidebook with suggestions about issues such as starting the school year, classroom management, lesson plans, assessment, and working with parents.

Choosing Rules and Procedures

CHAPTER OUTLINE

CHAPTER OBJECTIVES

This chapter provides information that will help you:

- Examine the need for classroom rules.
- Use guidelines for selecting rules and procedures.
- Determine ways to teach and review the rules.
- Examine the need for classroom procedures.
- Identify guidelines for ways to select, teach, and review procedures.
- Apply strategies to help students assume responsibility for their behavior.

Think about all the traffic laws that govern the use of motor vehicles. Guidelines are set for ways to signal, turn, yield the right of way, pass other vehicles, and numerous other aspects of driving. These laws have been established in each state to ensure the safety of the driver and others. In a similar way, guidelines are also needed in the classroom to govern how the teacher and the students conduct themselves so that the learning objectives are achieved and everyone is successful.

Rules and procedures are used to guide and govern student behavior in classrooms. Even in positive learning communities where students are actively involved in arranging their learning environment, rules and procedures are necessary to guide behavior. Teachers need to consider carefully what rules and procedures are needed in order to manage the class effectively.

Your philosophical perspective on the models of discipline will greatly influence how you select rules and procedures. As discussed in Chapter 2, teachers using the intervening model (high teacher control) would likely select rules and procedures without consulting students. Teachers using the interacting model (medium teacher control) would likely have a discussion with the students and then collaboratively decide on the rules and procedures. Teachers using the guiding model (low teacher control) would likely turn the discussion over to the students and let them determine the rules and procedures.

Many educators who have written about creating a learning community endorse student involvement in some classroom decision making, including the selection of rules and procedures. Alfie Kohn (2006), for example, maintains that teachers should create classroom learning communities by moving away from discipline through the use of student involvement. He would allow students to make choices, and says that teachers need to develop a caring community and provide an engaging curriculum. Kohn's principles are consistent with the guiding model (low teacher control). Some degree of student involvement in the selection of rules and procedures helps build ownership and commitment.

As you consider the information on rules and procedures, reflect on your philosophical perspective concerning discipline and classroom management. One model may represent your beliefs about child development and management of student behavior. That, in turn, will give you a perspective about the degree of control you would want to take when determining rules and procedures.

Basing your classroom decisions on the principles of freedom, justice, and equality helps students look beyond their own individual cultural needs and interests and into the realm of common societal values. Your rules and procedures should respect the individual nature of each student. At the same time, all students need and deserve information about classroom expectations so that they can equally participate in protecting the common welfare needs of the group (Brady, Forton, & Porter, 2011).

Rules in the Classroom

Rules refer to general behavioral standards or expectations that are to be followed in the classroom. They are general codes of conduct that are intended to guide individual behavior in an attempt to promote positive interaction and avoid disruptive behavior. Rules guide the way students interact with each other, prepare for class, and conduct themselves during class. They are commonly stated in positive terms. In addition to general rules, teachers sometimes state rules for specific situations (e.g., gum chewing is not allowed and cell phones must be turned off during class).

The effective use of rules involves several actions. You should examine the need for certain rules in the classroom, select appropriate rules, select the consequences, teach the rules to the students, obtain a commitment from the students about the rules, and then periodically review the rules throughout the school year.

Examine the Need for Rules

Rules provide guidelines for appropriate behaviors so that teaching and learning can take place. They should be directed at organizing the learning environment to ensure the continuity and quality of teaching and learning and not simply be focused on exerting control over students.

Rules are necessary to have teaching and learning take place, and they need to be realistic, fair, and reasonable. Rules that are selected should meet the following purposes: (1) the teacher's right to teach is protected; (2) the students' rights to learning are protected; (3) the students' psychological and physical safety are protected; and (4) property is protected (Levin & Nolan, 2014).

VOICES FROM THE CLASSROOM   Promoting Polite Behavior

David Young, third-grade teacher, Silverdale, Washington

During the first weeks of school, I work hard to create a positive atmosphere in my classroom and teach basic, polite behavior. As a class, we brainstorm and discuss what polite things students might do at school and in class. We then come up with a short list of things, such as saying please and thank you, waiting your turn patiently, and putting away someone else's things without even being asked.

After we have created our list, I try to catch students doing any of these polite behaviors, quickly get the class's attention, share the behavior I observed, and compliment the student. This quick celebration of polite behavior reinforces the behavior. As the year goes on, I cut back on these celebrations, but still do this occasionally. As a result, my classes have been better behaved and more polite, and I have been able to spend more time on teaching and less dealing with inappropriate behavior.

You need to examine the way you teach and the type of classroom environment you would like to maintain when considering rules. A number of factors should be considered, including your educational philosophy, the age and maturity of the students, school rules and expectations, the type of classroom climate to be developed, and the rationale for a particular rule.

Select the Rules

After considering the need for classroom rules, you are ready to select rules that are appropriate for your classroom. Sample rules include these:

- Follow the teacher's directions.

- Obey all school rules.

- Speak politely to all people.

- Keep your hands, feet, and objects to yourself.

These rules are probably appropriate for all grade levels (K–12).

Due to differences in student maturity and developmental levels, some rules may be needed for certain grade levels. For example, students in the primary grades (K–3) often need direct guidance on many matters. Some additional rules may be appropriate for these grades: (1) follow directions the first time they are given; (2) raise your hand and wait to be called on; (3) stay in your seat unless you have permission to get up; or (4) do not leave the room without permission.

For departmentalized settings and grade levels, some rules about materials and starting class are often used. For example, rules might include bringing all needed materials to class and being in your seat and ready to work when the bell rings at the start of the period. A number of guidelines for selecting classroom rules are displayed in Table 4.1.

1. **Make classroom rules consistent with school rules.** Before you identify classroom rules, you must become familiar with school rules and recognize your responsibilities to them. For instance, school rules may identify behaviors that are specifically forbidden (e.g., student may not wear flip-flop sandals, because they violate the school dress code) or specifically required (e.g., students need a hall pass when out of the classroom during class time). Some school rules, such as dress codes and cell phone use, may require a degree of interpretation when attempting to enforce the rules in the classroom. In these cases, it is useful to discuss the interpretation and enforcement of school rules with the building principal.

2. **Involve students in making the rules to the degree that you are comfortable and to the degree that the students' age level and sophistication permit.** Among other things,

■ TABLE 4.1 **Eight Guidelines for Selecting Classroom Rules**

1. Make classroom rules consistent with school rules
2. Involve students in making the rules to the degree that you are comfortable and to the degree that the students' age level and sophistication permit
3. Identify appropriate behaviors and translate them into positively stated classroom rules
4. Focus on important behavior
5. Keep the number of rules to a minimum (four to six)
6. Keep the wording of each rule simple and short
7. Have rules address behaviors that can be observed
8. Identify rewards when students follow the rules and consequences when they break them

student involvement in selecting rules will be affected by your philosophical perspective. Many teachers do not provide for student choice in rule setting; they may clearly present the rules and discuss the rationale for them. Other teachers find that students feel greater commitment and are more likely to adhere to the rules if they help formulate the rules and consequences. You can be an effective manager whether or not you involve students in identifying classroom rules.

If students are involved in selecting classroom rules, you can exert different degrees of direction during the discussion of them. You may begin with a general discussion of rules used in everyday life. Rich discussions can be prompted by questions such as: What is the purpose of traffic lights? Why do people need to pass a written test about laws and a driving test to obtain a driver's license? Why were rules established for sports such as basketball and football? What would a basketball game be like without the rules?

This can be followed by a guided discussion about appropriate rules to steer students' actions. Since students may not select all areas that you consider important, you may need to prompt the discussion at times. Teachers often guide students into selecting about five rules as a means to focus on important behavior. The degree of formality in managing the acceptance of the rules varies; you may want the class to vote on the list or you may prefer to handle approval by consensus.

VOICES FROM THE CLASSROOM   Involve Students in Selecting the Rules

Laurie Robben, fourth-grade teacher, Greenwich, Connecticut

When we discuss the rules on the first day of school, I begin with a discussion of what the lunchroom would be like with no rules. (No assigned tables, no order to buying lunch, no criteria for throwing away garbage.) Fourth graders are quick to surmise that lunch would be chaos. It might be fun for a while, but their lunch would soon become an unpleasant experience.

I then carry this discussion into the classroom. We brainstorm why we need rules. What problems would we face? They often say that everyone would talk at once, there would be little or no learning, and that it would be as loud as a gym. We then create a rule to avoid each possible negative outcome. We first list all possible rules and then reword the rules that are finally selected into positive statements.

Finally, I put the class into groups of four or five and have them illustrate a rule of their choice. While they perform this task, I neatly write the rules on a poster, which is displayed throughout the year.

Teresa Krell, fourth-grade teacher, Corpus Christi, Texas

On the very first day of a school year, I make sure that the students understand the guiding rule in my classroom—that no one in the class is allowed to do anything to keep them from learning. Students love the sound of this. They immediately get that they have rights in this new class. Through serious class discussions throughout the first week of school, we really nail down the implications and meanings of this rule. We talk about the hopes of their parents, grandparents, and guardians for their school year, and how none of these people would want anyone to hurt the students' feelings, hurt them physically, or keep them from learning what they need to learn on any given day of school.

After two or three days, the students write what they think the "small rules" should be for our classroom. I read these aloud, and students vote on a set of rules that will help the one big rule work. I type these up and make a poster for the room. All the students sign the poster showing that they agree, and we are off to a very problem-free year.

3. **Identify appropriate behaviors and translate them into positively stated classroom rules.** Since rules are a general code of conduct, they should focus on the conduct desired. Students respond better when the rule is stated in a way that expresses the desired behavior. To the extent possible, try to state rules positively. Instead of "No fighting," state the rule as "Keep your hands and feet to yourself." Instead of "No teasing, swearing, or yelling," state the rule as "Speak politely to all people."

4. **Focus on important behavior.** When identifying appropriate student behavior, you could make a list of student actions for various settings. Rules should focus on important behavior that meets one of the purposes of rules mentioned earlier. If you had a rule for every type of behavior, major and minor, you would have a very extensive list. Rules should focus only on important behavior.

5. **Keep the number of rules to a minimum (four to six).** By focusing on important behavior, the number of rules can be limited. Four to six rules is a good number for important behaviors. The rules can be written in broad enough language so they encompass related behaviors. For example, a rule about "Follow the teacher's directions" covers important behavior and is broad enough to cover a number of circumstances. By selecting rules with that degree of generality, the number can be limited to between four and six.

6. **Keep the wording of each rule simple and short.** A rule that has several conditions and qualifiers in its wording may be confusing. It is better to keep the wording simple and short so the meaning is clear and recognizable.

7. **Have rules address behaviors that can be observed.** Sometimes rules focus on an attitude, such as "Be kind to others." However, what constitutes being kind is open to many interpretations. One student might view a certain action as being unkind, whereas another student might not see it that way. To avoid problems of this nature, it is preferable that the rule address behaviors that can be observed. In this way, the behavior did or did not occur, and there is no gray area of interpretation.

8. **Identify rewards when students follow the rules and consequences when students break the rules.** Students need to know what will happen to them if they break the rules. They may then choose to follow the rule rather than incur the consequence. If the student chooses to break the rule, then that student must know that a consequence will be administered. Rewards for following the rules may include a variety of reinforcers such as social reinforcers, activities and privileges, tangible reinforcers, and token reinforcers (discussed more thoroughly in Chapter 5). Students need to be told that these reinforcers will be delivered if they follow the rules.

■ WHAT WOULD YOU DECIDE?   Selecting Your Classroom Rules

It is two weeks before school starts, and you are thinking about your classroom rules. You know some teachers select the rules themselves while other teachers involve their students in varying degrees. You think about your philosophical perspective on discipline and consider how you would like to conduct your class.

1. Do you intend to involve students in identifying rules? If so, how involved will you allow the students to be in the process?

2. How will you determine the consequences for the rules that are identified? Should students be involved in selecting consequences?

3. What type of discipline model does your approach to rule setting represent (see Table 2.1)?

Similarly, students need to be told what consequences will be delivered if they choose to break a rule. When a student gets off task, first provide situational assistance in an effort to get the student back to work. If the student stays off task, then you should deliver mild responses such as nonverbal and verbal actions. If that doesn't work, you can move on to logical consequences and other actions (discussed in Chapter 9).

Teach and Review the Rules

After the classroom rules have been identified, rules should be taught in the first class session as if they were subject matter content. This discussion should include an explanation of the rules, rehearsal, feedback, and reteaching. It is important that the students recognize the rationale for the rules and are provided with specific expectations for each rule. Specific guidelines for teaching and reviewing classroom rules are displayed in Table 4.2.

Presentation and discussion of the rules are intended to help students understand the rules, recognize their responsibilities in relation to them, and build a commitment to follow them. Consider the nine guidelines in Table 4.2 when teaching and reviewing classroom rules:

1. **Discuss the rules in the first class session.** When making plans for the first day of school, include time to discuss the classroom rules in the first class session in which teachers meet the students. Students need to know the rules from the very start. Some teachers, however, prefer to have an interesting activity on the first day and wait until the second day to address the rules. That approach also can be successful as long as the students know very early in the school year what the rules and expectations are for your classroom.

   You should teach the classroom rules as if they were subject matter content; this could include a handout, a transparency, discussion, practice, and even a quiz about the rules. This discussion should include an explanation of the rules, rehearsal, feedback, and repeat teaching. If different rules apply for various activities (e.g., large-group work, small-group work, labs, and independent work), these should also be clarified at this time.

2. **Discuss the reasons for the rules.** It is important the students recognize the rationale for the rules because it can build their understanding of and commitment to them. If there is a sound rationale for a rule, students are more likely to follow the rule and not challenge it. As mentioned earlier, this can start out as a general discussion about the need for rules in all aspects of life (e.g., for driving a car and for playing in a softball game). This discussion can then lead into the need for rules in the classroom to help teaching and learning.

■ TABLE 4.2   **Nine Guidelines for Teaching and Reviewing Classroom Rules**

1. Plan to discuss and teach the rules in the first class session
2. Discuss the reasons for the rules
3. Identify specific expectations relevant to each rule; provide examples and emphasize the positive side of the rules
4. Inform students of the consequences when rules are followed and also when they are broken
5. Verify students' understanding of the rules
6. Send a copy of your discipline policy home to families and to the principal
7. Post the rules in a prominent location
8. Remind the class of the rules at times other than when someone has just broken a rule
9. Review the rules regularly

3. **Identify specific expectations relevant to each rule. Provide examples and emphasize the positive side of the rules.** Examples of specific behaviors that meet or break a rule should be identified. This will help clarify your expectations. Since the wording of the rules is often brief and somewhat general, this discussion allows you to clarify what will be acceptable or unacceptable behavior for each rule.

4. **Inform students of the consequences when rules are followed and also when they are broken.** Point out to the students that you are helping them make good decisions about their behavior. When the students make good decisions about their behavior, positive results will occur. When students don't make good decisions, results will be negative. Appropriate decisions are rewarded; inappropriate decisions are not. After discussing the general reasons for providing consequences, you should discuss the specific consequences that will be used.

5. **Verify students' understanding of the rules.** As in any subject matter lesson, student understanding of the rules and consequences must be verified. This may take the form of questions, a game format, or even a quiz. If there is evidence that students do not fully understand the rules and consequences, repeat teaching may be needed.

6. **Send a copy of your discipline policy home to families and to the principal.** It is helpful to send a copy of the classroom rules and consequences to the families. Include a form for the families to sign indicating that they have read the discipline policy and have reviewed it with their child. This process helps develop understanding and commitment to the policy. The form could include space for the parents to write questions or comments. This signed form should be returned to you. It is helpful to provide the principal with a copy of your policy.

7. **Post the rules in a prominent location.** The rules should then be written on a poster and displayed in a prominent place in the classroom, perhaps on a side wall where students will easily see them. This display is a constant reminder that the rules exist to guide behavior.

8. **Remind the class of the rules at times other than when someone has just broken a rule.** Rather than waiting for a rule to be broken to remind the students about a particular rule, it is better to select a time when there have been no problems to remind students about the rules. It is helpful to anticipate potential problems and remind students of the rules before the problems occur. For example, before an activity that requires students to move around the classroom, it is a good idea to remind students about the rule "Keep your hands and feet to yourselves." You alert the students about the rule and the appropriate behavior, and this presumably will minimize poking and shoving during the activity.

9. **Review the rules regularly.** At all grade levels, it is important to review the rules frequently for several weeks at the start of the school year. Daily review during the first week, three times a week during the second week, and once a month thereafter is a good approach. In the first few weeks, it may be useful for the students to evaluate their behavior and consider whether improvement is needed. Periodic review throughout the school year is then appropriate, especially right after a holiday or after the winter or spring break. Review classroom rules with each new student who might transfer into the class after the start of the school year. In that case, it is often helpful to talk to the new student yourself and also assign him or her to a student who knows and follows the rules to help explain them to the new student.

VOICES FROM THE CLASSROOM   Discussing and Clarifying Rules

Beatrice Gilkes, high school computer science teacher, Washington, D.C.

To help maintain control in the classroom, I ask my students to discuss realistic expectations for all persons in the classroom, including myself, that will help lead to the students being successful. Next, we discuss and select specific rules of behavior that affect maximum learning success in the classroom. Throughout this discussion, we emphasize three key words—love, respect, and commitment. We then commit ourselves to these rules, and their recommendations for penalties are included in the agreement. Students place this list of rules in their notebooks. This approach to getting a commitment from the students about classroom conduct has been effective for me in 40 years of teaching.

Marjorie Marks, middle school communication arts teacher, Wixom, Michigan

My rules and procedures do not vary among the three grade levels I teach, and my students are told on the first day (through verbal discussion and succinct handouts) that respect is the critical aspect of our learning environment. I emphasize that each detail of behavior, work ethic, and project outcomes are directly influenced by the level of respect we show one another and our- selves. I talk to my classes openly and warmly about this, as I do not believe that being harsh or threatening elicits a respectful, unified classroom environment.

Together, we offer examples that illustrate respectful behavior, such as being on time to class, showing kindness to your peers, sticking to a project with effort, exhibiting energy and open- mindedness, and doing what you say you're going to do. All of these represent self-respect and respect toward others. My classroom quickly becomes a Safe Zone where we do our individual best and support one another.

Obtain Commitments

After initially teaching the rules to the students, have them express their understanding of the rules and indicate their intention to follow the rules. Although this can be done in a variety of ways, one of the most effective is to have each student sign a copy of the paper that lists the rules and includes a statement such as, "I am aware of these rules and understand them." Each student thus affirms understanding of the rules. You can keep these signed sheets. An extra copy of the rules could be given to students for placement in their desk or in a notebook.

As discussed earlier, sending the discipline policy home to the families is another means of obtaining a commitment to the policy. In this way, they are informed of the policy at the start of the school year. Include your email address and school phone number on the policy so that par- ents or guardians can contact you if they have any concerns or questions. If they do not, they are asked to sign and return a form that states that they are aware of the rules and understand them (similar to the form their child could sign at school).

Procedures in the Classroom

Procedures are approved ways to achieve specific tasks in the classroom. They are intended to help students accomplish a particular task, rather than prevent inappropriate behavior as in the case of rules. Procedures may be identified to direct activities such as handing in completed work, sharpening a pencil, using the restroom, or putting away supplies. The use of procedures, or routines, has several advantages: They increase the shared understanding of an activity between you and students, reduce the complexity of the classroom environment to a predictable structure, and allow for efficient use of time.

Some procedures may be sufficiently complex or critical, such as safety procedures for a laboratory or student notebook requirements, that you should provide students with printed copies of the procedures. Many procedures, however, are not written because they are very simple or their specificity and frequency of use allow students to learn them rapidly. Just as with rules, it is important to clearly state the procedures, discuss the rationale for them, and provide opportunities for practice and feedback, where appropriate (Harlacher, 2015).

Examine the Need for Procedures

As a first step, you must examine the need for procedures in your classroom. What activities or actions would benefit from having a procedure that would regularize student conduct in the performance of that action? To answer this key question, you might think about all the actions that take place in the classroom and identify those that would benefit from having an associated procedure (Smith, Fisher, & Frey, 2015).

Fortunately, you do not need to start from scratch in doing this assessment because research studies of classroom management in elementary and secondary classrooms have resulted in a framework that can be used to examine and identify typical classroom procedures. A number of the specific areas that might need classroom procedures are displayed in Table 4.3, some of which are adapted from Emmer and Evertson (2017), Evertson and Emmer (2017), V. F. Jones and L. S. Jones (2016), and Weinstein and Romano (2015).

Select the Procedures

When examining the items in Table 4.3, you need to consider the unique circumstances in your classroom. The grade level, maturity of the students, your preference for order and regularity, and other factors may be taken into account when deciding which items will need a procedure. It may turn out that you will select many items from the table because these items involve fairly standard actions in many classrooms.

■ TABLE 4.3   Areas Needing Classroom Procedures

1. Room Use Procedures
   a. Teacher's desk and storage areas
   b. Student desks and storage for belongings
   c. Storage for class materials used by all students
   d. Pencil sharpener, wastebasket, sink, and drinking fountain
   e. Restroom
   f. Learning stations, computer areas, equipment areas, centers, and display areas

2. Transitions In and Out of the Classroom
   a. Beginning the school day
   b. Leaving the room
   c. Returning to the room
   d. Ending the school day

■ TABLE 4.3   *(continued)*

3. Out-of-Room Procedures
    a. Restroom, drinking fountain
    b. Library, resource room
    c. School office
    d. School grounds
    e. Cafeteria
    f. Lockers
    g. Fire or disaster drills

4. Procedures for Whole-Class Activities and Instruction, and Seatwork
    a. Student participation
    b. Signals for student attention
    c. Talk among students
    d. Making assignments
    e. Distributing books, supplies, and materials
    f. Obtaining help
    g. Handing back assignments
    h. Tasks after work is completed
    i. Make-up work
    j. Out-of-seat procedures

5. Procedures During Small-Group Work
    a. Getting the class ready
    b. Taking materials to groups
    c. Student movement in and out of groups
    d. Expected behavior in groups
    e. Expected behavior out of groups

6. Beginning the Class Period
    a. Attendance check
    b. Previously absent students
    c. Late students
    d. Expected student behavior
    e. What to bring to class
    f. Movement of student desks

7. Ending the Class Period
    a. Summarizing content
    b. Putting away supplies and materials
    c. Getting ready to leave

8. Other Procedures
    a. Classroom helpers
    b. Behavior during delays or interruptions
    c. Split lunch periods

After selecting the items needing a procedure, decide specifically what each procedure will be. You could draw on your own experiences when deciding on the specific procedures. You might recollect your own schooling experiences, your observations of other classrooms, your conversations with other teachers, and your own teaching experience when determining what specific procedures would be appropriate and efficient.

Teach and Review the Procedures

Students should not have to guess whether they need to raise their hands during a discussion or how to interpret subtle signals from you to determine what you want them to do. From the very first day of school, teach and review the various procedures that are needed. Effective teachers spend more time during the first four days of school on management tasks than on academic tasks. Seven steps serve as guides when teaching and reviewing classroom procedures:

1. **Explain the procedure immediately prior to the first time the activity will take place.** Rather than explain procedures for many activities and actions on the first day, plan to space out your explanation over the first several days. It is often useful to wait for a situation to arise that provides an opportunity to explain the procedure. Some procedures will likely be taught early, such as asking to go to the restroom, while others, such as where to go during a fire drill, could be taught a few days later or just prior to the event.

2. **Demonstrate the procedure.** After the explanation, it is often useful to demonstrate what you want the students to do. For example, you could demonstrate how students are expected to use the pencil sharpener or how to get extra supplies. This will show students what actions are expected of them.

3. **Practice and check for understanding.** After your explanation and demonstration, students could then be asked to practice the procedure. They might be asked to line up in the manner explained to proceed to the next class. In this way, students actually go through the physical motions of the procedure. It is also useful to ask students about the procedures to see if they understand when and how the procedures need to be used.

4. **Give feedback.** As the students are practicing the procedure, observe carefully to determine whether they do it properly. If so, provide reinforcement. If there are some problems, constructively point this out and indicate how the procedure should be done.

VOICES FROM THE CLASSROOM   Procedures to Help Students Keep Track of Assignments

Destin Mehess, middle school science teacher, Pueblo, Colorado

I teach my students at the beginning of the school year to be responsible for their homework and assignments, and I show them the designated area where assignments are to be turned in. Each of my classes has an assignment box to place their homework and an assignment chart where the student is to check off when submitting an assignment. This chart is a visual aid that helps students keep track of what has or has not been turned in.

Students who are absent are held responsible for getting their assignments. As a result, I have an absent box that provides information about the assignments and a calendar showing the date when an assignment was given and when it is due.

The assignment box and absent box help students keep track and be responsible for their assignments. Students do not come to class and hand me assignments or come to me after an absence asking about new assignments. They know what is expected from the first day.

■ CLASSROOM CASE STUDY   Confusion about Procedures During Seatwork

Eric Johansson was eager to start the school year with his fourth-grade class. He spent a lot of time before the school year to prepare long- and short-range plans, determine the room arrangement, set up his plan for student assessment, and address many other instructional considerations.

On one of the first days of school, Mr. Johansson taught a math lesson and then asked the students to work on some sample math problems individually in seatwork for the last 15 minutes of the class session. That's when the confusion began. Several students needed some help from Mr. Johansson—some of them raised their hand to have Mr. Johansson come to their desk, other students walked to his desk to see the teacher, and still others asked a nearby student for help. Three students needed to sharpen their pencils, but they didn't know if they needed to ask permission to get out of their seats or if they could go directly to the pencil sharpener.

As students completed the math problems, some of them took their completed paper to the teacher, others tried to pass it up to the front of the row, and still others walked around the

room to see if there was a special basket to place completed seatwork.

At the end of the session, Mr. Johansson realized that he had not given consideration to procedures that were needed to provide clarity and guidance to the students. Then he also realized that he had not given prior thought to procedures for other classroom actions.

Focus Questions

1. For each episode of confusion in Mr. Johansson's class, what procedures would you have established if it were your classroom?

2. How might you go about teaching the seatwork procedures to your students?

3. Do you think you will have many specific procedures for the categories listed in Table 4.3 or will you have fewer, more relaxed procedures? Why? How might your students respond to your selections?

---

5. **Reteach as needed.** If a number of students have difficulty during the practice of the procedure, it may be necessary to reteach the procedure and perhaps explain it in a different way. It would then be useful to demonstrate the procedure once again and give the students another opportunity for practice.

6. **Review the procedures with the students prior to each situation for the first few weeks.** Rather than go through an activity and notice a student not following the procedure properly, it is better to remind students of the details of needed actions just before they are asked to perform them. At the end of class, for instance, you could remind students of the procedure for turning in their completed work just before you ask them to turn it in. Students appreciate the reminders instead of the criticism they might receive for not following the procedure. These reminders can be given for the first few weeks until the students have adopted the procedures.

7. **Review the procedures after long holidays.** After being away from school for many days, some students may forget some particular procedures. Therefore, reviewing the procedures after a long holiday is a useful step to reinforce them.

Helping Students Assume Responsibility for Their Behavior

Students should be given the message that they are responsible for their own behavior, and teachers should provide students with strategies and training to realize that control. Research on the impact of teaching strategies geared toward personal responsibility is strong (R. J. Marzano, J. S. Marzano, & D. J. Pickering, 2003). Positive benefits for using self-regulatory techniques include increasing competence in specific academic areas, increasing classroom participation, and reducing behavioral problems. Several approaches for helping students assume responsibility for their behavior are presented here.

1. **Use general classroom procedures that enhance student responsibility.** Without providing students with special training, teachers can enhance student responsibility with classroom meetings, the use of a language of responsibility, written statements of beliefs, and self-analyses.

   - **Have classroom meetings.** Classroom meetings can be used for a variety of purposes such as deciding about issues affecting the class, planning for various curricular or instructional issues, and reflecting on what has been learned. In relation to classroom management, these meetings can address causes and consequences of misbehavior and can lead to discussion, reflection, and resolution of problems. It is important to identify ground rules for the meetings to ensure that they achieve their intended purposes.
   - **Teach students the words concerning responsibility.** Certain words can be used to discuss classroom management and discipline issues, such as responsibility, rights, freedoms, and equality. To help students develop responsibility for their behavior, they need to know the vocabulary to explore and to discuss the concepts.
   - **Have students write statements of belief.** Some teachers have their students discuss and identify a classroom theme for the school year, such as "All students have a right to be treated with respect." When we take time to articulate our beliefs, we are forced to be specific about those beliefs. The class may include a narrative description in addition to the theme. Teachers also may have the class prepare a classroom constitution to outline rights and responsibilities.
   - **Use written self-analyses of behavioral incidents.** When misbehavior occurs, it is helpful to use a prescribed form to record the student's analysis of the behavioral incident. Information may include the date of the incident, location, others involved, and the nature of the incident. In addition, the form may have questions prompting the student's self-analysis and reflection of the incident with questions about how they believe they contributed to the incident, how it should be resolved, and how the student could stop this from happening again.

2. **Provide students with self-monitoring and control strategies.** Self-monitoring and control techniques are those in which students are taught to observe their own behavior, record it in some way, compare it with some predetermined criterion, and then acknowledge and reward their own successes. This is *not* a strategy to be used with an entire class. Rather, this strategy should be used with specific students for whom general management techniques are not working. This procedure involves record keeping of behavioral incidents, contingency management, monitoring, meetings, and often involvement of the parents or guardians. It follows many of the principles of behavior modification.

   Some students in your class may not regularly have behavioral difficulties, but they may benefit from your suggestions about self-control. One approach is to have students ask themselves questions when they are tempted to violate the rules or if they feel they are about to lose control. Students might ask themselves, "Is this worth the trouble it will cause me?" "Is this what I want to happen?" By pausing to question themselves, students will have an opportunity to assess the situation as well as calm down.

3. **Provide students with social skills training and problem-solving strategies.** Some students may violate classroom rules or procedures out of frustration due to poor social

interactions with other students. Other students may have difficulty with challenging situations and consequently may misbehave. The steps in social skills training and in problem-solving strategies are similar:

- When you feel like you might do something harmful or inappropriate, stop and think.
- What are some other things you can do?
- What will happen if you do them?
- Pick the best choice.

MAJOR CONCEPTS

1. Rules are general codes of conduct that are intended to guide individual behavior in an attempt to promote positive interaction and avoid disruptive behavior.

2. Rules that are selected should meet the following purposes: (a) the teacher's right to teach is protected; (b) the students' rights to learning are protected; (c) the students' psychological and physical safety are protected; and (d) property is protected.

3. To promote student commitment to their learning environment, involve students in making the rules to the extent that the students' age level and sophistication permit.

4. Procedures are approved ways to achieve specific tasks in the classroom.

5. Teachers must first select tasks that would benefit from procedures and then determine the particular actions that students will follow.

6. A number of guidelines can be considered when selecting, teaching, and reviewing classroom rules and procedures.

7. Helping students assume responsibility for their behavior can be achieved by using selected general classroom procedures, written self-monitoring strategies, and social skills and problem-solving training.

DISCUSSION/REFLECTIVE QUESTIONS

1. What are the advantages and disadvantages of involving students in the selection of classroom rules?

2. How might your teaching style and educational philosophy influence the way that you select your classroom rules? How might you need to alter these rules if you were using cooperative learning groups?

3. How could you develop student commitment to the classroom rules and procedures as a means to promote a positive learning environment?

4. What are the benefits and potential problems of having many very specific classroom procedures?

5. How might the grade level and subject area affect your selection of rules and procedures?

SUGGESTED ACTIVITIES

1. For your grade level or subject area, select the classroom rules that you prefer to use. Next, develop a plan for teaching these rules to the students on the first day of class.

2. Prepare a letter that you might send to parents describing your classroom discipline policy.

3. Talk to two or more teachers to determine what rules and specific procedures they use. Obtain any printed guidelines that they provide students.

4. Identify tasks you would like to have performed by classroom helpers. Establish a procedure for showing the students what to do in these roles. Establish a procedure for rotating these roles to other students every week or two.

5. Identify several techniques that you can use to maintain group accountability in your class.

FURTHER READING

Brady, K., Forton, M. B., & Porter, D. (2011). *Rules in school* (2nd ed.). Turners Falls, MA: Center for Responsive Schools.

Provides guidelines for creating rules with students, practicing rules, and dealing with students who break the rules. Offers guidance for dealing with unique aspects of grades K–8.

Thompson, J. G. (2013). *First-year teacher's survival guide* (3rd ed.). San Francisco: Jossey-Bass.

Provides an excellent, thorough, yet practical guide to all aspects of starting your school year. Many useful charts and specific guides. Covers planning for behavior, curriculum, and instruction.

Wong, H. K., & Wong, R. T. (2009). *The first days of school: How to be an effective teacher* (4th ed.). Mountain View, CA: Harry Wong Publications.

Is a highly popular guide for beginning teachers. Loaded with very practical guidelines on positive expectations, classroom management, lesson mastery, and other vital topics.

Maintaining Appropriate Student Behavior

CHAPTER OBJECTIVES

This chapter provides information that will help you:

- Build positive teacher–student relationships.
- Have a mental set for classroom management.
- Determine techniques to manage whole-group instruction.
- Apply techniques to maintain student attention throughout a lesson.
- Reinforce students effectively.

When you walk into a classroom where students are actively engaged in learning and are cooperating with the teacher and others, you can almost feel the good vibrations given off by the class. Students want to be involved and productive, and they enjoy working together. This type of classroom, however, doesn't happen by chance. Teachers take deliberate actions to establish a cooperative, responsible classroom so that students choose to cooperate and make efforts to be academically successful. Students need to feel that they are expected to be orderly, cooperative, and responsible. Developing a positive classroom climate is one of the most important ways to establish and maintain student cooperation and responsibility (Burke, 2008).

This chapter examines how you can develop a positive classroom climate and thus help maintain appropriate student behavior. Discussion in this chapter focuses on how to build positive teacher–student relationships, have a mental set for managements, manage whole-group instruction, maintain student attention and involvement, and improve classroom climate with reinforcers.

Building Positive Teacher–Student Relationships

Research studies on classroom management highlight the importance of having positive teacher–student relationships in promoting appropriate student behavior (Elias & Schwab, 2006; Hoy & Weinstein, 2006; R. J. Marzano, B. B. Gaddy, M. C. Foseid, M. P. Foseid, & J. S. Marzano, 2009). Building caring relationships between teachers and students is necessary for several reasons. First, when students sense that a teacher cares for them, they see the teacher as more credible and as an ally rather than a foe. This increases motivation to follow directions, adhere to rules, and put effort into classroom activities and academics (Elias & Schwab, 2006).

To address the issue of teacher–student relationships, this section begins with a discussion about how to communicate caring and support in the classroom. Then, making adjustments based on your students is addressed. Next, the issue of selecting appropriate levels of dominance and cooperation is explored when developing teacher–student relationships and maintaining appropriate student behavior.

Communicating Caring and Support

A significant body of research indicates that academic achievement and student behavior are influenced by the quality of the teacher–student relationship (Hoy & Weinstein, 2006; V. F. Jones & L. S. Jones, 2016). Students prefer teachers who are warm and friendly. Students who feel liked by their teachers reportedly have higher academic achievement and more productive classroom behavior than students who feel their teachers hold them in low regard. This research suggests that you need to learn and conscientiously apply skills in relating more positively to students.

Studies repeatedly attest to the importance students place on teachers' willingness to "be there" for them, to listen, and to show concern for students' personal and academic lives—in short, to *care* for them (Hoy & Weinstein, 2006). Developing a supportive community in the classroom helps to impart a sense of each student's belonging, to alleviate students' social anxieties and frustrations, and to motive students to comply with teacher's requests and act appropriately with peers (Elias & Schwab, 2006). Because of this, building caring relationships is the first step in the promotion of responsible behavior and prevention of misbehavior.

The guidelines listed below will help you build positive relationships and communicate your caring and support to students (Cassetta & Sawyer, 2015; Charles, 2014; Good & Brophy, 2008; V. F. Jones & L. S. Jones, 2016; Marlowe & Hayden, 2013; Weinstein & Novodvorsky, 2015).

1. **Learn about your students' lives.** Teachers can promote an invitational, caring classroom by understanding students and the social factors that influence their lives. This can be done through various means, such as questionnaires at the beginning of the school year and informal interactions.

2. **Use positive human relations skills.** When learning to manage the classroom climate, appropriate human relations skills are needed. There are four general human relations skills that apply to almost everyone in all situations: friendliness, positive attitude, the ability to listen, and the ability to compliment genuinely (Charles, 2014). When working with students, also give regular attention, use reinforcement, show continual willingness to help, and model courtesy and good manners.

3. **Enable success.** Students need to experience success. Successful experiences are instrumental in developing feelings of self-worth and confidence toward new activities, and this in turn positively affects the teacher–student relationship. Students need to be provided with opportunities to achieve true accomplishments and to realize significant improvements (Charles, 2014). Student learning is increased when they experience high rates of success in completing tasks (V. F. Jones & L. S. Jones, 2016). Students tend to raise their expectations and set higher goals. Failure, however, is met with lowered aspirations.

   To establish moderate-to-high rates of success: (a) establish unit and lesson content that reflect prior learning; (b) correct partially correct, correct but hesitant, and incorrect answers; (c) divide instructional stimuli into small segments at the learners' current level of functioning; (d) change instructional stimuli gradually; and (e) vary the instructional pace or tempo to create momentum.

4. **Communicate basic attitudes and expectations to students and model them in your behavior.** Students tend to conform not so much to what teachers say as to what they actually expect. You must think through what you really expect from your students and then see that your own behavior is consistent with those expectations. If you expect students to be polite to each other, for example, you should treat your students in the same manner.

5. **Communicate high expectations.** Teacher behaviors that create positive expectations almost always enhance the teacher–student relationship, and behaviors that create negative expectations result in poor relationships and poor student self-concepts, and thus reduce learning. For example, students often put forth a solid effort when you say that work may be hard but also express confidence that they will be able to do it.

6. **Give specific, descriptive feedback.** To be supportive of students' efforts, giving specific and descriptive feedback will help students take responsibility for their successes. They will link their effort to their successes.

VOICES FROM THE CLASSROOM   Helping All Students Feel Capable

Terri Jenkins, eighth-grade middle school language-arts teacher, Hephzibah, Georgia

Four years ago, I was teaching in an inner city school with 99 percent minority enrollment. From the beginning, I was convinced that all of these children could learn. My goal each day was to provide material and present it in such a way that ensured every student would experience some degree of success. I will never forget one particular series of lessons.

We began reading "The Graduation" by Maya Angelou, which recounts her own graduation and valedictory address. We then learned the Negro spiritual "We Shall Overcome." The story and song were inspirational, but they weren't enough. I wanted to make the entire experience personal. I told the class that one day someone sitting in that very classroom would be responsible for giving a valedictory address at his or her own graduation, and that their next assignment was to prepare a speech and present it in class. The speeches were wonderful as I introduced each and every one of them as the valedictorian of that year. As they spoke, I could hear a new determination in their voices; I could see a new pride in their posture.

Three weeks ago, there was a soft tap on my classroom door and a welcomed face appeared. Immediately I recognized Carol, one of those students who had given her valedictory address in my eighth-grade classroom almost five years ago. After a big smile and a warm hug, she quietly spoke. "I just had to come by and personally invite you to my graduation on June 5. I'll be giving the valedictory address, and I want you to be there." With that, an irrepressible smile burst across her face. After much earned congratulations, she looked at the tears in my eyes and said, "I did it just for you." Carol had become a believer in her dreams, a believer in herself.

Self-esteem and belief in oneself are essential. I firmly believe that self-esteem must be built through real achievement. I still strive to provide lessons designed to maximize student success and ensure achievement, and I continually verbalize my own convictions that they all can be winners. I make every effort to personalize success in the classroom. I realize that I cannot assure success for every student in my classroom, but I now know that I truly can make a difference.

7. **Maintain a high ratio of positive to negative statements.** Students are sensitive to praise and criticism. Too many negative statements will cast a cloud over the student's view of the classroom. Sprick (2013) recommends three positive, reinforcing statements to a student for every negative or corrective statement given. This will help teachers to be intentionally inviting (Purkey & Novak, 1996).

8. **Be fair and consistent.** Students want to be treated fairly, not preferentially. Your credibility is established largely by making sure that your words and actions coincide and by pointing this out to the class when necessary. If students can depend on what you say, they will be less likely to test you constantly.

9. **Show your respect and caring to students.** You must like your students and respect them as individuals. Your enjoyment of students and concern for their welfare will come through in tone of voice, facial expressions, and other routine behaviors. Middle and secondary teachers should make efforts to get to know students personally. Students who like and respect their teachers will want to please them and will be more likely to imitate their behavior and attitudes. Resources about developing caring relationships include Levine (2003) and Lundy and Swartz (2011).

10. **Listen to students.** Effective use of listening skills will help students express their real concerns, needs, and wants. Teachers can help students clarify their feelings and resolve their own conflicts.

11. **Be sensitive to cultural and ethnic differences.** The student population is diverse, and students may respond to teachers' words or actions in various ways due to their background. It is important to learn about your students and take that into account in your interactions. Useful resources are available, such as *How to Teach Students Who Don't Look Like You* (Davis, 2012).

12. **Create opportunities for personal discussions and interactions.** Beyond day-to-day activities, teachers often find it helpful to set time aside to get to know their students. Some possible approaches include the following: (a) talk with students before and after class; (b) demonstrate your interest in students' activities; (c) arrange for interviews with students; (d) send letters and notes to students; (e) use a suggestion box; and (f) join in school and community events (V. F. Jones & L. S. Jones, 2016).

Level of Dominance

Effective classroom managers use specific techniques to establish an appropriate level of dominance in the classroom. High dominance is characterized by clarity of purpose and strong guidance in both academic and behavioral aspects of the classroom (MacKenzie & Stanzione, 2010). Thus, the teacher provides guidance about the content to be addressed and the behavior to be expected in the class. A moderate to high level of dominance and a moderate to high level of cooperation (addressed later) provide the optimal teacher–student relationship for learning (Marzano et al., 2009). The proper level of dominance will help maintain appropriate student behavior and will not interfere with developing positive teacher–student relationships. You can express dominance in the following ways.

1. **Establish rules and procedures.** The rules and procedures that you determine will help establish your dominance in the classroom (discussed in Chapter 4).

2. **Use disciplinary interventions.** When misbehavior occurs, follow it with interventions to stop the inappropriate behavior. Your use of interventions is another expression of your dominance in the classroom (discussed in Chapter 9).

3. **Exhibit assertive behavior.** One of the best ways to communicate a proper level of dominance is to exhibit assertive behavior. *Assertive behavior* involves standing up for one's legitimate rights in ways that make it less likely that others will ignore or circumvent them. There are three primary ways that you can exert constructive, assertive behavior:

   • **Use assertive body language.** This includes making and keeping eye contact, maintaining an erect posture, facing the student but not too close, and having your facial expression match the content of your message.

■ WHAT WOULD YOU DECIDE?   Deciding How Much Personal Information to Share

You've started the school year, and you want to be friendly yet professional with your students. You want to tell the students a little about yourself, your background, your experiences, and your current activities. But you are concerned about telling too much and having students think more of you as a friend than as a teacher.

1. In your everyday interactions with your students, how personal will you be with your students, and what factors will you take into account when deciding on this?

2. To what extent will you relate personal experiences to the curriculum?

3. How might the grade level and ethnic diversity of your students affect your decisions?

- **Speak in an appropriate tone of voice.** This includes speaking clearly and deliberately, using a pitch slightly elevated from normal classroom use, and avoiding emotion in the voice.
- **Persist until the appropriate behavior is displayed.** This includes not ignoring an inappropriate behavior; not being diverted by a student denying, arguing, or blaming; and listening to legitimate explanations.

4. **Establish clear learning goals.** Another way to express a proper level of dominance is to be very clear about the learning goals to be addressed in a unit, a quarter, or semester. Clear learning goals can be communicated when you do the following:

- Establish learning goals at the beginning of a unit of instruction.
- Provide feedback on those goals.
- Continuously and systematically revisit the goals.
- Provide summative feedback regarding the goals.

Level of Cooperation

Effective classroom managers use specific behaviors that communicate an appropriate level of cooperation. High cooperation is characterized by a concern for the needs and opinions of others and a desire to function as a member of a team as opposed to an individual. A moderate to high level of dominance and a moderate to high level of cooperation provide the optimal teacher–student relationship for learning (Marzano et al., 2009). The proper level of cooperation will help maintain appropriate student behavior and will not interfere with developing positive teacher–student relationships. You can promote cooperation in the following ways.

1. **Provide flexible learning goals.** Although you will determine the learning goals for each lesson and unit, you may provide some flexibility by allowing students to set some of their own learning goals at the beginning of a unit or by asking students what they would like to learn. This conveys a sense of cooperation.

2. **Take a personal interest in students.** All students appreciate the personal attention of the teacher, and anything that you do to show interest in students as individuals has an impact on their learning. Here are some behaviors that communicate personal interest (R. J. Marzano, J. S. Marzano, & D. J. Pickering, 2003):

- Talk informally with students before, during, and after class about their interests.
- Greet students outside of school, at extracurricular events, or at stores.
- Single out a few students each day in the lunchroom and talk with them.
- Comment on important events in their lives, such as participation in sports, drama, or other activities.
- Compliment students on important achievements in and outside of school.
- Meet students at the door as they come into class and say hello to each student.

3. **Use equitable and positive classroom behaviors.** Teachers should ensure that their behaviors are equal and equitable for all students, thus creating an atmosphere in which all students feel accepted. These behaviors also foster positive teacher–student relationships. This can be done in many ways, such as the following:

- Make eye contact with each student in the room; freely move about all sections of the room.
- Over the course of a class period, deliberately move toward and be close to each student.
- Allow and encourage all students to be part of class discussions and interactions.
- Provide appropriate "wait time" for all students.

4. **Respond appropriately to students' incorrect responses.** When students respond incorrectly or make no response at all to a question you have posed, they are particularly vulnerable. Your appropriate actions at these critical points go a long way toward establishing a positive teacher–student relationship. Useful behaviors in these situations include the following (Marzano et al., 2009):

- Emphasize what was right. Give credit to aspects of the incorrect response that are correct.
- Encourage collaboration. Allow students time to seek help from peers.
- Restate the question. Ask the question a second time and allow time for the student to think before expecting a response.
- Rephrase the question. Ask the question in a different way or from a different perspective.
- Give hints or cues. Provide enough guidance so that students gradually come up with the answer.
- Provide the answer and then ask for elaboration. If the student cannot come up with the answer, state the answer yourself and then ask the student to say it in his own words.
- Respect the student's option to pass, when appropriate.

Having a Mental Set for Management

A review of research studies on classroom management has verified the importance and effectiveness of having a mental set about managing student behavior (Marzano et al., 2009). In relation to classroom management, a *mental set* is a teacher's heightened awareness of his or her surroundings and involves a conscious effort to control one's thoughts and behaviors in that setting. Using withitness and emotional objectivity will help you maintain appropriate behavior in your classroom.

Withitness

Use specific techniques to be aware of the actions of students in your classroom (withitness). Jacob Kounin (1970) is considered the first researcher to systematically study the characteristics of effective classroom managers. He coined the term *withitness* to describe a teacher's disposition (or mental set) to look at all parts of the classroom at all times to be aware of what is happening and then to demonstrate this withitness to students by quickly and accurately intervening when there is inappropriate behavior. Reflecting on the old adage, teachers who are "with-it" seem to have "eyes in the back of their heads." Such teachers do these things:

1. **Monitor regularly and react immediately.** To exhibit withitness, you should periodically and systematically scan your classroom, note the behaviors of individual students or groups of students, and respond quickly to inappropriate actions. When engaged in whole-group instruction, here are some specific techniques you can use to monitor students in the classroom (Marzano et al., 2003):

- Walk around the room, making sure you spend some time in each quadrant.
- Periodically scan the faces of the students in the class, making eye contact with each student if possible.
- As you scan the classroom, pay particular attention to incidents or behaviors that look like they could turn into problems.
- Make eye contact with those students involved in the incident or who are exhibiting the behavior.
- If this doesn't work, move toward the students. Say something to the students, if necessary.

■ **CLASSROOM CASE STUDY**   Poor Monitoring, Unfortunate Results

Abby Leibowitz's middle-level social studies class was completing a unit on the branches of the government and the role of political parties. Since an election for the state's governor was coming up, they had examined the candidates as a way to see the distinction between the parties. To summarize that information, Ms. Leibowitz split the class into four groups and asked each group to display the parties' similarities and differences on big Post-it sheets with the use of a graphic organizer, such as a compare/contrast chart or a Venn Diagram. After giving directions and forming the groups, Ms. Leibowitz was at her desk jotting some notes about a discipline incident from her last class period.

Some students were into the task, others were not. Some groups didn't know what a Venn diagram is or had disagreements about which graphic organizer to use. Some students started to doodle with the magic markers that were to be used on the poster paper. The students who wanted to get the poster prepared complained to the others who were off task. After a while, the noise increased, and most groups were not making much progress. Ms. Leibowitz had barely looked up during this time.

Focus Questions

1. How might Ms. Leibowitz improve her monitoring of the students' behavior and progress when they are in the groups? How could she show her withitness to the students during group work?

2. What problems might Ms. Leibowitz have foreseen with her plan? What adjustments might she have made before the lesson to have it work out better? (Foreseeing problems is part of withitness.)

2. **Foresee problems.**   Another aspect of withitness is the ability to foresee potential problems and make needed adjustments to minimize behavior problems. You should mentally review what might go wrong with specific students in specific classes and consider how you might address these potential problems.

When planning certain classroom activities, for example, you might recognize possible confusion or disruption when supplies are being distributed. With this advance thought, you could either modify the way you distribute the materials or take certain precautions when the materials are passed out. Also, you might know that specific students act in certain ways under particular conditions, such as a hyperactive student having difficulty focusing on tasks immediately after lunch. In these cases, you can give advance thought to ways to head off the potential problem behavior.

Emotional Objectivity

Use specific techniques to be emotionally objective with your students. When students misbehave, you may get upset and emotional to some degree. It is important that your disciplinary actions are not seen as an attack on the students involved, and you should try to be as objective as possible. *Emotional objectivity* is the ability to interact with students in a businesslike, matter-of-fact manner even though you might be experiencing strong emotions. This is particularly important when you are carrying out negative consequences for inappropriate behavior.

Your feelings of anger and frustration are only natural when dealing with misbehavior, but it is not useful to display these emotions when delivering consequences. Here are some techniques that you can use to help maintain a sense of emotional objectivity with students.

1. **Look for reasons for the misbehavior.**   Maintaining emotional objectivity is much easier if you don't personalize student misbehavior. Simply trying to understand the reasons for the misbehavior can help you maintain your businesslike manner.

2. **Monitor your own thoughts.**   Take time to monitor your attitudes about specific students. When your attitude about specific students is positive, it is fairly easy to interact with them. However, you might not be aware of the extent that negative attitudes about some students may get in the

VOICES FROM THE CLASSROOM   A Rubric for Participation to Guide Behavior

Lind Williams, High School English Teacher, Provo, Utah

At the start of each year, I teach my students about appropriate classroom behavior. To do this, I created a rubric that displays a scale between mature and immature behaviors—I call this my *Participation Grade Rubric*. The rubric helps clarify what I view as active, on-task, appropriate behavior for students in class, and the rubric helps students understand what appropriate and inappropriate behavior looks like. For each behavioral indicator on the rubric, a description is included to show a high range, a mid-range, and a low range of the behavior.

Students invariably chuckle at the descriptors in the low range of the rubric because the inappropriateness of the behavior is pretty obvious. I give examples or model some of the behaviors, such as laying heads on desks, putting unfinished work away when there is still class time, making comments that ruin or derail class discussions, and breaching conversational etiquette.

I present these behavioral expectations at the start of the school year, but it takes time for students to be fully independent and self-managed in their conduct. The rubric provides some guidance about appropriate behaviors and helps the students grow in that direction.

Students are assessed with this rubric throughout the school year. When I conference with a student with problem behaviors, we can read the descriptions to see where his or her behavior lies on the rubric.

way of interacting with them. To help avoid any negative bias, before class each day you could: (a) mentally review your students, noting those who you anticipate having problems; (b) try to imagine these problem students succeeding or engaging in positive classroom behavior; and (c) when you interact with these students, try to keep in mind your positive expectations.

Managing Whole-Group Instruction

In many classrooms, whole-group instruction takes place quite often. Special attention needs to be given to specific skills used in whole-class instruction that help maintain appropriate student behavior. In his widely respected book *Discipline and Group Management in Classrooms* (1970), Jacob Kounin reported how instructional techniques contribute to classroom management. The implications from his research can be organized into three areas: preventing misbehavior, managing movement through the lesson, and maintaining group focus.

Preventing Misbehavior

When approaching whole-group instruction, teachers can take a number of actions to prevent misbehavior based on Kounin's work.

1. **Exhibit withitness.** As discussed earlier in this chapter, a teacher who has withitness knows what is going on in the classroom at all times, notices who is misbehaving, and responds to the misbehavior in an appropriate and prompt manner. Systematic and periodic monitoring of each student in the class is a key part of withitness because it will help prevent misbehavior from occurring.

2. **Use overlapping.** Overlapping refers to teachers supervising or handling more than one group or activity at a time. For example, a teacher working with one group of students can notice and simultaneously address a behavior incident in another part of the classroom. Teachers who are skilled at overlapping are more aware of what is going on. Thus, they have good withitness as well. As a result, teachers who overlap can effectively monitor classroom

behavior and intervene when needed to keep students on task. When students know their teacher has withitness and is able to overlap, they are less inclined to get off task.

3. **Use desists.** Desists are statements by teachers to stop an inappropriate action or a misbehavior by asking or telling a student what to do. To be effective, desist statements should be specific and spoken clearly. A desist might be in the form of an appeal, such as, "Shanae, please put away the comb and continue with the class assignment." Or it could be in the form of a command such as, "Wayne, stop talking with your friends and continue with your calculations in the lab activity." Effective use of desists helps keep students on task and minimizes disorder and misbehavior.

4. **Avoid satiation.** Satiation occurs when the teacher asks the students to stay on a learning task too long, and then the students begin to lose interest and enthusiasm, make more mistakes, and misbehave. This can also occur if a certain type of activity or instructional approach is used over and over again. Teachers can prevent misbehavior by avoiding satiation and thus maintaining student interest and engagement. Satiation can be minimized by (a) highlighting progress and providing feedback; (b) providing variety in the content, group structure, level of difficulty, and instructional materials and activities; and (c) offering a challenging activity to promote a greater sense of purpose and accomplishment.

Managing Movement Through the Lesson

To minimize misbehavior and to promote learning, teachers need to have the lesson proceed at a reasonable pace and avoid having the lesson go astray with abrupt changes or shifts. Kounin (1970) described the movement of the lesson in terms of momentum and smoothness, as described next. Some problems with maintaining movement through a lesson are outlined in Table 5.1.

1. **Momentum.** Momentum refers to teachers starting lessons with dispatch, keeping lessons moving ahead, making transitions among activities efficiently, and bringing lessons to a satisfactory close. Momentum deals primarily with the pacing of the lesson, and the teacher needs to avoid slowdowns in the progression through the lesson. For example, one problem in momentum is jerkiness, where the teacher fails to develop a consistent flow of instruction, going too fast at some times and too slow at others.

■ TABLE 5.1 **Problems in Maintaining Movement Through a Lesson**

These are terms that Kounin (1970) used to describe problems in momentum and smoothness when progressing through a lesson.

Dangle: Occurs when a teacher leaves a topic or activity "dangling" before completion to do something else or to insert some new material. Later, the teacher may resume the first activity (also see *truncation*).

Flip-flop: The teacher is engaged in one activity and then returns to a previous activity that the students thought they had finished.

Jerkiness: The teacher fails to develop a consistent flow of instruction, thus causing students to feel jerks in the lesson momentum, from slow to fast (also see *thrust*).

Slowdown: When teaching, the teacher moves too slowly or stops instruction too often. Thus, students lose interest or learning momentum. Fragmentation and overdwelling are two types of slowdowns.

Fragmentation: This is a type of slowdown where the teacher breaks down an activity into subparts that could be taught as a single concept; all the subdivisions are unnecessary and slow down instruction.

Overdwelling: This is a type of slowdown where the teacher dwells on an issue and engages in a stream of talk that clearly lasts longer than the time needed for students' understanding.

Stimulus bound: The teacher is distracted by some outside stimulus and draws the students' attention to it and away from the lesson.

Thrust: The teacher inserts some new information at a point where students are involved in another activity, and the new material seems irrelevant to them.

Truncation: The teacher engages in a dangle, yet fails to resume the original activity (also see *dangle*).

2. **Smoothness.** Smoothness refers to staying on task in the lesson without abrupt changes, digressions, or divergences. Kounin described several problems when trying to maintain a smooth, continuous flow of activities throughout a lesson. Some of these problems include shifting from one topic to another, shifting back to earlier activities or content, or injecting unrelated information into a lesson.

Maintaining a Group Focus

Group focus occurs when a teacher makes a conscious effort to keep the attention of all students at all times. When this occurs, the teacher maintains efficient classroom control and reduces student misbehavior (Kounin, 1970). Group focus includes group alerting, group accountability, and high-participation formats.

1. **Use group alerting.** Group alerting refers to taking actions to engage the attention of the whole class when only individuals are responding. This includes a teacher's attempts to involve all students in learning tasks, maintain their attention, and keep them "on their toes." With group alerting, teachers create suspense before calling on a student to answer a question, keep students in suspense regarding who will be called on next, call on different students to answer questions, and alert nonperformers that they might be called on next.

2. **Maintain group accountability.** Group accountability takes place when the teacher lets the students know that their performance in class will be observed and evaluated in some manner. This assessment does not necessarily mean a grade will be recorded, only that the students' performance will be gauged. For example, the teacher might use record-keeping devices such as checklists and task cards. Other strategies include asking students to raise their hands in response to certain questions, asking students to take notes and then checking them, or asking students to write answers and then using various techniques to check them during the class session. Student misbehavior decreases when students know they are held accountable for their learning and behavior and that the teacher knows each student's progress.

3. **Use high-participation formats.** High-participation formats are lessons that have all students performing in some way even though they may not be involved in answering a teacher's question. High-participation formats occur when each student is expected to manipulate materials, solve problems, read along, write answers, or perform a concurrent task. In this way, students do not simply sit when others are answering questions; they are actively engaged as well.

Maintaining Student Attention and Involvement

To manage a group of students effectively, you need to capture and hold student attention and encourage ongoing involvement. *Attention* means focusing on certain stimuli while screening out others. General guidelines and specific techniques for maintaining student attention and involvement are offered below.

Securing and maintaining attention is an important responsibility. If students are not engaged in the learning process, it is unlikely that they will learn the material and it is possible that they will get off task and disrupt order. Preventive steps therefore need to be taken. In addition to techniques that promote student attention to class activities, you may consider motivational strategies (discussed in Chapter 8).

Recommendations for ways to maintain student attention and involvement come from a number of sources (Good & Brophy, 2008; V. F. Jones & L. S. Jones, 2016); some of the following guidelines come from these sources.

1. **Use attention-getting strategies.** You can use certain strategies to capture students' attention at the start of a lesson. These attention-getting strategies can be used throughout the lesson to maintain student interest, and they fall into four categories: physical, provocative, emotional, and emphatic. Overuse of any one approach, however, reduces its ability to arouse and maintain attention.

   • **Physical.** Attention getters deal with any stimulus that attracts one or more of the senses (sight, sound, touch, and taste). Pictures, maps, the chalkboard, music, and manipulative objects are examples. Even your movement and vocal expression can be considered to be physical stimuli.
   • **Provocative.** Attention getters involve the use of unique or discrepant events. To create them, you could introduce contrasting information, play the devil's advocate, and be unpredictable to the degree that the students enjoy the spontaneity.
   • **Emotional.** Attention getters are approaches aimed at involving students emotionally. This may be something as simple as calling the students by name.
   • **Emphatic.** Attention getters place emphasis on a particular issue or event. For example, you might cue students to an issue by saying, "Pay careful attention now. The next two items are very important."

2. **Arrange the classroom so that students do not have their backs to the speaker.** When presenting material during a lesson, students should be seated so that everyone is facing the presenter (who may be you, a student, or a guest). This may seem like a simple task, but too often classrooms are arranged so that students do not have a complete view of the presenter and the instructional medium. Not only is the presenter unable to see all of the students but also the students are not able to observe all of the presenter's nonverbal behaviors.

   You may prefer to have all the student seats facing the area where you spend most of your time in direct instruction, such as by the chalkboard or by the overhead projector. Or you may prefer to have them work in cooperative groups much of the time and thus arrange the desks in clusters. In that case, students can be asked to turn or move their chairs when you want their undivided attention.

3. **Select a seating arrangement that does not discriminate against some students.** Some teachers may spend as much as 70 percent of their time in front of the classroom. As a result, students at the back of the classroom contribute less to class discussions and are less attentive and less on task than those near the front. Involvement is more evenly distributed when high- and low-achieving students are interspersed throughout the room. You can enhance on-task behavior by carefully arranging the seating and moving around the room. You should experiment with seating arrangements to promote student attention and involvement.

4. **Monitor attention during lessons and provide situational assistance as necessary.** Students are much more likely to pay attention if they know you regularly watch them, both to see if they are paying attention and to note signs of confusion or difficulty. Regularly scan the class or group throughout the lesson.

   When students show signs of losing interest or getting frustrated, you should provide *situational assistance*—teacher actions designed to help students cope with the instructional situation and to keep students on task, or to get them back on task before problems become more serious. Situational assistance may include actions such as removing distracting objects, providing support with routines, boosting student interest, helping students over hurdles, altering the lesson, or even modifying the classroom environment.

5. **Keep lessons moving at a good pace.** Delays in a lesson may be caused by actions such as spending too much time on minor points, causing everyone to wait while students respond individually, passing out equipment individually, and so forth. Attention will wander while students are waiting or when something they clearly understand is being discussed needlessly (as in lengthy review lessons). You need to recognize what causes delays and minimize them in an effort to keep the lesson moving at a good pace.

6. **Vary instructional media and methods.** Monotony breeds inattentiveness, and the repeated and perhaps exclusive use of one approach to instruction will soon result in a classroom of bored students. Moreover, student achievement is increased when a variety of instructional materials and techniques are used (Good & Brophy, 2008). Varying media by using a projector, whiteboards, DVDs, web-based virtual field trips, and online resources provides a more interesting approach to teaching any lesson.

   You should use a variety of teaching methods to solicit students' attention through the use of demonstrations, small and large groups, lectures, discussions, field trips, and the like. Using a variety of instructional techniques helps. For example, lectures can be mixed with demonstrations, group responses with individual responses, and short, factual questions with thought-provoking questions. You should periodically review your instructional approaches to avoid falling into a dull routine. Not only does variability decrease boredom in students but it also appeals to the different student learning styles. One caution, however, is too much variety may distract students from the content and may decrease achievement. A happy balance must be struck.

7. **Stimulate attention periodically.** Student attention wanders when instruction becomes predictable and repetitive. You can promote continual attention as a lesson or an activity progresses. You can stimulate attention by cueing students through transitional signals that a new section of the lesson is coming up. For example, you might say, "We have just spent the last 15 minutes considering what running water erosion is. Now let's look at the ways that farmers and other people try to stop this erosion." Or you can use challenging statements such as, "Now, here's a really difficult (or tricky or interesting) question—let's see if you can figure it out."

■ WHAT WOULD YOU DECIDE?   Planning to Vary Your Methods and Media

You recognize that varying your instructional methods and media will help maintain student attention and involvement. You are now beginning to plan an eight-day unit, and you want to deliberately plan for much variety in methods and media. Even in each class session, you want to plan for variety. (Select a unit topic in your field for this exercise as you consider the following questions.)

1. Identify five instructional strategies that you would use at some point in the unit.

2. Identify several types of media that you and your students would use. Identify how you would use each type of media to teach the content.

3. How might you design your lesson plan template to prompt your attention to include variety in your instructional methods and media?

8. **Show enthusiasm.** Your own enthusiasm is another factor in maintaining student attention. Enthusiasm can be expressed through vocal delivery, eyes, gestures, body movement, facial expressions, word selection, and acceptance of ideas and feelings. Teacher enthusiasm has been related to higher student achievement (Good & Brophy, 2008). Students often learn more from lessons that are presented with enthusiasm and expressiveness than from dry lectures.

You do not need to express a high degree of enthusiasm all of the time. Depending on the circumstances of the lesson, you may vary the degree of enthusiasm being expressed. For example, there may be times during a lesson when you might be very animated and vocally expressive. Other times, you may choose to be very mild mannered.

9. **Use humor.** Students appreciate a certain amount of humor in the classroom, and it can help maintain student attention. You may enjoy making silly statements or sharing funny experiences with your students. Be cautious that jokes are not used to tease or demean any student, even if expressed in a funny way, because the student may interpret these statements as being serious.

10. **Use questions effectively to maintain attention.** You can use questions to achieve various academic objectives. To maintain attention and encourage ongoing involvement, consider the guidelines in Table 5.2.

11. **Maintain individual accountability.** Students should be accountable for being involved in lessons and learning all of the material. It is helpful to ask a question or require the student periodically to make some kind of response. An unpredictable pattern in the way you handle questions or responses helps maintain individual accountability and causes students to be mentally engaged in the lesson and to be more attentive.

12. **Pay close attention when students talk and answer questions.** Use active listening skills. This often entails using nonverbal skills that indicate that you are interested in what students are saying. If you do not give attention and show interest when students answer questions, you communicate to them that what they have to say is not very important, which, in turn, will discourage involvement. Nonverbal expressions of your interest might

■ TABLE 5.2 **Questioning Tips to Maintain Attention and Promote Learning**

1. Prepare key questions for each lesson to provide structure and direction
2. Phrase questions clearly and specifically
3. Ask questions logically and sequentially
4. Use questions that encourage wide student participation
5. Ask questions that relate to students' own lives
6. Vary the type of questions being asked
7. Use variety and unpredictability in asking questions
8. Ask the question before calling on a student
9. Wait at least five seconds after asking the question before calling on a student
10. Use random selection when calling on students
11. Have students respond to classmates' answers
12. Do not consistently repeat questions
13. Prompt students to elaborate on their answers through the use of follow-up questions and comments
14. When students fail to provide a complete and correct answer to your question, use cues, clues, and prompts to assist them in making connections that will lead to an answer

After teaching students about some strategies to solve math problems, you write five brief math problems on the whiteboard at the front of the room and ask five students to go to those problems and solve them while you and the rest of the class observe. You intend to provide commentary about how the students go through the mental process of solving the problems.

1. For those who are still in their seats, how might you hold them academically accountable for the material?

2. How could you provide feedback to the students at the board as well as to those still in their seats?

3. How might the lack of a procedure for academic accountability in this setting contribute to a loss of order in the classroom?

---

include nodding, moving toward the student, leaning forward, maintaining eye contact with the student, and showing interest in your facial expression. Verbal expressions of interest may include statements such as "Uh huh," "I see," "That's a thoughtful answer," or "I appreciate your thorough, insightful answer."

13. **Reinforce students' efforts and maintain a high ratio of positive to negative verbal statements.** Students attend more fully if a positive learning environment has been created. One of the best means for accomplishing this is to respond positively to their efforts. On the one hand, positive and encouraging statements are very important for all students, and they can be motivated by positive reinforcement. On the other hand, a teacher who consistently belittles students' efforts will create a negative learning environment that will likely lead to inattention and off-task behavior. Make many more positive and encouraging statements than negative statements. Think about it from the students' point of view—would you like to be in a classroom where you hear mostly negative statements or positive statements?

14. **Terminate lessons that have gone on too long.** When the group is having difficulty maintaining attention, it is better to end the lesson than to struggle through it. This is especially important for younger students, whose attention spans are limited. Nevertheless, some teachers continue lessons in order to maintain a certain schedule. This can be counterproductive since students may not learn under certain conditions and in any case will have to be taught again. It is always helpful to give advance thought to a backup activity for each lesson. For example, you may select a different instructional technique for covering the same lesson objectives.

Improving Classroom Climate with Reinforcers

A *reinforcer* is an event or consequence that increases the strength or future probability of the behavior it follows. Reinforcement is used to strengthen behaviors that are valued and to motivate students to do things that will benefit them. It is important to recognize the general principle of reinforcement: *Behaviors that are reinforced will be retained; behaviors that are not reinforced will be extinguished.* You need to carefully consider whom to reinforce, under what conditions, and with what kinds of reinforcement.

The awarding of reinforcers must be contingent on the student's behavior. If a student does what is expected, then an appropriate reinforcer can be awarded. Students are thus reinforced for their appropriate actions, and that behavior is strengthened. In the absence of the needed behavior, students do not receive reinforcers.

Types of Reinforcers

Several techniques of reinforcement are available, including recognition, activities and privileges, tangible reinforcers, and token reinforcers. Many of these reinforcers can be used with both individual students and the entire class.

Recognition

Recognition is a social reinforcer serving as a positive consequence to appropriate behavior. Social reinforcers may be expressed by verbal or written expressions, nonverbal facial or bodily expressions, nonverbal proximity, and nonverbal physical contact. Social reinforcers are especially valued by students when given by people important to them. Social forms of approval are especially useful when reinforcing student behavior if you and the students have a good relationship. *Praise* is an expression of approval by the teacher after the student has attained something, and social reinforcers are often used to express this praise.

Most recognition should be done privately with the student, but some may be done publicly. You need to consider carefully student characteristics when deciding how to deliver praise. A seventh grader, for example, might be somewhat embarrassed by being praised in front of the class.

Recognition should always be contingent on performance of appropriate behavior. You should be specific about the behavior that resulted in the praise and the reasons for giving it. With verbal expressions, the terms used, the inflection, and degree of enthusiasm should vary. Also, the type of praise (private, indirect, or public) should change. Social reinforcers should always be paired with other reinforcers. Systematic and appropriate reinforcement improves student behavior. It helps students know that their efforts and progress are recognized and appreciated.

Activities and Privileges

Activity reinforcers include privileges and preferred activities. After students complete desired activities or behave in appropriate ways, you can then reinforce them with various activities and privileges. Some of these reinforcers could be various jobs as a classroom helper. Activity reinforcers are often very effective for reinforcing the entire class. A list of sample activities and privileges that can be used as reinforcers is provided in Table 5.3.

It is important to verify that certain behaviors are desirable. When you and the student are on good terms, just performing certain tasks such as straightening the room or washing the whiteboards with you can be rewarding. Many other activities and privileges have an intrinsic value that doesn't depend on the student's relationship to you. Running errands, studying with a friend, going to the library, being first in line, or choosing an activity are each likely to be a positive incentive that produces satisfaction in its own right. You may have students fill out a sheet at the beginning of the school year to identify activities and reinforcers that they would appreciate.

Tangible Reinforcers

Tangible or material reinforcers are objects that are valued in and of themselves: certificates, awards, stars, buttons, bookmarks, book covers, posters, ribbons, plaques, and report cards. Food also may serve as a tangible reinforcer: cookies, sugarless gum, popcorn, jellybeans, candy, or raisins. If you are interested in using food (M&Ms, cookies, etc.), recognize some cautions. Some parents may object to certain foods (such as those high in sugar), and there may be cultural differences related to food. Students may be allergic to certain foods such as nuts, wheat, soy, or dairy, and there may be health and state regulations governing dispensing food in schools.

Since tangible reinforcers serve as external or extrinsic reinforcement, their use should be limited. Other types of reinforcers are generally more available and more reinforcing in natural settings than tangible reinforcers. When you give awards, it is a good idea to distribute them so as to include a good number of the students. Don't give awards only for outstanding achievement; award for improvement, excellent effort, good conduct, creativity, and so on.

■ TABLE 5.3   Examples of Activity and Privilege Reinforcers

Privileges
Playing a game
Helping the teacher
Going to the library
Decorating a bulletin board
Working or studying with a friend
Reading for pleasure
Exploring approved websites on the computer
Writing on the whiteboard
Earning extra recess time

Classroom Jobs
Distributing or collecting papers and materials
Taking attendance
Adjusting the window shades
Taking a note to the office
Watering the plants
Stapling papers together
Erasing the whiteboard
Operating the projector
Controlling the mouse for the SMART Board
Shutting down the computers

For example, you may select one or more students each week to receive awards for something of value that they have done. Awards may be in the form of a certificate accompanied by a pencil, poster, trading card, book, or other item. You may have students select their prize from a reward box that includes jewelry, magazines, cups, and other items students would value. This can also be done by teachers who are departmentalized and who work as a team with a larger group of students. Although at first glance this might seem too juvenile for middle and secondary students, it can be successful if the students value the awards.

Some schools have a student-of-the-month program, with the selection criteria being the most improved grade point average or other valued behavior. Members of the student council could select the winner, who might receive a T-shirt, a pin, a poster, or some other valued prize.

Token Reinforcers

A *token reinforcer* is a tangible item that can be exchanged for a desired object, activity, or social reinforcer at a later time. Tokens may be chips, points, stars, tickets, buttons, play money, metal washers, happy faces, or stickers. The backup reinforcer is the reward for which tokens can be exchanged. Token reinforcement is useful when praise and attention have not worked. Tokens are accumulated and cashed in for the reinforcer.

Using Reinforcers Effectively

It is important to recognize the general principle of reinforcement: behaviors that are reinforced will be retained; behaviors that are not reinforced will be extinguished. You need to consider carefully whom to reinforce, under what conditions, and with what kinds of reinforcement. Reinforcement is likely to be effective only to the extent that (1) the consequences used for reinforcers are experienced as reinforcers by the student; (2) they are contingent on the student achieving specific performance objectives; and (3) they are awarded in a way that complements rather than undermines the development of intrinsic motivation and other natural outcomes of behavior.

MAJOR CONCEPTS

1. Positive teacher–student relationships can be developed by communicating caring and support, adjusting to your students, and taking actions to create an appropriate level of dominance and cooperation.

2. An optimal teacher–student relationship consists of equal parts of dominance and cooperation.

3. Effective classroom managers have a mental set for management in which they consciously have high awareness of the actions in the classroom and respond quickly when misbehavior occurs.

4. Successful management of whole-group instruction can be achieved by deliberate actions to prevent misbehavior, manage movement through the lesson, and maintain a group focus.

5. A variety of approaches can be used that cause students to pay attention to the class activities at all times.

6. A reinforcer is an event or consequence that increases the strength or future probability of the behavior it follows. Reinforcement is used to strengthen behaviors that are valued and to motivate students to do things that will benefit them.

7. Recognition, activities and privileges, tangible reinforcers, and token reinforcers can be used to reinforce desired student behavior.

DISCUSSION/REFLECTIVE QUESTIONS

1. From your experiences and observations, what are the characteristics of good teacher–student relationships?

2. When considering the teacher–student relationship, give some examples of high and low dominance by a teacher. Also give some examples for high and low cooperation.

3. Describe some examples where a teacher does not have good momentum and smoothness when proceeding through a lesson.

4. Discuss how regular classroom meetings might help promote student on-task behavior. What guidelines would you establish for discussions in the meetings?

5. Why would attention-getting strategies promote student involvement? What precautions could you identify for their use?

6. How might your selection and use of reinforcers be affected by grade level or subject area?

SUGGESTED ACTIVITIES

1. Talk with several teachers and ask them to describe how they develop positive relationships with their students.

2. Ask several teachers how they maintain control of the class without being too dominant or negative.

3. Reflect on your schooling experiences and identify some strategies that your teachers used to successfully capture and maintain students' interest.

4. Talk with several teachers to see what they do to keep students on task and maintain appropriate behavior.

FURTHER READING

Bluestein, J. (2008). *The win-win classroom: A fresh and positive look at classroom management*. Thousand Oaks, CA: Corwin Press.
Offers guidance for restructuring power dynamics, establishing authority, creating a success orientation, and increasing positive classroom elements.

Burke, K. (2008). *What to do with the kid who . . .: Developing cooperation, self-discipline, and responsibility in the classroom* (3rd ed.). Thousand Oaks, CA: Corwin Press.
Examines ways to provide positive guidance for students for their behavior. Discusses setting the classroom climate, teaching social skills, teaching responsible behavior, and dealing with students with behavior problems or special needs. Includes useful lists and graphics.

Cushman, K. (2003). *Fires in the bathroom: Advice for teachers from high school students*. New York: The New Press.
Based on the candid discussions and recommendations from a number of urban high school students, insightful and practical recommendations are provided about topics such as knowing your students, respect and fairness, classroom behavior, a culture of success, motivation, teaching difficult academic work, and when things go wrong.

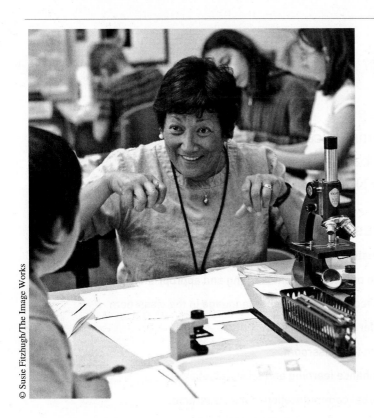

chapter 6

Communication Skills for Teaching

CHAPTER OUTLINE

CHAPTER OBJECTIVES

This chapter provides information that will help you:

- Use language effectively to promote student learning and appropriate conduct.

- Apply the guidelines for effective use of teacher language in the classroom.

- Communicate firm limits for student behavior.

- Use supportive language in the classroom.

- Apply listening skills to enhance learning and address behavior.

- Exhibit appropriate nonverbal communication in the classroom.

Teachers talk all day long. Everything they say communicates information and is designed to achieve certain purposes. Teacher talk can positively or negatively affect just about everything in the classroom—the classroom climate, student motivation, behavior, student performance, and other factors. With their language, teachers use can either support student decision making, responsibility, teamwork, and initiative or encourage students to be passive in the classroom to do only what they are told to do.

This chapter focuses on communication skills for teachers in relation to classroom management. The power of teacher language and the purposes of teacher communication in the classroom are first identified. Then there are separate sections concerning guidelines for teacher language, communicating firm limits for behavior, using supportive language, listening, and nonverbal communication.

The Power of Language

In recent years, there has been considerable interest in how teachers use their language to promote learning and to guide student behavior. Entire books have been written on this topic as illustrated by the following examples:

- *Positive Teacher Talk for Better Classroom Management* (Diffily & Sassman, 2006)

- *The Power of Our Words: Teacher Language that Helps Children Learn* (Denton, 2013)

- *Use Your Words: How Teacher Talk Helps Children Learn* (Mooney, 2005)

- *Choice Words: How Our Language Affects Children's Learning* (Johnston, 2004)

- *What Do You Say When . . .? Best Practice Language for Improving Student Behavior* (Holloman & Yates, 2010)

- *Inviting Students to Learn: 100 Tips for Talking Effectively with Your Students* (Edwards, 2010)

- *Talking, Listening and Teaching: A Guide to Classroom Communication* (Farrell, 2009)

The language that teachers use and the manner in which they express that language can profoundly affect students in the classroom. The term *teacher language* refers to the professional use of words, phrases, tone, and pace to enable students to engage in active, interested learning and develop positive behaviors (Denton, 2013, p. 3).

What teachers want to achieve in the classroom will influence their communication and their use of language. The overall role of the teacher is to guide and support student learning, which can be broken down into many smaller elements. In relation to classroom management, teachers try to achieve three important purposes in the classroom:

- To create a positive learning community

- To provide instruction and support student engagement

- To guide and correct student behavior

Teachers can achieve these purposes through the intentional use of language—this is the power of language. Learning to use teacher language to its full positive potential means becoming aware of your habitual ways of speaking and the positive and negative messages that these may be sending to students (Denton, 2013). It means stepping back to hear ourselves and to reflect "What did I say? What message did I convey? What tone did I use?" Teachers then can try and practice new words, phrases, tones, and pacings to replace any ineffective language patterns.

General Guidelines for Teacher Language

Students need to know that teacher words have meaning when providing instruction or addressing a misbehaving student. Students also need to know that words correspond with actions. Here are some general guidelines for using language to affirm meaning and action, to address various aspects of instruction and behavior management, and to engage in guidance and conversation with students. These guidelines underpin the additional, more specific strategies offered later in this chapter. These guidelines represent a synthesis of those offered by Charney (2002, pp. 235–245), Denton (2013, pp. 12–31), and Mooney (2005, pp. 18–20).

1. **Be direct and authentic; say what you mean.** When teacher language is direct and authentic, when we say what we mean and mean what we say, then students learn that they can trust us. Use direct language. Instead of an indirect statement such as "I like the way that Ethan and Joline are ready for our activity," say, "I would like everyone's attention before we start our activity." Use a warm, matter-of-fact tone since it conveys authenticity, respect, and directness (Denton, 2013). Deliver consequences for students who do not follow the directions.

2. **Use clear, direct language with off-task behavior.** If a student is not cleaning up after a classroom activity, it is generally not effective to ask, "Would you please clean up your area?" Nonnegotiable, direct statements are often needed, such as, "Ashley, you need to clean up your area now."

3. **Use words that invite cooperation and convey faith in students' abilities and intentions.** Because language is such a powerful shaper of identity and perceptions, it is important that teachers carefully use language to open, rather than close, the doors of possibility for students. Our language conveys our assumptions and expectations, which then influence students. "Show me how you will follow the rules in the hall," conveys an expectation that students know how to follow the rules they practiced and will do so. Also, take time to notice the positives that students exhibit and comment on them. This is reinforcing.

4. **Focus on observable words and actions.** Rather than use abstract terms, focus on concrete concepts and behaviors. Instead of saying, "Be responsible," teachers could tell the students specifically what is expected. If expectations include abstract concepts such as being responsible or treating each other with respect, teachers can have a discussion to clarify what those expectations look like in real words or actions. This helps communicate expectations more clearly.

5. **Keep it simple and brief.** When giving directions, long explanations are often counterproductive since students may not identify or remember all of the parts, and they may not even follow along during the entire explanation. Short, simple directions and explanations are essential if we expect specific actions.

6. **Know when to be silent.** The skillful use of silence can be just as powerful as the skillful use of language. Silence allows for students' voices. It allows for thinking, interacting, and decision making. When asking questions, provide wait time (i.e., teacher silence) for several seconds to enable students to think about the question and their possible response. Also, listen to what students have to say. Listening to what students have to say models respectful interaction in a community of learners, and it helps students learn when they need to formulate and express their ideas and knowledge.

7. **Make sure you have student attention before you proceed.** Whether talking with one student or the entire class, it is important to capture the students' attention before you proceed with what you plan to say. In a whole-class setting, teachers may use some type of signal, sound, movement, or statement to capture students' attention that the class is about to begin. When speaking to a single student, face-to-face communication works best along with eye contact.

8. **Be aware that body language, tone and volume of voice, and facial expression affects the message you deliver.** Your body language, tone of voice, and other nonverbal expressions should be consistent with your spoken words (discussed later in this chapter).

■ WHAT WOULD YOU DECIDE? Preparing Students for Computer Centers

You have two computer centers in your classroom, each with four computers. Since this is the first time students will be using the centers this year, you describe the guidelines for their use and your expectations about conduct before having the first group of students at the center. Then, you notice that two students at the computers are not following the behavioral guidelines you stated.

1. Identify specifically how you would apply the guidelines for effective teacher language when presenting the guidelines and behavioral expectations to the students.

2. Similarly, identify how you would apply the guidelines for effective teacher language when you noticed two students misbehaving at the computers.

Communicating Firm Limits for Behavior

Teachers identify rules for the classroom and then enforce the rules when necessary. When a student exhibits a behavior that violates a rule, teachers typically interact with the student verbally before delivering a consequence. However, many teachers hold up the wrong signals to stop misbehavior. They don't realize that their stop signs don't really require stopping or that their attempts to say no actually sound like "yes," "sometimes," or "maybe" to their students. In these cases, the teacher's limits are soft, not firm, and the students know it. *Setting Limits in the Classroom* (MacKenzie & Stanzione, 2010) provides the basis for much of this information, and it is a useful guide.

Soft Limits

Soft limits are rules in theory but not in practice. The verbal message seems to say stop, but the action message says stopping is neither expected nor required. Soft limits invite testing and power struggles.

Types of Soft Limits

Soft limits come in a variety of forms. They can be ineffective verbal messages or ineffective action messages. Sometimes they are both at the same time. Here are some examples:

Soft Limits—Examples of Ineffective Verbal Messages

- "Would you cooperate just once in a while?"

- "You'd better shape up."

- "Would you do me a favor and pay attention?"

- "Come on, get your act together."

Soft Limits—Examples of Ineffective Action Messages

- Allowing students to walk away from a mess.

- Cleaning up students' messes for them.

- Overlooking a misbehavior when you are in a good mood.

- Giving in to persistent nagging.

Examples of Soft Limits

Here are some typical examples of soft limits (MacKenzie & Stanzione, 2010). Realize that you should *avoid the following soft limit behaviors and use firm limits instead*. In most cases, the firm limits are simply the opposite of the soft limit behaviors that are noted.

1. **Wishes, hopes, and shoulds.** "I really wish you would put away your supplies before the end of class." Wishes, hopes, and shoulds are another way of saying, "Stopping is nice, but you really don't have to until you are ready."

2. **Repeating and reminding.** Teachers who repeat and remind are teaching students to ignore and tune out. For example, a teacher might ask a student to put away a personal booklet and then remind the student again when it is not done. When students wonder how far they can go, they simply do not comply until they realize they must do so.

3. **Speeches, lectures, and sermons.** If a student comes in from recess late, for example, the teacher might go on about how disruptive this is since the class has already begun and directions need to be restated for her. The student learns that showing up late is okay if she can tolerate the teacher's lectures about the event.

4. **Warnings and second chances.** Teachers sometimes give a student a warning before delivering a consequence. But if teachers give several warnings without a consequence, then students *will* probably continue to test until the consequence is delivered.

5. **Cooperate, okay?** "Amber, you're supposed to put away your materials before starting the next activity. Okay?" Okay to whom—the student or the teacher? Does that mean cooperation is optional? When teachers add "Okay" to the end of requests, the clarity of the message is obscured.

6. **Statements of fact.** Students at the beginning of class are talking with some not even in their seats. The teacher says, "I'm ready to start. It's too noisy. I can't get started until it's quiet." This soft message was intended to tell the students to stop talking and get in their seats, but many students continue to test the message. A clearer signal is needed. Statements of fact do not convey the intended message.

7. **Ignoring the behavior.** If a student is clowning around, for example, a teacher may ignore it with the hope that it will go away. Especially if the behavior shows up repeatedly, ignoring the behavior just gives a green light to the student. Instead, a teacher should tell the student to stop and should deliver appropriate consequences if the behavior continues.

8. **Unclear directions.** Sometimes teachers make statements that are open to interpretation. "Don't take too long on this task in your small groups." What does "too long" mean? Five minutes? Ten minutes? Unclear or open-ended directions invite testing and set up conflicts. It is better to be specific when stating expectations.

Firm Limits

In contrast to soft limits, firm limits are clear signals that students understand and that teachers enforce. When giving clear messages, it is best to (1) keep the focus of your words on behavior, (2) be direct and specific, (3) use your normal voice, (4) use nonthreatening body language, and (5) specify the logical consequence for noncompliance. Using firm limits will reduce testing. Using firm limits does not mean that a teacher is harsh or nasty with students.

Firm Limits—Examples of Effective Verbal Messages

- "I expect you to be back in five minutes."

- "If you shove, you will go to the back of the line."

- "You won't be ready to leave until your desk is clean."

Firm Limits—Examples of Effective Action Messages

- Removing an object from a student who does not put it away when asked.

- Separating a student from others for misbehaving in a small-group activity.

- Temporarily removing a privilege for abusing that privilege.

Opinions, Questions, Directives

When making statements to students about their behavior, teachers may state their opinions, ask questions, or give directives. The use of opinions and questions are indirect ways of guiding and correcting student behavior. Giving directives is more clear and straightforward.

If a student is making a tapping noise during a test, for example, the teacher may express an opinion ("I am concerned that this noise will distract other students"), ask a question ("Will you stop tapping?"), or give a directive ("Stop tapping now"). Using indirect language, such as

Near the end of some seatwork, you give directions to the students to soon be ready for their next large group activity. After a couple of minutes, you see an idle student and you say, "Austin, you are supposed to be getting ready for the next activity. Okay?" Even after you leave Austin's area, you then notice that he is not moving. But you decide not to go back to him because he might complain about you nagging him.

1. What specific problems with soft limits are illustrated in this example?

2. If you really were the teacher, how specifically might you have used firm limits to better address the situation?

with opinions and questions, may be a less harsh and sometimes easy way to gain compliance. However, soft commands such as those don't always lead to compliance. It is often better to be more clear and direct by stating a directive in a nonthreatening, matter-of-fact tone.

Think about these statements from the students' perspective at the end of small-group work: "I think it's time to get back to your regular seats" (opinion). "Will you get back to your regular seats?" (question). "Please go back to your regular seats now." (directive). There is less ambiguity and more clarity for the students when using a directive statement.

Using Supportive Language

Teachers can use supportive language to guide and support effective instruction, classroom management, and discipline. Language that expresses guidance, caring, and support can positively affect teacher–student relationships and the climate in the learning community. Although there are many dimensions of language for these purposes, the following sections offer suggestions for supportive language in relation to classroom management and discipline.

Being Intentionally Inviting

Establishing a positive classroom community is an important goal for all teachers, and many deliberate actions need to be taken to create this positive environment. To do so, teachers need to be intentionally inviting and supportive of students. In *Inviting School Success*, Purkey and Novak (1996) describe four types of teacher behaviors toward students: intentionally disinviting, unintentionally disinviting, unintentionally inviting, and intentionally inviting.

Inviting messages are intended to inform people that they are able, valuable, and responsible; that they have the opportunity to participate in their own development; and that they are cordially summoned to take advantage of these opportunities. Conversely, a disinviting message informs recipients that they are irresponsible, incapable, and worthless and that cannot participate in activities of any significance (Purkey & Novak, 1996). To create a positive, caring learning community, teachers need to use inviting messages and be intentionally inviting by giving deliberate attention to how they state and deliver their words. Teachers should strive to use inviting messages that express to students that they are able, valuable, and responsible.

In relation to classroom discipline, Purkey and Strahan (2002) state that there are four principles that give invitational teaching direction and purpose:

1. **Respect.** Students are to be seen as able, valuable, and responsible and should be treated accordingly.

2. **Trust.** Teachers establish trust through a pattern of inviting actions, rather than by a single inviting act.

3. **Optimism.** Teachers should take the optimistic view that students want to learn and they will learn in a cooperative and supportive environment.

4. **Intentionality.** By focusing on being intentional, teachers become more accurate and dependable in their decision making and behaviors, leading to a more clear purpose, direction, and control.

Reinforcing Language

Reinforcing language involves statements that identify and affirm students' specific positive work and behavior (Denton, 2013). We want to build on students' strengths, and reinforcing language helps achieve that purpose. Teachers can use reinforcing language in various situations such as: (1) to coach students on key behaviors when they practice social and academic skills ("That is the correct way to create a Venn diagram"); (2) to help a group move past a stuck point (by noticing and commenting upon correct behavior); (3) to point out an individual student's "leading edge" behaviors (by noticing and commenting on a student's important improvement in behavior or academic work); and (4) to make students aware of their growth by describing their learning histories (by drawing attention to how the student has changed from a previous time) (Denton, 2013).

Reinforcing language can be used to highlight many important student strengths. Here are some guidelines when using reinforcing language (Denton, 2013):

- Name concrete, specific behaviors.
- Use a warm and professional voice.
- Emphasize description of the action over your own personal approval.
- Consider adding a question to extend student thinking.
- Find positives to name in all students.
- Avoid naming individuals as examples for others.

Reminding Language

Reminders help us stay organized and on track with our activities. In everyday life, when we give reminders, we tell our listeners what it is they should remember. Reminders in classrooms, however, should prompt the students to do the remembering themselves ("What are some things we should remember about safety before we begin this lab activity?" "Jason, what are you supposed to be doing right now?").

Used in this way, reminding language helps students develop the feelings of autonomy and competence that lead to self-control and intrinsic motivation. These guidelines can make classroom reminders more effective (Denton, 2013):

- Start by establishing expectations clearly (by structured discussions, interactive modeling, and practice).
- Phrase a reminder as a question or a statement.
- Use a direct tone and neutral body language.
- Use reminders proactively before an event or reactively after an event to correct a behavior.
- Use reminders when the student and you are both calm.
- Keep reminders brief.
- Watch for follow through.

■ **CLASSROOM CASE STUDY**   Poor Use of Limit Setting and Supportive Language

Terrell Green planned some small-group activities for his tenth-grade geometry class. Instruction had been completed on a new topic, and Mr. Green wanted the students to work in small groups to work out some sample problems together. He provided each group with paper, rulers, compasses, and protractors to work out the problems.

After a while, some students in the groups were using the rulers to swat other students. Most students were on task, but one or two in each group were hitting with the rulers. Several times, Mr. Green said, "Rulers are not for hitting," but he didn't follow-up with any other statements or actions. Later, he said to two students, "Will you stop hitting with the ruler?" but he had no follow through. After about 10 minutes, he realized that he had not stated any guidelines or cautions with the use of the supplies at the start of the activity.

This activity disturbed Mr. Green, and he seemed to be at a loss for what to do. He didn't interact with the students who were on task, and he simply walked around to be physically close to those who were hitting. After the lesson, he reflected about what happened and what he might have done differently to get a better outcome.

Focus Questions

1. How did Mr. Green use opinions, questions, and directives? How should he have used those differently to get a better outcome?

2. How might Mr. Green have used reinforcing, reminding, and redirecting language to set the tone and also to correct misbehaviors?

3. Besides walking around, how could he have used nonverbal communication to better advantage?

Redirecting Language

Reinforcing positive behaviors and reminding students about how to behave can be very helpful in classroom management and discipline. However, there are times when teachers simply need to give students clear, nonnegotiable commands about what to do.

Redirecting statements should guide students to act differently while preserving their dignity and sense of belonging in the classroom. Here are some points to remember when using redirecting language (Denton, 2013):

- Be direct and specific. (Call the student by name and state exactly what you want the student to do.)

- Name the desired behavior. (Instead of, "Many of you are wasting time," state, "We will begin when you are all seated with your materials ready.")

- Keep it brief. (Get the students' attention in a few direct words.)

- Phrase redirections as a statement, not a question (Instead of, "Can you put your backpacks away?" say, "Put all backpacks on the hooks now.")

- Follow through after giving a redirection. (After giving redirecting language, observe the students and step in with clearer directions or consequences if students don't follow the redirection. This tells students we mean what we say.)

Listening

Effective communication is essential in the classroom for instruction and behavior management. Listening is a vital part of effective communication, and it is a key element in developing positive teacher–student relationships, addressing classroom problems, and enhancing instruction and supporting student learning.

What Is Listening?

Listening is more than passively receiving a student's words. It involves searching for the student's intended meaning, which means paying attention to what's being said beneath the works and using responding strategies to explore the words and the meaning. Listening and responding is actually a three-step process (Denton, 2013): (1) take in the words; (2) figure out the true meaning of the words by looking at tone, context, and other signals for clues; and (3) think about how to respond.

Listening involves more than hearing what the other person is saying. It is more than taking turns speaking, with responses sometimes unrelated to what the other person just said. The meaning of the words must be explored. There are four tools to develop the art of listening (Larrivee, 2009):

1. **Control the impulse to talk and just remain silent.** Avoid the tendency to jump in with your own ideas or solutions before hearing from the student.

2. **Demonstrate acceptance.** Provide verbal and nonverbal support for what the student is saying.

3. **Provide an invitation to talk.** This often involves open-ended, nonevaluative questions that invite the student to talk more.

4. **Use active listening skills.** Use listening strategies (discussed later) such as paraphrasing and clarifying to seek the real meaning of the messages.

Why Listen?

Teachers need to listen in order to communicate effectively when dealing with instruction and behavior management. Effective listening serves many purposes. In *The Power of Our Words*, Denton (2013) gives six reasons why we need to listen in the classroom:

1. **Listening lets us know the child.** Listening helps teachers understand their students, and this helps teachers make better decisions about curriculum, classroom management, and discipline. Students, then, are more likely to feel that they belong and are important in the classroom community.

2. **When we listen, children learn about themselves.** By listening to students and reflecting back to them what we heard, teachers can help students become more conscious of their own interests, talents, worries, and questions. This self-awareness is important if students are to learn at their best.

3. **Listening builds a sense of community.** When teachers listen and reflect back to students what they said, other students hear this interaction and thus understand each other better. Also, when teachers listen to all students, this sets a standard and a tone for respect and empathy that are fundamental to a strong learning community.

4. **Listening makes our questioning more effective.** When asking questions, it is important that teachers listen to the students' answers and follow-up as needed to identify and explore the meaning of their responses. If teachers do not show they listened and understood student replies, students will likely be less engaged in these interactions in the future.

5. **When we listen, students take their learning more seriously.** When teachers follow-up student statements with questions seeking meaning, students begin to take their ideas and words more seriously. They see that the teacher cares and is interested in them and their ideas.

6. **Our listening helps students become better communicators.** By listening and reflecting what we understood back to students, teachers can help students improve their communication skills. In this way, teachers model for students how to be good listeners themselves—how to take in a speaker's words, how to search for the intended meaning, and how to respond.

■ WHAT WOULD YOU DECIDE?   **Students Knowing Each Other Through Listening**

You know that there is a fairly high enrollment change each year in your school, so you realize that it is helpful at the start of the school year to help students in your class to get to know each other. Three important purposes of listening are to help the teacher to know the student, help students learn about each other, and help build a sense of community.

1. What might you do to listen and get to know individual students?

2. What might you do to help the students get to know each other?

3. How might this information help you when you plan for instruction and interact with the students?

Listening Strategies

Several listening strategies can be used to achieve the purposes just described. These strategies fall into four levels of listening: (1) *passive listening* in which the listener just listens without any interaction with the speaker; (2) an *acknowledgment,* which involves a response to indicate the teacher is really listening; (3) an *invitation to talk,* which is a deliberate encouragement to speak; and (4) *active listening,* which involves teacher responses that include additional interaction to more fully explore the meaning of the ideas being expressed (Larrivee, 2009).

Within these four levels of listening, there are nine listening strategies (Larivee, 2009):

1. **Silence.** Remaining a silent listener allows the person to express ideas and feelings. This is passive listening.

2. **Nonverbal support.** Nonverbal messages help communicate that you are really paying attention. These include nodding, smiling, or leaning forward. This is an acknowledgment of what the person is saying.

3. **Encouragers.** Minimal verbal expressions also can offer acknowledgment of what is being stated and serve as an encouragement to continue. Expressions such as "Oh," "I see," and "Un-huh" let the student know to continue.

4. **Opening.** A more deliberative invitation to talk involves asking open-ended, nonevaluative questions to encourage students to talk more. Some examples are "Would you like to tell me what happened?" "That's interesting. Want to tell me more?"

5. **Reflecting.** Reflecting and the next four strategies are those used in active listening. These strategies involve interaction with the student and provide feedback to the student that the teacher understands. With reflecting, teachers verbalize the feelings and attitudes that they perceive lie behind the message ("You seem disappointed with your assignment." "Paige really irritates you when she acts like that."). This interaction often leads to a discussion about the origin of a problem and can lead to a solution.

6. **Exploring.** This strategy calls for questioning in an open-ended way to extend a student's thinking and to expand a student's range of options. For example, "Can you tell me more about. . . .?" "What's causing you the most trouble?"

7. **Paraphrasing.** Paraphrasing calls for translating or feeding back to the student the essence of the message the teacher just heard, but in a simpler, more concise and precise way. In paraphrasing, you make sure that you are clear about what the student said. It demonstrates understanding of what was said and communicates that you care enough about what the student said to get it right.

8. **Perception checking.** The purpose of perception checking is to make sure you are interpreting what the student said in the way it was intended. To do so, you pose a question and

ask for feedback. After a student describes an incident, for example, the teacher might say, "I'm not sure I understand. Was it Tyler's statement that made you mad?"

9. **Clarifying.** Sometimes there is a need to sort out something that is confusing. Clarifying involves restating what the student has said to clear up any confusion. Often it involves stating your own confusion and asking for help to clarify your understanding. For example, "Can we stop here? I really don't understand what you mean. Can you tell me more?" "Earlier you said. . . . . Now you seem to be saying. . . . . I'm confused."

Using Nonverbal Communication

How teachers deliver their messages can be as significant as what information is being communicated. It is important to be aware of the types of nonverbal communication and the ways that you can use it in instruction and in addressing issues concerning classroom management and discipline.

Types of Nonverbal Communication

There are many aspects of nonverbal communication, commonly organized into two categories— proxemics and kinesics (Knapp & Hall, 2014). *Proxemics* deals with personal space, seating arrangements, and the general physical environment. *Kinesics* deals with the communication aspects of the body, such as facial expression, eye behavior, vocal intonation, touching, body movement and gestures, and dress and personal appearance (Leathers & Eaves, 2008). This section focuses on kinesics in which teachers communicate nonverbally to their students concerning classroom management issues.

Nonverbal communication does not occur in a vacuum, but instead occurs alongside verbal communication. We want our nonverbal and verbal communications to be congruent. In other words, if we are expressing positive ideas with our words, then our physical, nonverbal expressions should also send a positive message. Sometimes, however, the nonverbal message may not be consistent with the verbal message. In these cases, the recipient tends to see sarcasm in the message (Farrell, 2009).

Teachers' Use of Nonverbal Communication

As previously noted, teachers communicate nonverbally through their facial expressions, eye behavior, vocal intonation, body movements and gestures, and other ways. The use of nonverbal communication by teachers warrants additional discussion. Useful resources for teachers on nonverbal communication are available, including *Body Language: An Illustrated Introduction for Teachers* (Miller, 2005) and *Nonverbal Behavior in Interpersonal Relations* (Richmond, McCroskey, & Hickson, 2012).

Vocal Intonation

The tone of your voice is important when managing student behavior. Your normal voice tone expresses control, whereas your raised voice sends the opposite message—loss of control. Your tone should convey that you are firm, in control, and resolute in your expectations that the students do what you have asked (MacKenzie & Stanzione, 2010). Diffily and Sassman (2006) describe this as "developing your teacher voice." The best way to communicate this expectation is simply to state your message matter-of-factly in your normal voice, but with a noticeable degree of firmness.

Nonthreatening Stance

Our body language also conveys a message about our comfort level, feelings, and expectations in guidance and discipline situations. When our body language is congruent with a neutral or positive message, we increase the likelihood that the message will be received in a supportive manner.

Threatening body language, however, increases the likelihood of a defensive response by students. Glaring or staring at students, standing too close, standing rigidly with arms crossed, or looking down on students are examples of intimidating body language that raises the threat level and increases the likelihood of a defensive response from students (MacKenzie & Stanzione, 2010).

Gestures and Signals

Gestures and various types of signals can guide and direct students without any spoken word. Signals can be used to direct students to perform certain actions, but the signal and the action must be taught to students if they are expected to successfully follow them.

The simplest signals to use are those that just seem to come naturally. Holding up your hand with the palm facing out for stop, or an upraised index finger across your lips for quiet, or a crooked index finger curling back to you to come are signals that many teachers use (Diffily & Sassman, 2006). Teachers can identify situations that would benefit from a signal, select an appropriate signal, and then teach the students about the signal.

Cultural Differences in Nonverbal Communication

People from different cultures and ethnic groups may interpret nonverbal communication in a different way than the teacher. Gestures and the use of personal space, for example, may be interpreted quite differently by various cultures. Thus, it is important that teachers be familiar with the ways that culture influences communication in the classroom (R. G. Powell & D. L. Powell, 2015).

Nonverbal Aspects of Restoring Order

Teachers might consider the following nonverbal behaviors when trying to restore classroom control (Farrell, 2009):

- Use extended eye contact.
- Shake their head to indicate no.
- Use facial expressions of disapproval.
- Use gestures to put off the behavior.
- Move closer to the site of the disruption.
- Make use of approval facial expression when order is restored.

Awareness of One's Nonverbal Communication

As previously mentioned, we want our nonverbal and verbal communications to be congruent. When the messages are not congruent, the nonverbal signal is often the message that is recognized as the real message. Thus, it is important for teachers to examine and reflect on their use of words, but also to identify and reflect on their expression of nonverbal communication to effectively manage a classroom.

VOICES FROM THE CLASSROOM   Using Body Language and "The Teacher Look"

Lynne Hagar, high school history and English teacher, Mesquite, Texas

I am a small woman, but I can effectively control 30 senior students just by using my voice and my body language. When I want a certain behavior to stop, the first thing I do is to look at the student. Even if that student is not looking at me, he or she eventually becomes aware that I am staring. Then I point at the student and nonverbally indicate that the behavior is to stop. A finger placed on my lips indicates that talking needs to stop.

Often, a questioning or disapproving look or gesture can stop undesirable behaviors right there. I may have to move into a student's personal space or comfort zone to stop a behavior, but a combination of a look and physical proximity is effective about 90 percent of the time. I might even casually rest my hand on the student's desk, never stopping teaching, and stay put for a minute or so until I'm sure the student is back on task.

My advice is to practice "the look" in the mirror until you get it right. It shouldn't be a friendly look, but it doesn't have to be angry, either. Learn to say in your manner, "I am in charge here." Also, move around the classroom. Getting close to your students is essential, not only when you are correcting them but also when you want to reassure them or reinforce their positive feelings about you and your classroom. A friendly touch on the shoulder as you are helping a student with a problem or a hug when a student has a big success can go miles toward cementing your positive relationship with that student.

MAJOR CONCEPTS

1. The term *teacher language* refers to the professional use of words, phrases, tone, and pace to enable students to engage in active, interested learning and develop positive behaviors.

2. Teachers can follow general guidelines for using language to affirm meaning and action, to address various aspects of instruction and behavior management, and to engage in guidance and conversation with students.

3. Soft limits are rules in theory but not in practice. Firm limits are clear signals that students understand and that teachers enforce.

4. The use of opinions and questions are indirect ways of guiding and correcting student behavior. Giving directives is more clear and straightforward.

5. Teachers can use supportive language to guide and support effective instruction, classroom management, and discipline. Supportive language includes being intentionally inviting and using reinforcing, reminding, and redirecting language.

6. Listening is a vital part of effective communication, and it is a key element in developing positive teacher–student relationships, addressing classroom problems, and enhancing instruction and supporting student learning.

7. Teachers communicate nonverbally through their facial expressions, eye behavior, vocal intonation, body movements and gestures, and other ways. We want our nonverbal and verbal communications to be congruent.

DISCUSSION/REFLECTION QUESTIONS

1. Identify some ways that a teacher could capture students' attention at the start of a class.

2. Identify an example of a minor problem. Give examples for ways that a teacher may state an opinion, question, and directive in response to that problem.

3. Give some examples for ways that redirecting language can be used in instruction. And also when misbehavior occurs.

4. How can the active listening strategies of exploring and paraphrasing be used in an instructional situation? In a situation where a student has misbehaved?

5. From your experience, what are some ways your teachers have expressed nonverbal communication? What messages were they communicating in your examples?

SUGGESTED ACTIVITIES

1. Make a list of ten examples of classroom misbehaviors or situations where students need guidance. For each example, write an opinion, a question, and a directive that teachers might use in response to the behavior.

2. Identify two examples of positive student work and two examples of positive student behavior. For each, indicate how you could use reinforcing language for these behaviors.

3. View a video of a teaching episode (or observe in an actual classroom), and watch closely for the listening skills the teacher used in the episode. Identify the type of listening strategies used.

4. Talk with several teachers about how they use nonverbal communication in their teaching. Ask about facial expressions, eye behavior, vocal intonation, body movements and gestures, and other ways. Ask how they use this communication in instruction and behavior management.

FURTHER READING

Charney, R. S. (2002). *Teaching children to care: Classroom management for ethical and academic growth, K–8* (Rev. ed.). Turners Falls, MA: Center for Responsive Schools.
Three chapters address dimensions of teacher language in classroom management and instruction. Other chapters examine building and supporting classroom communities.

Denton, P. (2013). *The power of our words: Teacher language that helps children learn* (2nd ed.). Turners Falls, MA: Center for Responsive Schools.
Provides general guidelines for teacher language. Then discusses several specific areas: envisioning, open-ended questions, listening, reinforcing language, reminding language, and redirecting language. Very useful resource.

Diffily D., & Sassman, C. (2006). *Positive teacher talk for better classroom management.* New York: Scholastic.
Discusses the characteristics and importance of teacher language. Then provides guidance for language when welcoming students, setting the tone for the year, helping students manage their behavior, supporting learning, and using signals.

Edwards, J. (2010). *Inviting students to learn: 100 tips for talking effectively with your students.* Alexandria, VA: Association for Supervision and Curriculum Development.
Discusses reason for communicating invitationally with students, along with strategies and purposes. Then describes 100 specific tips to apply these strategies.

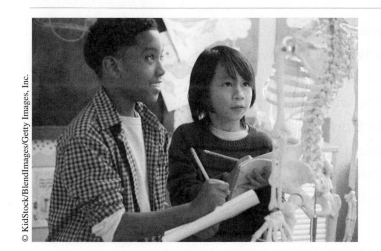

Knowing Your Diverse Students

CHAPTER OUTLINE

chapter

7

Creating a Responsive Classroom
    Create a Supportive, Caring Environment
    Vary Your Instruction
    Provide Assistance with the Response to Intervention
Getting to Know Your Students
    Types of Information
    Sources of Information
    Using the Information

CHAPTER OBJECTIVES

This chapter provides information that will help you:

- Describe multiple ways in which diversity is exhibited in student characteristics.

- Identify ways to address the diversity of students into your teaching.

- Create a supportive, caring classroom.

- Vary your instruction with student characteristics in mind.

- Provide assistance when needed by applying the Response to Intervention.

- Select ways to know your students and then use that information to enhance instruction.

Just think about the diversity apparent in a typical urban classroom. There may be a wide range of student cognitive and physical abilities. Students may have different degrees of English proficiency, and some may have a disabling condition such as a hearing disorder. A wide range of ethnic characteristics may be evident, and various socioeconomic levels are likely to be represented. The students may prefer to learn in different ways, such as in pairs, small groups, or independently. Some may prefer written work; others may learn best when performing an activity.

People differ in countless ways, and it is helpful to examine variables that account for human differences. Variables include human characteristics that differ or vary from one person to the next. For example, height, weight, and measured intelligence are variables. Gender, race, socioeconomic status (SES), and age also are variables. Less observable but equally important variables include self-esteem, confidence, anxiety, and learning style.

These examples are just a few of the human variables that create a wide range of individual differences and needs in classrooms. Individual differences need to be taken into account when instructional methods and procedures are selected for classroom management and discipline. What are the sources of student diversity? How can our understanding of these student characteristics help teachers to create an inclusive, responsive? How can you get to know your students? These issues are explored in this chapter.

Classroom Management Implications for Diverse Classrooms

Students who are in the classroom affect classroom management. Schools in the United States are very diverse and have students from different economic, cultural, ethnic, and linguistic backgrounds. In addition, you may find that your classroom has students with a range of ability levels or achievement, groups of students with skills below grade level, and students with special needs. All of these factors contribute to the diversity in your classroom.

For you and your students to be successful, you may need to make adjustments in instructional and management practices to meet the needs of different groups in your class. For example, you may find a wide variety of academic ability in your classroom and consequently need to vary your curriculum, instruction, and assessments. You also may have several students whose primary language is not English, and similar adjustments may need to be enacted. Your job is to enhance student learning, and adjustments based on student characteristics will be necessary.

As discussed in Chapter 1, there are several domains of responsibility for classroom management. Your understanding of your students will likely influence your decisions about ways that you will organize the physical environment, manage student behavior, create a supportive learning environment, facilitate instruction, and promote safety and wellness. To be an effective classroom manager in a diverse classroom, you should make a commitment to do these things:

- Get to know all of your students.

- Create an inclusive classroom by making instructional and management modifications based on an understanding of your students.

- Create a classroom environment that promotes positive behavior and enhances student learning.

Sources of Student Diversity

Individual differences abound, and adapting instruction to student differences is one of the most challenging aspects of teaching. The first step in planning to address the diversity of students is to recognize those differences. This section explores differences in development by age; differences in cognitive, affective, and physical areas; differences due to gender, sexual orientation, ethnicity, learning style, language, or creative potential; differences due to exceptionalities and at-risk characteristics; and other types of differences (Gollnick & Chinn, 2017). In the classroom, students rarely fall cleanly into one category or another, and may exhibit characteristics from several categories.

Developmental Differences by Age

Any elementary teacher can tell you that kindergarten students are profoundly different from sixth-grade students, and those differences need to be taken into account when planning and teaching. Similarly, any middle level or secondary teacher can tell you that eighth graders are quite different from seniors.

Students at the grade level you teach will be of a certain age and will possess certain developmental characteristics of that age. Those characteristics must be taken into account when planning and delivering instruction. Part of your review of contextual factors in your classroom, examined later in this chapter, includes careful identification of the characteristics of the students in your class.

It is beyond the scope of this book to review developmental characteristics of students at various age levels. However, it is important to alert teachers that those developmental characteristics must be taken into account when planning for instruction. College courses in human development examine characteristics of children as they grow older (Arnett, 2016; Boyd & Bee, 2015; Feldman, 2016). Educational psychology courses also consider various theories of development. Recall some of those developmental concepts, such as Jean Piaget's four stages of cognitive development; Eric Erikson's eight stages of psychosocial development; Lawrence Kohlberg's three levels and six stages of moral reasoning; and additional perspectives on the development of language, memory, and physical and emotional development.

Seek out resources that provide information about the developmental characteristics of children at the age of the grade level you teach. One such resource is *Yardsticks: Children in the Classroom, Ages 4–14* by Chip Wood (2007). In a separate chapter for each age, Wood describes the social, physical, and cognitive characteristics of children of that age. Dig out your educational psychology books (e.g., J. E. Ormrod, E. M. Anderman, & L. Anderman, 2017) to find useful reviews of developmental characteristics by age. All of these are useful resources to help you understand developmental characteristics by age and to take those characteristics into account when planning and delivering instruction and arranging for effective classroom management.

Cognitive Area

Cognitive ability includes information processing, problem solving, using mental strategies for tasks, and continuous learning. Children in a classroom will differ in their cognitive abilities to perform these tasks. Thus, students in a classroom might range from low academic ability to high academic ability. *Intelligence* involves the capacity to apprehend facts and their relations and to reason about them; it is an indicator of cognitive ability.

The work of Gardner (2006, 2011) on multiple intelligences and other cognitive psychologists provides ideas for teachers when selecting instructional techniques and differentiating instruction. There are many useful resource guides for addressing the diversity of students by applying the multiple intelligences concepts to lesson activities (e.g., Armstrong, 2009; Campbell, 2008; Fogarty & Stoehr, 2008). When considering the cognitive differences of your students, you should do the following:

1. Expect students to be different.

2. Spend the time and effort to look for potential.

3. Realize that student needs are not only in deficit areas. Development of potential is a need, too.

4. Be familiar with past records of achievement.

5. Be aware of previous experiences that have shaped a student's way of thinking.

6. Challenge students with varied assignments, and note the results.

7. Use a variety of ways of grading and evaluating.

8. Keep changing the conditions for learning to bring out hidden potential.

9. Challenge students occasionally beyond what is expected.

10. Look for something unique that each student can do.

Struggling Learners

A student who is considered a *struggling learner* cannot learn at an average rate from the instructional resources, texts, workbooks, and materials that are designated for the majority of students in the classroom. These students often have limited attention spans and deficiencies in basic skills such as reading, writing, and mathematics. They need frequent feedback, corrective instruction, special instructional pacing, instructional variety, and perhaps modified materials (Protheroe, Shellard, & Turner, 2004). Resources are available for supporting struggling readers in the secondary grades (McEwan, 2007).

In *How to Support Struggling Students*, Jackson and Lambert (2010) state that effective support is ongoing, proactive, targeted, accelerative (rather than remedial), learning focused, and managed by the teacher as an advocate. They suggest targeted strategies before, during, and after instruction to support struggling students.

For the struggling learners in your class, you should (1) frequently vary your instructional technique; (2) develop lessons around students' interests, needs, and experiences; (3) provide an encouraging, supportive environment; (4) use cooperative learning and peer tutors for students needing remediation; (5) provide study aids; (6) teach content in small sequential steps with frequent checks for comprehension; (7) use individualized materials and individualized instruction whenever possible; (8) use audio and visual materials for instruction; and (9) take steps to develop the student's self-concept (e.g., assign a task where the student can showcase a particular skill).

Gifted or Talented Learners

Gifted or talented learners are those with above average abilities, and they need special instructional consideration. Unfortunately, some teachers do not challenge high-ability students, and these students just "mark time" in school. Unchallenged, they may develop poor attention and study habits, form negative attitudes toward school and learning, and waste academic learning time. Resources about teaching gifted students are also available (e.g., Clark, 2013; Karnes & Stephens, 2008; Smutny & von Fremd, 2009, 2011; Sousa, 2009).

For these students, you should (1) not require that they repeat material they already have mastered; (2) present instruction at a flexible pace, allowing those who are able to progress at a productive rate; (3) condense curriculum by removing unneeded assignments to make time for extending activities; (4) encourage students to be self-directing and self-evaluating in their work; (5) use grading procedures that will not discourage students from intellectual risk taking or penalize them for choosing complex learning activities; (6) provide resources beyond basal textbooks; (7) provide horizontal and vertical curriculum enrichment; (8) encourage supplementary reading and writing; and (9) encourage the development of hobbies and interests.

Affective Area

Education in the *affective area* focuses on feelings and attitudes. Emotional growth is not easily facilitated, yet the students' feelings about personal skills or the subject being studied are at least as important as the information in the lesson (Slavin, 2015). Self-esteem, time management, confidence, and self-direction are typical affective education goals.

Although affective goals have generally played a secondary role to cognitive goals in school, they should be given an important place when planning and carrying out instruction. Love of learning, confidence in learning, and cooperative attitudes are important objectives that teachers should foster. You may find a range of affective characteristics exhibited in the classroom—from low to high self-esteem, confidence, cooperation, self-direction, and the like. To encourage affective development, you should take six steps:

1. Identify students by name as early as possible.

2. Accept the student as he or she is, for each has interesting, valuable qualities.

3. Be aware of previous experiences that have helped shape the student's feelings.

4. Observe students; notice moods and reactions from day to day.

5. Make observations over time, noting trends.

6. Observe changes, or stability, under different conditions.

Physical Area

Perhaps the best place to observe the wide range of physical differences among students is the hallway of any middle school. Tall and short, skinny and heavy, muscular and frail, dark and fair, active and quiet describe just a few of the extremes one can see there. Physical (psycho-motor) differences among students have sometimes been overlooked by teachers who are not involved in physical education (Woolfolk, 2016). *Psychomotor skills* involve gross motor skills and fine motor skills, such as dribbling a basketball or drawing a fine line. These skills are integral parts of most learning activities. Indeed, psychomotor and affective objectives often overlap.

Physical demands on learning are obvious in areas of handwriting, industrial arts, sewing, typing, art, and driver education. However, they must not be minimized in less obvious areas such as science labs, computer classes, speech and drama, and music. Vision and hearing deficiencies also contribute to individual differences. You should recognize the importance of physical skills in the total learning program and explore the possibilities for including psychomotor development activities in classroom objectives. You should follow these guidelines:

1. Remember that students come in many different sizes, shapes, colors, and physical states.

2. Be aware of previous experiences that have shaped physical performance and self-expression.

3. Know what the normal physical pattern is for each age level and note any extreme variations.

4. Provide materials for manipulation and observe carefully to see what skills emerge or are lacking.

5. Observe student responses to different environmental factors and different kinds of physical activities.

6. Give students a chance to express themselves physically.

Learning Styles

A *learning style* is an individual's preferences for the conditions of the learning process that can affect one's learning (Woolfolk, 2016), including where, when, and how learning takes place and with what materials. These styles may play an integral role in determining how the student perceives the learning environment and responds to it. Therefore, knowledge about learning styles can help you provide options in the classroom that would enhance students' learning.

Theories and research studies about learning styles are tentative and ongoing, though several promising areas of instructional assistance have emerged. These include cognitive style, brain hemisphericity, and sensory modalities. Students' learning styles can be addressed by using differentiated instructional techniques (Gregory & Chapman, 2012).

Cognitive Style

Cognitive style should be considered in planning. *Cognitive style* refers to the way people process information and use strategies in responding to tasks. Conceptual tempo and field dependence/field independence are two categories of cognitive style that educators may consider when planning instruction.

Conceptual tempo concerns students being impulsive or reflective when selecting from two or more alternatives. *Field dependence/field independence* deals with the extent to which individuals can overcome effects of distracting background elements (the field) when trying to differentiate among relevant aspects of a particular situation.

Brain Hemisphericity

In *How the Brain Learns*, David Sousa (2011) examines how the brain processes information and how teachers can promote student memory, retention, and learning. He supports the use of many instructional approaches and recommends a fairly explicit type of lesson delivery. In *Brain-Compatible Classrooms*, Robin Fogarty (2009) describes brain-friendly, practical strategies for differentiating instruction.

In *Designing Brain-Compatible Learning*, Gregory and Parry (2006) review the cognitive research and pedagogical theory of learning in relation to the brain. Many of the suggestions are consistent with those about differentiating instruction reviewed later in this chapter. Among the strategies they review and endorse are (1) creating classroom climates that support thinking,

---

VOICES FROM THE CLASSROOM   Learning Styles

Loraine Chapman, high school English teacher, Tucson, Arizona

Shortly after I began teaching, I noticed that students react differently to learning tasks. For example, Kelly stated that unless she can hear the words she reads, she has difficulty comprehending. Delila needs complete silence when she reads and will even put her fingers in her ears when reading to make it quieter. When given the option, some students will always select a partner for work while others will work alone.

After gathering more information about learning styles, I began to incorporate that information into my lesson plans and developed strategies to take into account the various cognitive learning styles of my students. For example, sometimes I let students choose from a list of activities that all fulfill the lesson's objectives, but each activity involves a different type of learning experience reflecting the various learning styles.

I also believe that students need to learn to stretch and use all learning styles. So within a class, or over a few days or a week, tasks using all learning styles will be incorporated into the lessons and each student must complete each activity, no matter what the learning style.

■ WHAT WOULD YOU DECIDE?   Providing Brain-Compatible Instruction

Students in your class don't seem to be paying much attention, and some students are getting off-task and misbehaving. You realize that you are not challenging them enough with the new content and are not making the material interesting. As a result, you decide to apply some of the instructional approaches endorsed by Gregory and Parry for brain-compatible learning to meet the learners' needs. You have a two-week unit coming up on the history of your state.

1. To apply some of Gregory and Parry's approaches, how might you specifically (a) use advance organizers, (b) use cooperative learning groups, and (c) promote creative problem solving?

2. How might you (a) use higher order questioning and (b) use graphic organizers?

(2) activating prior knowledge, (3) using advance organizers, (4) implementing cooperative group learning, (5) providing direct teaching of thinking, (6) using higher order questioning, (7) promoting creative problem solving, (8) using strategies for advancing concept development (e.g., concept attainment and concept development strategies), (9) teaching metacognition (e.g., students learning to examine and monitor how they think), and (10) using graphic organizers.

Sensory Modalities

Sensory modality is a third factor in students' preferences for a learning environment. A *sensory modality* is a system of interacting with the environment through one or more of the basic senses—sight, hearing, touch, smell, and taste. For teachers, the most important sensory modalities are the visual, auditory, and kinesthetic. Information to be learned is first received through one of the senses. The information either is forgotten after a few seconds or, after initial processing, is placed in short-term or long-term memory. Learning may be enhanced when the information is received through a preferred sensory modality. Use a variety of instructional approaches that enable the students to receive the content through one or more of the basis senses.

Creative Potential

Creativity is defined as the process of creating ideas or hypotheses concerning these ideas, testing the hypotheses, modifying and retesting the hypotheses, and communicating the results. Highly creative individuals sometimes demonstrate characteristics that are not always liked by others, such as independence of thought and judgment, courage of convictions, skepticism toward the voice of authority, and displays of nonconformity. Creative students process information differently and react to the world in ways unlike their peers.

You can nurture creativity in your students by learning about creative personalities and developing ability for divergent production. In this regard, you should take these steps (Davis, Rimm, & Siegle, 2011; Karnes & Stephens, 2008):

1. Listen for creative (unconventional) responses.

2. Reward creative responses by asking students to elaborate on those ideas.

3. Provide some learning activities in which students may be creative, not conforming.

4. Allow some work to be open-ended, perhaps messy, and ungraded, to encourage exploration, guessing, and playing with the material.

5. Set up flexible learning environments in which students are free to make choices and pursue areas of personal interest.

Gender

Differences between boys and girls exist, and some of those differences influence their performance at school. Researchers have found females generally are more extroverted, anxious, and trusting; are less assertive; and have slightly lower self-esteem than males of the same age and background. Girls' verbal and motor skills also tend to develop faster than do boys' (Berk, 2014; Berk & Meyers, 2016; Sadker & Silber, 2007).

These gender differences are caused by a combination of genetics and environment. These differences are examined in *Boys and Girls Learn Differently* (Gurian & Stevens, 2010), with discussions concerning elementary, middle, and high school classrooms. Concerns about the performance by boys in schools are examined in sources such as *The Minds of Boys* (Gurian & Stevens, 2007), *Teaching the Male Brain* (James, 2015), and *Teaching the Female Brain* (James, 2009).

You can make your classroom more gender friendly for all students by following these guidelines: incorporate movement in instruction, make learning visual, give students choice and control, provide opportunities for social interaction, find ways to make learning real, blend art and music into the curriculum, connect with your students, promote character development for the benefit of the individuals and the classroom environment, and encourage equal participation (Gurian, Stevens, & King, 2008; James, 2015).

Sexual Orientation

It is estimated that 5–10 percent of the population is lesbian, gay, bisexual, or transgender (LGBT) (Ost & Gates, 2004). As adults, LGBT individuals face discrimination in housing, employment, and social institutions. Society's prejudices and discriminatory policies result in many gays and lesbians hiding their sexual orientation. Early indicators of sexual orientation may show up in students in the elementary grades. During adolescence, about 8 percent of boys and 6 percent of girls report engaging in some same-sex activity or feeling strong attractions to same-sex individuals (Steinberg, 2014).

Loneliness and isolation are experienced by many gay and lesbian youth. If gays and lesbians openly acknowledge their sexual orientation or appear to be LGBT, they are likely to be harassed or bullied by peers. Sixty-four percent of LGBT students fear for their safety in schools. They feel more comfortable and safer in a school when faculty and staff are supportive, gay-straight alliance or similar clubs exist, and a comprehensive policy on harassment is enforced (Ost & Gates, 2004).

Teachers need to reach out to help students who are struggling with sexual identity and to address harassment and bullying (Biegel, 2010). First, listen to the students to allow them to vent or to express what is going on in their lives. Second, affirm to them that they are not alone and that others are dealing with the same issues. Third, refer the students to someone who is trained to deal with the issues. Fourth, address any verbal or physical harassment or bullying related to sexual orientation. Finally, follow up to be sure students' situations have improved and whether there is anything further you may be able to do. In addition to interacting with students who are addressing these issues, teachers may need to interact with parents who are gay or lesbian.

Language

There is tremendous language diversity in the United States, and it is not uncommon for a school district to have students representing numerous languages. According to the U.S. Census Bureau, in 2002, one in five U.S. residents aged five or older spoke a language other than English at home. The National Clearinghouse for English Language Acquisition reported in 2009 that about 5.4 million students have limited English proficiency. It has been estimated that about 10.8 percent of all public school students have limited English proficiency (National Clearinghouse for

English Language Acquisition [NCELA], 2009). The great majority spends most or part of their time in English-only classrooms (Nieto & Bode, 2012).

Some students whose first language is not English may have acquired sufficient English language skills to perform in English-only classes. Others have not acquired sufficient skill in speaking, reading, or writing English, and they need additional assistance. Schools have various types of programs to deliver assistance. If you have some students in your classroom who speak limited or no English, here are some strategies to use in communicating and teaching (Cary, 2007; J. A. Kottler & E. Kottler, 2007; E. Kottler, J. A. Kottler, & C. Street, 2008):

- Providing predictable, clear, and consistent instructions, expectations, and routines.

- Identifying and clarifying difficult words and passages.

- Providing extra practice in reading words, sentences, and stories.

- Provide a safe environment for language risk taking.

- Increase time and opportunities for meaningful talk.

- Encourage English speaking while honoring students' first language and culture.

- Offer periodic summaries and paraphrases.

- Emphasize collaborative over individual work.

- Emphasize process over product, wholes over pieces.

- Think aloud and model a variety of reading comprehension strategies.

- Use a variety of reading supports such as text tours and picture walks (to preview the material), graphic organizers (story maps, character analyses), and text signposts (chapter headings, bold print).

- Encourage students to write about topics of their choice for real-world purposes.

- Use a variety of writing supports, such as group composing, graphic organizers, and drawing-based texts.

- Use sheltered instruction, which focuses on core curriculum content and uses a rich variety of techniques and materials such as artifacts, visuals, videos, movement, roleplays, and collaborative learning.

Cultural Diversity

Cultural diversity is reflected in the wide variety of values, beliefs, attitudes, and rules that define regional, ethnic, religious, or other cultures. Minority populations wish their cultures to be recognized as unique and preserved for their children. The message from all cultural groups to schools is clear—make sure that each student from every cultural group succeeds in school.

■ WHAT WOULD YOU DECIDE?   Students with Limited English Proficiency

You've accepted a teaching position in a school district with much student diversity. At the start of the school year, you realize that several of your students have limited English proficiency and two students barely speak English at all. Besides English, there are four languages represented.

1. Where would you get resources for teaching students with limited English proficiency?

2. How might you use paraprofessionals, parent volunteers, and even the other students as assistants in your instruction of students with limited English proficiency?

■ CLASSROOM CASE STUDY   Adjustments for English Language Learners

Jason Kulpinski teaches high school history in an urban school in which 42 percent of the students are Hispanic and many are English language learners. To introduce his classes to some of the major events and themes of U.S. history, Mr. Kulpinski uses short texts, which are texts that can be read in one sitting and that combine both words and pictures to tell a story. He has found that all the students in his classes have benefited from reading the short texts.

The short texts provide ELLs with background knowledge on the content they will learn in the course. Without this background, many students would have no prior knowledge as a reference point for learning new content in the unit. With a design that incorporates both words and pictures providing context clues, the short texts help struggling readers and English language learners to negotiate meaning from the material.

Mr. Kulpinski has seen many of his hesitant readers grow in confidence after they have read several short texts and have been able to comprehend the content. Class discussions also have been enhanced by the use of short texts.

Focus Questions

1. How does Mr. Kulpinski's strategy of using short texts help him teach diverse learners?

2. How do all learners in the classroom benefit from this strategy?

3. If you had Mr. Kulpinski's class, what other strategies might you use to teach the content while reaching the English language learners?

Culturally responsive teaching is instruction that acknowledges cultural diversity (Gay, 2005, 2010). It attempts to accomplish this goal in three ways: (1) accepting and valuing cultural differences, (2) accommodating different cultural interaction patterns, and (3) building on students' cultural backgrounds. Culturally responsive teachers use the best of what is known about good teaching, including strategies such as these (Cole, 2008; Gallavan, 2011a, 2011b; Rothstein-Fisch & Trumbull, 2008):

- Connecting students' prior knowledge and cultural experiences with new concepts by constructing and designing relevant cultural metaphors and images.

- Understanding students' cultural knowledge and experiences and selecting appropriate instructional materials.

- Helping students to find meaning and purpose in what is to be learned.

- Using interactive teaching strategies.

- Helping learners construct meaning by organizing, elaborating, and representing knowledge in their own way.

- Using primary sources of data and manipulative materials.

In a culturally relevant classroom, the student's culture is seen as a source of strength on which to rely, not a problem to be overcome or as something to be overlooked (Ladson-Billings, 2009). Teachers can weave a range of cultural perspectives throughout the curriculum to make education more relevant for students who see their cultures recognized. Resources such as *Through Ebony Eyes* (Thompson, 2007a) and *Up Where We Belong* (Thompson, 2007b) provide information about helping African American and Latino students in school.

Many resources are available concerning cultural diversity (e.g., Banks, 2016; Gollnick & Chinn, 2017) and the instructional implications (Mazur & Doran, 2010; G. L. Thompson & R. Thompson, 2014). As you consider individual differences due to cultural diversity, you should do the following:

1. Examine your own values and beliefs for evidence of bias and stereotyping.

2. Regard students as individuals first, with membership in a cultural group as only one factor in understanding that individual.

■ **WHAT WOULD YOU DECIDE?**   **You Are Different from Your Students**

You accepted a teaching position in a different town from where you grew up. As you start the school year, you realize that you have students from several ethnic groups, three languages, various religions, and even several types of family arrangements. You are different from your students—they don't look like you, talk like you, or think like you. You feel the need to take steps to get to know your students to better meet their needs.

1. What can you do so that you and your students get to know each other and feel comfortable with one another?

2. What can you do so that the different backgrounds do not contribute to misunderstandings and off-task behavior?

3. Learn something about students' family and community relationships.

4. Consider nonstandard English and native languages as basic languages for students of culturally diverse populations, to support gradual but necessary instruction in the majority language.

5. Allow students to work in cross-cultural teams and facilitate cooperation while noting qualities and talents that emerge.

6. Infuse the curriculum with regular emphasis on other cultures, rather than provide just one unit a year or a few isolated and stereotyped activities.

Exceptionalities

Exceptional students include those who need special help and resources to reach their full potential. Exceptionalities include both disabilities and giftedness. About 10 percent of students in the United States are identified as having disabling conditions that justify their placement in a special education program (A. A. Turnbull, H. R. Turnbull, M. L. Wehmeyer, & K. A.Shogren, 2016). This figure increases to 15 percent when gifted children are counted as special education students. Categories for special education services include learning disabilities; speech or language impairment; mental retardation; emotional or behavioral disabilities; other impairments of health; multiple disabilities; impairments in hearing, orthopedics, or sight; deafness/blindness; traumatic brain injury; and autism spectrum disorder.

Teachers often make accommodations and modifications to their teaching to meet the learning needs of students with exceptionalities (Salend, 2016; Smith, Polloway, Patton, Dowdy, & Doughty, 2016). An *accommodation* is an adjustment in the curriculum, instruction, learning tasks, assessments, or materials to make learning more accessible to students. For example, a student might have an adapted test with fewer test items. The student may also have the same test but take it orally in a one-on-one situation with the teacher, or he or she might be given extra time to take a test. Different materials might be used to teach the same content, or additional practice or various instructional approaches may be used. In any case, accommodation is *not* a watering down or change in the content or a change in expected learner outcomes.

A *modification* is a change in the standard learning expectations so that they are realistic and individually appropriate. The curriculum or instruction is altered as needed. Modifications are used for students for whom all possible accommodations have been considered and who still need additional measures to help them progress. For example, students with skill deficits in reading or math may need modifications in assignments or the level of the content and reading materials, or they may need an alternative assignment or test.

Students at Risk

Other environmental and personal influences may converge to place a student at risk. *Students at risk* are children and adolescents who are not able to acquire and/or use the skills necessary to develop their potential and become productive members of society. Conditions at home, support from the community, and personal and cultural background all affect student attitudes, behaviors, and propensity to profit from school experiences.

Students potentially at risk include children who face adverse conditions beyond their control, those who do not speak English as a first language, talented but unchallenged students, those with special problems, and many others. At-risk students often have academic difficulties and thus may be low achievers.

Students at risk, especially those who eventually drop out, typically have some or all of the following characteristics (Ormrod et al., 2017): a history of academic failure, older age in comparison with classmates, emotional and behavioral problems, frequent interaction with low-achieving peers, lack of psychological attachment to school, and increasing disinvolvement with school. Here are some general strategies to support students at risk (Ormrod et al., 2017):

- Identify students at risk as early as possible.

- Create a warm, supportive school, and classroom atmosphere.

- Communicate high expectations for academic success.

- Provide extra academic support.

- Show students that they are the ones who have made success possible.

- Encourage and facilitate identification with school.

Socioeconomic Status

SES is a measure of a family's relative position in a community, determined by a combination of parents' income, occupation, and level of education. There are many relationships between SES and school performance (Woolfolk, 2016). SES is linked to intelligence, achievement test scores, grades, truancy, and dropout and suspension rates (Brown, Geor, & Lazaridis, 2014).

Students' school performance is correlated with their SES: Higher SES students tend to have high academic achievement, and lower SES students tend to be at greater risk for dropping out of school (Books, 2004; Lee & Bowen, 2006; Ormrod et al., 2017).

Taking these factors into account, you should (1) capitalize on students' interests; (2) make course content meaningful to the students and discuss the practical value of the material; (3) make directions clear and specific; (4) arrange to have each student experience some success; (5) be sure that expectations for work are realistic; and (6) include a variety of instructional approaches, such as provisions for movement and group work. Additional useful resources include *Teaching with Poverty in Mind* (Jensen, 2009), *Engaging Students with Poverty in Mind* (Jensen, 2013), *Why Culture Counts: Teaching Children of Poverty* (Tileston & Darling, 2008), and *Reaching and Teaching Students in Poverty* (Gorski, 2013).

In *A Framework for Understanding Poverty*, Ruby Payne (2005) describes how there are different hidden rules of behavior, depending on one's class and family income. She points out that many of the behaviors that children of poverty bring to school are necessary to help them survive outside of the school. Children of poverty may laugh when disciplined, argue loudly with the teacher, have angry responses, use inappropriate or vulgar language, be disrespectful to teachers, be disorganized, and talk a great deal. Payne maintains that offering structure and choice in the classroom are two aspects of a discipline plan that will help students move toward self-governance.

Often, children in low-income families, especially children of poverty, lag behind their more affluent peers in academic, physical, emotional, and social development. They may not have the going-to-school skills that many students have, and they will benefit from specific strategies and support from the teachers. Here are some suggestions (Hargis, 2006):

- **Provide free learning materials.** Seek out free resources or donations for extra instructional materials or special field trips or activities. Have extra supplies available in case some of your students don't have them.

- **Facilitate after-school programs.** Schools may be the only safe place in the neighborhood, and many students may not want to leave at the end of the school day. Provide opportunities for activities or study after school.

- **Subsidize school expenses.** Dances, sports, or other events can be expensive. Work with others in your school to find ways to keep costs low or to provide donations.

- **Treat students with respect.** Ensure that your classroom is emotionally and physically safe. Interact with your students in a respectful manner.

- **Teach procedures in a step-by-step manner to clarify expectations.** Point out expectations, describe why the procedure exists, and show how to complete the strategy.

- **Permit students to work together.** This enables students to discuss problems and solutions together, and also allows students to help another student with something they do well.

Students Who Are Troubled

You may have students who have difficulty with their academic work and their behavior due to exceptionally challenging circumstances in their lives. Some students may have been the victims of circumstances beyond their control, such as having been abused or neglected, living in extreme poverty, or having parents who are abusing alcohol or drugs. Other students may do things that place themselves at risk, such as being prone to violence, abusing alcohol or drugs, having eating disorders, or being depressed.

These are not your usual students, and the origins of their academic or behavioral problems initially may not be apparent. Significant deviations in a student's behavior may signal the presence of a problem. Some students exhibit those deviations from the first day they walk into your classroom.

When you notice atypical behavior, it is helpful to ask yourself a few questions to clarify the situation (J. A. Kottler & E. Kottler, 2007): What is unusual about this student's behavior? Is there a pattern to what I have observed? What additional information do I need to make an informed judgment? Whom might I contact to collect this background information? What are the risks of waiting longer to figure out what is going on? Does this student seem to be in any imminent danger? Whom can I consult about this case? These questions can provide guidance for analyzing the situation and deciding on a course of action.

Students may be troubled for a variety of reasons, including the following:

1. **Substance abuse.** Substance abuse can profoundly affect the behavior of individuals. Students may be affected in two ways—they may be the children of substance abusing parents or the students themselves may be abusing drugs and alcohol.

2. **Students who have been abused or neglected.** Many children suffer from physical, emotional, or sexual abuse, and many more may be the victims of neglect by their parents or guardian.

3. **Students prone to violence, vandalism, and bullying.** Violence and crime occur in communities, and that often shows up in schools to some degree. Some students seem prone to violent behavior, and they can cause considerable disturbance in schools. Some of these disruptive behaviors in schools are disturbing but not serious.

4. **Students living in poverty.** Many aspects of student behavior and performance may be influenced by conditions of poverty.

5. **Students facing serious challenges.** Some students face serious and exceptionally challenging situations in their lives that greatly influence their attendance and performance in school. Some of these serious challenges are homelessness, eating disorders, depression, and suicide.

Creating a Responsive Classroom

Understanding the sources of student diversity is not enough. You must use that information as the basis of many classroom decisions when creating a positive learning environment, selecting a responsive curriculum, determining instructional strategies, and providing assistance. A number of useful resources offer guidance about these issues, including *Culturally Proficient Instruction* (K. Nuri-Robins, D. B. Lindsey, R. B. Lindsey, & R. D. Terrell, 2011), *Building Culturally Responsive Classrooms* (Gaitan, 2006), and *How to Teach Students Who Don't Look Like You* (Davis, 2012).

Create a Supportive, Caring Environment

How students feel about the classroom can make a big difference in the way they participate in the classroom. Your attitude toward the students and the curriculum can influence these student feelings. To create a supportive, caring environment, you should translate your attitude into the following actions.

1. **Celebrate diversity.** Student diversity exists in many ways, as reviewed earlier in this chapter. Students don't want to be criticized because they have some characteristic that is different from others. Through your actions, recognize that each student contributes to the rich variety of ideas and actions in the classroom. Show that you appreciate and value the diversity that is reflected in the students in the classroom. In turn, students will feel appreciated rather than feeling different, and this will make them feel more comfortable in the classroom.

2. **Have high expectations for students, and believe all students can succeed.** Teachers may sometimes consider certain sources of student diversity—cognitive ability, language, disabilities, SES, for example—as having a negative effect on student performance. Thus, teachers may lower expectations and adjust the content and activities accordingly. However, this is a disservice to the students when they are not given the opportunity to address meaningful and challenging content and to develop their knowledge and skills. It is important to hold high expectations for all students and to believe all students can succeed. Students appreciate the challenge and will find the classroom more stimulating and worthwhile than a classroom with lowered expectations.

3. **Give encouragement to all students.** Students who perform well academically often receive words of praise, reinforcement, and encouragement from teachers. There may be many students in a classroom who do not perform at the highest academic levels, but they would appreciate hearing encouraging statements as well. Encouraging words and guiding suggestions will help all students feel that they are being supported in their efforts.

4. **Respond to all students enthusiastically.** When students see their teacher is welcoming and enthusiastic about each student, they feel more comfortable in the classroom and are more willing to participate fully. Warm greetings when students enter the classroom, conversations with individual students, and positive reactions when students contribute to classroom discussion are just a few ways that enthusiasm might be expressed. The main thing is that each student needs to feel valued, and they see this through enthusiastic teacher responses.

VOICES FROM THE CLASSROOM   Treat Students with Kindness

Sandra Allen-Kearney, fifth-grade teacher, Fort Pierce, Florida

At the beginning of every year, I give all students a fresh slate when they enter my classroom, regardless of their past experiences. I treat all children with kindness, fairness, and consistency. I work very hard to help my at-risk, behaviorally challenged students feel loved and cared for, while setting the limits they desperately seek.

This philosophy has taken time and patience to nurture, but the rewards are tremendous. One day, I went to pick up my students from physical education, and I saw one of my most challenging students wearing his jacket backward. I calmly asked him to put it on correctly, and he quickly complied.

At this, the physical education teacher's mouth dropped. She confronted the student in an angry voice, "I told you to put on your jacket properly in class several times, and you refused. I even put you in time-out for refusing to obey me, and you still wouldn't do it. Why did you put your jacket on the right way when Mrs. Kearney asked you to, when you wouldn't do it for me?"

His simple reply was, "Because she's nice to me." I will never forget that moment, or that young man, when all of my hard work paid off in that one sentence. As we walked back to class, I had to turn away and wipe my eyes when he wasn't looking.

5. **Show students that you care about them.** When students know that you care for them and that you are looking out for them, it makes all the difference in the world. Students then feel valued, regardless of their characteristics, and are more likely to participate actively in the classroom. Even when the teacher needs to deal with a student concerning a problem, the student recognizes that the teacher's actions are well intended.

6. **Create an antibias educational environment.** Sometimes when students interact with others who are different from them, they may talk or act in ways that express disapproval. Teachers need to take steps to overcome this bias. In an antibias classroom, teachers intervene with immediate actions and follow-up activities to counter the cumulative, hurtful effects of these messages. In an antibias classroom, children learn to be proud of themselves and of their families, to respect human differences, to recognize bias, and to speak up for what is right (Derman-Sparks & Edwards, 2010).

Vary Your Instruction

To meet the needs of the diverse students, instruction cannot be one dimensional. A variety of instructional approaches is needed to challenge all students and to meet their instructional needs. Useful resources include *The Differentiated Classroom* (Tomlinson, 2014), *Differentiated Instructional Strategies* (Gregory & Chapman, 2012), *So Each May Learn: Integrating Learning Styles and Multiple Intelligences* (Silver, Strong, & Perini, 2000), and *Planning and Organizing Standards-Based Differentiated Instruction* (Chapman & King, 2014). Several ways to vary your instruction are highlighted here.

1. **Challenge students' thinking and abilities.** Students have various learning styles, and they may learn best with their preferred learning style. However, should teachers always try to match student preferences and instructional methods? Probably not. You should (1) start where the learner is (i.e., in concert with the pupil's level of development), (2) then begin to mismatch (i.e., use a different approach from what the student prefers) by shifting to a slightly more complex level of teaching to help the student develop in many areas, and (3) have faith that students have an intrinsic drive to learn. These practices complement the

recommendations of Lev Vygotsky, Lawrence Kohlberg, and others to nudge students beyond comfort zones of learning into just enough cognitive dissonance to facilitate growth.

2. **Group students for instruction.** Grouping makes differentiation of instruction more efficient and practical. When each group is challenged and stimulated appropriately, students are motivated to work harder. Differentiated materials can be used more easily. On the other hand, labeling can be stigmatizing if grouping is based on variables such as ability or achievement. Grouping too much and changing groups too infrequently can obstruct student integration and cooperation.

   With the proper planning, structure, and supervision, grouping is a useful way to provide for individual differences. When using grouping arrangements, you should follow these guidelines:

   - Make liberal use of activities that mix group members frequently.

   - Adjust the pace and level of work for each group to maximize achievement. Avoid having expectations that are too low for low groups. Students tend to live up or down to teachers' expectations.

   - Provide opportunities for gifted students to work with peers at their own level by arranging cross-age, between-school, or community-based experiences.

   - Form groups with care, giving attention to culture and gender.

   - Structure the experience and supervise the students' actions.

   - Prepare students with necessary skills for being effective group members, such as listening, helping, cooperating, and seeking assistance.

3. **Consider differentiated assignments.** *Alternative or differentiated assignments* can be provided by altering the length, difficulty, or time span of the assignment. Alternative assignments generally require alternative evaluation procedures. Enrichment activities qualify as alternative assignments when directed toward the individual student's needs. Resources are available concerning ways to vary assessments, such as in *Differentiated Assessment Strategies* (Chapman & King, 2012).

4. **Have students participate in all class activities.** Regardless of the source of their diversity, all students like to participate in class activities such as discussions, projects, group activities, or computer-based activities. They enjoy the opportunity for involvement and interaction, and they seek the challenge. These activities also provide an opportunity for individual expression and serve as a vehicle for recognition and appreciation.

■ WHAT WOULD YOU DECIDE?   Varying Your Instruction to Meet Needs

Let's say you are planning to teach a lesson on soil erosion (or another topic that you think the students might not be too excited about). Yet you recognize that varying your instruction will help meet the learners' needs and may motivate them to be actively engaged.

1. What type of activities might you select to challenge students' thinking?

2. How might you use differentiated assignments and provide students with opportunities to try different types of activities?

3. How might you vary your assessment strategies?

4. How might you need to make adjustments for English language learners?

5. **Provide opportunities for students to try different types of activities.** Although certain class activities and instructional strategies may seem well suited for a particular student, it is important to involve the student in many different types of activities to challenge the student and the student's thinking and understanding. Project-based learning, for example, provides opportunities to differentiate instruction with a variety of activities and roles (Bender, 2012; Larmer, Mergendoller, & Boss, 2015).

6. **Use authentic and culturally relevant pedagogies.** Each instructional strategy has particular strengths, and some of the strengths may match up well with students with particular needs (Murawski & Spencer, 2011). Direct instruction, for example, has been used effectively in teaching basic skills to students with special needs. Cooperative learning has been shown to be effective in urban classrooms with diverse student populations and in positively changing the attitudes of nondisabled students toward their peers who have disabilities.

   Instructional approaches should be selected that develop classrooms that are multicultural and inclusive. Techniques can be used to anchor instruction in students' prior knowledge and help them learn the new content. Instructional approaches can be selected that are seen by the student as realistic and culturally relevant.

7. **Use authentic and fair assessment strategies.** Some students demonstrate their learning better through certain types of assessment. Since there are many types of students in classrooms, a variety of methods for evaluating student learning should be used. Using a variety of approaches, such as written or oral tests, reports or projects, interviews, portfolios, writing samples, and observations, will circumvent bias. In addition, evaluation of student learning should be at several levels—recall, comprehension, application, analysis, synthesis, and evaluation.

Provide Assistance with the Response to Intervention

Many classrooms include students who can benefit from special assistance in their learning. When creating an inclusive, multicultural classroom, these students cannot be overlooked because they may not advance in their learning without such assistance.

1. **Provide special individualized assistance to all students.** Teachers often provide individualized assistance to students who have difficulty learning. This assistance can make a big difference in helping the student overcome hurdles and can lead to better understanding. However, other students can benefit from this type of assistance as well. By providing assistance to all types of diverse learners, teachers express their interest in the student, provide support for student learning, and have the opportunity to challenge the students in new ways.

2. **Work with students with special needs.** As a first step, teachers need to know district policies concerning students with special needs and know what their responsibilities are for referrals, screening, and the preparation of individualized educational plans (IEPs). Learning materials and activities can be prepared commensurate with the abilities of students with special needs. Positive expectations for student performance are a means to promote student learning.

3. **Provide assistance through the response to intervention.** *Response to intervention* (RTI), as referenced in the Individuals with Disabilities Improvement Act of 2004, was conceived as a method to ensure that students receive early intervention and assistance before falling too far behind their peers. RTI requires that these students receive supplementary support, guided by regularly gathered assessment data, referred to as progress monitoring. When planning for instruction, teachers need to take into account the needs of all their students, and struggling students require extra attention and assistance. Thus, all levels of planning need to take these students into account as RTI is applied.

VOICES FROM THE CLASSROOM Using the Response to Intervention (RTI)

Margaret Price, first-grade teacher, West Bloomfield, Michigan

After administering district assessments, the data are analyzed and used to plan and implement interventions for those children who are not meeting the district standards. Based on the data, two children from my first-grade classroom were significantly below our district standard in reading.

With our RTI arrangements, Tier 1 intervention consisted of having these students meet with me five days a week for an individual 10-minute guided reading lesson. I would also individually conference with them either in reading or writing at least three days a week. In addition, they would have the lesson repeated another two times a week with one of our bilingual paraeducators.

Although the student needs were different, the lesson format is similar for each child. The lessons consist of reading or guided writing, working with the alphabetic principle (word study), and learning concepts about print. At the end of a six-week period, the students are assessed again to determine how much growth they have made. A determination is then made to continue the intervention or to alter it for more acceleration.

RTI requires that all teachers at all levels (K–12) assess students systematically and provide levels of support for students who need assistance (Allington, 2009; Howard, 2009). Most RTI models include three levels, or tiers (Fisher & Frey, 2010); see Figure 7.1.

- **Tier 1: Core instruction.** This is regular classroom instruction, and it involves assessing, instructing, and diagnosing learning difficulties. The focus is on quality teaching and implementing systems to determine which students respond to this instruction and which students do not. Approximately 75–85 percent of students should make sufficient progress through core instruction alone.

Intensive Intervention
- Conducted outside the regular classroom
- 5–10 percent of students need intensive intervention
- Individualized instruction and assessment based on needs
- Instruction provided by a specialist, not the regular classroom teacher

Supplemental Instruction
- In addition to regular instruction
- 10–15 percent of students need supplemental instruction
- Often in small groups
- More explicit instruction provided by the regular classroom teacher
- Frequent assessments to determine needs and progress

Core Instruction
- Instruction for all students in the regular classroom
- Is sufficient for 75–85 percent of the students
- Provides effective instruction for all

FIGURE 7.1 Response to Intervention: A Three-Tiered Model

- **Tier 2: Supplemental phase.** This phase can occur either in the regular classroom or as an adjunct to the classroom. In this phase, teachers begin to monitor how students respond to various interventions that are put in place to provide them with assistance. In Tier 2, students receive instruction in addition to that received in Tier 1, and assessment occurs more frequently in order to determine responsiveness and to plan subsequent interventions. This intervention often takes the form of additional small-group instruction, which complements the core instruction. About 10–15 percent of students at one time or another need supplemental interventions. These interventions may last up to 20 weeks, and more frequent assessments take place during this time. The regular classroom teacher typically provides this intervention, sometimes with guidance and support from other educators in the building.

- **Tier 3: Intensive intervention.** Some students do not benefit from the supplemental interventions in Tier 2 and will benefit from even more intensive interventions. Five to ten percent of students will require this level of intensive intervention. Students in Tier 3 often receive instruction on a one-to-one basis from a curriculum specialist, learning coach, speech-language pathologist, or related intervention specialists. The regular classroom teacher typically does not provide this intervention.

Getting to Know Your Students

The more information teachers have about their students, the better able they are to meet students' needs and support student learning. With a better understanding of their students, teachers can be more effective in their selection of instructional strategies, their adjustments for individual differences, and their interactions with the students and their families.

Types of Information

Several types of information would be useful for teachers to achieve these purposes. Teachers would benefit from information about each student concerning these areas:

1. **Academic abilities, needs, and interests.** Is the student a gifted or a struggling learner? What is the student's reading level? What is the student's performance on achievement tests? What are the student's strengths and weaknesses in relation to the academic work? What are the student's academic interests?

2. **Special needs, learning problems, or disabilities.** Are there any emotional or physical disabilities? Does the student have a learning disability of any kind? What accommodations or modifications are needed? Are there any health problems?

3. **Personal qualities related to diversity.** What is the student's preferred learning style? Is the student a second language learner? How does the student's culture or SES influence behavior or learning? Are there any gender or sexuality issues that might influence the student? Is the student considered at risk for any reason?

4. **The student's life and interests.** What are the student's interests? How do the family and community influence the student? What does the student like to do in spare time? What are the student's ambitions?

5. **Problematic or atypical parent custodial arrangements.** Many family arrangements and conditions exist, and it is useful for teachers to know which family member to contact, along with any other special considerations. One parent may have custody of a child with conditions to limit contact with the other parent. The student may be living with grandparents or other relatives. The student may have a parent away from the home, due to military obligations, prison, or other reasons. The student may have gay or lesbian parents.

Sources of Information

Some information about your students can be obtained from existing records, such as the student's cumulative record. Much information can be obtained directly from the students and their families. Although there are many ways you can obtain information about the students in your class, here are some commonly used sources:

- **Cumulative records.** The school office will have a cumulative record folder for each student. That folder includes personal information, home and family data, school attendance records, scores on standardized achievement tests, year-end grades for all previous years of schooling, and other teachers' anecdotal comments. Other types of additional information may be included, such as which family member to contact (or not to contact). Collectively, the cumulative record provides considerable information.

- **Using student questionnaires.** Asking students to fill out a questionnaire can provide much insight into their actions, interests, and skills. Include questions that provide helpful information as you (1) select curricular content, instructional activities, and strategies; (2) determine your way of interacting with the students in the class; (3) identify how to address the diversity of learners in the class; (4) address any challenges, problems, or disabilities the students may have; and (5) try to get to know all your student to enable their successful learning. Some open-ended questions can yield useful information (e.g., It helps me learn when . . ., or, What I appreciate about my family is . . .).

- **Using family questionnaires and contacts.** Information from families about their own children also can provide great insight into the qualities and needs of the students in your class. A brief questionnaire may be prepared for parents at the start of the school year. Items may include asking how parents describe their children, what makes their children special, what their children do at home, their children's strengths and weaknesses, and parents' hopes for their children during the school year. In addition, teachers may see some parents at back-to-school night or at parent-teacher conferences.

- **Observing and interacting with students.** Arrange for icebreaker activities for students to get to know each other at the start of the school year. Much information about each student can be learned simply by watching students interact during these icebreakers. Informal observation and interaction with students also provide opportunities to learn more about each student.

VOICES FROM THE CLASSROOM   Getting to Know Your Students from Their Parents

Lydia DiGiovanni, middle school science teacher, Union, New Jersey

During the first days of school, I have a homework assignment that the students' parents are asked to complete. I ask the parents to describe their child in a letter to me in any way they choose, with the goals of helping me better understand their child and giving me information that will assist me when creating unique and meaningful lessons which match their needs and interests. This also opens the line of communication with the families in a positive way.

I explain to the students that this parent homework helps me get to know them to the core, and this information helps me educate them to the best of my ability. I further explain that I do not want to let any of their earlier school activities or behaviors influence me; the parent homework allows students to start with a fresh slate, and I quickly gain their respect for that. They also realize that I genuinely care about them as individuals and that I take their education seriously.

I express to students the potential I see in them and how I hope to see those great qualities that their family member had written about them. I hold high expectations for my students; after this activity, every student tries to live up to those expectations. I have been told time after time, "Mrs. DiGiovanni, you are different, you care about us . . . you know us," and this makes them want to work hard in my class.

Using the Information

To know how to use the information you gather, think about the reasons you wanted that information in the first place—to be more effective in your selection of instructional strategies, adjustments for individual differences, and interactions with the students and their families. Gathering information is not sufficient. You must read, review, and mentally process the information to guide the decisions you will make in the classroom.

It may be useful to first summarize the information you have on each student, and perhaps on the class as a whole. Whether you have a class of 22 fifth-grade students or 143 high school students in several classes makes a big difference in how you might summarize the information. Some teachers may read through the information about each student from the various sources reviewed earlier and then simply make mental notations. Other teachers may want to summarize results of each question on a student questionnaire, for example, to get a picture of the entire class. Still other teachers may have a card for each student, with key information listed on the card. For certain types of information (e.g., the preferred type of learning approaches or styles), it may be helpful to make a list of students so that you pay proper attention to the students on that issue.

MAJOR CONCEPTS

1. Individual differences need to be taken into account when instructional methods are selected and procedures are determined for classroom management.

2. Cognitive, affective, and physical differences are only part of the array of variables that account for student diversity.

3. Diversity can be due to influences of learning style, creative potential, gender, language, and cultural diversity.

4. Diversity can be affected by disabilities, conditions placing the student at risk, and socioeconomic factors.

5. Some students may have been the victims of circumstances beyond their control, such as having been abused or neglected, living in extreme poverty, or having parents who are abusing alcohol or drugs. Other students may do things that place themselves at risk, such as abusing alcohol or drugs and being prone to violence.

6. Some students face serious and exceptionally challenging situations in their lives that greatly influence their attendance

and performance in school, including being homeless, having an eating disorder, and being depressed and considering suicide.

7. Information about the sources of student diversity can be used as the basis of classroom decisions to create a supportive, caring learning environment.

8. A variety of instructional approaches is needed to challenge all students and to meet their instructional needs.

9. Teachers can apply the steps in the RTI to provide special assistance to students in their learning.

10. In an effort to get to know students, teachers can select the types of information they need, identify the sources for that information, and then use that information to be more effective in their selection of instructional strategies, their adjustments for individual differences, and their interactions with the students and their families.

DISCUSSION/REFLECTIVE QUESTIONS

1. What types of student diversity were evident in classrooms in your own K–12 schooling experience? In what ways did your teachers seem to take those student characteristics into account in the selection of content and the use of instructional approaches?

2. What are some challenges you might experience in dealing with students with limited English proficiency? What could you do to overcome those challenges to promote student learning?

3. If you have a student who is prone to physical behavior and violence, what can you do in your classroom to protect the other students and secure their safety?

4. How might you recognize and celebrate the diversity of students in your own classroom, and even use this information to enhance instruction?

5. Should you have different expectations and evaluation standards to reflect the diverse students in your classroom? Why or why not?

6. What is the value of obtaining information about your students? How might you use that information to improve your instruction and your management of the classroom?

SUGGESTED ACTIVITIES

1. Using the categories of differences addressed in this chapter as a guide, ask several teachers to describe individual differences they notice in their students. How do the teachers take these differences into account? What difficulties have they experienced?

2. Imagine that the students in your class have a wide range of academic abilities. Consider ways that you could be responsive to those differences and still help all students learn. Consider some curricular and instructional variations that you might use.

3. Select the topic of a daily lesson that you might teach and identify five things that you could plan into the lesson to make appropriate adjustments for limited English proficient students.

4. Select a unit that you might teach, and identify specific ways that you could vary your instruction over a two-week unit when taking student diversity into account.

FURTHER READING

Davis, B.M. (2012). *How to teach students who don't look like you: Culturally relevant teaching strategies* (2nd ed.). Thousand Oaks, CA: Corwin Press.

Provides background knowledge about diverse learners and understanding our own perspectives about diversity. Provides guidance for creating a supportive learning community and for selecting instructional strategies for diverse learners.

Fisher, D., & Frey, N. (2010). *Enhancing RTI: How to ensure success with effective classroom instruction and intervention*. Alexandria, VA: Association for Supervision and Curriculum Development.

Describes the steps of RTI and the ways instruction and assistance can be offered at each step.

Gollnick, D. M., & Chinn, P. C. (2017). *Multicultural education in a pluralistic society* (10th ed.). Boston: Pearson.

Provides descriptions of human differences due to class, ethnicity and race, gender, exceptionality, religion, language, and age. Discusses education that is multicultural.

Tomlinson, C.A., & Imbeau, M.B. (2010). *Leading and managing a differentiated classroom*. Alexandria, VA: Association for Supervision and Curriculum Development.

Provides reasons and background for differentiating classrooms. Offers specific ideas for managing a differentiated classroom with the learning environment, routines, and other suggestions.

Vaughn, S., Bos, C. S., & Schumm, J. S. (2014). *Teaching students who are exceptional, diverse, and at-risk in the general education classroom* (6th ed.). Boston: Pearson.

Provides a comprehensive discussion about diverse student characteristics and thoroughly describes instructional modifications that are suitable. Also examines inclusive instructional approaches for the subject areas and for reading.

Planning and Conducting Instruction

CHAPTER OBJECTIVES

This chapter provides information that will help you:

- Select ways to structure lessons and group students.

- Identify ways to hold students academically accountable.

- Determine ways to motivate your students.

- Address administrative actions that are commonly taken at the start of a lesson.

- Take actions that can be used at the start of a lesson to capture student interest and focus attention on the learning objectives.

- Take actions that contribute to effective group management during the middle part of a lesson.

- Conduct actions at the end of a lesson to provide for lesson summary and enable students to prepare to leave.

- Manage seatwork, assignments, records, and paperwork.

When planning for a vacation trip, you often need to plan ahead. Do you want to stay in one place and relax, or do you want to visit a number of areas? Would you like to schedule several events for each day, or would you like to leave the daily schedule open? What types of accommodations would you like? To ensure an enjoyable vacation, you need to give these questions attention.

Similarly, you need to give advance thought to the type of classroom you would like to have. How structured do you want your classroom and lessons? How do you want to group your students for instruction? How will you hold the students academically accountable? How can you motivate your students to learn? How will you handle various aspects of lesson delivery? How will you manage student work? These issues will be explored in this chapter. How you attend to these issues will make a difference in managing instruction and student behavior.

Planning Decisions Affect Behavior Management

Preparing daily lesson plans is a vital task for effective classroom management and discipline because effective, engaging lessons can keep students on task and can minimize misbehavior. You need to consider the degree of structure that will occur in each lesson. The grouping planned for the instructional activities will also affect student interaction. Furthermore, students are more likely to stay on task and be engaged in instruction when they know that they will be held academically accountable. Also, decisions need to be made about motivating students to learn.

The Degree of Structure in Lessons

Many instructional strategies can be used, ranging from teacher-centered, explicit approaches to the presentation of content to student-centered, less explicit approaches. *Teacher-centered approaches* include lectures, demonstrations, questions, recitations, practice and drills, and reviews. *Student-centered approaches* include inquiry approaches, discovery learning and problem solving, role-playing and simulation, gaming, laboratory activities, computer-assisted instruction, and learning or activity centers. Various types of grouping and discussion methods may be student or teacher directed, depending on how they are used. Teacher-centered approaches are often more structured than student-centered approaches. As a result, the management issues will vary depending on the approach used.

When deciding on your instructional strategy, you need to weigh the advantages and disadvantages of the various strategies along with the lesson objectives. Effective teachers use several strategies, ranging from teacher directed to student directed. The lesson objectives may determine what type of approach is most appropriate. Some content may lend itself to inquiry and discovery techniques, whereas other content may be better handled with direct instruction. Over time, students should be given the opportunity to learn through a variety of instructional strategies.

Grouping Students for Instruction

Group students in the way most appropriate for the instructional strategies and objectives. Focus on a group as a collection of individuals who learn. Within groups, each individual student observes, listens, responds, takes turns, and so on. Groups can be large or small. Whole-group, small-group, and independent work are options to consider; each affects student conduct and order.

Whole-Group Instruction

In *whole-group instruction*, the entire class is taught as a group. It allows you to (1) lecture, demonstrate, and explain a topic; (2) ask and answer a question in front of the entire class; (3) provide the same recitation, practice, and drill exercises; (4) work on the same problems; and (5) use the same materials. Although instruction is directed to the whole group, you can still ask individual students to answer questions, monitor students as they work on assigned activities, and work with individual students. Even with whole-group instruction, however, you need to consider individual student differences.

Small-Group Instruction

There are times when the objectives can be better met with small groups called *small-group instruction*. In small-group instruction, students tend to be more actively engaged, and teachers can better monitor student progress. Groups of four students often work well. If there are more than six in a group, generally, not everyone will actively participate.

Since group work helps develop relationships, it is useful to vary the membership of the groups based on gender and ethnicity. Students with disabilities can be placed in groups with nondisabled students to integrate them into the mainstream classroom. Although there may be good reasons for planning a homogeneous group for certain activities, educators in general recommend the use of heterogeneous groups (D. W. Johnson & F. P. Johnson, 2013; Slavin, 2015).

There are three types of groupings: ability grouping, cooperative learning, and peer tutoring. An explanation of each follows:

1. **Ability grouping.** *Ability grouping* involves the clustering of students who are judged to be similar in their academic ability into classes for instruction. There are two common types of ability grouping: between-class grouping and within-class grouping.

    Between-class grouping involves having separate classes for students of different abilities. When reporting research on between-class ability grouping, Slavin (2015) noted that grouping arrangements made on the basis of standardized test scores are not effective in reducing the range of differences that affect the specific class. In addition, the quality of instruction often is lower in lower track classes, and students feel stigmatized by their assignments to low tracks. The disadvantages of between-class ability grouping suggest that it should be avoided when possible (Oakes, 2005).

    Within-class grouping involves creating subgroups within a class, with each subgroup being fairly homogeneous in terms of ability. A small number is better than a large number

---

VOICES FROM THE CLASSROOM   Grouping Students for Instruction

Saralee Wittmer, second-grade teacher, Amarillo, Texas

Students in my room are arranged in small groups of four students according to ability. I shuffle the mix every four to six weeks. Students get the chance to work with all other students and can sit close to the teacher, at the back of the room, close to the door, and up by the chalkboards.

Students are encouraged to discuss lessons with each other within their groups. It's amazing how much they learn from each other if we will only give them the opportunities. I can tell what the class might not have gotten from my lesson presentations by listening carefully to them when they are in their groups.

Gladis Diaz, fifth-grade teacher, Reno, Nevada

When preparing to group my students, I have them complete some cooperative activities so that I can see their skills and personalities. This helps me place them in homogeneous groups and establish the roles for each person in a group. Each group has a leader, a recorder, a go-getter, a speller, and an organizer. I choose the leader who remains in that role throughout the school year. The roles of the others rotate four times during the school year. I meet with the group leaders at least twice a week to discuss their role for the week and to be sure everything is running smoothly.

---

of groups. In this way, group assignments can be flexible, role models for low achievers are available, teacher morale is higher, and the stigmatizing effect is minimized (Slavin, 2012). Within one classroom, you may group students for various activities or subjects. For example, middle school and secondary teachers may use ability groups for only part of a class period and whole-group activities or other approaches for the rest of the class time. You may group students to work on selected projects or activities.

2. **Cooperative learning.** *Cooperative learning* is a grouping in which students work in small, mixed-ability learning teams to help one another learn academic content. Such groups can be formed at various grade levels and in different subject areas. Through cooperative learning, students understand that they are responsible not only for their own learning but also for the learning of their team members. Cooperative learning approaches are often used to supplement other instructional practices.

Cooperative learning occurs in three different ways: (1) assignment of individual students to specific responsibilities within a larger group task or project; (2) assignment of students to a shared project or task; or (3) assignment to groups to study and be responsible for group members' learning. There are several common types of cooperative learning techniques. Additional resources on cooperative learning include Gillies (2007), Jacobs, Power, and Inn (2003), D. W. Johnson, R. T. Johnson, and E. J. Holubec (2007, 2009), Jolliffe (2007), Slavin (2015), and Udvari-Solner and Kluth (2008).

3. **Peer tutoring.** *Peer tutoring* involves students teaching students. The two types of peer tutoring are (a) cross-age tutoring, in which older students work with younger ones and (b) peer tutoring, in which students within the same class work together. There are several advantages of peer tutoring (D. W. Johnson & F. P. Johnson, 2013): (a) peer tutors are often effective in teaching students who do not respond well to adults; (b) peer tutoring can develop a bond of friendship between the tutor and tutored, which is important for integrating slow learners into the group; (c) peer tutoring allows the teacher to teach a large group of students while giving slow learners the individual attention they need; and (d) tutors benefit by learning to teach.

Peer tutoring can be used at all grade levels. Before having students work in pairs, you will need to clarify the purposes of the tutoring, obtain the necessary materials, and provide an appropriate work area where the students can work without disturbing other students. You might offer some guidance about working and studying together.

Independent Work

You might give students opportunities to work on tasks of their own choosing, or you may assign activities that enable students to work alone. This is *independent work*. Good and Brophy (2008) found that one-third of elementary teachers attempt to individualize instruction and that one-fifth of secondary teachers attempt to do so.

When assigning independent work, you may involve students in any of a number of instructional strategies. In inquiry and discovery instructional approaches, students learn about the process of discovery by collecting data and testing hypotheses. Teachers guide students as they discover new meanings, practice the skills, and undergo the experiences that will shape their learning. These approaches include computer-assisted instruction, learning centers, learning stations, laboratories, discovery techniques, and others.

Holding Students Academically Accountable

Procedures to help manage student work must be selected. *Academic accountability* means that the students must complete certain activities related to the instructional objectives. Teacher responsibilities for holding students academically accountable are displayed in Table 8.1, some of which are adapted from Emmer and Evertson (2017), Evertson and Emmer (2017), and V. F. Jones and L. S. Jones (2016).

Consider these five guidelines when holding students academically accountable:

- **Determine a system of grading (e.g., letter grades or numerical grades and measures for nonachievement outcomes).** This decision may have been made for you by the school district as reflected in the report card format. Use a variety of evaluation measures (e.g., tests, written or oral reports, homework, ratings, and projects) throughout the marking period and describe the grading system to the students.

- **Make decisions about assignments.** Decide on where and how you will post assignments, as well as the requirements and criteria for grading. Students should understand that completed assignments are part of the grading system.

■ TABLE 8.1   **Holding Students Academically Accountable**

Take into account the grade level and subject area when decisions are made on the following issues in an effort to hold students academically accountable.

1. The Grading System
   a. Select a grading system.
   b. Select types of evaluation measures.
   c. Determine how grades will be assigned.
   d. Address nonachievement outcomes.
   e. Communicate the grading system to students.
   f. Design a gradebook.
   g. Report grades and communicate to parents.

2. Assignments
   a. Post assignments.
   b. State requirements and grading criteria for assignments.
   c. Make long-term assignments.

(continued)

■ **TABLE 8.1**   *(continued)*

3. Work and Completion Requirements
   a. Identify work requirements.
      (1) Use of pencil or pen
      (2) Headings on papers
      (3) Writing on the back of the paper
      (4) Neatness and legibility guidelines
   b. Identify completion requirements.
      (1) Due dates
      (2) Late work
      (3) Incomplete work
      (4) Missed work
   c. Make provisions for absent students and make-up work.
      (1) Assignment lists or folders
      (2) Due dates
      (3) Places to pick up and drop off absent assignments
      (4) Regular times to assist students with make-up work

4. Monitoring Progress and Completion of Assignments
   a. Determine when and how to monitor in-class assignments.
   b. Determine when and how to monitor longer assignments, projects, or works in progress.
   c. Determine when and how to monitor in-class oral participation or performance.
   d. Determine which activities will receive a grade and which will be used only for formative feedback for the student.
   e. Select checking procedures that will be used in class.
      (1) Students exchanging papers
      (2) Marking and grading papers
      (3) Turning in papers

5. Providing Feedback
   a. Decide what kind of feedback will be provided to students, and when it will be provided.
   b. Determine what records students will keep concerning their progress.
   c. Select incentives and rewards.
   d. Record scores in the gradebook.
   e. Post selected student work.

- **Decide on work and completion requirements.** Students need to have guidelines or work requirements for the various assignments. Details about due dates, late work, and missed assignments due to absence should be explained. The relevant procedures will help students understand expectations held of them and should minimize questions on a case-by-case basis.

- **Monitor student progress and completion of the assignments.** You may want to use some in-class activities as formative exercises for students but not count performance on these in your grading. The activities may be written, oral, or performance demonstrations. Student progress should be monitored. In many cases, the entire class is at work on the designated activity; this enables you to walk around and observe each student carefully to see how the student is progressing.

VOICES FROM THE CLASSROOM   Promoting Student Accountability
by Posting a Weekly Agenda

James Roussin, grades 7–12 English and literature teacher, Big Lake, Minnesota

I have found that it is important for students to be aware of the classroom agenda for the week so they can take appropriate actions to prepare for tests or turn in assignments. I post a weekly agenda on the blackboard every Monday morning. I have found this to be extremely useful. In this way, students have a clear idea of what the week will look like and what is expected of them. This weekly agenda also helps if students are absent; they just need to look at the board to see what was missed.

If we cannot get to everything that has been scheduled in the weekly agenda, I collaborate with the class to determine what should be deleted or extended; this allows the students to feel that they are part of the overall planning in the class.

The best part of this agenda is that it keeps me organized for the week. I can glance at the board and it will reveal to me if I have a variety of different activities for the lessons that week. One primary "learning goal" is also listed for each day, and this helps the students and me know what is essential in the lesson for that day.

- **Provide students with feedback about their progress.** Feedback on in-class activities may take the form of statements to the individuals or to the class. Students may exchange papers to evaluate progress on formative exercises. Papers or projects that are to be part of the report card grade should be collected, graded, and returned promptly. In this way, students receive regular feedback about their progress throughout the marking period. Computer programs available for maintaining a gradebook can easily generate progress reports for both students and teacher.

Planning for Motivation

Many educators use the word motivation to describe those processes that can arouse and initiate student behavior, give direction and purpose to behavior, help behavior to persist, and help the student choose a particular behavior. Of course, teachers are interested in a particular kind of motivation in their students—the motivation to learn (E. M. Anderman & L. H. Anderman, 2014; Gregory & Kaufeldt, 2015; Middleton & Perks, 2014; Wentzel & Brophy, 2014).

Before examining specific motivational strategies, it is important to consider three aspects of planning for motivation:

1. **Develop a comprehensive approach to motivation.** The message about motivation from research and best practice is clear—develop a comprehensive approach to motivate students to learn instead of looking at one or two classroom variables in isolation. Much of the information about motivation addresses important topics such as needs, satisfactions, authority, and recognition. These issues should not be considered in isolation, and the ways teachers address these issues show up in their decisions about instructional tasks, evaluation, recognition, and other areas.

2. **Adjust motivational strategies to your instructional situation.** Motivational strategies discussed in this chapter come from research and best practice, and thus they provide a framework for classroom decisions. It is likely, however, that you will need to evaluate your own situation—grade level, subject area, student characteristics—to determine which strategies are most appropriate in your context. Some strategies might need to be modified to work successfully in your classroom. Some strategies might be used a great deal while others might not be used at all. Your professional assessment of your situation will guide the selection and use of the motivational strategies.

3. **Build motivational issues into all levels of your instructional planning.** Your instructional planning actually includes many time frames: the course, the semester, the marking period, each unit, each week, and each lesson.

As you consider how to incorporate the motivation concept of relevance, for example, into your instruction, you would think about ways to apply that concept in each time frame listed here. How might you help students see the relevance of the entire course, and how might that be reflected in your course syllabus and introduction to the course? How might you highlight the relevance of the content during each marking period and each unit? Similarly, students would appreciate seeing the relevance of the content that is covered in each week and in each lesson.

You need to think globally to help students see the big picture as well as the importance of each smaller piece of content. Your long-range planning should take the topic of relevance into account, and the relevance should be apparent in each unit and lesson. Therefore, your planning for motivation needs to be conducted for all levels of planning.

There are various ways to organize the way you incorporate motivational aspects into your instruction. Based on the research on motivation, Wentzel and Brophy (2014) organized strategies in two categories: (1) strategies for increasing expectations for success and (2) strategies for increasing perceived value. Quate and McDermott (2009) suggest the six Cs for creating a context that motivates students and nurtures engagement: (1) caring classroom community, (2) checking in and checking out (i.e., assessment), (3) choice, (4) collaboration, (5) challenge, and (6) celebration. Sullo (2009) offers suggestions centering on relationships, rules and procedures, rewards, enthusiasm, expectations, and student characteristics and needs.

The instructional strategies that you use, the tasks that you ask the students to complete, and the way that you interact with students during instruction all influence students' motivation to learn (Reeve, 2006; Schunk, Meece, & Pintrich, 2014). As you prepare your plans, try to incorporate the following 12 motivational strategies into your instruction. Table 8.2 summarizes the motivational strategies for instruction.

■ TABLE 8.2 **Motivational Strategies for Instruction**

1. Capture Student Interest in the Subject Matter

   a. Take time to understand what students perceive as important and interesting.

   b. Select topics and tasks that interest students.

   c. Set the stage at the start of the lesson.

   d. State learning objectives and expectations at the start of the lesson.

   e. Use questions and activities to capture student interest in the subject matter.

   f. Introduce the course and each topic in an interesting, informative, and challenging way.

2. Highlight the Relevance of the Subject Matter

   a. Select meaningful learning objectives and activities.

   b. Directly address the importance of each new topic examined.

   c. Adapt instruction to students' knowledge, understanding, and personal experience.

   d. Have students use what they previously learned.

   e. Illustrate the subject matter with anecdotes and concrete examples to show relevance.

3. Vary Your Instructional Strategies to Maintain Interest

   a. Use several instructional approaches throughout the lesson.

   b. Use games, simulations, or other fun features.

   c. Occasionally do the unexpected.

■ TABLE 8.2   (continued)

4. Plan for Active Student Involvement

   a. Try to make study of the subject matter as active, investigative, adventurous, and social as possible.

   b. Vary the type of involvement when considering the students' learning and cognitive styles.

5. Select Strategies That Capture Students' Curiosity

   a. Capitalize on the arousal value of suspense, discovery, curiosity, exploration, and fantasy.

   b. Use anecdotes or other devices to include a personal, emotional element in the content.

6. Select Strategies with an Appropriate Degree of Difficulty

   a. Assign moderately difficult tasks that can be completed with reasonable effort.

   b. Divide difficult tasks into smaller parts that are achievable without requiring excessive effort.

   c. Focus on higher order learning outcomes.

   d. Monitor the level of difficulty of assignments and tests.

7. Group Students for Tasks

   a. Plan to use a variety of individual, cooperative, and competitive activities.

   b. Promote cooperation and teamwork.

8. Design the Lesson to Promote Student Success

   a. Design activities that lead to student success.

   b. Adapt the tasks to match the motivational needs of the students.

   c. Communicate desirable expectations and attributes.

   d. Establish a supportive environment.

   e. Use familiar material for initial examples, but provide unique and unexpected contexts when applying concepts and principles.

   f. Minimize performance anxiety.

9. Allow Students Some Control over the Lessons

   a. Promote feelings of control by allowing students a voice in decision making.

   b. Monitor the difficulty of the goals and tasks that students choose for themselves.

10. Express Interest in the Content and Project Enthusiasm

   a. Model interest and enthusiasm in the topic and in learning.

   b. Project enthusiasm.

   c. Introduce tasks in a positive, enthusiastic manner.

   d. Expect interest, not boredom, from the students.

11. Provide Opportunities to Learn

   a. Focus lessons around mid-level concepts that are substantive but not overwhelming to students.

   b. Make the main ideas evident in presentations, demonstrations, discussions, and assignments.

   c. Present concrete illustrations of the content and relate unfamiliar information to your students' personal knowledge.

   d. Make explicit connections between new information and content that students had learned previously, and point out relationships among new ideas by stressing similarities and differences.

   e. Elaborate extensively on textbook readings rather than allowing the book to carry the lesson.

   f. Guide students' thinking when posing high-level questions.

   g. Ask students to summarize, make comparisons between related concepts, and apply the information they were learning.

12. Support Students' Attempts to Understand

   a. Model thinking and problem solving, and work with students to solve problems when the students have difficulty.

   b. Keep the procedures in instructional tasks simple.

   c. Encourage collaborative efforts by requiring all students to make contributions to the group.

Managing Lesson Delivery

You've finished your planning. You've selected the instructional strategies. You've prepared and gathered the instructional materials. Now it is the day of your lesson. You're all ready to begin, but wait. You also must recognize that you can take certain actions during your instruction that will help students stay on task and achieve the lesson objectives.

You can use a number of strategies at certain points in a lesson to manage the group effectively, maintain order and control, and fulfill various administrative and academic objectives. If these actions are not handled appropriately, it is likely that students will be more inclined to be off task and possibly misbehave. As a result, it is important to examine these lesson delivery tasks from the perspective of management and order in the classroom.

The Beginning of a Lesson

A successful lesson beginning can greatly contribute to a meaningful learning experience for students. The beginning of a lesson should be designed to handle various administrative tasks, capture the students' interest, and focus their attention on the learning objectives to be addressed during the lesson. An effective beginning can increase students' ability to focus on the objectives.

Actions you take at the start of a lesson help establish an atmosphere in which students have the "motivation to learn" (Wentzel & Brophy, 2014). *Motivation to learn* draws on the meaningfulness, value, and benefits of the academic task to the learner. For example, math problems may be developed relating to student interests, such as selling products for a youth-group fundraiser. Thus, the focus is on learning rather than on merely performing. Often, students can be motivated at the beginning of a lesson by emphasizing the purpose of the task or the fact that students will be interested in the task.

Prior to beginning the substance of a lesson, take attendance and solicit student attention. At the beginning of the lesson, your actions include providing daily review, providing a set induction, introducing lesson objectives, distributing and collecting materials, and giving clear, focused directions.

Taking Attendance

Elementary teachers in self-contained classrooms commonly take attendance first thing in the morning, whereas middle school and high school teachers take attendance at the start of each class. Tardiness also must be noted, and teachers need to follow school policies when recording and responding to tardy students. It is helpful not to hold up the beginning of class to take attendance.

You should plan an opening activity for students to do while you take attendance. Some teachers have the first activity posted on the board for the students to do while attendance is taken. It is important to have a seating chart for each class; a substitute teacher will find this to be especially useful.

Getting Attention

Students should understand that they are expected to give full attention to lessons at all times. A lesson should not begin until you gain their full attention. There should be a predictable, standard signal that tells the class, "We are now ready to begin the lesson." The type of signal will vary with teacher preferences. For example, you can raise your hand, ring chimes or a bell, stand in a certain location, or make a statement. After giving the signal, pause briefly to allow it to take effect. Then when you have attention, move quickly into the lesson.

There are at least three ways to solicit attention at the beginning of a lesson. These approaches are designed to secure the students' attention and reduce distractions that might occur at the beginning of a lesson (V. F. Jones & L. S. Jones, 2016).

1. **Select a cue for getting students' attention.** Students often need a consistent cue to focus their attention. These cues may include a special phrase that the class has chosen to indicate that you want immediate attention, or it may be a nonverbal cue such as closing the door at the beginning of class.

2. **Do not begin until all students are paying attention.** It is important not to begin a lesson until all students are paying attention to the teacher. Teachers who begin lessons without the attention of all their students spend much more time repeating directions. Also, a teacher who begins a lesson in such a fashion is a poor role model since this indicates that it is all right to talk while others are talking. Teachers sometimes just stand silent, waiting—students soon get the message.

3. **Remove distractions.** Some students cannot screen out distracting stimuli. You can help remove distractions by closing the door, having the students remove unnecessary materials from the tops of their desks, adjusting the blinds, or taking other appropriate actions.

Providing Daily Review

A lesson can start with a brief review of previously covered material, correction of homework, and review of prior knowledge that is relevant to the day's lesson. The purpose of daily review is to determine if the students have obtained the necessary prerequisite knowledge or skills for the lesson. This review may last from three to eight minutes, and the length will vary according to the attention span of the learners and the nature of the content. Daily review is especially useful for teaching material that will be used in subsequent learning. Examples include math facts, math computation and factoring, grammar, chemical equations, and reading sight words.

You can conduct daily review at the beginning of a lesson to provide additional practice and overlearning for previously learned material and to allow the teacher to provide corrections and reteaching in areas where students are having difficulty. Vary the methods for reviewing material.

Checking homework at the start of class is one form of review. Game formats, such as a trivia game, can be used as a means for review. You can conduct review through discussion, demonstration, questioning, written summaries, short quizzes, individualized approaches, and other methods of instruction. During reviews, students might answer questions at the chalkboard, in small groups, or as a whole class. Some additional techniques include asking questions about concepts or skills taught in the previous lesson, having students meet in small groups of two to four to review homework, and having students prepare questions about previous lessons or homework and ask them to one another or the teacher can ask them to the class.

In addition to daily review, the learning of new material is also enhanced by weekly and monthly reviews. Weekly reviews may occur each Monday, and monthly reviews every

VOICES FROM THE CLASSROOM   Using Clickers for Daily Review

Cindy Burkes, third-grade teacher, Las Vegas, Nevada

We use a classroom performance system (CPS) for a variety of purposes, including daily review. This system enables me to enter a series of questions into a PowerPoint presentation, and it includes a handheld "clicker" (like a remote control) for students to record their answers to these questions. On my computer screen, I can immediately see the results for each question and each student.

I begin each day with "The Daily Four," which are two review questions and two preview questions that students answer using their clickers. The instant feedback on student performance provided by the clickers helps me determine if remediation is needed or if future lessons can be pared down, thereby eliminating the need for in-depth lessons when a quick overview will be sufficient.

fourth Monday. These reviews provide additional opportunities for you to check for student understanding, ensure that the necessary prior skills are adequately learned, and also check on your pace of instruction.

Establishing Set

Set induction is the activity at the beginning of the lesson that is used to induce students to a state of wanting to learn. This activity helps establish the context for the learning that is to follow and helps students engage in the learning. Typically, the set is brief, lasting only long enough to develop student readiness to accomplish the lesson's objective. Set induction helps students see what the topic of the lesson is in a way that is related to their own interests and their own lives. Madeline Hunter (1994) used the term *anticipatory set* to describe this concept, pointing out that the activity is intended to develop a mental readiness (or "set") for the lesson.

For example, a health lesson on the topic of first aid might begin with the reading of a newspaper report about a recent fire or accident. After reading the article, you could ask the students what they would do if they were the first ones to arrive after the accident. A number of ideas are likely to be generated in this discussion. Then you could bring that opening discussion to a close by saying that today's lesson will be about that exact topic—what type of first aid to administer for various conditions. Then you would move into the first part of the lesson. This set induction activity helps create interest in the lesson in a way that students can relate to their own lives.

Effective set induction activities should meet four criteria:

1. **Get the students interested in what is to be taught during the lesson.** This is referred to as an initiating activity. For example, you might begin a lesson on creative writing by turning off the lights in the room and explaining to the students that you will take them on an adventure to a distant planet. As the room remains dark, they are to imagine their trip into outer space.

2. **The set induction activity must be connected to the lesson.** An activity that is designed to get the students' attention but is not connected to the lesson does not meet this criterion.

3. **Students must understand the material and/or activity.** The information contained in the initiating activity must be stated in a clear manner so students will not only understand the activity but also know how it is connected to later content. Later, the set induction activity can be referred to while teaching the lesson.

4. **The set induction and the content of the lesson should be related to the students' lives or to a previous lesson.** Students will be more interested in a lesson if they can relate the material to their own lives. For example, a lesson concerning measurement might include measuring ingredients to bake a cake or some other practical application. Also, you can reduce anxiety by relating the lesson to material already learned by the students.

Introducing Lesson Objectives

At the start of a lesson, you should clearly describe its purpose. In addition, it is helpful to discuss the activities and evaluation process, since these procedures help reduce student anxiety about the lesson. At the beginning, some teachers will clearly explain the objectives, the activities, and evaluation procedures to be used; others will write these elements on the board for the students, or they will wait for an appropriate point in the lesson, such as after the set induction.

By using set induction activities and introducing lesson objectives, a teacher gives students an *advance organizer* that provides a framework for the new content and helps the students relate it to content they already know. Advance organizers help students by focusing their attention on the subject being considered, informing them where the lesson is going, relating new material to content already understood, and providing structure for the subsequent lesson. Students learn more, in less time, when they are informed of the lesson objectives. Furthermore, students are more likely to become involved and derive more satisfaction and enjoyment from an activity that has a definite aim.

Consider the alternative if you do *not* clearly communicate the learning goals to enable the students to understand the goals. Students may go through the motions of an activity without understanding its purpose or its relationship to other content. Students may be concerned only with completing the assignment, rather than attempting to understand the purposes and objectives behind the assignment. Some students, in fact, may become passive when they see no academic purpose and consider assignments to be busywork with no specific learning objective.

Distributing and Collecting Materials

Teachers often need to distribute materials to students. Students' maturity should be considered when determining the most appropriate time and way to do so. Handouts, maps, and student guides can be distributed at the beginning of class to focus student attention on important material and to avoid disruptions during the lesson. Materials can be handed to students as they enter the room to save time during the lesson. You may prefer to distribute materials at the point in the lesson when they are actually needed.

Materials should be strategically located in the classroom to provide easy distribution and to minimize disruptions. For example, frequently used resource books should be located where there is sufficient room when the books are needed. Procedures should be established for their distribution. You may have one row of students at a time get the resource books, have one student in each row get enough copies for that row, have students pick up a copy as soon as they enter the room, or give each student a copy as soon as they enter the room.

Some materials that are distributed need to be collected later in the lesson, and appropriate ways to collect these materials should be selected. The manner of collecting the materials may be the same as or different from the way they were distributed.

Giving Clear, Focused Directions

To give clear and focused directions, you first must carefully plan them. Directions are often given at the beginning of a lesson; of course, directions might also be given for activities throughout a lesson.

> **VOICES FROM THE CLASSROOM   Giving Directions**
>
> **Ron Butler, high school social studies teacher, Gillette, Wyoming**
>
> There are several parts of giving directions for class activities. First, I give detailed, step-by-step descriptions for what I want the students to do. This may include mentioning the pages in the textbook and the specific actions that I want the students to take. Second, I seek feedback from the students to see if they understand the directions. Especially when there are several steps in the directions, I ask a randomly selected student to repeat the directions to ensure that the students hear them again. At any time, I can correct any misunderstandings they have. Third, I screen the steps on the overhead projector so the students can refer to them as they move along.

When *planning for directions*, you should (1) have no more than three student actions that are required for the activity to be described; (2) describe the directions in the order that students will be required to complete the tasks; (3) clarify what type and quality of product is expected; (4) make the description of each step specific and fairly brief; (5) provide written (on the chalkboard, a transparency, or a handout) and oral directions; (6) give the directions just before the activity; and (7) make provisions for assisting students who have difficulty.

When actually *giving directions*, you need to (1) get student attention; (2) present the directions; (3) check to see if students understand the directions ("Do you have any questions about what you need to do?"); (4) have the students begin the tasks; and (5) remediate if necessary if one or more students are not following directions. Clearly state what books and materials are needed.

It is often helpful to demonstrate the actions expected of the students by doing one problem or activity together. Students then see what is expected of them before they begin to work independently. Once students begin work, you should walk around to see if they are following the directions and to be available to answer student questions. If many questions arise, it may be useful to gain everyone's attention for further explanation.

The Middle of the Lesson

A number of teacher behaviors during lesson delivery contribute to effective group management. These include pacing the lesson, providing smooth transitions, avoiding satiation, having a task orientation, ensuring academic learning time, being clear, and exhibiting enthusiasm.

Pacing the Lesson

Pacing is the speed at which the lesson proceeds. It is the rhythm, the ebb and flow, of a lesson. Effective pacing is neither too slow nor too fast. Adjustments in the pace of the lesson are made as the need warrants. To pace a lesson effectively, you should not dwell too long on directions, should distribute papers in a timely and efficient manner, and should move from one activity to another smoothly and without interruption. Classrooms that lack effective pacing will drag at times or will move along at a pace where the students are unable to grasp the material. You should, however, recognize that it takes more time for students to mentally and physically transition from one activity to another than it does the teacher.

Use the following guidelines to pace a lesson effectively (Good & Brophy, 2008; V. F. Jones & L. S. Jones, 2016).

1. **Develop awareness of your own teaching tempo.** As you gain more experience in the classroom, you will be more aware of your own personal pace in the classroom. A good means of determining your pace is to audio- or videotape your performance. In this way, you

will be able to determine how fast you talk, how you move around the classroom, and how much wait time you provide your students.

2. **Watch for nonverbal cues indicating that students are becoming puzzled or bored.** Monitor student attentiveness and then modify the pacing of the lesson as needed. If high-achieving students are looking puzzled, they and perhaps most of the class may be lost. The content may be too complex or it is being covered too quickly. A good indication that your pacing is too slow is if students are becoming restless and inattentive—looking out the window or fiddling with materials on their desks. You might select several students to notice on a regular basis throughout the lesson as indicators of your pacing.

3. **Break activities up into short segments.** Many teachers go through an entire activity before beginning discussion or review. However, it is more effective to break the activities up into shorter segments and to ask questions or review these shorter segments rather than the entire activity.

4. **Provide short breaks for lessons that last longer than 30 minutes.** Long lessons can cause inattentiveness and disruptive behavior. A three- to five-minute break can allow the students to return fresh to the activity. These breaks can be short games related to the activity or a stand-up-and-stretch interlude. A brief activity where students can get up to mingle or just stand up and stretch can also provide enough of a break.

5. **Vary the instructional approach as well as the content of the instruction.** Students often become restless with only a single instructional approach. A lesson plan that incorporates several instructional strategies will result in better attentiveness.

6. **Avoid interrupting the flow of the lesson with numerous stops and starts.** *Jerkiness* is a term that refers to behaviors that interfere with the smooth flow of the lesson. This occurs when the teacher (a) interrupts an ongoing activity without warning and gives directions to begin another activity; (b) leaves one activity dangling in midair, begins another, only to return to the first; or (c) leaves one activity for another and never returns to the first activity. In such instances, students never experience closure to the activities they were engaged in prior to the switch. Sudden reversals of activities tend to leave students flustered over not completing the previous activity and unprepared to begin the new activity.

7. **Avoid slowdowns that interfere with the pace of the lesson.** *Slowdowns*, or delays in the momentum or pace of a class, can occur due to overdwelling or fragmentation. *Overdwelling* occurs when too much time is spent on directions or explanations. Overdwelling also occurs when the teacher becomes so enthralled with the details of the lesson or a prop being used for a demonstration that students lose sight of the main idea. For example, an English teacher may get so carried away describing the details of an author's life that the students barely have time to read the author's works. Another example is a science teacher who gets carried away describing the laboratory equipment so that the students have little time to conduct any experiments.

   Fragmentation is another form of slowdown in which the lesson is divided into such minute fragments that some of the students are left waiting and become bored. For example, the directions for an experiment may be broken down into such minute, simple parts that the students feel belittled, or an activity may be done by one row of students at a time, leaving the rest waiting.

8. **Provide a summary at the end of a lesson segment.** Rather than plan for a single summary at the end of a lesson, it might help the pacing of the lesson to provide a summary after each main point or activity. For example, students might be asked to write a one-sentence summary of each scene as the class reads a play orally.

Providing Smooth Transitions

Transitions are movements from one activity to another. A smooth transition allows one activity to flow into another without any breaks in the delivery of the lesson. Transitions that are not smooth create gaps in delivery.

Transition time can occur when (1) students remain at their seats and change from one subject to another; (2) they move from their seats to an activity in another part of the classroom; (3) they move from somewhere else in the classroom back to their seats; (4) they leave the classroom to go outside or to another part of the school building; or (5) they come back into the classroom from outside or another part of the building.

Disorder and misbehavior can arise during transition times. More disruptions occur during transitions (including hitting, yelling, and other inappropriate actions) than during nontransition time. There are several reasons why transitions can be problematic. First, you may have difficulty getting the students to finish an activity, especially if they are deeply engaged in it. Second, transitions are more loosely structured than instructional activities, and there typically is more freedom to socialize and move around the room. Third, students may "save up" problems or tensions and deal with them during the transition time. For example, a student may ask to use the restroom, complain to you about another student, or ask permission to get something from a locker. Finally, there may be delays in getting students started in the new activity.

To reduce the potential for disorder during transitions, you should prepare students for upcoming transitions, establish efficient transition routines, and clearly define the boundaries of lessons. V. F. Jones and L. S. Jones (2016) offer several suggestions for effective transitions:

1. **Arrange the classroom for efficient movement.** Arrange the classroom so you and the students can move freely without disturbing those who are working.

2. **Create and post a daily schedule and discuss any changes each morning.** Posting a daily schedule will aid in the elimination of confusion in the students.

3. **Have material ready for the next lesson.** Prepare and gather materials for the next lesson to ensure that class time is not taken and that activities flow smoothly.

4. **Do not relinquish students' attention until you have given clear instructions for the following activity.** All too often, teachers allow the class to become disruptive while they pause between activities or lessons to prepare for the next lesson. It requires considerable time and energy to regain students' attention.

5. **Do not do tasks that can be done by students.** Have students take responsibility for their own preparations for the next class session. This will enable you to monitor student actions.

6. **Move around the room and attend to individual needs.** By moving around the room, you will be able to notice any minor disturbances that might expand into major problems.

7. **Provide students with simple, step-by-step directions.** Clearly state exactly what you want your students to do during the time given for the transition.

8. **Remind students of key procedures associated with the upcoming lesson.** Reviewing standard procedures and discussing unique procedures for an upcoming activity help promote smooth transitions because students know what is expected of them.

9. **Develop transition activities.** After lunch or physical education, for example, students are excited and may not be ready for quieter work. Given this, you could choose structured transition activities to prepare the students for the next class session. These might include reading to students, discussing the daily schedule, having students write in a journal, or doing some type of activity that may not necessarily deal with the content of the next class session. After this transition time, they will likely be more ready to begin the next class session.

VOICES FROM THE CLASSROOM   Transitions Between Activities

Carla Roman, kindergarten teacher (National Board Certified Teacher), Miami, Florida

After providing whole-class instruction, I often ask students to work in small groups. I have found it is useful to provide a break from their small-group work when they are getting tired or having trouble staying focused on what they are doing.

Providing a break as a transition to another activity can take many forms. Sometimes, it may be just some time to rest. Other times, it may involve singing and asking the students to do certain actions. In this way, they are provided a "break" from what they are currently doing, and to them it seems like a game. Actually it provides an opportunity to listen and to follow directions, and students are more ready to get back on task for the next activity.

Avoiding Satiation

Satiation means that students have had enough of something, and this may lead to boredom, restlessness, and off-task behavior. For example, students may enjoy seeing a video, writing a creative story, or working in pairs on a project. When those activities are used too often or for too much time, however, students will start to lose interest, become bored, and will likely get off task. You need to guard against planning activities that will lead to satiation.

There are three ways to avoid satiation (Kounin, 1970). First, have students experience progress, which is the feeling they get when steadily moving toward some significant objective. Pacing and group focus help achieve this sense. To promote feelings of progress, you need to avoid dwelling on one topic too long. Second, provide variety as an effective way to avoid satiation. At the same time, classroom routines are necessary to preserve order and organization. You need to sense when enough is enough. Instructional variety helps invite inquisitiveness, excitement, and interest.

Third, select an appropriate degree of challenge in the students' academic work. Students do not tire of success if the success is a genuine test of their abilities and culminates in personally relevant accomplishments. When the challenge is sufficient to court and fortify the best efforts of students, satiation is seldom a problem.

Being Task Oriented

Task orientation has to do with your concern that all relevant material be covered and learned as opposed to being mired in procedural matters or extraneous material. The more time dedicated to the task of teaching a specific topic, the greater the opportunity students have to learn. Task-oriented teachers provide an appropriate amount of time lecturing, asking questions, and engaging students in activities directly related to the material that is to be learned. Students have higher rates of achievement in classrooms of task-oriented teachers.

Task-oriented teachers are goal oriented, and they plan instructional strategies and activities that support these goals. In addition, task-oriented teachers have a high, but realistic, set of expectations for their students. To be task oriented in the classroom, you should (1) develop unit and lesson plans that reflect the curriculum; (2) handle administrative and clerical interruptions efficiently; (3) stop or prevent misbehavior with a minimum of class disruption; (4) select the most appropriate instructional model for objectives being taught; and (5) establish cycles of review, feedback, and testing.

Ensuring Academic Learning Time

Academic learning time is the amount of time students are successfully engaged in learning activities. However, the amount of time that students are actively engaged, or on task, can vary greatly across and within classrooms. On the one hand, low-achieving students often go off task due to

■ WHAT WOULD YOU DECIDE?   Having Smooth Transitions

Assume that you have planned a lesson in which your students viewed a video, then had small-group discussions about the video, and finally individually outlined some content and answered some questions from the textbook.

1. What arrangements would you need to make to ensure smooth transitions throughout the lesson?

2. How might the directions that you select for the lesson promote smooth transitions?

frustrations about not understanding class material. High-achieving students, on the other hand, tend to go off task after they have completed their assigned work. Therefore, you should ensure that all students can be successfully engaged in classroom tasks while also ensuring that high-achieving students are engaged throughout the lesson. Provide feedback and correctives to students who need assistance, and at the same time, monitor the rate of student progress through the lesson.

For new material that students have not yet mastered, expect a lower success rate initially but set a goal of higher success rates as students receive feedback on their performance and gain confidence. As a general rule, students should have a success rate of approximately 80 percent on most initial tasks. The rate of success should be somewhat higher when students are engaged in independent work, such as homework or independent seatwork. The goal is to ensure that students are given meaningful tasks to complete, are given feedback and correctives when needed, and are ultimately able successfully to complete all assigned tasks.

Being Clear

Clarity refers to the precision of your communication to your students regarding the desired behavior. Clarity in teaching helps students understand better, work more accurately, and be more successful. Effective teachers exhibit a high degree of clarity by providing very clear and explicit directions, instructions, questions, and expectations. If you are constantly asked to repeat questions, directions, and explanations, or if your students do not understand your expectations, you are not exhibiting clarity in your instructional behavior.

Clear directions, instructions, and expectations need to be given. Students then know what is expected of them and can act accordingly as they work on classroom activities, assignments, and other tasks. If you are not very clear when giving directions, for example, the student may not complete the assignment in the way you intended, may become confused, and may need additional time and attention later to complete the assignment in the manner intended.

To be clear in the classroom, (1) inform the learners of the objective; (2) provide learners with advance organizers; (3) check for task-relevant prior learning at the beginning of the lesson; (4) give directions slowly and distinctly; (5) know the ability levels of students and teach to those levels; (6) use examples, illustrations, and demonstrations to explain and clarify; and (7) provide a review or summary at the end of each lesson.

Exhibiting Enthusiasm

Enthusiasm is an expression of excitement and intensity. It is quite obvious that a teacher who is enthusiastic and vibrant is more entertaining to observe than an unenthusiastic teacher. However, teacher enthusiasm has also been related to higher student achievement (Good & Brophy, 2008). Enthusiasm has two important dimensions: (1) interest and involvement with the subject matter and (2) vigor and physical dynamism. Enthusiastic teachers are often described as stimulating, dynamic, expressive, and energetic. Their behavior suggests that they are committed to the students and to the subject matter. While teachers often expect students to be interested in *what* they say, students more often react to *how* enthusiastically it is said.

Enthusiasm can be conveyed in a variety of ways. These include the use of animated gestures, eye contact, voice inflection, and movement around the room. A teacher who is enthusiastic in the classroom often manages to develop enthusiastic students. Constant, highly enthusiastic actions are not necessary and, in fact, may be counterproductive. Instead, a variety of enthusiastic actions, ranging from low to high degrees of enthusiasm, would be appropriate.

The Ending of a Lesson

As stated earlier, an effective lesson has three important sections: a beginning, a middle, and an end. All three sections must be planned and implemented effectively if a lesson is to be successful. Simply ending a lesson when the bell rings or when you have covered the planned material is not appropriate. In such cases, students are not given the opportunity to place the lesson in a context with other related lessons or are not permitted to ask questions that might clarify a misunderstood point from the lesson. Providing a summary is imperative for a successful lesson. Furthermore, students need time at the end of the lesson to get ready to leave the classroom.

Providing Closure to Part of a Lesson

Closure refers to actions or statements that are designed to bring a lesson presentation to an appropriate conclusion. Closure has three purposes (Shostak, 2014):

1. **Draw attention to the end of a lesson segment or the lesson itself.** Often students need to be cued that they have arrived at an important segment of the lesson or that it is time to wrap things up. They might be cued with a statement that it is time to summarize key concepts.

2. **Help organize student learning.** It is the teacher's responsibility to relate the many pieces of the lesson to the whole. Some students are able to see this by themselves while others need assistance. To accomplish this purpose, you might provide a diagram, illustration, outline, or other type of summary indicating how all the content of the lesson is related.

3. **Reinforce the major points to be learned.** You might emphasize or highlight certain concepts at this point. The major objective is to help the student retain the information presented in the lesson for future use.

Closure is important because students instinctively structure information into patterns that make sense to them. If a learning experience is left with some uncertainties, students may draw inaccurate conclusions as they create their own patterns of understanding from the material, thus detracting from future learning.

■ WHAT WOULD YOU DECIDE?   **Providing Closure**

Let's assume that you are teaching a history lesson in which a series of significant dates have been identified and related events have been discussed.

1. How might you bring closure to this part of the lesson in a way that helps students see how all the dates and events are related?

2. How might you involve students in this closure?

3. How might you take into account students' varied learning styles?

The second and third purposes involve summarizing, which is addressed later. The time at the end of a lesson segment or the lesson itself can be used to make homework assignments. Between lesson segments, students may be given 5–10 minutes to start the homework assignment while you move around the room to answer questions that might arise.

Summarizing the Lesson

Providing a *summary* of the main points of a lesson can help students gain a better idea of the content and clarify any misunderstandings. You should plan to stop the lesson several minutes before the bell rings to begin the summation. Make sure that you have the attention of all students before the summary begins. You should avoid merely reiterating the content covered during the lesson. Ask several questions that encourage the students to relate key aspects of the lesson or to evaluate key points. Also ask their opinions about what they believe are the key points.

To add interest and variety, vary the way that the lesson summary is conducted. Some days may involve simply a series of questions for students. On other days, you may ask several students to go to the chalkboard to solve a problem and discuss the thought process involved. A game format could be used as a means of summary, such as questions out of a hat or a "Trivial Pursuit" type of approach. Several creative approaches could offer the desired variety of lesson summaries.

The summary should be used to determine if the students have grasped the main ideas of the lesson. For example, your summary might reveal that several students do not understand the key concepts of a math lesson. It would be foolish to teach the next math lesson as though all students understand the concept. Therefore, you can use the information gathered during the summary to adjust the next day's lesson plan.

Getting Ready to Leave

At the end of the lesson, middle, junior high, or senior high school students usually need to leave the classroom and go to their next class. The bell will ring at the end of the class period and students will have just a few minutes to get to their next class in another room in the building.

You should plan to complete all instruction and lesson summary by the end of the class period so students are not delayed in moving to the next class. You should not teach right up to the bell because time needs to be allowed for several other events.

First, you must allow time for students to return any books, supplies, or materials to the appropriate locations. Also, students need time to throw away any scrap paper and to straighten up the classroom. They need time to put away their own books, papers, pencils, or other materials before leaving. You may plan to reserve from one to four minutes at the end of a lesson to allow sufficient time for these final actions to be completed before the bell rings. Students then should be dismissed on time. You need to schedule this time when planning lessons.

Managing Student Work

Students prepare homework and seatwork as a regular part of their instruction. To effectively manage this student work, guidelines are offered here for managing seatwork effectively, collecting assignments and monitoring their completion, maintaining records of student work, managing the paperwork, and giving students feedback. It is helpful to develop a plan to organize your instructional records, grading and assessment records, classroom management records, parental contact records, and special needs and accommodation records (Mierzwik, 2005).

Managing Seatwork Effectively

Seatwork involves students working on assignments during class that provide practice or review of previously presented material. Students spend hundreds of hours during a school year doing seatwork privately at their desks. It is imperative that you structure seatwork so that it is done effectively while enabling students to experience a high rate of success.

Guidelines for successfully implementing seatwork in the classroom come from a variety of sources (V. F. Jones & L. S. Jones, 2016; Weinstein & Novodvorsky, 2015; Weinstein & Romano, 2015). The following 12 recommendations represent a synthesis from these sources:

1. Recognize that seatwork is intended to practice or review previously presented material. It is not suited for students to learn new material.

2. Devote no more time to seatwork than is allocated to content development activities.

3. Give clear instruction—explanations, questions, and feedback—and sufficient practice before the students begin their seatwork. Having to provide lengthy explanations during seatwork is troublesome for both you and the student. In addition to procedural directions, explain why the activities are being done and how to do the seatwork.

4. Work through the first few problems of the seatwork together with the students before having them continue independently. This provides a model for completing the work and provides an opportunity for the students to ask questions for clarification about the content or procedures.

5. Decide if you will allow talking during seatwork. It is often desirable to start out with no talking during seatwork to have students work alone. After a month or two, teachers sometimes allow students to talk quietly with others to seek or provide help. Clarify when quiet talking is allowed.

6. Circulate from student to student during seatwork, actively explaining, observing, asking questions, and giving feedback. Monitoring students to provide this positive and corrective feedback is very important.

7. Determine how students will seek your help. When students are working at their seats and need help, ask them to raise their hands. You can then go to them or signal them to come to you at an appropriate time.

8. Determine when students can get out of their seats. To eliminate unnecessary wandering around the room during seatwork, decide when and for what purpose students can get out of their seats. For example, students may get supplies, sharpen pencils, or turn in papers only when necessary.

9. Have short contacts with individual students (i.e., 30 seconds or less).

10. Break seatwork into short segments rather than one long time slot. Rather than having one lengthy presentation of content followed by an extended period of seatwork, break up instruction into a number of segments, followed by brief seatwork after each segment.

11. Arrange seats to facilitate monitoring the students (e.g., face both small groups and independently working students).

12. Establish a routine to use during seatwork activity that prescribes what students will do when they have completed the exercises. Students may complete an additional enrichment assignment for extra credit, or they may use the time for free reading or to work on assignments from other classes.

■ **CLASSROOM CASE STUDY**   Managing Lesson Delivery

Logan Reynolds's 12-grade English class just finished reading George Orwell's *1984*, one of his favorite books to teach. The students participated in panel discussions and debates, and the desks were arranged in a circle to promote discussion. Mr. Reynolds encouraged lively conversations by asking probing questions and engaged his students in role-playing and simulation activities. His animated nature during class discussions motivated the students to become actively involved. Students also responded to a number of journal prompts at the beginning of each class session just prior to discussion. These prompts required students to reflect on the underlying ideas presented in their readings and to make connections to present-day concerns.

The class next moved to a unit on Shakespeare. Although Mr. Reynolds was not particularly interested in the works of Shakespeare, he understood the importance of introducing his class to classics such as *Macbeth*. Since Mr. Reynolds was concerned about the complexity of Shakespeare's works, he decided that lecturing about the material was the best way to promote student learning, and the desks were put into rows for this approach. As a result, student interactions were minimal, with no room for debate, role-playing, and simulation games. Mr. Reynolds felt those activities would only complicate study of an already obscure literary subject. Mr. Reynolds conducted all of his class meetings in a similar fashion, asking students to read a certain number of pages for homework and be prepared for the lectures, with only brief opportunities for discussion. Mr. Reynolds became concerned when his students were not very engaged in the brief class discussions and seemed to lose focus and interest.

Focus Questions

1. What factors contributed to the high level of student involvement in the unit on *1984?* To the low level of student involvement in the unit on Shakespeare?

2. Based on what you know about managing lesson delivery and other instructional factors, what suggestions do you have for Mr. Reynolds when teaching the unit on Shakespeare?

Collecting Assignments and Monitoring Their Completion

Whether it is homework or seatwork, you need to establish a process for collecting assignments and monitoring their completion.

- **Institute a regular procedure for collecting assignments.** Papers can be collected during class by asking students to pass them in a given direction until you have all papers in your hands. As an alternative, students may be asked to place their completed assignments in certain basket, tray, or drop box at a designated time during class. Once students know this collection procedure, assignments can be gathered quickly and efficiently.

- **Have a procedure for grouping papers by subject or class session.** In an elementary classroom, assignments on a variety of subjects may be submitted during the day. It is useful to have a separate drop box for each subject. In this way, only papers of a certain subject are in a drop box, and you don't need to spend time sorting through all the papers to pick out just the math papers or just the social studies papers. Similarly, middle and secondary classrooms should have a different drop box for each class period. Thus, students in the fourth hour would place their assignments in the box for their class period.

- **Keep a record of whose papers have been turned in.** If you evaluate the papers quickly, you will know who has or who has not submitted the assignments when you record the grades in your gradebook. If there is a delay in grading, you may have a checklist to record who has submitted the assignments. In this way, you can follow up with students who did not submit the materials. Some teachers also have students keep an assignment notebook for homework and seatwork to record the items that were due and what was turned in.

Maintaining Records of Student Work

Records of student progress and completion are entered in your gradebook. For elementary classes, you may organize your gradebook by having a separate section for each subject area. The date and description of the assignment can be entered at the top as a subject heading, and each students' scores can be placed in the appropriate column on the line for his or her name. Similarly, middle level and secondary teachers can have separate sections of the gradebook for each of their class sections. It is useful to establish a coding system to indicate a student absence or other information related to the assignment.

Gradebook software can be used to record the submission of assignments and the scores that students received. Progress reports for individual students can be easily prepared, and these are useful to show the students and parents.

Managing the Paperwork

Homework and seatwork involve a lot of paperwork, and it is easy to become overwhelmed by the volume of papers you deal with on a regular basis. Here are five guidelines to effectively manage your handling of the papers:

- **Assess, record, and return assignments quickly.** Make a commitment to assess and return all assignments in a day or two. Delays in your return of assignments often lead to a backlog of assignments to be graded. That situation puts a lot of pressure on you, and it is not fair to the students because they need to receive feedback as quickly as possible.

- **Be realistic about your grading capabilities.** Plan sufficient time in your schedule to assess and record the assignments. If you are making frequent assignments and getting behind in the grading, it is time to reassess your use of assignments. Strategically, space out the assignments that are to be graded. Long assignments take time to assess. Instead, short and specific assignments may be effective in monitoring student learning, and they take less time to assess.

- **Recognize that every seatwork assignment does not need to have a grade.** Every subject or every class period does not need an assignment that must be graded by you every day. Therefore, you do not need to receive papers each day. Students can be assessed in class and given feedback in various ways without asking them to submit the paperwork to you to be assessed. For example, you can assign seatwork and then check each student's work and give feedback during class.

- **Institute a system for coding the papers for each subject or class section.** As mentioned previously, have a system for collecting assignments from your students. Using color-coded folders for each subject or each class period can be a helpful technique for organizing the paperwork.

- **Have a predetermined way to return papers to the students.** When returning papers to students, keep them in labeled folders by the subject or class period. You could organize the papers by rows or groups to facilitate the return. Plan a certain way to return the papers each time. You may choose to use student helpers in returning the papers.

■ WHAT WOULD YOU DECIDE?　　Giving Students Feedback

You regularly use seatwork in your classroom, and you provide prompt feedback. However, three students often have difficulty with the seatwork and need more feedback and guidance.

1. What are some ways that you can provide these students with the extra feedback that they need?

2. How might you use other students in the class to provide this needed guidance and feedback?

Giving Students Feedback

You will assign seatwork and homework to help students learn, and it is important that students receive feedback about this work. Follow these guidelines for giving students feedback:

- **Provide frequent and regular feedback.** Students need fairly immediate feedback about their performance so they have an opportunity to correct any errors in their knowledge or skills before moving ahead to new material. Thus, plan for ways for students to demonstrate their learning and for ways that you can provide frequent and regular feedback about their learning.

- **Develop ways to provide feedback to students in class.** To provide prompt feedback and to avoid assigning homework every day, develop ways to provide feedback to students after instruction and practice have taken place in class. For example, you could have students work on problems at the board and give feedback, show answers on an overhead screen, or have students help review one another's work.

- **Take corrective actions promptly with students who do not perform well.** Don't wait until several poor assignments have been turned in or until it is time to submit the report card grade before meeting with a student who is not performing well. Some students may need more assistance to learn the content, and this feedback and assistance should come early without delay.

MAJOR CONCEPTS

1. The degree of structure in a lesson and the manner in which students are grouped for instruction need to be taken into account when managing instruction and promoting appropriate behavior.

2. Students are more likely to stay on task when they are held academically accountable for their work.

3. When beginning a lesson, teachers need to take attendance, solicit attention, provide daily review, provide a set induction, introduce lesson objectives, distribute materials, and give clear, focused directions.

4. When conducting a lesson, effective teachers pace the lesson appropriately, provide smooth transitions, avoid satiation, have a task orientation, ensure academic learning time, and exhibit clarity and enthusiasm.

5. An effective teacher ends a lesson with a summary of important concepts and allows students time to get ready to leave the room after the lesson.

6. Managing student work involves managing seatwork effectively, collecting assignments and monitoring their completion, maintaining records of student work, managing the paperwork, and giving students feedback.

DISCUSSION/REFLECTIVE QUESTIONS

1. What are the merits of whole-group, small-group, and independent work? What might teachers do to minimize misbehavior with each strategy?

2. In what ways might the selection of the various accountability procedures be affected by differences in grade level and subject areas?

3. From your own school experiences, what approaches to review did you find the most useful? What are the merits of using different approaches for review?

4. Recall several examples when your teachers were not clear in providing directions, instructions, or expectations. What effect did this lack of clarity have on you as a student?

SUGGESTED ACTIVITIES

1. Look at Table 8.1 concerning ways to hold students academically accountable. Then identify ways that you would make assignments and determine work and completion requirements.

2. Talk with several teachers to determine the various ways that they begin and end a lesson. How are these actions affected by the type of instructional strategy they use?

3. List a number of approaches that you could use to summarize a lesson. You could direct some of the techniques and some could involve students in an active way.

4. Establish some guidelines for yourself in how you assign, monitor, and assess seatwork in your classroom.

5. Talk with several teachers about the procedures they use to manage seatwork, collect and monitor assignments, maintain records, and manage paperwork. Then outline the ways that you will handle these responsibilities.

FURTHER READING

Burden, P. R., & Byrd, D. M. (2016). *Methods for effective teaching* (7th ed.). Boston: Pearson.

Provides an overview of all aspects of teaching methods including topics such as planning, classroom management, instructional strategies, and assessment. Includes content on lesson delivery.

Dean, C. B., Hubbell, E. R., Pitler, H., & Stone, B. (2012). *Classroom instruction that works: Research-based strategies for increasing student achievement* (2nd ed.). Alexandria, VA: Association for Supervision and Curriculum Development.

Provides a thorough yet concise review of proven instructional strategies to promote student learning. Examines homework and practice, cooperative learning, cues, questions, advance organizers, summarizing, and other strategies.

Marzano, R. J. (2007). *The art and science of teaching: A comprehensive framework for effective instruction*. Alexandria, VA: Association for Supervision and Curriculum Development.

Provides research-based guidelines for many aspects of lesson delivery, planning, management, student involvement, and assessment.

Thompson, J. G. (2009). *The first-year teacher's checklist*. San Francisco: Jossey-Bass.

Offers concise recommendations about many aspects of lesson delivery and related issues such as planning, instruction, classroom climate, management, and behavior. Based on her 2013 book, *The First-Year Teacher's Survival Guide*.

chapter

9

© Lisa F. Young/iStockphoto

Responding to Inappropriate Behavior

CHAPTER OBJECTIVES

This chapter provides information that will help you:

- Describe the principle of least intervention.
- Identify ways that situational assistance can be provided.
- Apply mild and moderate responses to misbehavior.
- Avoid certain disciplinary practices.
- Recognize the limitations of punishment and guidelines for its effective use.
- Identify ways to address chronic misbehaviors.
- Confront bullying.

Even with an effective management system in place, students may lose interest in a lesson and get off task. You must be prepared to respond with appropriate strategies to restore order. How should you respond to students who are simply off task? What options do you have when a student misbehaves? What are some practices to avoid? What are some guidelines in the use of punishment? How can chronic misbehavior be addressed? How can bullying be confronted? This chapter addresses these issues.

A Three-Step Response Plan

The teacher must decide when and how to intervene when students are off task or are misbehaving. An *intervention* is an action taken by the teacher that is intended to stop the disruptive actions and return the student to the academic activities.

Intervention decisions are typically based on the teacher's knowledge of who is misbehaving, what the misbehavior is, and when it occurs. Decisions about the type of intervention may depend on the student's history of inappropriate behavior. However, you should not automatically jump to conclusions if an incident involves a student with a history of behavior problems. It is helpful to discuss the problem with the student to clarify the problem from both your perspective and the student's before considering possible interventions.

The *principle of least intervention* states that when dealing with routine classroom behavior, misbehaviors should be corrected with the simplest, least intrusive intervention that will work (Slavin, 2015). If the least intrusive intervention does not work, then you move up to a more intrusive approach. The main goal is to handle the misbehavior in an effective manner that avoids unnecessarily disrupting the lesson. To the extent possible, the lesson should continue while the misbehavior is handled.

How do you apply this principle of least intervention? When you notice students starting to lose interest in the lesson or beginning to get off task, you can provide situational assistance— these are actions to help the student cope with the situation and keep the student on task. Then if the student is still off task, you can select mild responses to get the student back on task. If mild responses are not effective, next you can use moderate responses. Based on the principle of least intervention, this three-step response plan is displayed in Table 9.1.

■ TABLE 9.1   A Three-Step Response Plan to Misbehavior Using the Principle of Least Intervention

Teacher Response	Step 1: Provide Situational Assistance	Step 2: Use Mild Responses	Step 3: Use Moderate Responses
Purpose	To help the student cope with the instructional situation and keep the student on task	To take nonpunitive actions to get the student back on task	To remove desired stimuli to decrease unwanted behavior
Sample Actions	• Remove distracting objects • Provide support with routines • Reinforce appropriate behaviors • Boost student interest • Provide cues • Help students over hurdles • Redirect the behavior • Alter the lesson • Provide nonpunitive time-out • Modify the classroom environment	**Nonverbal Responses** • Ignore the behavior • Use nonverbal signals • Stand near the student • Touch the student **Verbal Responses** • Call on the student during the lesson • Use humor • Send an I-message • Use positive phrasing • Remind students of the rules • Give students choices • Ask "What should you be doing?" • Give a verbal reprimand	**Logical Consequences** • Withdraw privileges • Change the seat assignment • Have the student write reflections on the problem • Place student in a time-out • Hold student for detention • Contact the family • Have the student visit the principal

Situational Assistance

Students sometimes pause from the instructional task to look out the window, daydream, fiddle with a comb or other object, or simply take a brief mental break from the work. In these examples, students are not misbehaving—they are simply off task for a short time. You should take steps to draw students back into the lesson and to keep students on task.

Some inappropriate behaviors are of such short duration and are so insignificant that they can be safely ignored. Your use of situational assistance might be considered a "forgiveness step" for the student by recognizing that the off-task behavior is minor or fleeting and by allowing the student to get back on task without penalty.

To communicate to the student that you have noticed off-task behavior, you should first provide *situational assistance*—these are actions designed to help the students cope with the instructional situation and to keep them on task or to get them back on task before problems worsen. Problem behaviors thus can be stopped early before they escalate or involve other students.

If students remain off task after situational assistance has been provided, move on to *mild responses*. These nonverbal and verbal nonpunitive responses are designed to get the student back on task. The continuum of responses to misbehavior (see Table 9.1) illustrates that situational assistance is the starting point when dealing with off-task behavior. The following techniques can be used to provide situational assistance to help get students back on task.

1. **Remove distracting objects.** Students sometimes bring objects to school that may be distracting, such as combs, key, or magazines. When you see that such an object is keeping the students from the assigned tasks, simply walk over to the student and collect the object. The student should be quietly informed that the object can be picked up after class. Be kind and firm; no discussion is necessary. Inform students that they should store such objects in an appropriate place before school.

2. **Provide support with routines.** Students appreciate and often find comfort in knowing what is going to happen during the class period or during the day. They like to know where,

when, why, and with whom they will be at various times. It is helpful to announce and post the daily schedule. Changes in the schedule should be announced in advance, if possible. Even for a single lesson, students often appreciate knowing at the start what activities are planned for the lesson. Knowing the schedule provides students with a sense of security and direction. Routines for entering and leaving the classroom, distributing classroom papers and materials, and participating in group work contribute to this sense of security.

3. **Reinforce appropriate behaviors.** Students who have followed the directions can be praised. This communicates to the student who is off task what is expected. A statement such as "I'm pleased to see that Juan has his notebook ready for today's lesson" communicates to others what is expected. Appropriate behavior is reinforced while giving a signal to students who are off task. While commonly used in elementary classrooms, this approach may be considered a little juvenile by middle and secondary students.

4. **Boost student interest.** Student interest may wane in time as the lesson proceeds. You should express interest in the student's work when he or she shows signs of losing interest or being bored. Offer to help, noting how much work has been completed, noting how well done the completed part of the task is, or discussing the task. These actions can help bring the student back on task. Interest boosting is often needed when students do individual or small-group class work.

5. **Provide cues.** Sometimes, all the students are asked to do one thing, such as to prepare their materials or to clean up at the end of class, and cues can be given in these cases. *Cues* are signals that it is time for a selected behavior. For example, you may close the door at the start of class as a cue that instruction is about to begin and that everyone is expected to have all materials ready. The lights could be flipped or a bell sounded to signal time to begin cleanup or to finish small-group work. You can select an appropriate cue and explain its use to the students. This conveys behavioral expectations and encourages constructive on-task behavior.

6. **Help students over hurdles.** Students who are experiencing difficulty with a specific task need help in overcoming that problem—help over a hurdle—to keep them on task. Hurdle helping may consist of encouraging words from you, offering to assist with a specific task, or making available additional materials or equipment. For example, in a seatwork activity in which students need to draw several elements, including some straight lines, you might notice that one student is becoming upset that his or her lines are not straight. You could help by handing the student a ruler. In this way, you help before the student gives up on the assignment or becomes disruptive.

7. **Redirect the behavior.** When students show signs of losing interest, you can ask them to answer a question, do a problem, or read as a means of drawing them back into the lesson. Students should be treated as if they were paying attention and should be reinforced if they respond appropriately. It is important not to embarrass or ridicule students by saying that they would have been able to answer the question if they had been paying attention. Simply by asking a content-related question, you will show students that you are trying to draw them back into the lesson. Redirecting student behavior back into the lesson discourages off-task behavior.

■ WHAT WOULD YOU DECIDE?   **Using Cues or Signals**

Imagine that your students are working in cooperative learning groups on a seven-day project. When they come into the room, they immediately go to their groups and start work. On some days and during some of the class sessions, you need to give some information to all students.

1. How can you use a cue as a signal for students to stop work at that point and pay attention to you?

2. How can you give a cue that it is time to prepare to leave the class at the end of the class period?

8. **Alter the lesson.** Lessons sometimes do not go as well as you would like, and students may lose interest in the lesson for a variety of reasons. The lesson needs to be altered in some way when students are seen daydreaming, writing notes to friends, yawning, stretching, or moving around in their seats. When altering the lesson, select a different type of activity from the one that has proven unsuccessful. For example, if a whole-class discussion proves unsuccessful, you might have students work in pairs on a related issue that still deals with the lesson's objectives.

   In your initial planning, take student interests and abilities into account and provide a variety of activities in each lesson. The need to alter the lesson once underway is thereby minimized. It is helpful to have several types of activities planned in each lesson, some requiring active student participation. Consider the length of time allocated to each activity by taking into account students' age and maturity.

9. **Provide nonpunitive time-out.** Students who become frustrated, agitated, or fatigued may get off task and become disruptive. When you notice this happening, provide a nonpunitive time-out. A *time-out* is a period of time that the student is away from the instructional situation to calm down and reorganize his or her thoughts. The student then returns to the task with a fresh perspective. This time-out is not intended to be punishment for the off-task behavior. When a time-out is needed, you can ask the student to run an errand, help you with something, go get a drink, or do some other task not related to the instructional activity. Be alert to students showing signs of frustration and agitation and be ready to respond quickly.

   Sometimes, it is useful to have a small area of the room specifically designated for time-outs. This could be a desk placed off in a corner, partly hidden by a filing cabinet. The student could go to this semiprivate area in an effort to calm down and prepare to continue with the lesson. You could suggest that the students be allowed to go to this area when they think they need it. Students who use the corner for nonpunitive time-out should be allowed to decide themselves when they are ready to return.

10. **Modify the classroom environment.** The classroom environment itself may contribute to off-task behavior. The arrangement of desks, tables, instructional materials, and other items in the classroom may give rise to inefficient traffic patterns or limited views of the instructional areas. Other factors include the boundaries between areas for quiet student and group projects and access to supplies. In addition, both your actions and those of your students may affect their behavior. Once misbehavior develops, you may need to separate the students or change the setting in some way. Examine the disturbance and identify the element that contributes to it. Modification in the classroom arrangement may include moving tables, student desks, or the storage area.

Mild Responses

Students may misbehave even after you have developed a system of rules and procedures, provided a supportive instructional environment, and given situational assistance to get misbehaving students back on task. In that case, mild responses should be used to correct the student's behavior. *Mild responses* are nonpunitive ways to deal with misbehavior while providing guidance for appropriate behavior. Nonverbal and verbal mild responses are meant to stop the off-task behavior and to restore order. The three-step response plan shown in Table 9.1 illustrates the movement to more directive responses if situational assistance is not successful.

Nonverbal Responses

Even with situational assistance, students may get off task. Nonverbal responses are taken as a nonpunitive means to get the student back on task. *Nonverbal responses* may include ignoring the behavior, nonverbal signals, standing near the student, and touching the student. These approaches are taken in increasing order of teacher involvement and control.

1. **Ignore the behavior.** Intentionally ignoring minor misbehavior is sometimes the best course of action as a means to weaken the behavior. This is based on the reinforcement principle called *extinction*; that is, if you ignore a behavior and withhold reinforcement, the behavior will lessen and ultimately disappear. Minor misbehaviors that might be ignored are pencil tapping, body movements, hand waving, book dropping, calling out an answer instead of raising a hand, interrupting the teacher, whispering, and so on. Behaviors designed to get your attention or that of classmates are likely candidates for extinction or ignoring the behavior.

    Ignoring the behavior is best used to control only behaviors that cause little interference to teaching/learning, and it should be combined with praise for appropriate behavior. Extinction is inappropriate for behaviors (e.g., talking out and aggression) reinforced by consequences that you do not control and behaviors (violence) that cannot be tolerated during the time required for extinction to work (Kerr & Nelson, 2010). If the behavior continues after a reasonable period of planned ignoring, you should be more directive.

    There are limitations to ignoring the behavior. One risk is that students may conclude that you are not aware of what is happening and may continue the behavior. Although you may ignore the behavior and not give the student the desired attention, other students may give such attention. Furthermore, the student may continue the behavior for a while after you ignore it, and thus the time taken for correcting the problem will be too long. Hostile or aggressive behaviors may be too dangerous to ignore.

2. **Use nonverbal signals.** A nonverbal signal can be used to communicate to the disrupting student that the behavior is not appropriate. Signals must be directed at the student. They let the student know that the behavior is inappropriate and that it is time to get back to work. Nonverbal signals may include making eye contact with the student who is writing a note, shaking a hand or finger to indicate not to do some inappropriate action, holding a hand up to stop a student's calling out, or giving "the teacher look." These actions should be done in a businesslike manner. You need to move to the next level of intervention if these disruptive behaviors persist.

3. **Stand near the student.** Using your physical presence near the disruptive student to help him or her get back on task is *proximity control*. This is warranted at times when you can't get the student's attention to send a signal because he or she is so engrossed in an inappropriate action. For example, a student may be reading something other than class-related material or may be writing a note. While doing this, the student may not even look up at you.

■ WHAT WOULD YOU DECIDE?   Using Nonverbal Responses

Students are working in small groups on an activity, and you notice a group in which two students are off task. They are not misbehaving or causing disruption; they just are not working on the activity.

1. How can you respond nonverbally to get these two students back on task? What factors might affect your decision on the particular method?

2. At a later time, you are making a presentation to the whole class when you notice two other students off task. What nonverbal responses might you make in that situation?

As a result, signals will not work. While conducting the lesson, walk around the room and approach the student's desk. The student will then likely notice your presence and put the material away without a word being spoken.

Some proximity control techniques are somewhat subtle, such as walking toward the student, while other approaches such as standing near the student's desk are more direct. If students do not respond to proximity control, you need to move to a more directive level of intervention.

4. **Touch the student.** Without any verbal exchange, you may place a hand on the student's shoulder in an effort to achieve calm, or take the student's hand and escort the student back to his or her seat. *Touch control* involves mild, nonaggressive physical contact that is used to get the student on task. It communicates that you disapprove of the action. Talk to your principal to be certain you understand the guidelines and legal considerations of appropriate touching.

When deciding whether and how to use touch control, you may take into account the circumstances of the behavior and the characteristics of students. Students who are angry or visibly upset sometimes do not want to be touched, and some do not want to be touched at any time. How well touch will be received depends on where it occurs and how long it lasts. A touch on the back, hand, arm, or shoulder is acceptable to many students, whereas touch to the face, neck, leg, chest, or other more personal area are often unacceptable. Brief touch is considered acceptable; the longer the touch is, the more it becomes unacceptable.

Verbal Responses

Although nonverbal mild responses may be effective, verbal responses can be used as nonpunitive, mild responses to misbehavior. Their purpose is to get the student back on task with limited disruption and intervention. Various verbal responses are described as follows.

1. **Call on the student during the lesson.** You can recapture a misbehaving student's attention by using his or her name in the lesson, such as "Now, in this next example, suppose that Kimberly had three polygons that she. . . ." You can then ask a question of the student to recapture his or her attention. Calling on the student in these ways allows you to communicate that you know what is going on and to capture his or her attention without citing the misbehavior. Be cautious—student dignity should be preserved. If you call on students in these ways only when they misbehave, they will sense that you are just waiting to catch them misbehaving, and this strategy will backfire by creating resentment.

2. **Use humor.** Humor can be used as a gentle reminder to students to correct their behavior. Humor directed at the situation or even at yourself can defuse tension that might be created due to the misbehavior. It can depersonalize the situation and thus help resolve the problem. You must be careful that the humor is not sarcastic. *Sarcasm* includes statements that are directed at correcting or making fun of the student; these statements are intended to criticize or embarrass the student. Instead, humor is directed at or makes fun of the situation or the teacher. The student may then reconsider his or her actions and then get back on task.

3. **Send an I-message.** An *I-message* is a statement you make to a misbehaving student that prompts appropriate behavior without giving a direct command (Gordon, 2003). An I-message has three parts: (a) a brief description of the misbehavior; (b) a description of its effects on you or other students; and (c) a description of your feelings about the effects. For example, you might say, "When you tap your pen on the desk during the test, it makes a lot of noise and I am concerned that it might distract other students." I-messages are intended to help students recognize that their behavior has consequences for other students and that you have genuine feelings about the actions. Since I-messages leave the decision about changing the behavior up to the student, they are likely to promote a sense of responsibility.

4. **Use positive phrasing.** *Positive phrasing* is used when inappropriate off-task behavior allows you to highlight positive outcomes for appropriate behavior. This usually takes the form, "When you do X (behave in a particular appropriate way), then you can do Y (a positive outcome)." For example, when a student is out of her seat, you might say, "Renee, when you return to your seat, then it will be your turn to participate in the activity." Through the use of positive phrasing, you redirect students from disruptive to appropriate behavior by simply stating the positive outcomes.

5. **Remind students of the rules.** Each classroom needs to have a set of rules that govern student behaviors, along with a set of consequences for breaking them. When students see that consequences of misbehavior are in fact delivered, reminders of the rules can help them get back on task because they want to avoid the consequences. When one student is poking another student, for example, you might say, "Delores, the classroom rules state that students must keep their hands and feet to themselves." This reminder often ends the misbehavior because the student does not want the consequence. If the inappropriate behavior continues, you must deliver the consequence; otherwise the reminder will be of little value because students will recognize that there is no follow-through.

6. **Give students choices.** Some students feel defensive when confronted about their misbehavior. As a result, you can give them choices about resolving the problem. This allows the student to feel that he or she settled the problem without appearing to back down. All of the choices that you give to the student should lead to resolution of the problem. If a student is talking to another nearby student, you might say, "Harvey, you can turn back in your seat and get back to your project, or you can take the empty seat at the end of the row." In this way, Harvey has a choice, but the result is that he gets back to work in his seat or in the seat at the end of the row.

7. **Ask "What should you be doing?"** Glasser (1998a) proposes that teachers ask disruptive students questions in an effort to direct them back to appropriate behavior. When a student is disruptive, you might ask "What should you be doing?" This question can have a positive effect because it helps redirect the student to appropriate behavior. Of course, some students may not answer this question honestly or may refuse to reply at all. In that case, you should make statements related to the question, for example, "Keith, you were swearing and name-calling. That is against our classroom rules. You should not swear or call others names." If the student continues to break the rule, then appropriate consequences should be delivered.

8. **Give a verbal reprimand.** A straightforward way to have students stop misbehaving is to simply ask or direct them to do so. This is sometimes called a *desist order* or a *reprimand*, and it is given to decrease unwanted behavior. Verbal reprimands are effective with many mild and moderate behavior problems, but by themselves are less successful with severe behavior disorders (Kerr & Nelson, 2010).

   A *direct appeal* involves a courteous request for the student to stop the misbehavior and to get back on task. You might say "Martina, please put away the comb and continue with the class assignment." A direct appeal often gives the student a sense of ownership for deciding to get back on task and to do as you requested. The student feels a sense of responsibility.

   As an alternative, you could use a *direct command* in which you take the responsibility and give a direction in a straightforward manner, such as "Wayne, stop talking with your friends and get to work on the lab activity." With the direct appeal and the direct command, the student is expected to comply with your directions. If the student defies your request or command, you must be prepared to deliver an appropriate consequence.

   Soft reprimands, audible only to the misbehaving student, are more effective than loud reprimands in reducing disruptive classroom behavior (Kerr & Nelson, 2010). Soft, private reprimands do not call the attention of the entire class to the misbehaving student and also may be less likely to trigger emotional reactions.

Moderate Responses

Following situational assistance and mild nonverbal and verbal responses, students might continue to misbehave. In that case, moderate responses should be used to correct the problem. The three-step response plan shown in Table 9.1 illustrates the movement to more directive responses if mild responses are not successful.

Moderate responses are intended to be punitive ways to deal with misbehavior by removing desired stimuli to decrease the occurrence of the inappropriate behavior. Moderate responses include logical consequences and behavior modification techniques. Because student behaviors that warrant moderate responses are more problematic than mild misbehaviors, it is often useful to discuss specific problems with the principal, other teachers, or the school counselor. The family can be contacted at any point to inform them of their child's actions and to solicit their help.

A *logical consequence* is an event that is arranged by the teacher that is directly and logically related to the misbehavior (Dreikurs, Grunwald, & Pepper, 1998). The consequence should be reasonable, respectful, and related to the student action. For instance, if a student leaves paper on the classroom floor, then he or she must pick the paper off the floor. If a student breaks the rule of speaking out without raising his or her hand, you will ignore the response and call on a student whose hand is up. If a student marks on the desk, then he or she will be required to clean the marks off. Students are more likely to respond favorably to logical consequences because they do not consider the consequences mean or unfair.

You may tell the student what the consequence is right after the behavior occurs—for example, "Milton, you left the study area a mess. You need to clean it up at the end of class." As an alternative, you may give the student a choice when inappropriate behavior is noticed. This tells the student that the inappropriate behavior must be changed or, if it isn't changed, that a particular consequence will occur. For example, you may say "Joellen, you have a choice of not bothering students near you or having your seat changed."

When given a choice, students will often stop the inappropriate behavior. This approach can be very effective because the student feels a sense of ownership in solving the problem, and the issue is over quickly. Of course, if the problem behavior continues, you must deliver the consequence that you stated to the student.

At the start of the school year, you should think of two or three logical consequences for each of the classroom rules and inform students of them. When logical, reasonable consequences are preplanned, you are not under the pressure of thinking up something appropriate at the time the misbehavior occurs. Some examples of logical consequences include the following:

- **Withdraw privileges.** As a regular part of the classroom activities, you may provide your students with a number of special privileges such as a trip to the library, use of a computer, use of special equipment or a game, service as a classroom helper, or other valued privilege. If the misbehavior relates to the type of privilege offered, a logical consequence would be to withdraw the privilege. For example, if a student mishandles some special equipment, then the student would lose the privilege of using the equipment.

- **Change the seat assignment.** Students may talk, poke, or interact with other students in nearby seats. Sometimes, a problem occurs because certain students are seated near each other. Other times, just the placement of seats enables easy interaction. If inappropriate interaction occurs, a logical consequence would be to relocate the student's seat.

- **Have the student write reflections on the problem.** It is often useful to ask the student to reflect on the situation to help him or her recognize the logical connection between the behavior and the consequences. You may ask the student to provide written responses to certain questions; this might be done during a time-out.

  These questions may include the following: What is the problem? What did I do to create the problem? What should happen to me? What should I do next time to avoid a problem? Other questions may require the student to describe the rule that was broken, why he or she chose to misbehave, who was bothered by the misbehavior, what more appropriate behavior could be chosen next time, and what should happen to him or her the next time the misbehavior occurs.

  Written responses to these or similar questions help students see their behavior more objectively and promote more self-control. You may choose to have the student sign and date the written responses for future reference. The written responses can be useful if family members need to be contacted at a later time.

- **Place the student in a time-out.** Sometimes, a student is talking or disrupting the class in such a way that interferes with the progress of the lesson. In such a case, the student can be excluded from the group; this is called a *time-out*. Removing the student from the group is

---

VOICES FROM THE CLASSROOM   Using an OOPS Sheet for Reflections

Lisa Bietau, fourth-grade teacher, Manhattan, Kansas

When my students misbehave, I sometimes ask them to fill out an OOPS sheet to have them reflect on their behavior. OOPS stands for "Outstanding Opportunity for a Personal Stretch." The sheet has a place for their name and date at the top. Then there are several other areas that the student needs to fill in: (1) Describe the problem. (2) What other choices did you have to settle the situation without difficulty? (3) How might you handle this differently if it happens again?

After the student fills out the OOPS sheet, I meet with the student privately to discuss the situation briefly and to review the options and solutions that the student wrote. This reflection and discussion with me helps the students understand my expectations and recognize that they have a responsibility to consider reasonable options when they meet a challenging situation.

I sign the OOPS sheet and make a copy for my files. The original is then sent home with the student to obtain the parent's signature. All of the student's privileges are suspended until the signed sheet is returned. If the sheet is not returned the next day, I call the parents and another copy is sent home if necessary. I have found that students show more self-control after completing the OOPS sheet.

a logical consequence of interfering with the group. An area of the room should be established as the time-out area, such as a desk in a corner or partly behind a filing cabinet. As a general rule, a time-out should last no longer than 10 minutes.

- **Hold the student for detention.** *Detention* means detaining or holding back a student when he or she normally would be free to go and do other things. The student is deprived of free time and perhaps the opportunity to socialize with other students. Detention may include remaining after class or staying after school.

  Detention can be a logical consequence for student behaviors that waste class time. A student might be asked to work on the social studies paper that wasn't completed during class due to inappropriate behavior. Students will soon see the logic that time wasted in class will have to be made up later, on their own time in detention.

  Make sure the student understands the reasons for the detention. It should logically fit the offense and the time should not be excessive—20–30 minutes after school would be reasonable. Confer with the student and work out a plan to help him or her avoid detention in the future and move toward self-control.

- **Contact the family.** If a student shows a pattern of repeated misbehavior, then you may need to contact the family. The logic here is that if all earlier attempts to extinguish the misbehavior do not work, it is appropriate to go to a higher authority. Parents, guardians, or other family members may be notified by a note or a letter to inform them of the problem and to solicit their involvement or support. You may choose to call them instead. If the situation is fairly serious, a conference with the parents may be warranted.

- **Have the student visit the principal.** In cases of repeated misbehavior or serious misbehavior, such as fighting, students may be sent to the school office to see the principal. The principal may talk with the student in an effort to use his or her legitimate authority to influence the student to behave properly. Some schools have specific procedures to be followed when students are sent to the principal. When the behavior problems reach this point, additional personnel, including the school counselor or psychologist and the family, need to be consulted to help the student.

Cautions and Guidelines

Before school starts, it is best to have a plan to address off-task behavior and misbehavior when it occurs. However, teachers may make decisions in the heat of the moment when responding to misbehavior, and these responses may not be appropriate. You should be aware of some disciplinary practices to avoid and some guidelines for using punishment.

Some Practices to Avoid

Research and practice suggest that some interventions are inappropriate or unsuccessful when trying to restore control. Disadvantages outweigh advantages in the use of harsh reprimands, threats, and physical punishment. Furthermore, practitioners have identified additional approaches that have questionable effectiveness. The message is clear—teachers should avoid the following practices.

1. **Harsh and humiliating reprimands.** A harsh reprimand is very negative verbal feedback. Teachers may be carried away with this verbal thrashing and humiliate the student. Research reports suggest that the use of harsh reprimands is a very ineffective, inefficient, and costly strategy. Harsh reprimands include speaking to the student in an exceptionally stern manner, yelling, and screaming. All of this may progress to the point where the student is humiliated.

2. **Threats.** A threat is a statement that expresses the intent to punish the student if he or she does not comply with the teacher's wishes. Most practitioners and researchers believe the disadvantages of using threats outweigh any possible benefits. Teachers may warn students to alert them to potential consequences, but a threat often expresses more severe consequences than would normally be expected and may be stated when the teacher has lost emotional control.

3. **Nagging.** Continual or unnecessary scolding only upsets the student and arouses the resentment of other students. The teacher may consider these scoldings as mini-lectures, but they are seen as nagging from the students' point of view.

4. **Forced apologies.** Forcing a student to express an apology that is not felt is a way of forcing him or her to lie. This approach solves nothing.

5. **Sarcastic remarks.** Sarcastic remarks are statements that the teacher uses to deride, taunt, or ridicule the student. While the teacher may consider these statements as a means of punishment, they create resentment; they may lower the student's self-esteem and may lower the esteem of the teacher in the eyes of students.

6. **Group punishment.** Group punishment occurs when the entire class or group is punished because of the misbehavior of an individual. The intent is for peer pressure to help modify the individual's behavior. Group punishment is difficult to use effectively, however; the undesirable side effects are likely to outweigh the advantages. It forces students to choose between the teacher and a classmate. Many students will unite in sullen defiance of the teacher and refuse to blame the classmate if group punishment is used. Even if they go along with the teacher, the punishment engenders unhealthy attitudes.

7. **Assigning extra academic work.** When assigning extra academic work as a punishment, the teacher implies that the work is unpleasant. It is often in the form of homework that is not normally required. The student then associates schoolwork with punishment. This is not a message teachers should convey.

8. **Reducing grades.** Penalizing a student academically for misbehavior again creates an undesirable association. Students who are penalized for misbehaving may develop an attitude of "What's the use?" toward academic work. Furthermore, reducing grades for misbehavior confounds the grade, which is intended to report only the student's academic progress.

9. **Writing as punishment.** After students misbehave, teachers may have them copy pages out of a dictionary, encyclopedia, or other book, or have them write a certain statement ("I will not do such and such again.") a number of times. Unfortunately, this approach leads to hostility from students, gives the impression that writing is a bad thing (English teachers will get upset about the message being conveyed here), and is not logically linked to what students may have done.

10. **Physical labor or exercise.** A teacher may use push-ups or some other physical action as punishment. However, the teacher may not be familiar with the student's physical abilities, and the student could get hurt. In addition to concerns about the student's safety, having students do extra exercises in physical education in response to misbehavior may cause the student to lose interest in the physical activities when the teacher assigns them as punishment.

11. **Corporal punishment.** Corporal punishment is a strategy in which the teacher inflicts physical pain on the student to punish him or her for misbehaving. Paddling, spanking, slapping, and pinching are examples. There are many disadvantages to using physical consequences (Hyman, 1997). Other negative behaviors often emerge, such as escape (running away from the punisher), avoidance (lying, stealing, cheating), anxiety, fear, tension, stress, withdrawal, poor self-concept, resistance, and counter-aggression. Many districts have a policy either prohibiting the use of corporal punishment or establishing specific guidelines for its limited use.

■ **WHAT WOULD YOU DECIDE?** **Creating a Learning Community**

In *Beyond Discipline: From Compliance to Community* (2006), Alfie Kohn makes an articulate and passionate argument for the reduction of punishment. He challenges educators to ask this question when planning to work with students: "What do they require in order to flourish, and how can we provide those things?" Kohn says teachers should focus on developing caring, supportive classrooms where students participate in problem solving, including problems about behavior. He advises teachers to develop a sense of community in their classrooms.

1. If you were to adopt Kohn's ideas, how would that affect your selection of rules and procedures and your selection of consequences for infractions?

2. To contribute as members of the learning community and participate in decision making, what knowledge and skills would students need to have?

3. How would you justify to parents your classroom approaches where students have so much say in how the class is run?

Guidelines for Punishment

The later steps of the principle of least intervention may involve punishment. *Punishment* is an act of imposing a penalty with the intention of suppressing undesirable behavior. There are two procedures for achieving this purpose: (1) withholding positive reinforcers or desirable stimuli through techniques such as logical consequences and behavior modification approaches such as time-out and loss of privileges and (2) adding aversive stimuli through actions where students receive a penalty for their misbehavior. Withholding positive reinforcers is considered to be less harmful than adding aversive stimuli.

Especially for beginning teachers, dealing with misbehavior that requires moderate or severe responses can be very troubling. It is often helpful to talk with the principal, other teachers, or school counselors to obtain ideas and advice for dealing with students who exhibit more serious misbehavior. In addition, it is often useful to contact the student's parents at any point to inform them of any concerns you might have and to solicit their help in working with the student.

You should express confidence in students' ability to improve and punish only as a last resort when students repeatedly fail to respond to more positive treatment. Apply punishment as part of a planned response, not as a means to release your anger or frustration.

The following factors are important to consider when effectively using punishment:

1. **Discuss and reward acceptable behaviors.** Acceptable behaviors should be emphasized when classroom rules are first discussed. Make it clear to students why the rules exist. Discuss the reasons for not engaging in the behavior considered to be inappropriate. Most students will behave appropriately if they know what is expected.

2. **Clearly specify the behaviors that will lead to punishment.** Clarifying acceptable behaviors for the students may not be enough. To help the students understand, identify, and discuss examples of behaviors that break the rules and lead to punishment.

3. **Use punishment only when rewards or nonpunitive interventions have not worked, or if the behavior must be decreased quickly because it is dangerous.** Punishment should be used as a last resort when other techniques have failed.

4. **Administer punishment in a calm, unemotional manner.** If you deliver punishment while still emotionally upset, you may select an overly harsh punishment and may also provoke the student into further inappropriate reactions. Punishment should not be an involuntary emotional response, a way to get revenge, or a spontaneous response to provocation.

5. **Deliver a warning before punishment is applied to any behavior.** The warning itself could reduce the need for punishment. If the student does not correct the behavior after the warning, punishment should be delivered at the next occurrence.

■ **CLASSROOM CASE STUDY**   Responding to a Classroom Incident

Marilyn Schmidt is a middle school social studies teacher who just started her second year of teaching. On one of the opening days, she was presenting some new material to the entire class when she noticed three students talking near the back of the classroom, and one of them was also sending a text message.

Ms. Schmidt decided not to wait for anything more to happen before acting since she wanted to show that she was in control. She already was somewhat upset from her previous class period when the students were unruly, so she wanted to send a strong message that nonacademic talking would not be tolerated in this class. So she told the three students that they would need to come after school for a half hour of detention. The three students protested this decision and began to argue with Ms. Schmidt. She told them if they did not agree to come in for detention, then the whole class would have an additional project to complete.

After one of the three students said a few more words in protest, Ms. Schmidt demanded that the student apologize for those statements. If the student did apologize, Ms. Schmidt said that she would remove the whole class punishment. The student ended up apologizing, but didn't really mean it. There seemed to be a lot of tension for the rest of the class period. Ms. Schmidt got the three students to stop talking, but at what price?

Focus Questions

1. In what ways did Ms. Schmidt *not* follow the sequential steps in the three-step response plan when addressing misbehavior?

2. Identify the disciplinary practices that she used but should have avoided.

3. Identify the ways she did not follow the guidelines for the use of punishment.

4. How might Ms. Schmidt have addressed the situation more appropriately and successfully?

---

6. **Apply punishment fairly to everyone who exhibits the targeted behaviors.** You should treat both genders the same way, and low-achieving and high-achieving students the same way.

7. **Apply punishment consistently after every occurrence of the targeted misbehavior.** Behaviors that reliably receive punishment are less likely to be tried by students than behaviors that occasionally go uncorrected.

8. **Use punishment of sufficient intensity to suppress the unwanted behaviors.** Generally speaking, the greater the intensity, the longer lasting the effect. But this does not mean that you need to resort to extreme measures. For example, the loss of positive reinforcement because of inappropriate behavior is better than shouting "Don't do that!" with increasing intensity.

9. **Select a punishment that is effective, that is not associated with a positive or rewarding experience, and that fits the situation.** Not all aversive consequences that you select may be seen as punishment. Some students, for instance, might think that it is a reward to be placed in a time-out area in the classroom. In that case, a different consequence should be used that is not seen by the student as being positive or rewarding. Also, don't overreact to mild misbehavior or underreact to serious misbehavior. The seriousness of the misbehavior, the student, and the context of the situation need to be taken into account.

10. **Avoid extended periods of punishment.** Lengthy, mild punishment such as missing open study time for a week may have a boomerang effect. Punishment with a short duration is more effective.

Dealing with Chronic Misbehaviors

Chronic misbehaviors are troublesome behaviors that students repeatedly or compulsively perform. They include tattling, clowning, cheating, lying, stealing, profanity, rudeness toward the teacher, defiance or hostility, and failure to do schoolwork. This behavior is recurring and inappropriate, and teachers can take actions to minimize their presence in the classroom (Crowe, 2009; Foley, 2012; Gootman, 2008; Kapalka, 2009; Khalsa, 2007b). Strategies to address a number of common chronic misbehaviors are presented here.

1. **Tattling.** Tattling occurs when students report minor infractions or perceived injustices to the teacher. Tattling is not disruptive, but it can become a problem when students commonly report minor, petty complaints. To prevent tattling from occurring in the first place, let students know what kinds of information they should and should not report to you. You need to know about an incident where a student got hurt, for example, but not when some other student is not doing the schoolwork.

   Many teachers, especially in the primary grades, have an explicit lesson about tattling. They describe the difference between reporting important information to the teacher and reports that are tattling about minor infractions. Numerous examples can be provided and discussed for each category. Students can offer examples as well. It is important to convey to students that you will be available to help them with important matters, but that you are not interested in minor complaints.

2. **Clowning.** Students who clown behave in silly or funny ways or may play practical jokes. This clowning is disruptive to the class. Figuring out the source of the student's clowning can help determine what to do about it (Gootman, 2008). Some students may use clowning to cover up a deficiency; they may clown during a math lesson because they are weak in math. Clowning may also be a vehicle for a student to achieve success—to gain some recognition, fame, and popularity among other students. Still, clowning may be a way of venting frustrations and pressures that students may experience from school, home, or other factors.

   Keeping a record of who, what, when, where, and how for clowning incidents can help pinpoint the source. Then you can meet privately with the student to discuss the pattern of the clowning behavior and why it is disruptive. Help the student figure out ways to meet his or her needs without being disruptive.

3. **Cheating.** Cheating involves students getting answers or projects from someone else and turning them in as their own. Students may cheat for several reasons. They may cheat if teachers' expectations are too high and they may not be capable of mastering the material. Students then may see cheating as a way out. Other students may simply not be prepared or they may have test anxiety.

   It is best to minimize the temptation to cheat by determining the difference between helping and cheating, demonstrating expected behaviors for various activities, and having students identify appropriate and inappropriate actions. In addition, it is important to minimize the opportunity to cheat by determining desk placement during tests and by giving attention to policies, procedures, and submission guidelines for other types of student products.

   If you catch a student cheating, you can talk to the student privately, present your reasons for suspecting cheating, express concern and try to find out why the student cheated, explain the consequences, and then discuss the consequences for subsequent cheating (Weinstein & Romano, 2015). Rather than give the student a zero on the assignment, you may ask him or her to complete the test or assignment again under controlled conditions where cheating cannot occur. Some schools have predetermined consequences for cheating, such as parental notification.

4. **Lying.** Lying involves saying something that is not true in a conscious effort to deceive somebody. Students may have many reasons for lying, such as trying to protect their self-image, to mask their vulnerable points, or to inflate their image in front of others. They may feel afraid, feel insecure, or fear rejection. Students may lie to protect themselves from punishment or if we are too strict with them.

■ WHAT WOULD YOU DECIDE?   **Addressing Cheating in Your Classroom**

On three successive quizzes in your class, you notice that four students have always received the same score. You are suspicious that this is more than a coincidence.

1. Under what circumstances would you talk with these four students about their scores?

2. What could you do about the questions and the formatting of the quiz to minimize cheating?

3. What could you do about room arrangement and your monitoring of students during a quiz to minimize cheating?

The best response is to express concern about the student's need to lie by saying "I wonder why you couldn't tell me what really happened." This approach makes it easier for the student to talk about the reason he or she felt compelled to lie. Stay calm and encourage them to discuss why they felt they needed to tell a lie. In doing so, try not to overreact or get angry with the student. Focus on the student's reasons and feelings that led to the lie. You might encourage the private conversation with a statement such as "If you tell me what really happened, we can figure out what to do about this situation and perhaps I can help you not let this happen again." Encourage students to be honest about their feelings, and use a calm problem-solving approach to help students address a problem that caused them to lie in the first place.

5. **Stealing.** Stealing involves taking something that belongs to somebody else without the owner's permission. Students in early grades may still be learning the difference between sharing and taking what doesn't belong to them. Students may impulsively steal because they want something, or they may take something from another student because they are angry with the other person.

If an incident of stealing takes place and you know the culprit, you can have a private conversation with the student about what happened. Describe what you saw and have the student return the item, replace it, or make restitution. Help the student figure out options other than stealing. You may need to respond more forcefully, depending on the value of the property and the frequency of stealing. In such cases, you may need to contact the principal and the family. Because of legal implications, it is wise to discuss an incident with the principal before conducting a search of backpacks, lockers, or a student's clothing.

6. **Profanity.** Profanity occurs when students use abusive, vulgar, or irreverent language. Age plays a role in the use of profanity. Young children may simply be restating language they heard on television, by family, or by friends with little or no understanding of the meaning. An instructional response is appropriate here, rather than a disciplinary one (e.g., "We don't use words like that in school"). For older students, such language may have become a regular part of their vocabulary, or they may use profanity when they are angry with another person. In such cases, students need to see what is acceptable and unacceptable in school. Stress that using language to hurt others will not be permitted and that there are other acceptable ways to express anger.

7. **Rudeness toward the teacher.** Students may be rude to the teacher by using disagreeable or discourteous words or actions that are outside acceptable standards. Rudeness may be expressed in talking back, arguing, making crude remarks, or showing inappropriate gestures. It is best to avoid overreacting, arguing, or getting into a power struggle. A low-key, respectful response is more suitable. When rude behavior is first evident, you should inform the student that the behavior is inappropriate, and you might refer to a classroom rule that relates to respectful behaviors. If the actions continue, you should meet with the student privately to identify the reason for the behavior and possibly to deliver consequences. If the rude behavior continues, you may need to consult with the principal or counselors about additional responses.

8. **Defiance or hostility toward the teacher.** Defiance occurs when a student refuses to obey or conform to teacher directions. These actions may be open, bold, or even hostile, and defiance may be in the form of a confrontation with the teacher during a class session. The best way to deal with defiance is to try to defuse it by keeping it in private and handing it individually with the student. Put the student off by saying that you will discuss the situation in a few minutes when you have time. Avoid a power struggle and remain objective. Listen to the student's point of view but don't engage in an argument. State the consequence clearly and implement it.

Here are some guidelines when students become defiant. First, stay in control of yourself. Direct the rest of the class to work on something while you speak to the student in a private area away from the rest of the students. Stand a few feet away from the defiant student (i.e., don't get in his face). Acknowledge the student's feeling by saying something like "I can see that you are really angry." Avoid a power struggle in the conversation (e.g., "I am the boss here, and I am telling you what to do"). As a means to defuse the situation, offer the student a choice of actions for what the student needs to do next (Weinstein & Romano, 2015).

9. **Failure to do work in class or homework.** You may have some students who regularly do not complete seatwork or homework. You should first examine how you hold students academically accountable in your class (see Chapter 8) and make any needed adjustments to ensure accountability. Next, you should plan to maintain accurate records of the schoolwork and respond early when you recognize students who are regularly not completing their class work.

You also should examine the nature of assignments and homework. Is the material too difficult to be completed independently? Is it too boring? Is it too long? Could the material be mastered with a shorter assignment? Was there sufficient preparation in class before students were to do the seatwork or homework? Are there other ways to provide practice and to assess student progress without having seatwork and homework every day? Your reflection on these questions may lead to your adjustment of the assignments and expectations.

When selecting seatwork and homework, it is often helpful to break it up into parts whenever possible. Work on first few questions in class as a group before asking students to complete the rest on their own. Monitor students closely to see that they are able to handle the work independently. Be sure to review, collect, and grade all assignments. Many teachers have homework planners where they list the assignments and due dates somewhere in the classroom.

10. **Inappropriate use of electronic devices.** Millions of students of all ages carry their cell phones and other electronic devices (e.g., iPods and MP3 players) to school each day. Student use of these devices during school hours has the potential for creating problems, so many schools have adopted schoolwide policies for their use.

Cell phones can create distractions that disrupt the class. Students may misuse their phones by texting, bullying other students (i.e., cyberbullying), or taking unflattering photographs or recordings of teachers. Phones are attractive targets for thieves, and they also can be used to cheat on tests and other assignments (Thompson, 2011). Students also may use headphones to listen to music rather than participate in academic activities.

Teachers should take a common-sense approach when dealing with these electronic devices. First, follow the guidelines in your schoolwide policy for these devices. Second, make sure all students are aware of the policy, understand when they can and cannot use these devices, and are aware of the consequences for not following the school policy. Third, be consistent in your enforcement, and students should be self-disciplined about the use of these devices.

If there is no school policy, it is useful to establish a policy for your classroom. For example, you may have a clear and consistent expectation that phones will be silenced during class and stored in a backpack, unless they are being used in classwork. To discourage cell phone use, teachers may require that backpacks be placed on the floor, and the teachers may walk around the room during class to monitor this. Moving around will also help teachers notice students using headphones for music.

Bullying

Bullying is when a person, or group of persons, uses power to harass or intimidate one or more people who have less power. Bullying takes the form of belittling weaker students, calling them names, and threatening or harassing them. For elementary students, the bully may be the student who pushes them out of the cafeteria line or bothers them on the school bus. For older students, bullying might even be in the form of harassment on the Internet through photographs or text messages (Hyman et al., 2006).

Characteristics of Bullying

Regardless of the type of bullying, three characteristics are apparent:

1. **Imbalance of power.** People who bully use their power to control or harm, and the people being bullied may have a hard time defending themselves.

2. **Intent to cause harm.** The person bullying has a goal to cause harm. Actions done by accident are not bullying.

3. **Repetition.** Incidents of bullying happen to the same person over and over by the same person or group.

Bullies may do many things to harass or dominate others, such as make verbal threats, boss people around, take people's money, put people down, make obscene gestures, attack people physically, intimidate people, gossip, leave people out, spread rumors, tease, hit, or hurt others in many possible ways.

There are no differences in rates of bullying for urban, suburban, or rural communities. The overall percentage of students being bullied does not vary based on school size, although bullying does happen more often in larger schools. Boys and girls are just as likely to be involved in bullying. However, forms of bullying vary by gender. Some research has found girls are more likely to bully others socially (U.S. Department of Education, 2011b).

Bullies tend to be average students academically. Bullies have an inflated self-concept but usually have low self-esteem or feel inferior to others, which reflects a strong need to dominate with threats. Bullies lack empathy for their victims and feel justified in their actions. Reciprocal aggressive behavior by the victim usually does not stop the bully (Khalsa, 2007a).

Bullying is most commonly learned, with modeling and reinforcement by parents and peers playing major roles and influences (Roberts, 2006). Bullies tend to come from homes whose parents are authoritarian, hostile, and rejecting. Parents may have poor problem-solving skills and use fighting as a solution to conflicts; their children then imitate these behaviors. Bullies are often emotionally underdeveloped, and they are unable to understand or empathize with others' perspectives or regulate their own behavior (Berk, 2013; Berk & Meyers, 2016).

People who bully take advantage of imbalances in power, such as greater size or strength, higher status, or the support of a peer group. Surveys indicate that nearly 75 percent of 8- to 11-year-olds and more than 85 percent of 12- to 15-year-olds report bullying at their school

(Roberts, 2006). In other studies, nearly one third of students reported that they had bullied, been a victim of bullying, or both within the last month (Viadero, 2003). Bullying is most prevalent at the middle school level, with more than 40 percent of students reporting at least one incident of bullying a week, compared to slightly more than 20 percent at both the elementary and high school levels (National Center for Education Statistics, 2007).

Incidents of bullying may actually be higher than reported because it most commonly occurs in areas where students interact informally, such as playgrounds, school buses, hallways, cafeterias, and places where they have little adult supervision (Siris & Osterman, 2004). Students are often hesitant to report bullying because they fear reprisals or don't want to appear weak or unable to solve their own social problems (Newman, 2008).

Effects of Bullying

Bullying has serious and long-lasting effects for both bullies and their victims. Students who are bullied have a higher risk of depression and anxiety that may persist into adulthood, including feelings of sadness and loneliness, changes in sleep and eating patterns, and loss of interest in activities. They are more likely to have health complaints, decreased academic achievement and school participation, and increased thoughts about suicide that may persist into adulthood; they are also more likely to skip or drop out of school, and to retaliate through extremely violent measures (Hoglund, 2007; U.S. Department of Education, 2011a).

People who bully others are more likely to get into fights, vandalize property, and drop out of school; have a higher risk of abusing alcohol and other drugs in adolescence and as adults; are more likely to engage in early sexual activity; are more likely to be abusive toward their romantic partners, spouses, or children as adults; and are more likely to have criminal convictions and traffic citations as adults (U.S. Department of Education, 2011a).

Bullying is linked to a number of antisocial and aggressive behaviors that can have negative consequences for bullies and their victims (Raskauskas & Stoltz, 2007). Studies suggest bullying is a major factor in many school-shooting incidents (Fast, 2008). Another study found that both bullies and victims were more likely to carry a weapon to school and become involved in serious fights (Viadero, 2003).

Types of Bullying

There are several types of bullying (S. Breakstone, M. Dreiblatt, & K. Dreiblatt, 2009; Khalsa, 2007a):

1. **Physical bullying** is action oriented. It includes hitting, shoving, kicking, pushing, spitting, or taking or damaging a person's property.

2. **Verbal bullying** involves the use of words to hurt or humiliate another person. It includes teasing, name-calling, insulting, put-downs, and making threats or rude comments.

3. **Relational bullying,** also known as social aggression, is the use of relationships to hurt others. It includes preventing people from playing with others, using the silent treatment, and spreading rumors and lies.

4. **Sexual bullying** involves hurtful teasing and comments about sexuality, sexual preference, physical development, and sexual experiences as a way to undermine an individual's self-esteem and self-confidence. Victims may even be physically threatened or injured. Some experts would not consider these actions sexual bullying; they would call them sexual harassment. Harassment of girls and young women ranges from name-calling to touching, and even rape. Lesbian, gay, bisexual, or transgender (LGBT) youth report

VOICES FROM THE CLASSROOM   Bullying Students Who Are LGBTQ

Ken Jackson, high school counselor, Atlanta, Georgia

Students who are lesbian, gay, bisexual, transgender, or queer/questioning (LGBTQ) are often the targets of bullies. Since these characteristics are not typically exhibited until adolescence, bullying of LGBTQ students occurs more often in middle school and high school.

I am a high school counselor, and I recently needed to address an incident with two students. Claudia is a self-identified lesbian, rather small in stature, and a relatively successful student taking advanced placement courses. One day, she approached me relatively timidly but very upset. She explained that she was experiencing harassment in one of her classes from a varsity football player. He was talking to her in class telling her to have sex with him, using explicit language to describe what he wanted them to do. He spoke softly so the teacher could not hear, and he had a female varsity athlete giving him support for his taunting. After Claudia kept refusing, the other student then began making statements about her being a lesbian and continued to mess with her.

As the school counselor, I gave Claudia some options and strategies. With her permission, I met with the classroom teacher to discuss how to help Claudia without making things more difficult since the teacher had not heard any of the remarks. The teacher decided to rearrange some classroom groupings to separate the students, place Claudia closer to the teacher's desk, and make the commitment to monitor students more closely. With these adjustments, Claudia felt that she could trust the teacher and go to the teacher for support should there be a recurrence. I followed up with Claudia several times to make sure she felt supported, and the situation had significantly improved.

verbal, sexual, and physical harassment that ends in physical assaults for one in five LGBT students. The most common harassment experienced by LGBT students is in the form of verbal abuse, with sexist and homophobic name-calling such as "faggot" or "dyke." These homophobic remarks are applied to both LGBT and non-LGBT students as derogatory terms meant to call into question a student's masculinity or femininity (Greytak, Kosciw, & Diaz, 2009).

5. **Cyberbullying** involves the use of technology to hurt or humiliate others. It includes using computers and the Internet, emails, cell phones, text messaging, Facebook, Weblogs, and digital photography to embarrass or exclude others. The anonymity of the Internet distinguishes cyberbullying from other types of bullying. This anonymity can make bullies even more insensitive to the hurtful nature of the bullying incidents (Willard, 2006). While cyberbullying is hard to measure, experts estimate that between 10 and 30 percent of students are victims of online harassment (Stobbe, 2007).

Confronting Bullying

Adult intervention is one of the best defenses against bullying. Teachers need to recognize the warning signs of bullying and intervene when it happens, sending the message that bullying is not acceptable. Although there is no set formula for how teachers should respond to bullying incidents, here are some actions to consider:

- **Intervene immediately.** Separate the students involved. Do not immediately ask about or discuss the reason for the bullying.

- **Get the facts.** Speak to the students involved, both participants and observers, and ask what happened. Request more information. Get all sides of the story before taking any action.

- **Tell the students you are aware of their behavior.** Talk to the students involved separately. Make it a teachable moment. Helping the students and bystanders understand what happened and why it happened may help prevent future incidents.

- **Consider an appropriate intervention.** Base your decision on the circumstances, the severity and history of the incident, and the students involved.

- **Follow up with the students.** Follow up on the incident and monitor the students involved to ensure the bullying does not continue.

- **Report the incident to the right person.** The school may have a reporting policy about bullying incidents, and a report may need to be submitted to the school administrator, a counselor, or a member of the school safety committee. This report will help the school track the incidents and the responses. Some states have laws that require incidences to be reported.

Teachers can take steps to deal with aggression and to encourage cooperation. Teachers can present themselves as a nonaggressive model. They can ensure that their classroom has enough space and appropriate materials for all students, thus minimizing the source of some conflicts. They can make sure students do not profit from aggressive behaviors by delivering appropriate consequences. They can teach directly about positive social behaviors. Teachers can also provide opportunities for learning tolerance and cooperation. Furthermore, states and school districts are developing safe school laws and policies that promote changing the behaviors of bullies. They include procedures for reporting and investigating incidents.

A number of books are available for teachers with information along with classroom activities and discussions to address bullying. These include *How to Stop Bullying and Social Aggression* (Breakstone et al., 2009), *No Kidding about Bullying* (Drew, 2010), *Break the Bully Cycle* (Khalsa, 2007), and *Bully Prevention* (Barton, 2006). Useful sources also include Coloroso (2015), Dillon (2012, 2015), Hoover and Oliver (2008), Kaiser and Raminsky (2017), and Swearer, Espelage, and Napolitano (2009). A search of the Internet will reveal a number of sources to address bullying.

MAJOR CONCEPTS

1. The principle of least intervention states that when dealing with routine classroom behavior, misbehavior should be corrected with the simplest, least intrusive intervention that will work. If that doesn't work, then move up to a more intrusive, directive approach.

2. Situational assistance is designed to help students cope with the instructional situation and to keep them on task.

3. Mild responses are nonpunitive ways to deal with misbehavior while providing guidance for appropriate behavior. Nonverbal and verbal approaches can be used.

4. Moderate responses deliver punishment by removing desired stimuli as a means of decreasing inappropriate behavior.

5. Research and practice suggest that some interventions are inappropriate or unsuccessful when trying to restore order, and these practices should be avoided.

6. Due to inherent problems in the use of punishment, teachers should follow certain guidelines when using punitive responses.

7. Chronic misbehaviors are troublesome behaviors that students repeatedly or compulsively perform. They include tattling, clowning, cheating, lying, stealing, profanity, rudeness toward the teacher, defiance or hostility, and failure to do schoolwork.

8. Bullying is when a person, or group of persons, uses power to harass or intimidate one or more people who have less power. Bullying may be physical, verbal, relational, sexual, or cyber.

DISCUSSION/REFLECTIVE QUESTIONS

1. What are some positive aspects of the principle of least intervention?

2. What are the benefits of providing situational assistance?

3. What student misbehaviors would you be willing to deliberately ignore for a short time? What situations would you not ignore?

4. What inappropriate interventions have you experienced or observed? What were the effects on the students?

5. Can chronic or challenging misbehaviors be adequately addressed in the three-step response plan shown in Table 11.1, which applies the principle of least intervention?

6. What difficulties might teachers experience when trying to identify and address problems with cyberbullying done by their students?

SUGGESTED ACTIVITIES

1. Ask several teachers to describe how they deal with misbehavior. Do they have an overall plan such as the principle of least intervention that escalates the interventions?

2. Identify examples of consequences and punishments that teachers might deliver. Determine where those actions fall in the three-step response plan and judge whether the punishments are appropriate.

3. Ask teachers what types of chronic misbehavior they encounter and discuss how they address these misbehaviors.

4. Search the topic of bullying on the Internet. From the many resources and the many topics, identify ten significant guidelines that teachers might follow in addressing bullying.

FURTHER READING

Burke, K. (2008). *What to do with the kid who . . . : Developing cooperation, self-discipline, and responsibility in the classroom* (3rd ed.). Thousand Oaks, CA: Corwin Press.

Examines ways to provide positive guidance for students for their behavior. Discusses setting the classroom climate, teaching social skills, teaching responsible behavior, and dealing with students with behavior problems or special needs. Includes useful lists and graphics.

Foley, D. (2012). *Ultimate classroom management handbook.* (2nd ed.). Indianapolis, IN: JIST Publishing.

Offers many practical suggestions concerning managing student behaviors, seat assignments, peer pressure, common problems, dealing with disruption, incentives, connecting with your students, preparing students for work, providing an environment for achievement, rewarding success, and managing the classroom.

Khalsa, S. (2007). *Break the bully cycle: Intervention techniques and activities to create a respectful school community.* Tucson, AZ: Good Year Books.

Describes bullying and offers suggestions for creating a respectful school community, helping the victims, helping the bullies, keeping schools safe, and addressing cyberbullying.

Thompson, J.G. (2011). *Discipline survival guide for the secondary teacher* (2nd ed.). San Francisco: Jossey-Bass.

Provides thorough coverage of many topics including developing a comprehensive plan for classroom management and discipline, developing a positive classroom environment, promoting self-discipline, maintaining order with effective instruction, and preventing and addressing misbehavior.

© Mike Abrahams/Alamy Limited

Dealing with Challenging or Violent Students

CHAPTER OUTLINE

CHAPTER OBJECTIVES

This chapter provides information that will help you:

- Identify characteristics of challenging and violent students.
- Develop a plan for working with challenging students in your classroom.

- Teach students alternatives to disruption and violence.
- Develop an action plan for responding to disruption in your classroom.
- Determine when and how to seek outside help.

It's bound to happen. You have planned an exciting lesson for your students, and two students who often cause disturbances create some problems partway through the lesson. You have to stop what you are doing to deal with these students. Since they don't respond well to some of your usual disciplinary techniques, you know that they will disturb tomorrow's class and that of the day after. Some of the students, in fact, may have a tendency to be physical and violent. What do you do with these challenging students?

The first step is to understand these challenging students—their behaviors and the influences on their behaviors. Next, you need to make a commitment and a plan to work with them. Furthermore, you can teach students alternatives to disruption and violence. Finally, you need to be ready to respond to disruptive or violent behavior if it does occur.

Understanding Challenging and Violent Students

Challenging students are constantly disruptive, demand attention, openly confront your authority, or do not complete any assigned work. They disrupt learning, interfere with the work of others, and may prompt other students to misbehave. Your regular classroom management system may not work with challenging students. Before considering how to deal with these students, it is helpful to identify the behaviors challenging students actually exhibit, recognize influences that may have contributed to the development of the difficult behaviors, and understand that the behaviors of challenging students may be the early signs of serious problems.

Behaviors

According to R. L. Curwin, A. N. Mendler, and B. D. Mendler (2008), 80 percent of students rarely break classroom rules, 15 percent break rules on a somewhat regular basis, and 5 percent are chronic rule breakers and are generally out of control most of the time. Rhode, Jenson, and Reavis (2010) estimate that about 2 to 5 percent of all students meet their definition of a *tough kid* who has excessive noncompliant and aggressive behavior or behavior deficits in self-management, social, and academic skills. In some school environments, percentages for difficult students may be even higher. Tough kids who persistently break rules and sometimes become involved in serious misbehavior are an ongoing challenge in the classroom.

Characteristic behaviors of challenging and violent students are outlined in Table 10.1. These include *behavior excesses* where students do too much of a behavior. This may include noncompliance and aggression. The behaviors also include *behavior deficits* where students are unable to adequately perform a behavior (e.g., self-management, social skills, and academic skills).

Schools reflect society. If there are problems in the school community, similar problems may show up in schools. Violent or challenging students may be involved with thefts, robbery, assaults, bullying, gangs, drugs, hate-related words or graffiti, fights, weapons, illegal substances,

■ TABLE 10.1   Characteristic Behaviors of Challenging or Violent Students

1. Behavior Excesses: Too Much of a Behavior
   a. Noncompliance
      (1) Does not do what is requested
      (2) Breaks rules
      (3) Argues
      (4) Makes excuses
      (5) Delays
      (6) Does the opposite of what is asked
   b. Aggression
      (1) Tantrums
      (2) Fights
      (3) Destroys property
      (4) Teases
      (5) Verbally abuses
      (6) Is cruel to others
2. Behavior Deficits: Inability to Adequately Perform a Behavior
   a. Self-management skills
      (1) Cannot delay rewards
      (2) Acts before thinking; impulsive
      (3) Shows little remorse or guilt
      (4) Will not follow rules
      (5) Cannot foresee consequences
   b. Social skills
      (1) Has few friends
      (2) Goes through friends fast
      (3) Noncooperative; bossy
      (4) Lacks affection
      (5) Has few problem-solving skills
      (6) Constantly seeks attention
   c. Academic skills
      (1) Generally behind in academics, particularly reading
      (2) Off task
      (3) Fails to finish work
      (4) Truant or frequently tardy
      (5) Forgets acquired information easily

alcohol, and marijuana. However, many indicators of school crime and safety show a *decrease* in recent years in the occurrence of many indicators (National Center for Education Statistics [NCES], 2010). The most serious forms of violence (robbery, aggravated assault, homicide, rape, and sexual assault) rarely occur in schools (Centers for Disease Control and Prevention, 2007). There are schools where violence and fear are prevalent, but these schools are the exception rather than the rule.

Here are some crime and safety indicators for schools in the United States (NCES, 2010):

- **Victims.** The overall percentage of students ages 12–18 who were victimized at school decreased between 1995 and 2005 from 10 to 4 percent. (Theft was the most frequent type.)

- **Victims.** In 2007, 4 percent of students ages 12–18 reported being victimized at school during the previous six months. About 3 percent of students reported theft, 2 percent reported violent victimization, and less than half a percent reported serious violent victimization. (*Violent crimes* include violent incidents and simple assault. *Serious violent crimes* include rape, sexual assault, robbery, and aggravated assault.)

- **Victims.** In 2007, 75 percent of public schools recorded one or more violent incidents of crime, 17 percent recorded one or more serious violent incidents, and 47 percent recorded one or more thefts.

- **Gangs.** In 2007, 23 percent of students reported that there were gangs at their schools during the school year. A higher level was reported for grades 9–12.

- **Drugs.** The percentage of students in grades 9–12 who reported that drugs were offered, sold, or given to them decreased from 32 percent in 1995 to 23 percent in 2009.

- **Hate language.** In 2007, 10 percent of students ages 12–18 reported that someone at school had used hate-related words against them, and 35 percent had seen hate-related graffiti at school.

- **Bullying.** In 2007, about 32 percent of 12- to 18-year-old students reported having been bullied at school during the school year and 4 percent reported having been cyberbullied.

- **Fights.** The percentage of students in grades 9 through 12 who reported being in a physical fight on school property decreased between 1993 and 2009 from 16 to 11 percent.

- **Weapons.** Between 1993 and 2009, the percentage of students in grades 9–12 who reported carrying a weapon at least one day anywhere during the past 30 days declined from 22 to 17 percent, and the percent carrying a weapon on school property declined from 12 to 16 percent.

- **Alcohol.** In 2009, about 42 percent of students in grades 9–12 reported having at least one drink of alcohol anywhere in the past 30 days, while 4 percent had at least one drink on school property.

- **Marijuana.** In 2009, 21 percent of students in grades 9–12 reported using marijuana anywhere at least one time in the past 30 days, while 5 percent reported using marijuana at least one time on school property.

- **Fear.** In 2007, approximately 5 percent of students ages 12–18 reported that they were afraid of attack or harm at school.

There are many useful websites providing information to help understand disruptive and violent student behavior and providing guidance about solutions. Some sites are Safe Schools and Violence Prevention Office (www.cde.ca.gov/ls/ss), the National School Safety Center (www.schoolsafety.us), and Stop Bullying (www.stopbullying.gov).

Influences

In many of these students, there are underlying influences that may contribute to their persistent misbehavior. Many of these students come from homes where they have been emotionally or physically abused or neglected. Some of them may have had traumatic childhoods as a result of suffering from organic conditions, such as attention deficit-hyperactivity disorder (estimated to affect 4 percent of school-age children), fetal alcohol syndrome, or the effects of being born to mothers addicted to cocaine. Some of the students may live in a home environment where one or more adults are addicted to alcohol, crack, or other drugs. Many students come from home environments where parents have little influence or control over their children's behavior.

Many students who chronically misbehave come from home environments in which the parents themselves have had a negative school experience. The student then carries this distrust to school with the expectation that school will not be a positive experience. The student also may have limited trust in adults and teachers. Thus, the student enters school with negative influences and expectations. Every failure diminishes his or her self-esteem and often leads to anger and distrust. These are the difficult students, the tough kids who must be reached. Some students may have emotional and behavioral problems that contribute to their challenging actions (Cole & Shupp, 2012).

The risk of violent behavior in schools is heightened with the increased occurrence of gangs and weapons. A street gang is a group of people who form an allegiance for a common purpose and engage in violent, unlawful, and criminal activity. Many gang members are of school age, and when they come to school, confrontations often arise.

Schools have struggled over how to address the influence of gangs. Strategies fall into three categories: (1) prevention—stopping the problem before it begins by teaching children skills so they will never become violent; (2) intervention—singling out those kids who have shown violent behavior and working one on one to change their ways; and (3) suppression—keeping weapons out of schools by using police-style tactics to make schools safe. Many educators maintain that we must teach children how to avoid violence—how to keep conflicts from escalating, how to deal with anger, how to recognize dangerous situations, and how to avoid weapons. Resources are available for dealing with gangs and school violence (Jimerson, Nickerson, Mayer, & Furlong, 2012).

Early Signs of Serious Problems

Some of the behaviors exhibited by challenging students are troublesome while others are quite serious. Aggressive behaviors such as fighting, throwing tantrums, vandalizing, stealing, and exhibiting abusive behavior very seriously affect the student and the learning environment. Because of the immediacy of the events, you cannot ignore these actions. Immediate attention is needed.

Some challenging students, however, exhibit behaviors that may not demand immediate attention, yet they also may be a sign of serious problems. A student who does not comply with directions, has limited self-management skills, or has limited social or academic skills may be considered a challenging student. Whether overtly aggressive or passively noncompliant, challenging students exhibit behaviors that can disrupt their learning and that of others. Some students may show early signs of serious problems through their behavior in the following ways.

1. **Changes in physical appearance.** Students may reveal underlying problems through sudden changes in their physical appearance. This may be evident in deterioration in posture, dress, and grooming habits, or in changes in weight. Bruises and cuts may be signals of abuse, neglect, or even self-mutilation.

2. **Changes in activity level.** Excessive tardiness, lethargy, absenteeism, and sleepiness may result from various problems, including depression and substance abuse. Students may also deal with problems by exhibiting hyperactivity, overaggressiveness, impulsivity, or lowered frustration and tolerance levels.

3. **Changes in personality.** When students experience emotional disturbances, they may express uncharacteristic personality characteristics. These may include sudden expressions of sadness, easy agitation, or anger.

■ TABLE 10.2   Early and Imminent Warning Signs of Violence

Early Warning Signs
- Social withdrawal
- Excessive feelings of isolation and being alone
- Excessive feelings of rejection
- Being a victim of violence
- Feelings of being picked on and persecuted
- Low school interest and poor academic performance
- Expression of violence in writings and drawings
- Uncontrolled anger
- Patterns of impulsive and chronic hitting, intimidating, and bullying behaviors
- History of discipline problems
- Past history of violent and aggressive behavior
- Intolerance for differences and prejudicial attitudes
- Drug use and alcohol use
- Affiliation with gangs
- Inappropriate access to, possession of, and use of firearms
- Serious threats of violence

Imminent Signs of Violence
- Serious physical fighting with peers or family members
- Severe destruction of property
- Severe rage for seemingly minor reasons
- Detailed threats of lethal violence
- Possession or use of firearms and other weapons
- Other self-injurious behaviors or threats of suicide

4. **Changes in achievement.** When students are dealing with problems, they may have a decline in their ability to focus on the school activities, to complete the activities, or to perform at their previous achievement level.

5. **Changes in health or physical abilities.** Complaints about frequent headaches, stomachaches, dizziness, unhealed sores, and frequent bathroom use lead to a concern about a student's health. These changes may be an indication of other difficulties the student is experiencing.

6. **Changes in socialization.** Although students who are suddenly quiet and withdrawn may not cause disruption in the classroom, this change might signal a problem in the student's life that may be later expressed in more outward and potentially disruptive behavior. Contributing factors to these changes could be very serious and beyond your influence to address or remedy. You should be prepared to contact other specialized professionals in an effort to help students who show signs of serious problems. Professionals may include counselors, psychologists, nurses, social workers, or even police officers. It is often helpful to consult with the school principal before making contacts with those outside the school.

Students who are prone to violent behaviors often exhibit a number of behaviors prior to any violent acts. The U.S. Department of Education and the Department of Justice published a guide for schools (Dwyer & Osher, 2000; Dwyer, Osher, & Warger, 1998) that contains a list of early warning signs that can alert teachers to a student's potential to violence, as well as signs that violence is imminent (see Table 10.2).

Planning to Work with Challenging and Violent Students

Many schools have taken actions to address violent behavior with formal violence prevention programs, increased school security, zero-tolerance policies, and programs in character development, problem resolution, and anger control. To be successful with challenging and possibly violent students in your own classroom, you must assume responsibility for addressing the situation and take steps to have the student behave within acceptable limits (Applebaum, 2009; L. Canter & M. Canter, 2008; Kaiser & Rasminsky, 2017; Mendler & Curwin, 2007). Resources such as *Motivating Defiant and Disruptive Students to Learn* (Korb, 2012) link motivation with classroom management and discipline strategies. There are several things that you could do to meet that challenge.

1. **Establish rules, procedures, consequences, and reinforcements for the classroom.** It is vital to develop a comprehensive classroom management and discipline system for all students in the classroom. This is the foundation for any additional actions that you need to take when addressing the special challenges of working with difficult students.

2. **Make a commitment to help challenging students succeed.** These students are sometimes accustomed to teachers trying to help them but then later giving up. Actually giving up on the student only reinforces and perpetuates the problem behavior; it will not go away without intervention. The inappropriate behavior will continue unless you make the commitment to help the challenging student.

   In doing so, you must clearly communicate your concern to these students. They must know that you will do everything possible to help them succeed. Since you may not be in a position to change any of the underlying contributing factors for the misbehavior, you should focus on the inappropriate classroom behaviors. This commitment is a vital step in overcoming problem behaviors.

3. **Establish a plan to deal with each challenging student.** Because there are different types of challenging students, you may need to use a different approach with each type. In addition, each student has his or her own personality, academic history, and circumstances to be considered. For these reasons, it is helpful to establish a plan to deal with the unique characteristics of each challenging student.

   Handling each incident as a separate act is not sufficient. Preplanned, sequential actions are needed to address the problem behaviors systematically. Approaches to be used in the classroom as part of this plan are addressed in the next section. Fortunately, some useful guidelines and materials are available (e.g., Colvin & Scott, 2015; Jenson, Rhode, & Reavis, 2009; Morgan, Young, West, & Smith, 2012; Rhode et al., 2010).

4. **Keep documentation and anecdotal records.** It is important to keep a written record of the incidents of misbehavior and the actions you have taken in a separate folder for each challenging student. This documentation will help you see any patterns in the behavior. If at a later point you need to consult the parents, principal, counselor, psychologist, or others about the student, this documentation will help them better understand the nature and scope of the problems.

   There are several types of documentation. First, keep a written *anecdotal record* to document specific events of misbehavior. An anecdote is a brief, narrative description of an incident. Anecdotal records can be quite simple in design and may include a column format on a page. Information that is recorded should include the student's name, the date and time of the incident, the location of the incident, a brief description of the student's behavior, and a brief description of your response.

   Second, you might ask the student to fill out an *incident reaction sheet* outlining an incident of misbehavior. Students could write this while in time-out. The incident reaction sheet provides the student with an opportunity to evaluate his or her behavioral choices while calming down. Questions may require the student to describe the rule that was broken, why the student chose to misbehave, who was bothered by the misbehavior, what more appropriate behavior could be chosen next time, and what should happen to the student next time the misbehavior occurs. This reaction sheet should be kept on file as documentation of the incident, and it may be shown to others such as the family, principal, or counselor as the need warrants.

   Third, keep a record of any *one-on-one meetings* with the student as a means to document the series of interactions and decisions that were made in consultation with the student.

Two students in your classroom are involved in a heated argument about a lost notebook. One student has no previous problems in class, whereas the second student has had a series of difficulties getting along with others in the classroom.

1. Will you make a written anecdotal record of this incident for both students' files?

2. What factors will you take into account as you decide whether or not to have a written record?

3. Why is it important to have a written record of certain incidents?

Fourth, keep a copy of any *behavioral contracts* that were developed with the student or in consultation with others.

In addition to these four types of documentation, your folder of documentation might include notes or records of phone conversations concerning the student.

5. **Focus attention on preventing disturbing or violent behavior.** Think comprehensively about prevention strategies. These may include teaching students alternatives to disruption and violence, knowing the early warning signs for violent behavior, being attentive to student interactions, building a positive classroom community, and taking actions to de-escalate confrontational situations.

6. **Make plans for ways to respond to disruptive or violent behavior.** Decide how you will address aggressive behavior and even how you will respond to physical fights. Thinking about these issues in advance will enable you to make quick, appropriate decisions in the event of an incident.

Teaching Students Alternatives to Disruption and Violence

When confronted with a challenging conflict, students may not have the skills to defuse a situation and thus may resort to disruption and violence as a first step. Students, however, can be taught strategies that emphasize self-control and problem solving. Students can be taught ways to deal with anger, use problem-solving strategies, and use new behavioral skills such as social skills, conflict resolution skills, and self-management skills. By using these skills, students are less likely to exhibit disruptive behaviors or become violent.

Dealing with Anger

Anger is a feeling indicating the person feels frustrated and thwarted. Everybody gets angry at some time or other, and figuring out what to do with anger is the tough part. Hidden anger often leads people to a breaking point where they explode with pent-up feelings, but letting anger get out of hand also can lead to many problems. In the classroom, help students manage anger constructively, calm their own anger, and deal with other people's anger (Gootman, 2008).

Managing Anger Constructively

People who are angry may take actions without thinking much about the situation. Here are some ways to manage anger constructively (D. W. Johnson & R. T. Johnson, 2005):

1. **Recognize and acknowledge your anger.** Anger is a natural, normal human feeling. It does not need to be feared or rejected. Repressed anger does not vanish: It may erupt suddenly in physical or verbal assaults or as overreactions to minor provocations. Recognize how you get angered and what your responses are.

VOICES FROM THE CLASSROOM   Guidelines for Working with Challenging Students

Michael Abbott, teacher in an alternative high school, Livonia, Michigan

Our alternative high school has a high percentage of students who would be considered at risk and challenging to work with. There is a sign in the school that says, "Soft on people, hard on issues." Probably nothing has helped me in my relationships with my students as much as this simply stated philosophy. To me, it says a great deal about human relationships and provides the following guidance as I work with challenging students:

- Self-esteem is easily damaged.
- People respond well to gentleness.
- It is not necessary to be cruel to be effective.
- People respond well if they know the issues.
- Expectations must be clear.
- Anticipate problems (be proactive rather than reactive).
- State consequences before anything has happened.
- Be consistent.
- Follow through.

2. **Decide whether or not to express your anger.** You may find something upsetting, but you may or may not want to express your anger. Clarify the situation to be certain someone has done something aggressive or provocative in nature. Then decide whether to express your anger directly or keep it hidden. Detach and let go if you decide not to express your anger.

3. **Express your anger directly and descriptively when it is appropriate to do so.** Express your anger to the appropriate person and make your point in descriptive, accurate, and brief terms as a means to describe your concerns and to lay the groundwork for settling the difficulty.

4. **When direct expression is not appropriate, express your anger indirectly or react in an alternative way.** When not expressing anger openly, you may still have feelings that need to be expressed. This can be done privately by some verbal or physical expression, physical exercise, psychological detachment, or relaxation.

5. **When the other person is angry, focus on the task or issue.** You can control and contain your anger and better manage the situation by staying focused on the goal to be achieved, not on what the other person is saying or doing.

6. **Analyze, understand, and reflect on your anger.** Get to know yourself so that you recognize the events and behaviors that trigger your behavior and the internal signs that signal you are becoming angry. This will help you understand your anger and stop anger before it develops.

Calming One's Own Anger

There are many easy-to-learn things that make it possible to calm yourself when you are angry (Curwin & Mendler, 1997). These include the following:

1. **Count from 1 to 10.** Plan on this counting before doing anything when you are upset. You may repeat this counting if you are still feeling angry. What did you say or do to the person who upset you? After the counting, how did your feelings change?

2. **Count from 10 to 1.** Counting backward from 10 to 1 works the same way as counting from 1 to 10, but just in reverse order.

3. **Count backward by 5, starting at 100.** This type of counting requires a little more thinking and thus helps calm the anger.

4. **Breathe in deeply.** Just breathe in deeply and then let the air out slowly. Repeat this several times. By focusing on your deep breathing for three to five minutes, you can calm your anger.

5. **Breathe in deeply and count together.** This approach combines deep breathing and counting. Silently say the number "one" each time you exhale. Doing this for two minutes or more can slow down and calm the anger.

6. **Count by fives and breathe.** This is similar to the exercise in which you say "one" when exhaling. In this exercise, you silently count to five while inhaling, count to five while briefly holding your breath, and count to five while exhaling.

7. **Use calming words.** Many students find that they can calm themselves down by silently saying words that make them feel better. This approach could be combined with deep breathing. For example, students might think of words such as *calm down*, *chill out*, *stay cool*, or *relax*. Students could silently say the first word (e.g., *calm*) when inhaling and the second word (e.g., *down*) when exhaling. This can be repeated several times.

Dealing with Another Person's Anger

It is important to not let other people's anger make you angry. There are many things you can do to keep calm when someone is bothering or threatening you. Here are some ways to respond to other people's anger constructively (D. W. Johnson & R. T. Johnson, 2005):

1. **Let others feel angry.** Remember that anger is a natural human feeling, and that everyone feels angry at some time. It is better for the anger to be expressed than hidden, as long as there is no violence or aggression.

2. **Don't get angry back.** When another person is angry, the first step is to control your own feelings. Losing your temper will only escalate the problem.

3. **Recognize that the use of aggression by the other person is an expression of feeling weak and helpless.** The angry person probably does not know what to do when angry and thus may be aggressive. Help the person back off, cool down, and try something else.

4. **Focus attention on the task, not on the anger.** Focus both your attention and the attention of the angry person on the task to be completed. Don't get sidetracked or baited into a quarrel when the other person is angry.

5. **Explain the situation.** Your explanation of the situation can help the angry person see the circumstances from a new perspective, understand the cause of his or her anger, and lead to calming of the anger.

Techniques for Solving Problems

In addition to dealing with anger, students need to be good at figuring out how to solve problems that they have or that others give them. When students confront a conflict, they need problem-solving strategies to help them act effectively without doing damage to themselves or others. Students can use a 10-step process for dealing with problem situations before they do something hurtful to themselves or others (Curwin & Mendler, 1997).

VOICES FROM THE CLASSROOM   Dealing with an Angry Student

Lynne Hagar, high school history and English teacher, Mesquite, Texas

John walked into my classroom at the start of the school year ready to fight me all the way. This pugnacious redhead walked, talked, and acted tough as nails, but when I spoke to him sharply, he blushed.

How should I handle this firecracker of a student? Experience had taught me that a lot of love and consistency would solve many of his problems. I tried to react calmly to John's insulting comments, trusting that once he began to respond to my teaching, he would show more respect. When he became disruptive, I asked him privately to tell me if I had done something to offend him or to lose his respect. John was surprised that a teacher would be concerned about the reasons for his behavior and astonished that I had admitted I was capable of doing something wrong.

Once we had a basis for our relationship, I found something to say to John every day—not necessarily a compliment, just an acknowledgment that I recognized he was there. I tried my best to really listen when John talked to me, making eye contact and coming close to his desk. Sometimes I touched his arm in a friendly way when he entered the room, or laid my hand on his shoulder as I passed his seat. I put long comments on his papers and added stickers when his work began to show improvement.

I soon realized that John attended school every day without fail; it was the best place in his life—the only place where he felt safe enough to express his feelings. I gave John opportunities to let his anger out on paper and to write about his feelings. I found out about things he was proud of and then built writing lessons around subjects such as rodeo-riding and fast cars.

There's something about struggling with a difficult student and succeeding in gaining his or her trust that gives a teacher a special warmth for that student. It's very rewarding in a unique way.

1. **Stop and calm down.** Give yourself time to think and respond when something upsetting occurs. Pay attention to the signs that your body gives you when it feels tense. If angered, use some technique previously discussed to calm your anger.

2. **Identify what the problem is.** Clarify your concerns in specific, behavioral terms. Think about the causes of the problem, who was involved, and whether you contributed to the problem in some way. Consider whether you need to talk to others to help come up with a solution.

3. **Decide on your goal.** Determine specifically what you want to have happen.

4. **Think of as many solutions to the problem as you can.** Brainstorm about the many different actions you can choose to take to solve the problem.

5. For each possible solution, think of all the things that might happen next. Anticipate consequences for these possible solutions.

6. **Choose the best solution.** From your list of possible solutions, select one solution that has the most desired consequences.

7. **Choose a back-up solution in case the first one doesn't work out.** Always have a back-up plan ready. You need to have at least one more possible solution ready in case the first one doesn't work out.

8. **Plan your solution and make a final check.** Mentally rehearse when, where, and how a best solution will be implemented. Also anticipate potential obstacles and how to deal with them.

9. **Carry out your solution.** Carry out your decision and see how it works. If it does not work, then try another solution.

10. **Evaluate.** When evaluating your decision making concerning a particular problem, there are three important questions to consider: Did I reach my goal? If the same problem occurs again, what will I do? Are there any people (parents, friends, and teacher) who might help me as I figure out the best solution?

Developing New Behavioral Skills

Another way to help students seek alternatives to disruption and violence is to teach them new behavioral skills that help them effectively function in the classroom. A number of authors have developed programs in which students are taught new behavioral skills, such as social skills, conflict resolution skills, and self-management skills. Although it is beyond the scope of this book to provide a detailed description of each of these programs, a brief description is provided for a representative sample of the available programs.

- **Social skills.** Cooperative skills are those that help students get along socially. These skills include communication, cooperation, problem solving, conflict resolution, and team building. Burke (2008) provides comprehensive descriptions and specific activities to teach cooperative social skills to K–12 students. Her program addresses basic interactions, communication skills, team-building skills, and conflict resolution. Separate sections of Burke's book discuss students who have trouble accepting responsibility, students who need help with their inter-personal skills, students with behavior problems, and students with special needs. Activity descriptions, checklists, forms, and related transparency masters are included.

- **Conflict resolution and self-management skills.** Some programs provide a set of individual or interactive activities for students to complete to develop self-management and conflict resolution skills (e.g., Henley, 2003; Morgan et al., 2012).

  Conflict resolution programs help students develop skills to deal with conflicts they might experience in the classroom. Conflict resolution programs typically involve instruction about the steps in dealing with conflict and the related skills necessary to work through the conflicts (Winslade & Williams, 2011). In *Creating the Peaceable School*, Bodine, Crawford, and Schrumpf (2003) organize their instruction of the skills into the following units: building a peaceable climate, understanding conflict, understanding peace and peacemaking, mediation, negotiation, and group problem solving. They also offer guidance for professional development of the staff and implementation of the program.

■ WHAT WOULD YOU DECIDE?   Teaching Students Conflict Resolution and Self-Management Skills

Students in your fourth-grade class seem to have disagreements all the time. Even during recess and noninstructional time, they pick at each other and say mean things. They don't seem to have the social skills and the ability to settle disagreements in a reasonable manner. You've reached the point where something must be done. You decide to find instructional materials to teach your students how to deal with conflicts themselves.

1. After selecting some ready-made instructional lessons on conflict resolution (e.g., Bodine, Crawford, & Schrumpf,

2003), you must take class time for this instruction and the student interaction. How can you justify taking time away from content instruction?

2. Why don't teachers teach some of these skills even when there are no major problems?

3. What is the value of teaching conflict resolution and self-management skills?

- **Reducing school violence through conflict resolution.** D. W. Johnson and R. T. Johnson (2005) also offer specific guidance to help students deal with conflicts in a constructive manner. In *Teaching Students to be Peacemakers* (2005), D. W. Johnson and R. T. Johnson examine conflicts in a comprehensive way and then provide guidance in teaching students skills in the following areas: negotiating, conflict strategies, managing anger, mediating conflicts, managing developmental conflicts, and peacemaking. Conoley and Goldstein (2004) also provide abundant guidance for school violence intervention.

Responding to Disruptive or Violent Behavior

Teachers who have a plan to respond to disruptive or violent behavior are often more successful than teachers who do not have a plan. Without a plan, teachers continually feel stressed and ill-equipped to deal with challenging students, and this may contribute to teachers leaving teaching. A number of specific approaches can be used to respond to disruptive behavior (Colvin & Scott, 2015). Outside help is available if necessary.

Approaches to Use in the Classroom

The goal is to help challenging students be successful. To achieve that goal, you need to be committed to a preplanned, sequential set of actions to have the student stop misbehaving and get back on task. A set of actions is discussed here to achieve that goal. Communication with parents is vital when dealing with difficult students. One of the following steps is to consult and inform parents, but this contact can occur at any point as the need warrants, even when you are assessing the situation.

Assess the Situation

Before taking any actions to remedy the situation, it is vital to gather information and be reflective about the student, the behaviors, the environment, and yourself.

1. **Find out about the characteristics of the challenging students and the influences in their lives.** In this way, you will have a better understanding of the students, and this information may help you decide on appropriate actions to help the student succeed. You may obtain this information by talking with the student, through a questionnaire about interests, by asking other teachers who come in contact with the student, or other means.

2. **Examine your classroom management system.** This is a necessary step to see if there are any factors in the classroom contributing to the misbehavior of challenging students. This should include a review of rules and their consequences, procedures, space usage, motivation, lesson delivery, reinforcement, and efforts to monitor students and promote cooperation.

3. **Analyze the problem behavior and your response.** It is important to identify precisely what the student is doing to create a problem. Some of the student behaviors may be similar to those listed in Table 10.1. Various checklists and observation systems are available to help record the behaviors (Rhode et al., 2010). One useful format is to list the type of student behavior and your related response.

   This step of looking at your own actions can be quite enlightening. To borrow from William Glasser (1969), ask, "What am I doing? Is it working?" If it is not working, stop doing it! When asking these questions, your attention is focused on selecting an appropriate, workable response. By looking at the student's behaviors and your related responses, you can often determine the reason for the misbehavior. You then can act in ways not to reinforce the motive behind the student's misbehavior.

This step of self-examination can help determine if your expectations of the student are reasonable. For example, many individual differences may be apparent in students in your class due to factors such as ethnicity, learning styles, academic ability, language, disabling conditions, socioeconomic status, and at-risk status. When considering students who are different from you, it is important to maintain reasonable expectations given their characteristics. Just because a student is different doesn't mean that he or she is a behavioral problem.

Meet with the Student

Some consequences used to stop misbehavior may have only short-term effects with challenging students. These students need help in making better decisions about their behavior. Thus, a one-to-one conference with the student is needed when the behavior is chronic or serious, or if there is a sudden change in behavior. The purpose of the conference is to provide caring and guidance to the student. You should listen to the student's concerns, firmly clarify your own expectations, and then work together to arrive at a practical course of action. There are several guidelines to consider when meeting with the student (L. Canter & M. Canter, 2008).

1. **Meet with the student privately.** The conference should be confidential, and there should be no other students around to overhear or disrupt the meeting. The conference should also be brief, with a maximum of 10–15 minutes.

2. **Show empathy and concern.** The conference is intended to help the student explore alternative, more appropriate behaviors. Therefore, you should help the student gain insight into his or her present behavior and choose more responsible behavior. The student should understand that this meeting is to help him or her, rather than punish. The student should also know that you are concerned and that you care.

3. **Question the student to find out why there is a problem.** It is important to listen to the student's point of view rather than assume you know why the student is misbehaving. Question the student about what the problem may be. It might be that the work is too hard or that there is something happening at home or with other students who are contributing to the misbehavior.

    Questions should be stated in a caring, nonaccusational manner. Avoid questions such as "What is your problem?" Instead, use questions such as "Did something happen today to get you so upset?" or "Can you tell me what's causing you to be so upset?" After asking the question, listen carefully to the student and don't interrupt. Let the student talk. By doing so, you will have more information and fuller understanding of the student and the circumstances that contribute to the misbehavior.

4. **Determine what you can do to help.** Based on the answers to your earlier questions, you may discover there is a simple method to get the student back on track, such as moving his or her seat away from another student. In most cases, however, the solution is more difficult to find.

■ WHAT WOULD YOU DECIDE?   Meeting with a Disruptive Student

A student has been misbehaving in your class, primarily due to limited self-management and social skills. It has reached the point where you decide that a special, private meeting is warranted to express your concern, provide guidance, clarify your expectations, and seek a practical course of action to overcome the problems.

1. What materials might you need to gather, and how might you prepare for this meeting?

2. How might you prepare for and conduct the meeting differently if the student instead showed behavior excesses such as noncompliance and aggression?

5. **Determine how the student can improve his or her behavior.** Part of the meeting should focus on what the student can choose to do differently in the future to avoid problem behaviors. Talk about the situation and listen to the student's input.

   At this time, it may be necessary to reteach appropriate behaviors for certain classroom activities. Most students need only a single explanation of procedures for classroom activities such as independent seatwork, discussion, cooperative groups, and entering and leaving the room. Other more difficult students need to be taught how to behave and be reminded often. While you will have previously taught appropriate procedures to the entire class, this one-to-one meeting with the difficult student provides an opportunity to reteach and clarify these procedures and expectations.

6. **State your expectations about how the student is to behave.** The student must understand that you are very serious about not allowing the misbehavior to continue. While expressing a caring attitude to work with the student to solve the problem, the student must realize that predetermined consequences will be used if he or she chooses to continue to misbehave. Therefore, near the end of the meeting, you might say something like: "I'm going to work with you to solve this problem. I know that you can behave responsibly. But you must remember that fighting is not acceptable. Anytime you choose to fight, you will be choosing to go to the principal."

7. **Disarm criticism.** Some difficult students may become argumentative and critical and may actually blame you for all the problems they have in class. In that case, take steps to disarm the criticism by letting the student speak. Also, ask the student for more information concerning why he or she is upset with you. This approach can help calm the student down, and he or she will see you as being concerned. This additional information will likely help address the problem.

8. **Document the meeting.** In addition to anecdotal records you keep concerning the student's behavior in class, it is important to keep records of any one-to-one meeting you have with the student. This documentation should include the date of the meeting, a summary of the ideas generated in the meeting, and any conclusions that were drawn.

Consult and Inform Others

You may want to consult with others to get more information or advice about how to deal with the challenging student in the classroom. The principal, school counselor, psychologist, or other teachers who currently or previously came in contact with the student may be consulted for more information. They could also share their experiences in dealing with the student and perhaps offer recommendations for strategies that you could take in the classroom. The student's family members are also a source of information about the student. Consultations are intended to help you deal with the student in the classroom; no referrals for outside services are made at this point.

   Rather than wait until the behavior becomes very serious, inform the principal or family members about the problems. They will then know what you are doing and may be able to support you as the situation warrants. If the problems become more serious, the principal and family will appreciate this earlier contact rather than being surprised by a crisis at a later time. At a later time, the principal and parents may be involved in actions to address the problems if they persist or become more severe.

Provide Positive Support

Students need to receive reinforcement for their appropriate behavior through social reinforcers, activities and privileges, tangible reinforcers, and token reinforcers. Reinforcement encourages the student to continue the rewarded behavior. Challenging students especially need to be reinforced for their appropriate behavior. Even though it may be easy to overlook delivering reinforcement to difficult students, they need to receive their fair share of rewards for their appropriate behavior. You may choose to make notes in your plan book as reminders to reinforce difficult students at regular intervals.

Challenging students need to receive additional positive support beyond what is given to all students in the class (Canter, 2010; Rhode et al., 2010). One way is to call the student at home before the school year begins. (You will know which students to call based on information you hear from the student's teachers from the previous year.) In this way, you can ask the student for ideas about how the school year could be successful and to express your confidence that you and the student will work together to have a good year.

You could contact the student's family to express your caring about their child, get input about the student's experiences the previous year, get input on what the child needs from you this year, emphasize that the student will be most successful if you and the family work together, and express confidence that by working together the child will have a more successful experience at school. This early contact helps build a positive relationship with the family before problems arise.

Another approach that can be used with all students but is especially useful with challenging students is to have them fill out a student interest inventory at the start of the school year. Based on the questions you ask and the responses provided, you will have a fuller understanding of the student's interests. Furthermore, personal attention and welcoming words should be given to the challenging child when coming into the classroom. If problems occur during the day, you could call the student at home in the evening to express concern and inquire about the problem.

Relating to the student as an individual is important. Take time to talk with the student or involve yourself with him or her in school activities. The individual attention of a caring adult can make a big difference. Visiting the student at home is another way of showing your concern.

■ CLASSROOM CASE STUDY   A Class with a History of Disruption

David DeFranco had some concerns when preparing his fifth-grade classroom for the new school year. This particular class of students had a reputation from their previous grades for teasing, arguing, insulting, and pushing each other to the limits. Mr. DeFranco followed the guidelines for effectively starting the school year by making management and instructional preparations, establishing rules and procedures, and so on.

Despite his preparation and guidance, within a couple weeks his students started to exhibit the same challenging behaviors he heard from the students' previous teachers. They argued with each other and just didn't seem to like or respect each other. This led to disturbances and conflicts during instructional time and also transition times. Three students, in particular, seemed to be the ones encouraging this disruptive behavior by needling others and provoking reactions. All of this led to a significant decrease in quality instructional time, and the classroom atmosphere always seemed tense since another disruption could occur at any moment.

Mr. DeFranco decided he couldn't continue with his typical instruction and his typical responses to student misbehavior any longer. The students just didn't appear to have the social and interpersonal skills to effectively deal with conflict. After assessing the situation, Mr. DeFranco decided to take a multipronged approach. First, he decided to meet individually with the three students who were the ring-leaders, and set up behavioral contracts for each which included rewards and penalties. By checking the behavior of these students, he reasoned much provocation would be reduced.

Second, Mr. DeFranco decided the entire class would benefit from some training on social skills, conflict resolution, and self-management skills. He located some commercially prepared materials that included lesson plans and discussion guides to teach these skills. He planned to use regular class time to discuss the problems the class was experiencing and to have the students go through the training materials. Third, Mr. DeFranco talked with the principal and school counselor to inform them of the situation and to seek any advice and assistance they might offer.

Focus Questions

1. Do you agree or disagree with the three actions that Mr. DeFranco selected? Why?

2. What other approaches might you suggest to Mr. DeFranco to address the problem?

3. With an understanding of these incoming students, would you start the school year differently from what you typically might do?

Decrease Inappropriate Behavior

Your rules and consequences for the class should be used for all students, including challenging students. Since the consequences selected may not work for challenging students, you may need to select alternative consequences for these students only. Some discipline plans include the delivery of a series of consequences based on the number of rule infractions the student has made. Several consequences are discussed below.

1. **Loss of privileges.** A number of special privileges may be provided for students. Withdrawing privileges can be an effective consequence, but you need to determine which privileges will have the most influence on correcting the student's behavior if the privilege is withdrawn.

2. **Time-out.** Time-out involves removing the student from the instructional setting. Thus the student is not given the opportunity to obtain reinforcement for the misbehavior. There are several types of time-out. One of the most effective approaches is to remove the student from the instructional situation to be seated apart from the rest of the class; however, the student is expected to continue to do the work or listen to the lesson. In this way, the disruption stops, the rest of the class gets back to work, and the disrupting student is given an opportunity to calm down and get back to the instructional activities. You may ask the student to complete an incident reaction sheet during the time-out.

3. **Time after class.** Keeping the student for about a minute after class can be an important consequence for students moving on to another classroom after your class. This separates the student from peers, which can be perceived as a big penalty, and provides you with an opportunity to speak to the student about his or her behavior and the better choices that could have been made. At this time, you could give the student an index card on which to write a brief description of what was done in class to warrant staying after class. He or she could then sign and date the card for you to use as documentation in the event that the principal, parents, or others need to be contacted.

4. **Detention.** Detention involves the loss of free time and the opportunity to socialize with other students. Loss of recess time and staying after school are two common types of detention. Students should understand the reasons for the detention, and the time should not be excessive. You may ask the student to complete an incident reaction sheet during detention.

5. **Student calls a family member.** Having the student call his or her family at home or at work in your presence can be a strong deterrent. The student is expected to explain the problem behavior and what will be done to improve. The call should be made as soon as possible after the incident when both you and the student can get to a phone in the building. This may take place at recess, at lunch, or at the end of the class period.

6. **Time-out in another classroom.** If a student is highly disruptive, it may be useful to send him or her to another classroom at the same or higher grade level for a specified amount of time. This approach is useful for students who seek attention, because they are removed from the peers whose attention they seek. It is important that participating teachers discuss and agree to arrangements for sending and receiving disruptive students for a time-out. If students disrupt the classroom where they are sent for the time-out, they should know that the next consequence will be delivered, which may be a trip to the principal's office.

Prepare a Behavioral Contract

A *behavioral contract* is a written agreement between you and the student that represents a commitment for the student to behave more appropriately. A contract commonly includes (1) a statement of the expected, appropriate behavior; (2) a specified time period during which the student is to exhibit such behavior; (3) rewards or positive support for exhibiting the appropriate behavior;

■ **WHAT WOULD YOU DECIDE?**   **Preparing a Behavioral Contract**

Students in your classroom are working in small groups when you notice that one student argues with others in the group, delays completing expected group work, and does the opposite of what is expected. This student consistently displays this behavior when there is small group work; it is a pattern with her behavior. She displays these actions even when there is whole-class instruction. You decide that something must be done to deal with this challenging student. You decide to prepare a behavior contract for her, and you consider the four parts that are in a typical contract.

1. What is the expected, appropriate behavior that you would include in the contract?
2. What rewards or positive support would you identify when she exhibits the appropriate behavior?
3. What penalties or corrective actions would you include?
4. Would you decide on all of these items yourself or would you involve the student in the discussion? Why would you handle it yourself? Why would you involve the student?

and (4) penalties or corrective actions that will be taken if the student does not exhibit the appropriate behavior.

Behavioral contracts are not necessary for all challenging students. Some students may respond favorably to the approaches that have been discussed up to this point. A behavioral contract should be prepared for students who do not respond to the techniques previously described, or if you are delivering more and more consequences for a particular student or are getting frustrated or angry. A behavioral contract should then be drawn up.

Behavior contracting can be used at any grade level, but is often more appropriate and effective with elementary and middle level students, as older students may resent obvious attempts to manipulate their behavior. This contract is also effective with special education students.

Know When to Involve Others

Consultations made earlier with the principal, school counselor, or psychologist were intended to provide information and advice as you deal with the challenging student. Sometimes, however, students do not respond to any of your strategies, and the misbehavior may continue to be chronic and serious. In such cases, it is necessary to involve others in helping the student. Deviant and disruptive behavior warrants referrals to outside help.

Prior informal contacts, telephone calls, and conferences with family members informed them of the student behaviors and your actions. Now, you need formal contact with the principal or counselors to solicit their assistance.

The principal can counsel or intervene in various ways when handling a challenging student. A referral to the school counselor or psychologist is warranted when you recognize that a developing problem is beyond your professional expertise. Remember that you have not been trained to be a psychologist, counselor, or social worker, and you should not view yourself as a failure when referring the student to receive help from someone with appropriate training. Some districts use an intervention assistance team approach. Many district and community agencies work with schools and families, and these agencies also might be contacted.

Be Ready for Urgent Action

It is important to have a thoughtful, deliberate plan to deal with challenging or violent students, as outlined earlier. However, unexpected, disturbing events may occur in your classroom that require immediate action. For example, students may become involved in a physical fight, have a tantrum, destroy property, exhibit bullying behavior, tease others in a mean way, show cruel behavior, or carry a weapon.

Give advance thought to how you would deal with disturbing events that might occur and decide on the general ways that you will respond to those events. For example, if there is a physical fight, you may tell students to stop, disperse the other students, do not physically intervene, and get help. You cannot foresee every type of incident, but your advance thought and decision making will enable you to be ready for urgent action if it is needed.

Seeking Outside Help

After deciding to seek outside help, you first need to gather all the documentation that you have prepared up to this time. You then need to select the most appropriate person to contact. When outside help is needed, it is common practice in many schools to first contact the principal, who may take some actions or recommend that you contact the counselor or psychologist. Family members may be involved at any point, depending on the recommendations of the principal, counselor, or psychologist.

Principal

When dealing with chronic or serious misbehavior, the principal has the authority to make certain decisions. The principal may counsel or intervene when dealing with challenging students, including rewarding positive behavior. In consultation with you, the principal may be helpful in giving words of praise or other rewards when the student's behavior has improved. The principal might counsel the student by talking with the student. This additional guidance about the consequences of the student's choices can make a difference in turning the behavior around.

The principal might contact the family. This keeps the family informed of actions taken up to that time and they can be asked to support those actions at home. The principal might recommend that the family members come to the school for a conference with the teacher or others. The principal might approve new placements, services, or suspensions. Depending on the circumstances, the principal may take several actions such as changing the classroom placement, arranging for in-school suspension in a separate room, or referring the student to a counselor or psychologist. In more serious cases, the principal has the authority to seek placement in specialized educational settings outside the school, arrange for long-term suspension, or contact the police or other appropriate community agencies.

Sometimes a student's problems are rooted in deeper and more pervasive personality disturbances or family problems. The school psychologist can provide more intensive evaluation and diagnostic study. The psychologist will use the anecdotal and other records that you have accumulated concerning the student and will supplement them with other tests, interviews, and observations. This analysis can lead to recommendations for actions to be taken by those at the school or may result in referrals to outside agencies or resources.

Counselors and Psychologists

Other than the principal, the school counselor is often one of the first people contacted when outside help is needed for dealing with challenging students. The counselor may explore the student's behavior, the classroom environment, your teaching style, the classroom management plan, or a variety of related issues. The counselor then tries to provide objective feedback and suggestions for new approaches to deal with the problems. By considering the viewpoints of both you and the student, the counselor can serve as an intermediary for any potential conflicts.

Problem-Solving Teams

Some schools have a committee that assists teachers in dealing with classroom problems. *Problem-solving teams* consist of groups of educational personnel, parents, and other involved parties that meet systematically to discuss problems referred to them by other educational personnel within their school. The teams provide collegial assistance for teachers with a minimum of bureaucracy. The teams also increase commitment, communication, and morale by involving teachers and families as expert resources and collaborators in problem solving.

The problem-solving team identifies the needs, receives referrals, and plans and coordinates interventions with teachers, family members, other educational personnel, and community agencies. Some teams become involved in preventive interventions, crisis intervention, and inter-agency coordination. Teams can provide (1) help for teachers in dealing with educational, behavioral, and discipline problems; (2) early identification and schoolwide prevention of the problems; (3) a means of in-school intervention for the problems; and (4) a mechanism for referral to appropriate educational resources.

Families

Many teachers, principals, counselors, and psychologists prefer that they be contacted before the families are contacted. In this way, those at the school can explore all appropriate interventions without prematurely involving the parents. If it becomes necessary to contact the family members, they are often more responsive when they learn that steps have been taken already. Family members may then visit with you or others in the school. This is a more formal meeting than previous informational contacts, and the principal or others at the school may participate.

The initial meeting with the family gives all parties the opportunity to share information about the student and formulate a common information base. Teachers and counselors, for example, may review the set of documentation about the series of incidents and actions that have taken place. Family members may share information about the child's attitudes and behaviors at home. Together, those present at the meeting can develop a plan of action. Depending on the nature of the problem, they may conclude that some outside agency should be consulted.

The student may be asked to attend this meeting or will be informed by the teacher, counselor, or principal about the results of this meeting shortly after the meeting occurs. The primary purposes of this meeting are to share information, develop a plan of action to help the child be successful, and gather the support of the family.

District or Community Agencies

Community agencies work with schools and families to help each child be successful. For example, Cities in Schools is a national nonprofit organization dedicated to decreasing the dropout rate. Its mission is to assist a targeted group of children to achieve academic and social success

---

VOICES FROM THE CLASSROOM   A Meeting with the Family

Beth Schmar, sixth-grade teacher, Topeka, Kansas

In the middle of March, my principal and I realized that Brad had taken control of the classroom. The other students hung on his every word and followed each of his actions. Brad was constantly seeking the other students' attention by rotating between being the class clown and the class bully. Either way, he had their admiration or awe.

From the start of the school year, the principal and I tried many behavior-management approaches, from a contract to suspension. In an act of desperation, we requested a meeting with Brad and his family. We decided to include Brad for the entire meeting and to speak to him frankly. The principal and I shared our expectations for Brad's behavior and explained how his current behavior fell below these expectations. With the help of Brad and his family, we developed a behavior plan that we all could live with.

We expressed to Brad genuine caring and concern about his future, along with our own frustrations about his lack of success. Our honesty helped Brad react differently. He even commented to his family later, "At least now I know the principal and teacher don't hate me." The meeting was the beginning of a new understanding that made our time together more positive.

by coordinating existing community services to them and their families through the schools. That agency might be contacted to assist in some way.

Many districts or city governments have an office of substance abuse and violence prevention and intervention, and its resources may be useful. Social workers are available in various community agencies. Other types of offices and organizations within the district or community might also be contacted for help.

MAJOR CONCEPTS

1. Challenging students often have excessive noncompliant and aggressive behavior or behavioral deficits in self-management, social, and academic skills.

2. Underlying influences that may contribute to persistent misbehavior include emotional or physical abuse or neglect, organic conditions, drugs or alcohol, or gangs.

3. A commitment and a plan must be made to help each challenging student succeed.

4. Specific strategies can be used to help students manage their anger constructively, calm their anger, and deal with another person's anger.

5. Students can be taught new behavioral skills, such as social skills, conflict resolution skills, and self-management skills,

as a means to help them seek alternatives to disruption and violence.

6. Documentation of the student's behavior and the teacher's actions is needed. This may include anecdotal records, incident reaction sheets, or records of meeting and contracts.

7. The plan of action for the classroom involves assessing the situation, meeting with the student, consulting and informing others, providing positive support for the student, taking steps to decrease inappropriate behavior, preparing a behavioral contract, and knowing when to involve others.

8. The principal, counselor, psychologist, problem-solving teams, or family members may be contacted if actions taken in the classroom are not successful.

DISCUSSION/REFLECTIVE QUESTIONS

1. Should teachers deal only with the student's problem classroom behavior or should they also try to address the underlying influences? What are your reasons?

2. Why might teachers sometimes have difficulty in making a commitment to help challenging kids?

3. How might your grade level and the characteristics of your particular students affect how you select and teach strategies to

deal with anger, solve problems, and develop new behavioral skills?

4. What might affect the successful implementation of a behavioral contract with a challenging student?

5. How might the principal help or hinder the handling of challenging students?

SUGGESTED ACTIVITIES

1. Ask several teachers about any overall plan or particular strategies they use in dealing with challenging students in their classrooms.

2. Prepare the format for an anecdotal record form and a behavioral contract that you will use in your classroom.

3. Reflect on what makes you upset and angry and also how you respond when you are upset. What guidelines can you establish

for yourself when you might get upset about something that happens in your classroom?

4. Obtain and read resource material on teaching students new behavioral skills such as social skills, conflict resolution skills, and self-management skills.

FURTHER READING

Bodine, R. J., Crawford, D. K., & Schrumpf, F. (2003). *Creating the peaceable school: A comprehensive program for teaching conflict resolution* (2nd ed.). Champaign, IL: Research Press.

Addresses building a peaceable climate, understanding conflict, mediation, negotiation, and group problem solving. Focuses on teaching students necessary conflict resolution skills.

Canter, L., & Canter, M. (2008). *Succeeding with difficult students: New strategies for reaching your most challenging students*. Bloomington, IN: Solution Tree.

A useful, practical guide with content about reaching out to difficult students, meeting their special needs, communicating with them, and using individualized behavior plans.

Kaiser, B., & Rasminsky, J. S. (2017). *Challenging behavior in elementary and middle school* (4th ed.). Boston: Pearson.

Provides comprehensive discussion of risk factors, influences, relationships, culture, preventive strategies, guidance and other disciplinary strategies, bullying, and working with families.

Swearer, S. M., Espelage, D. L., & Napolitano, S. A. (2009). *Bullying prevention and intervention: Realistic strategies for schools*. New York: Guilford Press.

Describes bullying behaviors, influences, and consequences. Describes an antibullying policy, practical strategies to reduce bullying, and resources to help.

© Michael Newman/PhotoEdit Inc.

Collaborating with Colleagues and Families

CHAPTER OBJECTIVES

This chapter provides information that will help you:

- Collaborate with colleagues for assistance and professional development.

- Describe the reasons for contacting and interacting with families.

- Recognize the reasons some families resist involvement.

- Determine ways to work through cultural and language differences.

- Communicate with families though a variety of approaches.

- Prepare for and effectively conduct parent–teacher conferences.

Can you imagine how challenging it must have been to teach in a one-room school-house? There were so many responsibilities and challenges with the curriculum, instructional materials, and student behavior, and no one to turn to for help. Fortunately, teachers today have a number of colleagues to whom they can turn for assistance concerning a variety of issues.

Families can also be contacted for assistance when working with their children. In addition, teachers must take a variety of steps to contact and communicate with families about the school program and the progress of their children. This chapter addresses ways to work with both colleagues and families.

Working with Colleagues

Teachers don't teach in isolation. They need to interact with others in various ways to meet the needs of the students in their classroom. There has been increasing recognition of collaboration in the profession. For example, when the InTASC standards for teachers were revised in 2011, a new standard was included concerning leadership and collaboration (see those standards in this book on pages xvii–xxi) (Council of Chief State School Officers [CCSSO], 2011). The number of professional education resource books on collaboration has also increased in recent years. This is happening because collaboration is needed in schools, and educators are looking for resources to be successful in their collaborative activities.

What Is Collaboration?

Collaboration is a style of interaction between individuals engaged in shared decision making as they work toward a common goal. People who collaborate have equally valued resources to contribute, and they share decision-making authority and accountability for outcomes (CCSSO, 2011, p. 20).

Teachers often need to turn to others for assistance when dealing with student behavior problems, reading or language problems, media and instructional technology, students with special needs, curricular issues, instructional strategies, and numerous other issues. Depending on the issue, teachers may turn to one or more of these colleagues and resource people: principals, counselors or psychologists, reading specialists, special education resource teachers, librarians, media specialists, curriculum specialists, school or district committees, or district or community agencies.

Sometimes, this interaction is only to obtain information from a colleague; at other times there is genuine interaction and shared decision making toward a common goal about an issue—this is collaboration. But collaboration is not only about addressing an issue concerning a certain student; there are several purposes of collaboration, as noted in the next section.

Why Collaborate?

There are several reasons for going out of your own classroom to interact and collaborate with others. You might be applying your school's response to intervention (RTI) plan when addressing the learning needs of several students in your class, and you need to arrange for intensive intervention by another educator. You might have three students with disabilities, and you need to interact with the special education teacher. You might have a student who is having trouble dealing with a family problem, and you need to contact the school psychologist or counselor. You might be seeking information on how to use formative assessment, and you choose to work with another teacher on this topic. You might be asked to serve on a schoolwide committee addressing student dropouts in high school.

Many more examples could be provided, but the reasons for collaborating fall into the following categories:

1. **To meet the needs of the students.** Let's say you are dealing with a student who has significant misbehavior problems. It is wise to consult with the principal, school counselor, and/or psychologist to obtain information and advice as you work with this challenging student. Sometimes, however, students do not respond to any of your strategies, and the misbehavior may continue to be chronic and serious. Deviant and disruptive behavior warrants referrals to outside help. In such cases, you may need to refer this student to the school counselor or psychologist when you recognize that a developing problem is beyond your professional expertise. Remember that you have not been trained to be a psychologist, counselor, or social worker, and you should not view yourself as a failure when referring the student for help from someone with appropriate training.

   Before students' problem behavior gets serious enough for these referrals, it is often helpful to have telephone calls and conferences with families to inform them of the student behaviors and your actions and to solicit their assistance. In addition, the principal can counsel or intervene in various ways when handling a challenging student.

   In serious cases, district and community agencies might need to be contacted to work with the school and the family. Many districts or city governments have an office of substance abuse and violence prevention and intervention, and its resources may be useful. Social workers are available in various community agencies. Other types of offices and organizations within the district or community might be contacted for help.

   This example of misbehaving students is one way to illustrate actions that teachers could take to meet the needs of the students. Depending on the need, teachers may interact and collaborate with many different people. These actions may involve working with other members of an instructional team, paraprofessionals, or other colleagues. Through collaboration, teachers can take responsibility for student learning and ensure learner growth.

2. **To improve professional competence by engaging in professional development activities.** Ongoing professional development is crucial when trying to meet the needs of all students. Teachers need to learn about new aspects of the curriculum, how to apply new instructional techniques, how to effectively check for student understanding, how to integrate technology into their instruction, how to provide better guidance to read in the content area, and a host of other interests and needs. Therefore, teachers seek out collaborative opportunities to increase their knowledge and skills in any number of areas. Some of these collaborative approaches to professional development include mentoring programs, co-teaching, peer coaching, teacher support groups, and teacher centers.

3. **To provide leadership when addressing a school improvement issue.** Teachers can be agents for change and for school improvement by serving on schoolwide or districtwide

committees or task forces. Many types of special task forces or ongoing committees exist in schools and districts. They deal with issues such as discipline, textbook adoptions, curriculum development and revisions, improving reading ability, professional development programs, assisting English language learners, and a variety of other topics. By working in a collaborative way on these committees, teachers can address important school issues and be advocates for the students.

Collaborate with Whom?

To serve the three reasons for collaboration, teachers interact and collaborate with a variety of people. The particular need or circumstance will typically dictate whom the teacher may contact.

Other Teachers

When trying to meet the learning needs or the behavior of their students, teachers often turn to colleagues as a source of ideas and support. This may take place in an informal manner but also may occur in grade-level or subject-area teams in more formal structures.

When trying to improve professional competence or to address a school improvement issue, teachers work with other teachers in many different ways, such as mentoring teams, peer coaching, lesson study groups, professional learning communities, action research groups, and co-teaching arrangements. Resource books are available on these approaches, as illustrated by these examples:

- *Teacher Collaboration for Professional Learning* (Lassonde, Israel, & Almasi, 2009)
- *Mentoring as Collaboration* (Blank & Kershaw, 2009)
- *Leading Lesson Study* (Stepanek, Appel, Leong, Mangan, & Mitchell, 2007)
- *A Guide to Co-Teaching* (Villa, Thousand, & Nevin, 2013)
- *Collaborative Teaching in Secondary Schools* (Murawski, 2009)
- *Collaborate, Communicate, and Differentiate* (Murawski & Spencer, 2011)
- *The Practice of Authentic Professional Learning Communities* (Venables, 2011)
- *Action Research* (Mertler, 2014)

Other School Professionals

Teachers collaborate with many other school professionals, including counselors or psychologists, reading specialists, special education resource teachers, librarians, media specialists, and curriculum specialists. Educators in these other roles have specialized training for their particular responsibilities. Thus, they are an important source of information and expertise as teachers collaborate with them.

Teachers often interact with other school professionals when they have questions or needs related to teaching and meeting the needs of their students. In addition to working with individual teachers concerning specific needs, these other school professionals may also be involved in professional development efforts for large groups of teachers and service on schoolwide committees.

VOICES FROM THE CLASSROOM   Collaborating with Colleagues for Data-Driven Decision Making

Wendy Whitten-Lavery, third-grade teacher, Ocala, Florida

My third-grade team recently collaborated with our reading coach to develop a systematic approach to data-driven planning. First, our reading coach analyzes the data for the upcoming skill we are going to teach. She checks to see how our grade level did with the skill on assessments, reviews the types of questions that seemed to be a challenge for students, and then sends a list of the types of essential questions that we should have our students become familiar with.

Then our data groups meet. We divided our third-grade team into two data groups, which meet once per week. One group focuses on finding or developing skill-related activities, while the other group creates data-driven essential questions to go along with the reading materials for the skill. Finally, the information is shared through email so that all of the teachers in the grade level are given input and have access to a wide variety of materials and approaches to teach the skill. This approach divides a task among many people so that all students in the grade level can receive a well-formulated plan of instruction. This collaboration to inform our decision making has made a big difference.

School Administrators

Each school will have a school principal. Depending on the size of the school and the level of complexity, there may be additional school administrators such as an assistant principal or a director of the reading program. Teachers may need to consult and collaborate with one or more of these administrators concerning the students in their class, their professional development, or their involvement in school improvement opportunities.

Schoolwide Committees or Teams

There may be various types of schoolwide committees or task forces to deal with issues such as discipline, textbook adoptions, curriculum development and revisions, improving reading ability, professional development programs, assisting English language learners, and a variety of other topics. Teachers are often members of such committees. If not a member, teachers may need to consult or interact with the committees if they have a need to be addressed.

Students

Although the degree of collaboration may not be the same as with other educators, teachers can collaborate with their students in various ways. If a teacher is conducting action research in her own classroom, for example, the students may be involved in the process. Collaboration can also occur with students as co-teachers in cooperative learning groups (Villa, Thousand, & Nevin, 2010).

Families

When considering the purposes of collaboration, teachers most often collaborate with families to support the learning of their children. There should be more than communication by the teacher to the families; there should be interaction and collaboration to promote the learning of the students. Parents can be partners in supporting the learning of their children.

Due to the nature of the condition and the learning needs, teachers may need to interact and collaborate more often with the parents of students with disabilities or special needs.

Fortunately, there are some useful resources available to provide guidance (e.g., Cramer, 2006; Dardig, 2008). In addition, extra efforts need to be made to provide culturally responsive family involvement and collaboration (Grant & Ray, 2015).

School–Community Partnerships

Schools sometimes reach out to community agencies to capture support for student learning and to address certain problems. For example, it is becoming increasingly common for businesses to financially support certain school interests, needs, or programs. They might purchase necessary school equipment, such as computers, or support certain school programs, such as the theater department. Common community partnerships with schools include the following (Sanders, 2006):

- Businesses and corporations
- Universities and other institutions of higher learning
- National and local volunteer organizations
- Social service agencies and health partners

These partnerships are often coordinated by a school administrator, but teachers are typically involved in developing the school–community partnership proposals and in conducting the actions designated in the partnership. Roles, responsibilities, and relationships between the school professionals, community agencies, and service providers must be carefully defined if the partnerships are to succeed (Kochhar-Bryant & Heishman, 2010).

Collaboration Skills and Dispositions

What skills are needed to effectively collaborate with others? InTASC Standard #10: Leadership and Collaboration provides a perspective on what teachers might be expected to do when providing leadership and collaborating with others (CCSSO, 2011). Clues about necessary collaboration skills can be inferred from those performance statements. Here are some representative performances from that standard requiring collaboration:

- Take an active role on the instructional team, give and receive feedback on practice, examine learner work, analyze data from multiple sources, and share responsibility for decision making and accountability for each student's learning.

- Work with other school professionals to plan and jointly facilitate learning on how to meet diverse needs of learners.

- Work collaboratively with learners and their families to establish mutual expectations and ongoing communication to support learner development and achievement.

- Work with school colleagues to build ongoing connections with community resources to enhance student learning and well-being.

- Engage in professional learning, contribute to the knowledge and skill of others, and work collaboratively to advance professional practice.

When examining these representative performances, some broader skills necessary for effective collaboration become apparent. These collaboration skills include the following:

1. **Communication skills.** Effective verbal and nonverbal communication skills are needed. How a person uses these skills also makes a difference in collaboration. Active listening, providing information, and asking questions are part of good interpersonal relations that are based on communication skills.

2. **Problem-solving skills.** There are several steps in problem solving: identify the problem, generate potential solutions, evaluate potential solutions, select the solution, implement the solution, and evaluate the outcome. Collaboration often involves addressing problems, and problem-solving skills are needed for effective collaboration.

3. **Conflict resolution skills.** Collaboration with others may be needed to address a conflict situation with students or others. Also, conflicts might arise with your collaborative partners when addressing issues of attention or concern. Mediation and negotiations skills may be need to resolve the conflict.

4. **Administrative and management skills.** Skills are needed to coordinate and implement the actions identified from the collaborative discussions. This may involve practical matters such as scheduling and coordinating services. When interacting with other school professionals on an ongoing basis, additional skills may be needed. When working with a paraprofessional, for example, a teacher will need skills related to training, planning, assigning responsibilities, communicating, supervising, and evaluating the work of the paraprofessional (Ashbaker & Morgan, 2013; Friend & Cook, 2017).

Dispositions. In addition to the skills just reviewed, certain dispositions are needed for effective collaboration. Here are some representative dispositions:

- Takes the initiative to grow and develop with colleagues through interactions that enhance practice and support student learning.

- Respects families' beliefs, norms, and expectations and seeks to work collaboratively with learners and families in setting and meeting challenging goals.

- Willing to be helpful in making necessary compromises to accomplish a common goal. Willing to assume shared responsibility for collaborate work.

- Values the individual contributions made by each team member.

- Willing to participate in respectful and reciprocal communication.

Many schools have various types of committees and task forces, and collaboration takes place in those venues. These groups may meet in an ongoing basis, and certain skills are needed to conduct these committees in an effective manner (Glaser, 2005). The responsibility for conducting these committees falls to the group leader. The skills of effective group processing are also needed for collaboration in this context.

Working with Families

Imagine that you are a parent and that you and your family just moved into a new community during the summer. You have one child in third grade and another in seventh grade. Because you moved from another state, you are concerned that the curriculum might be quite different in this new district, and you wonder how your children will adjust to the new community and their new school and teacher. Wouldn't you want to talk to the teachers to share some of these issues? Wouldn't you like to hear about the curriculum and how the teachers will handle instruction? Wouldn't you like to maintain ongoing contact throughout the school year? Yes, of course!

Good communication with families should be a priority because it keeps teachers and families informed about what is happening. It also builds trust so that there can be a working partnership in the event there are difficulties with the students. Although a teacher's primary responsibility is to work with students, it is important to communicate and interact with the students' families throughout the school year. The reason for the communication will often determine the timing of the contact and the means by which the contact will be made.

■ **CLASSROOM CASE STUDY**   Working with Colleagues and Families

Hui Chen is an eighth-grade mathematics teacher at a middle school. At a grade-level team meeting about six months into the school year, Ms. Chen and her colleagues discussed issues of concern. They noted that one of their students, Miranda, had been struggling in all of her classes all year. Miranda was on the verge of failing three of these classes, and she would likely have to repeat the eighth grade unless her performance improved. Even when the teachers had discussed Miranda in previous team meetings, they had agreed that her poor organizational and study skills contributed to her current academic standing.

Ms. Chen and her colleagues scheduled a student–teacher meeting with Miranda, where they discussed ways to improve her organizational and study skills. Miranda was given a booklet to record her homework assignments, and she was encouraged to attend after-school homework sessions. Despite these efforts, Miranda continued to struggle in all of her classes, and her grades worsened. After determining that Miranda was

on the verge of being held back, Ms. Chen and her colleagues decided to contact Miranda's family.

When Ms. Chen telephoned Miranda's family, the conversation was tension-filled and awkward. Miranda's parents were frustrated that they had not been contacted sooner. They stated that Miranda had never performed at the top of her class but that she always earned passing marks. Even though Ms. Chen attempted to address the issues and schedule a meeting about the concerns, Miranda's parents refused and declared that they would go straight to the school administration to discuss their daughter's situation.

Focus Questions

1. What errors did the teachers make in handling the situation with Miranda?

2. How could the teachers have handled the situation differently to establish better communication and collaboration with Miranda's parents from the start?

At the start, we must recognize that children come from many types of family settings. While some students come from traditional or nuclear families (47 percent), others come from single-parent families (27 percent), blended families (16 percent), extended or multigenerational families (6 percent), or other types of families such as gay and lesbian families, families headed by grandparents, families with adopted or foster children, and even homeless families (P. Barbour, C. H. Barbour, & H. Roberts-King, 2015; Olsen & Fuller, 2012). As a result of these various family settings, the term *parent* is used throughout this book to represent the adult or adults who have parental responsibility. Thus, this definition of a parent could include the biological parents, foster or stepparents, a grandparent, an aunt or uncle, an older sibling, or a guardian.

Families want their children to succeed in school and generally appreciate teachers' efforts to keep them informed and involved about academic and behavioral issues (Berger & Riojas-Cortez, 2016). Families' reactions to problems vary widely. Reactions are largely determined by individual experiences, life experiences, education and training, expectations, socioeconomic circumstances, and other factors. The reactions of the child, the teacher, and others also have a bearing on how the problem will be handled (Shae & Bauer, 2012).

It is important to listen carefully to families to identify their concerns and suggestions. Trust is developed when they know that their ideas are recognized and understood. The full benefits of parent–school relationships are not realized without this interaction and collaboration. Fortunately, a number of useful resources provide guidance when working with families (e.g., L. Canter & M. Canter, 2001; National PTA, 2000; Olender, Elias, & Mastroleo, 2010; Olsen & Fuller, 2012). In *Working with Families*, Hanson and Lynch (2013) provide important foundational information about many types of families and ways to communicate and collaborate with them to benefit their children.

What are the reasons for working with families? Why is it important to understand them and their point of view? When should families be contacted? What are the ways that teachers might communicate with families? We will examine these questions in this chapter.

Reasons for Working with Families

Students ultimately benefit from good communication and effective working relationships between the school and home. Families' involvement in their children's schooling has been associated with better attendance, more positive student attitudes and behavior, greater willingness to do homework, and higher academic achievement. There are several reasons why you should communicate with parents:

1. **To create open, two-way communication and to establish friendly relations.** Positive contacts with families early in the year help establish positive, friendly relations. In this way, families see each other not as adversaries but as allies in helping the student be successful. Two-way communication can be fostered, and that will result in appropriate school–community relations that will benefit everyone involved.

2. **To understand the student's home condition.** Information about a student's home setting can help you decide on an appropriate course of action with the student. You may learn the parents are having marital problems, have limited ability to read or speak English, exert excessive pressure for the child to excel academically, or tend to be abusive to the student when there are problems at school. Such factors can be important as you decide how best to help each student academically and behaviorally.

3. **To inform families of academic expectations and events as well as student performance.** Families appreciate knowing your policy concerning homework, late papers, and grading guidelines. Informing parents at the start of the school year helps prevent misunderstandings about your expectations. They also like to know what content will be covered, when the quizzes or tests are scheduled, and what special events are scheduled. Introductory letters or a back-to-school night is helpful, as are newsletters devoted to special events, units to be covered, or the academic schedule. Finally, families want to know how their children are doing. Report cards and conferences provide information periodically, but families appreciate learning about early indications of academic difficulties.

4. **To enlist help from families about academic issues.** Teachers often seek help from families at the start of the year. They may send a list of needed classroom and instructional supplies home to the families to supplement purchases made by the school district. You may want to identify family members who might be available to serve as classroom aides or chaperones for regular or special events. This assistance may include preparing materials for bulletin boards, assisting during a field trip, and the like.

5. **To inform families of disciplinary expectations and actions.** At the start of the year, teachers often inform families of their disciplinary policy and their expectations for student conduct. As with the academic information at the start of the year, this communication is often accomplished through an introductory letter or a newsletter, or at the back-to-school night. If students misbehave, you may need to inform the families of the situation.

6. **To enlist help from families about dealing with their children.** When a student has difficulties, the family should be contacted to identify ways they might help. When a student misbehaves, the family should be contacted so that you can work together to help the student stay on task and be successful. Families exert much influence on their children, and they can cooperate and support your actions. You and the families may agree on strategies to help the child and to build the child's cooperation and commitment to address any problems.

VOICES FROM THE CLASSROOM   Communicating with Parents

Kaye Lynn Mazurek, high school German teacher, Commerce, Michigan

When a parent contacts me for any reason, my first response is to say, "Thanks for your email, for your phone call, for coming to conferences . . .." If the parent expresses a concern, my second response is to ask, "What can I do to help?" I've found that these two responses to parents have been the key to setting a positive tone for a discussion, which will lead to a productive outcome. Finally, I ask, "What suggestions do you have for me to help your child be successful in my class?"

Of course, I have to be willing to listen to and accept the parent's suggestions. In nearly all cases, I've found that the parent request ends up being as simple as wanting the student to retake a quiz, hand in a late assignment, stay after school, or have a seat moved. I firmly believe that a teacher who is interested in the academic success of a student should be willing to make any of these adjustments in order to establish a foundation of trust. It's important for both the parent and the student to realize that the teacher is invested in the student's academic success instead of focusing on a particular rule such as "no late work" that may result in the student's academic failure.

Why Some Families Resist Involvement

As much as you would like the cooperation and support of families when dealing with a student with academic or behavioral difficulties, you may find families apathetic or resistant to involvement. There also may be circumstances in the lives of the families that create barriers to good communication and involvement, such as work schedules or English language limitations. There are several possible barriers or reasons for family resistance to involvement (Applebaum, 2009; McEwan, 2005):

- Some adults may have had unhappy experiences when they were students. They may view school as being oppressive and not a place of hope for their children. These families may consider it unlikely that school personnel can solve the problems.

- Families of children who have a history of misbehavior may adopt coping mechanisms in an effort to deal emotionally with the problems (Shae & Bauer, 2012). Their responses may point to self-doubt, denial, withdrawal, hostility, and frustration. These families may resist involvement with all school personnel.

- Some families view teachers, principals, counselors, and other school personnel as the experts in addressing issues such as misbehavior (A. A. Turnbull, H. R. Turnbull, E. J. Erwin, L. C. Soodak, & K. A. Shogren, 2015). Consequently, they may resist involvement because they do not want to interfere with the actions taken by the teacher or other officials.

- Some families are threatened by the school itself and by the bureaucracy. They may be intimidated by the size of the school, the need to report to the school office when visiting the school, the busy nature of the school, the lack of private areas for discussion, and other physical aspects of the school. As a result, those families may resist involvement because they have a sense of discomfort about the school.

- Diversity among the families, population, and the sense of being different from school personnel may make families uncomfortable in seeking contact with teachers or administrators. For example, Asian immigrant parents may think that communication with teachers is considered to be "checking up on them" and an expression of disrespect. Members of other ethnic groups, likewise, may feel out of place.

- Some families don't know what is expected of them or how they might contribute to their child's education. They may withdraw or become angry or frustrated when the school seems to be failing to meet their child's needs. They do not realize that the school would value their involvement.

- Some families don't become involved with the school for practical reasons. They may not speak English or may have limited competency in English. They may not drive a car, or they may have limited access to transportation. They may not have access to a babysitter or cannot afford one. Or they may simply be too tired after long days at work themselves.

- Teachers or administrators may have done things in the past to upset family members, and now they may not want to get involved or may participate in an angry manner. In previous interactions, educators may have failed to communicate with the family, held stereotypes, broken promises, or been rude, condescending, dishonest, or unprofessional in various ways (McEwan, 2005).

- Schools may have not met the families' expectations for various reasons, and this may influence their involvement. Some families' concerns may be about a lack of student learning in the school, poor behavior in the school, a lack of competent teachers, erosion of values, a lack of safety, or even a feeling of having to settle for financially poor schools (McEwan, 2005).

- Some families may have personal problems themselves, and these factors may interfere with good communication and involvement with the school. There may be separated or divorced parents or problems such as abuse, addiction, dysfunction, and mental illness. There are also some who simply must complain (McEwan, 2005).

Working through Cultural and Language Differences

An increasing number of students are from culturally and linguistically diverse families. It is imperative that you make adjustments in how you approach and interact with the families to develop successful home–school communication and partnerships (Grant & Ray, 2015):

1. **Learn about the cultures of the families of students.** Information is available about families of different cultures. For example, Lynch and Hanson (2011) provide detailed cultural descriptions on families with Anglo-American, American Indian, African American, Latino, Asian, Filipino, and Middle Eastern roots. *Involving Latino Families in Schools* (Gaitan, 2005), *Teaching Hispanic Children* (Jones & Fuller, 2003), and *Educating Immigrant Students in the 21st Century* (Rong & Preissle, 2009) are examples of books addressing specialized cultures.

2. **Use school resources and interpreters to communicate with families who have limited English language proficiency.** With increasing student diversity, many schools have forms, letters, policies, and other types of communication translated into one or more languages beyond English to facilitate communication with families. In addition, schools sometimes have interpreters available for one or more other languages. Classroom teachers need to use these school resources to effectively communicate with the families of students in their classrooms.

3. **Acknowledge and adapt to cultural differences in social etiquette and ways of communicating and expressing respect.** If you do not speak the same language as the family, your nonverbal messages become more important. Use positive body language when you meet family members at an open house or other school event. Greeting families at the door,

for example, expresses respect. Any notes, letters, or newsletters sent home should be translated into the home language.

4. **Have early and frequent teacher–family contacts.** Initiate positive home–school contact and dialogue by chatting, making phone calls and home visits, talking with community workers, and arranging for afternoon homework help or tutoring to promote student success.

5. **Provide families with information about the school.** Keep families informed (in the home language, if possible) about important classroom, school, and community events; help available in the school or from community-based organizations; and sources of academic support. Communicate through student-produced newsletters, telephone calls, and other notices. Provide materials in the home language.

6. **Encourage family participation at the school and in the home.** Encourage and welcome families to come to school meetings and social events and even come to the classroom. Encourage family members to come to class to share skills or to discuss their culture. Provide suggestions for ways families can enable their students' learning by supporting homework and creating a positive learning environment at home.

7. **Adjust how you conduct family–teacher conferences.** Schedule time for the conference that is convenient for family members, and show them a portfolio of the student's successes. By also including the student, this three-way conference can promote a dialogue about schooling. The use of an interpreter is sometimes necessary, and this shows respect for the home language of the family. Watch for any facial expressions, voice intonations, and body movements to extend communication (Diaz-Rico, 2013).

Contacting and Communicating with Families

As discussed previously, there are several reasons for working with families. The timing of the contact will depend on the reason for it. There are three points to consider when contacting families:

1. **Initial contact with all families.** This contact should occur at the start of the year. It would be designed to inform families about the academic program, grading guidelines, the homework policy, rules and procedures, and other academic and behavioral expectations. Requests for additional classroom supplies and for volunteers for activities are generally made at this time. You can make these contacts through an introductory letter, a newsletter, a back-to-school night, or other means.

■ WHAT WOULD YOU DECIDE?   Families Not Attending

Let's assume that you teach in a school that has much ethnic diversity, and that some families do not attend the back-to-school night or the parent–teacher conferences at the end of the report card periods.

1. How can you find out why the families do not attend?

2. How can you communicate to those families that it is acceptable to attend such sessions and that their child will ultimately benefit from their attendance?

3. What are some alternative ways that you can communicate important information to the families who do not attend these events?

2. **Ongoing contact with all families.** This contact occurs throughout the year to provide information about content being covered in class, the schedule for tests or other evaluation requirements, field trips, the progress of the students, and so on. You may need additional volunteers throughout the year and may contact family members at various times as the need arises. These ongoing contacts could be made through a newsletter or information sheet, an open house, report cards, or other means.

3. **Contact with selected families.** This contact needs to occur to inform them about concerns unique to their child's progress. It could occur when there is both positive and negative news to report. You will often contact families when there is a problem, yet it is easy to overlook contacting them when there is good news to report. Families especially appreciate reports of good news; if a problem arises later, they are often more willing to support and cooperate with the teacher. Guidebooks are available for advice on working with parents of students with special needs (e.g., Dardig, 2008) and even for working with parents of bullies and victims (e.g., Roberts, 2008).

Ways to Communicate with Families

There are many ways to communicate with families, and the method may be affected by its purpose. To discuss a serious act of misbehavior, for example, you would probably not wait for a parent–teacher conference scheduled at the end of a report card period to contact the family but would likely call them immediately.

Much communication with families occurs at the start of the year in the form of an introductory letter, a letter about classroom management and discipline, a back-to-school night, and information sheets. Ongoing communication may be through an open house, newsletters, notes and letters, phone calls, special events and informal contacts, sending home student work, report cards, and parent–teacher conferences. To contact families about their child's academic work or behavior, you could call them or arrange for a special conference. In *Engage Every Family*, Constantino (2015) advocates reaching out to every family in a variety of ways.

Introductory Letter

Teachers sometimes send an *introductory letter* home with the students to give to their parents or guardians during the first week of school prior to the back-to-school night. This letter is intended to serve as a brief welcome to the new year, include some basic information about the class, and invite the family members to the back-to-school night that will soon follow.

The letter may include some information about classroom and school policies such as the schedule, homework, absences, and the curriculum. You may mention in the letter that more will be said about these and other issues at the back-to-school night. A sample introductory letter to families is displayed in Figure 11.1. You can adapt this letter for your particular situation.

Newsletters

At the start of the school year or a new course, teachers sometimes prepare a newsletter that will go to the families of all the students in the class. An initial newsletter may be sent instead of an introductory letter to the families. This newsletter often includes information about the course content, instructional activities, and grading procedures and student requirements. Of course, the nature of the initial newsletter will vary with the grade level and the type of teaching assignment. As a guide, though, the initial newsletter may include a description of the following:

1. Course title or subject area(s).

2. Brief course or subject area description.

September 4

Dear Parents:

Now that the school year has begun, I'd like to introduce myself. I am Melissa Riley, and I am your child's ninth-grade algebra teacher this year. I have taught in this school district for 14 years and have taught pre-algebra, algebra, geometry, and trigonometry. I completed my undergraduate work at the University of Illinois and my master's degree at Kansas State University.

I want this to be a successful school year for you and your child. To ensure this success, it is important that we maintain open communication. Please do not hesitate to contact me if you have any questions or concerns. You could call me at school after dismissal between 3:30 and 4:30 p.m. at 555-7308. Or you could call anytime during the day and leave a message for me to call you back. My email address is mriley@centralschooldistrict.org.

At various times throughout the school year, I will be sending a newsletter home with your child to provide information about classroom activities and special events. On a regular basis, your child will bring home graded assignments for you to look at. I also look forward to seeing you at the conference session that we schedule at the end of each report card period.

The annual back-to-school night for this school is scheduled for next Thursday, September 12, from 7:30 to 9:15 p.m. On that evening, you will have the opportunity go through your child's schedule of classes in shortened 10-minute class periods. When you meet me during algebra class, I will share information about the curriculum, my approach to instruction, my academic expectations and procedures, my policy on discipline, and other issues. The books and materials that we will be using this year will also be on display. I encourage you to attend back-to-school night because it will give you an opportunity to understand the mathematics program and become better acquainted with me.

By working together and keeping in good contact, I'm confident that this will be an exciting and successful school year. I look forward to meeting you at back-to-school night.

Sincerely,

Melissa Riley

FIGURE 11.1   Sample Introductory Letter to Families

3. Course objectives.

4. A brief content outline.

5. Typical learning activities.

6. Grading procedures. This could include a listing of the types of evaluation measures to be used and the proportion of the marking term grade that each measure will carry. For example, tests (40 percent), homework (20 percent), projects (20 percent), and quizzes (20 percent). In addition, the grading scale could be included indicating the percentages for each letter grade.

7. Materials that the student will need.

8. Behavioral guidelines and expectations.

9. The school telephone number and your district email address. Contact information is included as a convenience to make it easy for parents/guardians to communicate with you.

It is important that you convey this initial information to the students as well. Students especially need to know grading procedures and guidelines and also behavioral expectations. During the school year, additional newsletters might be sent to all families with information about special events, programs, content to be covered in the curriculum, tests or quizzes that are coming up, student projects, and other issues. Newsletters can be as brief as one page or longer,

> **VOICES FROM THE CLASSROOM   Ways to Communicate with Parents**
>
> **Ana Bermudez, second-grade teacher (National Board Certified Teacher), Miami, Florida**
>
> I believe that most parents want to be involved in their children's education. Due to different circumstances, however, they may not be able to fully engage in the process. As a teacher, I understand the importance of parent–teacher communication and how it benefits the students. Therefore, I make it a priority to communicate with parents constantly. I keep all my contact records in Microsoft Outlook; it is a great way to keep track of everything and to have it readily available.
>
> There are many different ways I reach out to parents. I send *weekly notes* reminding them of events and activities. Every time there is a new concept introduced in math, I send them a *letter* with family activities that deal with the new skill. I *email* parents back and forth, which I find is the fastest and best way to reach many of them. I make *good news phone calls* to share positive information about student behavior or performance. I *meet with parents* before the report cards go home so they have an opportunity to help their child. I also *send tests home* so parents can see the mistakes and then better guide their children.
>
> I basically have constant contact with parents, and they are so appreciative of this. By keeping them informed, I start a blossoming relationship with many of the parents that ultimately affects their children in a positive way. Parents need to see how much a teacher cares for their child.

according to need. You can report accomplishments of the class and of individual students. Computers can be used to prepare the newsletters. Students can prepare the newsletter as a group or class project, under suitable circumstances.

Letter about Classroom Management and Discipline

You need to share your plan for classroom management and discipline with the families and the principal. If you expect them to be involved when you need them, they need to know that you have a plan and to be aware of your rationale for rules, positive recognition, and consequences.

At the start of the school year, you need to discuss rules, consequences, and other aspects of management with the students. A copy of this information sheet should be given to the students to take home to their parents. The letter should provide details of the classroom management and discipline plan and should explain why it is important. Ask the parents to discuss the plan with their children, sign the plan, and return the signature portion to you. A sample letter to families about classroom management and discipline is displayed in Figure 11.2. You may adapt that letter for your particular situation.

If the back-to-school night is scheduled early in the year, you may ask the families to return the signature portion at that time. Or you may prefer to wait and present the letter to the families at the back-to-school night and get the signatures at that time. Letters can then be sent home to families who did not attend that evening.

Back-to-School Night

Many schools schedule a *back-to-school night* or family night during the first or second week so families can receive information about the academic program, grading guidelines, homework policy, rules and procedures, and other expectations. Requests for additional classroom supplies and for volunteers for activities are generally made at this time.

Some schools do not schedule a back-to-school night or, if they do, it comes later than the first or second week of school. You may find other ways to communicate with families since it is important to establish contact as early as possible. For example, a letter about classroom

Dear Parents:

Now that the school year has begun, I'd like to introduce myself and give you some information about how I conduct my classes. My name is Keith McKinsey, and I am your child's fifth-grade teacher. I have taught in this school district for eight years. I completed my undergraduate work at Florida State University and my master's degree at Kansas State University.

To maintain an appropriate learning environment, I have established the following classroom rules that all students are expected to follow:

1. Follow the teacher's directions.

2. Keep your hands, feet, and objects to yourself.

3. Do not swear or tease.

To encourage students to follow the rules, I will recognize appropriate behavior with praise, various types of reinforcement, and notes or calls home to you. If students choose to break the rules, I have established an escalating series of responses ranging from gentle prompts and reminders to the use of logical consequences, and to detention. In class, we have discussed these rules, the reinforcement for following the rules, and the consequences if the students choose to break the rules. My goal is to ensure success for your child. Working together, I'm confident that it will be an enjoyable and productive school year.

Please indicate that you understand this discipline plan by signing your name below and indicate the phone numbers where you can be reached during the day and evening. You might also discuss the rules to make sure your child understands them.

Please do not hesitate to contact me if you have any questions or concerns. You could call me at school after dismissal between 3:30 and 4:30 p.m. at 555-6188. Or you could call anytime during the day and leave a message for me to call you back. My email address is Kkeith@centralschooldistrict.org.

Sincerely,

Keith McKinsey

(Please tear off the bottom part and return it to Mr. McKinsey.)

I have read and understand the classroom management plan in Mr. McKinsey's classroom, and I have discussed it with my child.

Parent/Guardian

Signature_____ Date_____

Comments:

FIGURE 11.2   Sample Letter to Families About Classroom Management and Discipline

management and discipline might be expanded to include information that is commonly covered at a back-to-school night.

The scheduling of the back-to-school night is handled in different ways. For middle, junior high, and senior high schools, families are often given their child's schedule, and they follow it just as the student would, but in shortened class sessions of 10–15 minutes. In this way, they see every teacher in the way that their child would during the school day. Teachers often use this time to present information to the families about academic and behavioral guidelines and expectations.

Preparing for Back-to-School Night

A back-to-school night is often your first contact with families, so thorough preparation is necessary. There are many ways to prepare for this evening.

- **Prepare your own introductory letter to families about the back-to-school night in your classroom.** See the sample introductory letter in Figure 11.1. Do not rely only on notices that the school sends home. Some teachers like to have their students prepare special invitations for their own families.

- **Make sure the classroom looks attractive and neat.** Post your name and room number prominently on the door and the front chalkboard. Display samples of work by all students. Display copies of the textbooks and other instructional materials.

- **Prepare a list of any instructional supplies or materials that families might be able to provide.** This list will vary, depending on the subject and grade level. It may include such items as rulers, buttons, a box of facial tissues, or other supplies. Have enough copies of the list to give to all families.

- **Prepare separate sign-up sheets for families.** These may concern the need for a private, follow-up conference about their child; volunteers to help at special events such as field trips; volunteers such as guest speakers in class; or volunteers to provide various instructional supplies requested by the teacher.

- **Plan a well-organized, succinct presentation.** Families want to hear about your background and experience, behavioral and academic expectations, procedures for issues such as homework and absences, and other policies. Be sure to plan for time at the end of the presentation for questions.

- **Prepare handouts for your presentation.** Families will receive the handouts at the back-to-school night. Have enough copies of this material to give to all of them. A sample content outline of the presentation is shown in Table 11.1; your handout should include details about issues such as those listed in that table. On the front page of the handout, include your name, the school phone number, your school email address, and the times at which you can be reached. Attach other related materials to this handout; these materials may include a sheet showing the daily or weekly class schedule, a sheet of needed instructional materials and supplies, or a sheet concerning the classroom management and discipline policy. To simplify distribution, staple all the handouts together as one set of materials sequenced in the order that you will cover the material during the presentation.

Conducting the Back-to-School Night

Take several guidelines into account when conducting the back-to-school night. Since your presentation is usually limited, possibly to only 10–15 minutes, it is important to plan how to conduct yourself. Greet families at the door, introduce yourself, and ask them to be seated. Begin your presentation using the handout that you previously prepared concerning your background, the daily and weekly schedule, the curriculum, academic goals and activities, academic expectations and procedures, discipline, and other issues. At the start, give a copy of the handout to each family member.

Have parents sign up for individual follow-up conferences if they want to talk with you at length about their child. Back-to-school night is not intended to deal with concerns about individual students. Allow time for family members to ask questions. This will be an opportunity for you to provide clarification about issues and to hear families' concerns.

■ TABLE 11.1   Sample Content Outline for Your Back-to-School Night Presentation

1. Background About Yourself
   a. College training and degrees earned
   b. Professional experience, including length of teaching service, grade levels taught, where taught
   c. Personal information (e.g., family, hobbies, special interests, or experiences)

2. The curriculum, academic goals, and activities
   a. Overview of the curriculum and the topics to be covered (refer to the textbooks and related instructional materials on display in the room)
   b. Your approach to instruction
   c. Instructional activities and any special events such as field trips or unique programs

3. Academic expectations and procedures
   a. Grading guidelines and procedures (how grades are determined)
   b. Grading requirements (e.g., tests, quizzes, homework, and projects)
   c. Homework (purposes, how often, make-up policy, absences)
   d. When report cards are delivered
   e. Parent–teacher conferences

4. Discipline
   a. Classroom rules
   b. Positive rewards
   c. Consequences for breaking the rules
   d. Incremental steps taken when misbehavior continues
   e. When parents will be contacted
   f. Sheet concerning the classroom management and discipline policy that parents need to sign

5. Ask parents to sign up for selected issues
   a. For a private, follow-up conference about their child
   b. For parent volunteers for providing instructional materials and supplies
   c. For parent volunteers to help at special events such as field trips
   d. For parent volunteers such as guest speakers in class

6. Express an interest in hearing any ideas and concerns from families at any time

7. Time for questions at the end of the session (save several minutes if possible)

Information Sheets

Not all schools schedule a back-to-school night, and not all families attend a scheduled night. As a result, you can prepare a packet to send home that provides information about the curriculum, grading expectations and requirements, rules and procedures, the discipline plan, and other matters. The sheets may be the same as those given to families who attend the back-to-school night, or a shortened version.

Open House

Once or twice a year, most schools schedule an open house for families to visit the classrooms during a particular evening to see their child's teacher, observe the classroom and samples of student work, and learn about books and materials being used. Some districts do not have a back-to-school night but instead schedule the first open house in mid to late September. At open house, teachers may give a formal presentation about the program. Or schools may allow family members to drop in at any time during open house to discuss issues informally with the teacher.

Since open houses are conducted well into the school year, materials and projects that students have prepared can be displayed. Science fairs, for example, may be scheduled at the same time as an open house to provide an opportunity for families to see students' science displays. Since some of the families attending the open house may not have attended the back-to-school night, it is often useful to have extra copies of the handout provided at the back-to-school night to describe your policies.

Assignment Sheets

Another way to communicate with families is through an assignment sheet that describes the assignments for the next week or two. Students are asked to show it to their families. Some teachers prefer that parents sign the sheet and return it to school. The assignment sheet also helps students recognize the assignments that are due in the next week or two and enables the students to make plans to complete the assignments on time. Especially when students have many school-related activities or other outside-school activities, they can plan which day or days they will work on school-related assignments while still participating in their other activities.

Individual Notes and Letters

Notes and letters are written to individual parents to discuss some particular issue about their child. You can use them to request that a conference be arranged with you, to invite family members to class functions, to inform them about their child's work, or to offer suggestions. Notes should be carefully written. They should be free of errors in spelling, grammar, and sentence structure. Furthermore, they should be brief, clear, honest, and factual. Educational jargon should not be used. Notes and letters are especially useful for contacting family members who are hard to reach by telephone.

Make sure that you address the letter correctly since the parent and child may not have the same last name. If the family members do not read English, try to take needed steps to write the letter or note in their native language. Avoid writing a letter when you are upset about a classroom event; calm down first. Try to end with a positive statement about working together for the benefit of the child.

Be cautious about sending notes home to families only when there is bad news to deliver. Certainly, there are times when such notes need to be sent. You should also send notes home to families with good news about the child's academic work or behavior. Briefly, positive notes take only a few minutes to write to express pleasure about the child's performance. By systematically writing one or two notes to different parents each day, you will provide good news and help build positive relationships with them. Family members will usually talk with their child about the note, and the child may come to school the next day with a more positive attitude.

■ WHAT WOULD YOU DECIDE?   Sending Notes or Letters Home

Sending notes or letters home to families is one way to communicate with them about classroom issues or their child's performance.

1. What types of information might you convey in the notes or letters?

2. What guidelines will you establish for yourself about the content, the writing form, the frequency, and other factors for the notes or letters?

3. How might you modify your procedures if a number of the families have limited English proficiency or if several ethnic groups are represented?

Phone Calls

Like notes and letters, telephone calls are made to families to discuss a particular issue. The phone call could request that a conference be arranged with you, invite the family to class functions, inform them about their child's work, or offer suggestions. As with notes and letters, be cautious about calling families only when you have bad news. Also call them when there is good news to report.

Phone calls can be quite brief because you only need to have two or three positive statements to share. They are not intended to be a lengthy discussion about the student. The parents should be asked to tell the child about the phone call.

There are times when you need to contact the family about the child's misbehavior. You need to plan ahead before making the call. The call should begin with a statement of concern, such as, "Mrs. Erickson. I am Kristina's teacher, and I need your help. I care about Kristina and I feel that her behavior in the classroom is not in her best interest." You then should describe the specific problem and present any pertinent documentation. You should go on to describe what you are doing and have done to deal with the misbehavior. At this point, it is helpful to invite the family's input by asking questions such as, "Has Kristina had similar problems in the past? Why do you feel she is having these problems at school? Is there something going on at home that could be affecting her behavior?"

It is then useful to get input about how to solve the problem. State what you will do to help solve the problem and explain what you want the parent to do. Before ending the telephone conversation, you should let the family know that you are confident that the problems can be worked out and tell them that there will be follow-up contact from you. Then recap the conversation.

Websites and Email

Increasingly, schools are using the Internet to make information available to parents, students, and the public. A school's website might include the school calendar; directories for teachers, administrators, and the staff; school policies; information about athletics and extracurricular activities; special events; and other information. Some school districts also communicate through Twitter, Facebook, and text messages directly to cell phones.

Some schools make provisions so that each teacher has a webpage for his or her classroom. In these cases, teachers can place information on their classroom website to communicate to students and families about their syllabus, rules and procedures, notices about special events, listing of assignments or homework, Web links to useful resources, and much more. These classroom websites can be prepared, developed, and tailored by each teacher, and they can be a fine

---

VOICES FROM THE CLASSROOM   Making "Good News" Phone Calls to Families

Bernadette Hampton, high school mathematics teacher, Beaufort, South Carolina

To build positive relationships with parents and students, I call home for the top three students after a quiz or a test. I do this to encourage and motivate the student to excel. You can also select other criteria for the phone calls, such as most improved, most creative, or others to include most students over time.

Parents are often surprised to receive this phone call, especially when they usually receive phone calls with negative news. Students return to school with much appreciation for the good news call. The student's self-esteem is increased, and support is gained from the parent. If I need to call the parent about difficult behavior or another troublesome issue, I then have the support of the parent. The "good news" phone calls help me develop a positive relationship with the parents as well as the students.

■ WHAT WOULD YOU DECIDE?   Creating Your Own Classroom Website

Many schools make provisions so that each teacher has a webpage for his or her classroom. Teachers may post their syllabi, rules and procedures, notices about special events, listing of assignments or homework, links to useful resources, and much more.

1. If you had a webpage available for your use for your classroom, how might you use it? What information might you post?

2. Would you want to only post information, or would you want the webpage to have interactive capability (like a blog)? What advantages or problems might there be with a classroom blog?

source of information for the students and families. Since these classroom websites are on the district's website, they typically are not blocked by firewalls and thus are easily accessible for good communication.

As computer use has become more common, many families have email capability. Teachers can provide students and families with their email address to open this type of communication. Families can contact the teacher with questions or comments through email, and teachers can report student progress and other information to parents through email. When sending emails to students or families, word your messages carefully to avoid any misinterpretation. Clearly state your message, and check your spelling and grammar. Also, be cautious about sending out emails with negative messages. It often is better to deal with individuals directly if there are some concerns that need attention.

Some schools and districts, however, have firewalls or other protections to limit emails. In these cases, teachers need to maintain communication through other approaches.

Special Events and Informal Contacts

Throughout the year, teachers and families may attend many special events. These may include sporting events, concerts, plays, carnivals, craft displays, and others. Contacts with family members at these events may provide brief opportunities to share a few words about their child's work. These contacts are especially useful as progress reports and as a means of discussing a particular issue. You might say something about the student's interests, such as "Josh's work during our unit on Australia focuses on the animal life. He is very interested in animal life in all of our studies."

Sending Home Student Work

You can inform families about their child's academic progress by sending home completed and graded student work. They can see what you have covered, the child's work, and any notes or remarks you have made.

Sending home only completed worksheets may not be very enlightening for families. It is useful to send home a variety of materials including worksheets, tests, quizzes, homework, projects, lab reports, writing samples, artwork, or other types of student products. Be sensitive about notes or remarks you place on the papers. These notes are evaluative statements, but they should also include comments about good points and improvement, as well about areas still needing attention.

Papers that are sent home with students to show their parents may not even get home, and those that do get home may not be shown to the family members. To overcome these problems, you might devise various ways to have family members sign a sheet to indicate that they have seen the material. For example, a parent response sheet might list the material being sent home, with a blank space for parents to sign and date indicating that they discussed the piece with their child. The form could also include space for the family members to write any comments. The student then returns the response sheet to you.

Report Cards

Families are informed of their child's academic performance when report cards are distributed. Most report cards have an area where you can either write a statement or indicate a code for a statement concerning effort and citizenship. As with notes, letters, and phone calls, you should avoid making only negative notes on report cards. Deserving students should receive positive notes.

When warranted, include notes on the report card to indicate the need to improve and the actions needed to improve the situation. Families may call teachers shortly after report cards have been delivered if they have any questions about them. Have documentation ready to justify what you have noted.

Gradebook software often provides the capability to print out reports for individual students, which display each assessment measure, points earned, and point tallies. These individual student printouts can be useful if family members inquire about their child's grade. The printouts can also be generated for individual students for parent–teacher conferences, which are considered in the next section.

Parent–Teacher Conferences

Another important way of communicating with families is through *parent–teacher conferences* to report information about progress, academic performance, or behavior. Many school districts schedule a day or two at the end of each report card period for parent–teacher conferences so parents can meet individually with the teachers. Conference days are typically scheduled only for elementary grades; all parents are invited to attend these individually scheduled conferences.

Many middle schools, junior high schools, and high schools do not schedule parent–teacher conferences, but instead arrange for a block of time on one day at the end of the report card period for families to visit with each teacher on a drop-in basis. The ways to prepare for and conduct this session will be somewhat different from those used at the elementary level, but the general principles discussed here for preparing for this contact still apply.

In addition to the conferences conducted at the end of report card periods, parent–teacher conferences are held with particular parents as the need warrants. When a student persistently misbehaves or has academic problems, you may ask the family of that child to come to the school for a conference. Prior to having such a conference, you may want to meet with the student to work out a plan to address the problem. If this meeting with the student does not lead to resolution, then a meeting with the family is warranted, and the student may be asked to also attend.

To have effective parent–teacher conferences, teachers should thoroughly prepare for the conference, take certain actions when conducting the conference, and provide appropriate follow-up. Guidelines discussed in the following sections center primarily on parent–teacher conferences to address academic issues. These guidelines would need to be adapted somewhat to address individually scheduled parent–teacher conferences concerning academic or disciplinary issues.

Preparing for the Conference

Preparation for a drop-in conference with the family at the end of the report card period will be different from preparation for an individually scheduled parent–teacher conference. Administrators in middle schools, junior high schools, and high schools commonly take steps to inform families about the day and time for the drop-in conferences at the end of the report card periods. Since these teachers have responsibility for many students, it is usually not feasible to have sample materials available for all of them. Instead, teachers often have the gradebook on hand, along with sample tests, quizzes, homework, and projects that students completed throughout the marking period.

If an individual parent–teacher conference is needed, the teacher often calls the family to select a day and time. Before the conference, the teacher may gather pertinent materials about the student and the situation. If it is an academic issue, the teacher may collect the gradebook and a sample of work done by the student, including tests, projects, and homework to be shown to the family during the conference. If it is a behavioral issue, anecdotal record sheets and other documentation may be gathered.

Whether for a drop-in conference at the end of the report card period or for an individually scheduled conference, the physical environment needs to be prepared for the session. You can arrange for these materials: (1) a table for the conference; (2) three or four adult-sized chairs for the table; and (3) a clean, tidy room. Be sure to allow enough time for the conference, and do not overwhelm parents with the presence of other school personnel or irrelevant materials.

Conducting the Conference

Discussion and questions in the conference should be sequenced to develop rapport, obtain information from the family, provide information to them, and summarize and follow up. The following guidelines include a technique to "sandwich" your main messages between good news or positive statements at the start and at the end of the conference. The parents who hear good comments at the start will be in a comfortable frame of mind. As the conference comes to a close, it is useful to summarize your main points and then conclude with additional positive statements. Consider these guidelines:

1. **Begin the conference in a positive manner.** Walk up to the family members, introduce yourself, and welcome them into the room. Start the conference with a positive statement about the student, such as "Emily really enjoys providing leadership for students in her small group when working on projects."

2. **Present the student's strong points before describing the matters needing improvement.** Highlight the student's strengths as you move into a discussion about his or her performance. Show samples of the student's work to the family. Later, identify matters that need further improvement.

3. **Present documentation for the student's grades.** Review the assessments that were conducted and identify the student's grades for the assessments.

4. **Encourage the family to participate and share information.** Allow opportunities to ask questions and share information about the student. Pose questions to parents at various points of the conference to encourage their input.

5. **Plan a course of action cooperatively.** If the student needs to work on a particular issue, discuss the possible actions that you and the parents could take. Come to agreement about the course of action that each of you will take.

6. **End the conference with a positive comment.** Thank the family for coming, and say something positive about the student at the end of the conference.

7. **Use good human relations skills during the conference.** To be effective, you should be friendly and informal, positive in your approach, willing to explain in understandable terms, willing to listen, willing to accept parents' feelings, and careful about giving advice. You should avoid the following: arguing and getting angry; asking embarrassing questions; talking about other students, teachers, or families; bluffing if you do not know an answer; rejecting parents' suggestions; and being a "know-it-all" with pat answers (Miller, Linn, & Gronlund, 2013).

■ TABLE 11.2   Fourteen Ways to Communicate with Families

1. An introductory letter
2. Newsletters
3. A letter about classroom management and discipline
4. Back-to-school night
5. Information sheets
6. Open house
7. Assignment sheets
8. Individual notes and letters
9. Phone calls
10. Websites and email
11. Special events and informal contacts
12. Sending home student work
13. Report cards
14. Parent–teacher conferences

Handling Conference Follow-Up

During the conferences, it is useful to make a list of follow-up actions. These actions may include providing more thorough feedback to the student during the next marking period, recommending additional readings to some students, providing certain families with periodic updates on their child's performance, or a host of other actions. It is important to follow up in the ways that were identified during the parent–teacher conference.

MAJOR CONCEPTS

1. Teachers often need to turn to others for assistance when dealing with student behavior problems, reading or language issues, media and instructional technology, special needs, curricular issues, instructional strategies, and numerous other issues.

2. Collaboration is a style of interaction between individuals engaged in shared decision making as they work toward a common goal.

3. Teachers collaborate with others to: (a) meet the needs of their students, (b) improve professional competence by engaging in professional development activities, and (c) provide leadership when addressing a school improvement issue.

4. Teachers work with families to (a) understand the student's home setting; (b) inform parents of academic expectations and events as well as student performance; (c) enlist family members' help with academic issues; (d) inform them of disciplinary expectations and actions; and (e) enlist their help in dealing with their children.

5. Families' resistance may be due to (a) their unhappy experiences when they were students; (b) their coping mechanisms in dealing with ongoing problems with their children; (c) their view that educators are the experts; or (d) their perception of the intimidation and bureaucracy of the school.

6. To accommodate differences in culture and language, teachers must adjust how they approach and interact with families to develop successful home–school communication and partnerships.

7. The timing of the contact with the families will be determined by the reason for the contact. The three main times of family contact are (a) initial contacts with all families at the start of the school year; (b) ongoing contacts with all families throughout the school year; and (c) contact with selected families concerning their child's academic or behavioral progress.

8. Initial communication with the family occurs at the start of the school year in the form of an introductory letter, a letter about classroom management and discipline, a back-to-school night, and information sheets.

9. Ongoing communication throughout the school year may occur with an open house, newsletters, assignment sheets, notes and letters, phone calls, websites and email, special events, informal contacts, sending home student work, report cards, and parent–teacher conferences.

10. To contact individual families about their child's academic work or behavior, teachers often call the parents/guardians and sometimes arrange for a special parent–teacher conference to address issues.

DISCUSSION/REFLECTIVE QUESTIONS

1. If a student in your class has been causing serious disruptions, which colleagues in your school might you collaboration with for assistance? How might those colleagues help?

2. If a student in your class has been having serious emotional problems, who might you turn to for help? Why?

3. How might information about a student's home setting help you as a teacher decide on an appropriate course of action with the student? How might this information create some problems for you?

4. When is an appropriate point to contact families if a student is exhibiting mild misbehavior? Moderate misbehavior?

5. In what ways did your teachers in the middle and secondary grades contact and interact with your parents? When and how did this communication occur?

6. What are some ways that teachers can communicate with families about academic expectations and events?

SUGGESTED ACTIVITIES

1. Talk to a school counselor or a school psychologist to find out what services they provide for students and teachers. Ask how they collaborate with teachers to address problems.

2. Talk with several teachers and ask who they turn to for assistance when dealing with instructional or disciplinary problems. Ask them to describe the type of assistance they provide.

3. Ask several teachers to describe the ways that they prepare for and conduct the back-to-school night. What recommendations do they have to aid your preparation?

4. Think about the reasons that families may not attend parent–teacher conferences. Identify ways that you might communicate to those particular families.

FURTHER READING

Canter, L., & Canter, M. (2001). *Parents on your side: A teacher's guide to creating positive relationships with parents* (2nd ed.). Bloomington, IN: Solution Tree.

Provides thorough, practical guidance about ways to communicate, to establish positive relationships, and to solve problems that may occur.

Friend, M. D., & Cook, L. (2017). *Interactions: Collaboration skills for school professionals* (8th ed.). Boston: Pearson.

Provides comprehensive discussion about many aspects of collaboration, such as interpersonal communication and problem solving, teams, meetings, consultations, co-teaching, paraeducators, and dealing with difficult interactions.

McEwan, E. K. (2005). *How to deal with parents who are angry, troubled, afraid, or just plain crazy* (2nd ed.). Thousand Oaks, CA: Corwin Press.

Describes why parents may be angry or troubled. Offers suggestions to defuse and disarm emotionally charged behavior, engage in productive problem solving, create a healthy school culture and climate, and be proactive when dealing with parents.

National PTA. (2000). *Building successful partnerships: A guide for developing parent and family involvement programs*. Bloomington, IN: Solution Tree.

A practical resource that provides a blueprint for developing quality parent involvement programs. Includes discussion of issues such as communicating, parenting, student learning, and volunteering.

Stein, J., Meltzer, L., Krishnan, K., Pollica, L. S., Papadopoulos, I., & Roditi, B. (2007). *Parent guide to hassle-free homework*. New York: Scholastic.

Offers guidance about the home study environment, ways to support the child, motivation, and communicating with the teacher.

References and Further Readings

Albert, L. (2003). *A teacher's guide to cooperative discipline: How to manage your classroom and promote self-esteem* (Rev. ed.). Circle Pines, MN: American Guidance Service Publishing.

Allington, R. L. (2009). *What really matters in response to intervention*. Boston: Pearson.

Anderman, E. M., & Anderman, L. H. (2014). *Classroom motivation* (2nd ed.). Boston: Pearson.

Applebaum, M. (2009). *How to handle the hard-to-handle student, K–5*. Thousand Oaks, CA: Corwin Press.

Armstrong, T. (2009). *Multiple intelligences in the classroom* (3rd ed.). Alexandria, VA: Association for Supervision and Curriculum Development.

Arnett, J. J. (2016). *Human development: A cultural approach* (2nd ed.). Boston: Pearson.

Ashbaker, B. Y., & Morgan, J. (2013). *Paraprofessionals in the classroom* (2nd ed.). Boston: Pearson.

Ashbaker, B. Y., & Morgan, J. (2015). *The paraprofessional's guide to effective behavioral interventions*. New York: Routledge.

Banks, J. A. (2016). *Cultural diversity and education: Foundations, curriculum, and teaching* (6th ed.). New York: Routledge.

Barbour, P., Barbour, C. H., & Roberts-King, H. (2015). *Families, schools, and communities: Building partnerships for educating children* (6th ed.). Boston: Pearson.

Barton, E. A. (2006). *Bully prevention: Tips and strategies for school leaders and classroom teachers* (2nd ed.). Thousand Oaks, CA: Corwin Press.

Bender, W. N. (2012). *Project-based learning: Differentiated instruction for the 21st century*. Thousand Oaks, CA: Corwin Press.

Berger, E. H., & Riojas-Cortez, M. R. (2016). *Parents as partners in education: Families and schools working together* (9th ed.). Boston: Pearson.

Berk, L. E. (2013). *Child development* (9th ed.). Boston: Pearson.

Berk, L. E. (2014). *Development through the lifespan* (6th ed.). Boston: Pearson.

Berk, L. E., & Meyers, A. B. (2016). *Infants, children, and adolescents* (8th ed.). Boston: Pearson.

Biegel, S. (2010). *The right to be out: Sexual orientation and gender identity in America's public schools*. Minneapolis, MN: University of Minnesota Press.

Blank, M. A., & Kershaw, C. A. (2009). *Mentoring as collaboration*. Thousand Oaks, CA: Corwin Press.

Bluestein, J. (2008). *The win–win classroom: A fresh and positive look at classroom management*. Thousand Oaks, CA: Corwin Press.

Bluestein, J. (2010). *Becoming a win–win teacher: Survival strategies for the beginning teacher*. Thousand Oaks, CA: Corwin Press.

Bodine, R. J., Crawford, D. K., & Schrumpf, F. (2003). *Creating the peaceable school: A comprehensive program for teaching conflict resolution* (2nd ed.). Champaign, IL: Research Press.

Bongalan, R., Moir, E., & Baron, W. (2010). *Keys to the secondary classroom: A teacher's guide to the first months of school*. Thousand Oaks, CA: Corwin Press.

Books, S. (2004). *Poverty and schooling in the U.S.: Contexts and consequences*. Mahwah, NJ: Lawrence Erlbaum Associates.

Bosch, K. A. (2007). *Planning classroom management* (2nd ed.). Thousand Oaks, CA: Corwin Press.

Bosch, K. A., & Bosch, M. E. (2015). *The first-year teacher: Be prepared for your classroom*. Thousand Oaks, CA: Corwin Press.

Boyd, D., & Bee, H. (2015). *Lifespan development* (7th ed.). Boston: Pearson.

Brady, K., Forton, M. B., & Porter, D. (2011). *Rules in school* (2nd ed.). Turners Falls, MA: Center for Responsive Schools.

Breakstone, S., Dreiblatt, M., & Dreiblatt, K. (2009). *How to stop bullying and social aggression*. Thousand Oaks, CA: Corwin Press.

Brown, E. L., Geor, P. C., & Lazaridis, G. (Eds.). (2014). *Poverty, class, and schooling*. Charlotte, NC: Information Age Publishing.

Burden, P. R., & Byrd, D. M. (2016). *Methods for effective teaching* (7th ed.). Boston: Pearson.

Burke, K. (2008). *What to do with the kid who…: Developing cooperation, self-discipline, and responsibility in the classroom* (3rd ed.). Thousand Oaks, CA: Corwin Press.

Campbell, B. (2008). *Handbook of differentiated instruction using the multiple intelligences*. Boston: Pearson.

Canter, L. (2010). *Assertive discipline: Positive behavior management for today's classroom* (4th ed.). Bloomington, IN: Solution Tree.

Canter, L. (2014). *Classroom management for academic success*. Bloomington, IN: Solution Tree.

Canter, L., & Canter, M. (2001). *Parents on your side: A teacher's guide to creating positive relationships with parents* (2nd ed.). Bloomington, IN: Solution Tree.

Canter, L., & Canter, M. (2008). *Succeeding with difficult students: New strategies for reaching your most challenging students.* Bloomington, IN: Solution Tree.

Cary, S. (2007). *Working with English language learners: Answers to teachers' top ten questions* (2nd ed.). Portsmouth, NH: Heinemann.

Cassetta, G., & Sawyer, B. (2015). *Classroom management matters: The socio-emotional learning approach children deserve.* Portsmouth, NH: Heinemann.

Causton-Theoharis, J., & Kluth, P. (2009). *The paraprofessional's handbook for effective support in inclusive classrooms.* Baltimore, MD: Paul H. Brookes Publishing.

Centers for Disease Control and Prevention. (2007). *The effectiveness of universal school-based programs for the prevention of violent and aggressive behavior. Morbidity and Mortality Weekly Report, 56,* RR-7.

Chapman, C., & King, R. S. (2012). *Differentiated assessment strategies: One tool doesn't fit all* (2nd ed.). Thousand Oaks, CA: Corwin Press.

Chapman, C., & King, R. S. (2014). *Planning and organizing standards-based differentiated instruction* (2nd ed.). Thousand Oaks, CA: Corwin Press.

Charles, C. M. (2014). *Building classroom discipline* (11th ed.). Boston: Pearson.

Charney, R. S. (2002). *Teaching children to care: Classroom management for ethical and academic growth, K–8* (Rev. ed.). Turners Falls, MA: Center for Responsive Schools.

Clark, B. (2013). *Growing up gifted: Developing the potential of children at school and at home* (8th ed.). Boston: Pearson.

Cole, A. J., & Shupp, A. M. (2012). *Recognize and respond to emotional behavioral issues in the classroom: A teacher's guide.* Baltimore, MD: Paul H. Brookes Publishing.

Cole, R. W. (Ed.). (2008). *Educating everybody's children: Diverse teaching strategies for diverse learners* (rev. 2nd ed.). Alexandria, VA: Association for Supervision and Curriculum Development.

Coloroso, B. (2002). *Kids are worth it! Giving your child the gift of inner discipline* (Rev. ed.) New York: HarperCollins.

Coloroso, B. (2015). *The bully, the bullied, and the bystander* (Revised and updated ed.). New York: HarperCollins.

Colvin, G., & Scott, T. M. (2015). *Managing the cycle of acting-out behavior in the classroom* (2nd ed.). Thousand Oaks, CA: Corwin Press.

Conoley, J. C., & Goldstein, A. P. (2004). *School violence intervention: A practical handbook* (2nd ed.). New York: Guilford Press.

Constantino, S. M. (2015). *Engage every family: Five simple principles.* Thousand Oaks, CA: Corwin Press.

Council of Chief State School Officers (CCSSO). (2011, April). *Interstate Teacher Assessment and Support Consortium (InTASC) model core teaching standards: A resource for state dialogue.* Washington, DC: Author. Retrieved from www.ccsso.org/Documents/2011/InTASC_Model_Core_Teaching_Standards_2011.pdf.

Cramer, S. F. (2006). *The special educator's guide to collaboration: Improving relationships with co-teachers, teams, and families* (2nd ed.). Thousand Oaks, CA: Corwin Press.

Crowe, C. (2009). *Solving thorny behavior problems: How teachers and students can work together.* Turners Falls, MA: Center for Responsive Schools.

Curwin, R. L., & Mendler, A. N. (1997). *As tough as necessary: Countering violence, aggression, and hostility in our schools.* Alexandria, VA: Association for Supervision and Curriculum Development.

Curwin, R. L., Mendler, A. N., & Mendler, B. D. (2008). *Discipline with dignity* (3rd ed.). Alexandria, VA: Association for Supervision and Curriculum Development.

Cushman, K. (2003). *Fires in the bathroom: Advice for teachers from high school students.* New York: The New Press.

Dardig, J. C. (2008). *Involving parents of students with special needs.* Thousand Oaks, CA: Corwin Press.

Davis, B. M. (2012). *How to teach students who don't look like you: Culturally relevant teaching strategies* (2nd ed.). Thousand Oaks, CA: Corwin Press.

Davis, G. A., Rimm, S. B., & Siegle, D. (2011). *Education of the gifted and talented* (6th ed.). Boston: Pearson.

Davis, H. A., Summers, J. J., & Miller, L. M. (2012). *An interpersonal approach to classroom management: Strategies for improving student engagement.* Thousand Oaks, CA: Corwin Press.

Dean, C. B., Hubbell, E. R., Pitler, H., & Stone, B. (2012). *Classroom instruction that works: Research-based strategies for increasing student achievement* (2nd ed.). Alexandria, VA: Association for Supervision and Curriculum Development.

Denton, P. (2013). *The power of our words: Teacher language that helps children learn* (2nd ed.). Turners Falls, MA: Center for Responsive Schools.

Derman-Sparks, L., & Edwards, J. O. (2010). *Anti-bias education for young children and ourselves.* Washington, DC: National Association for the Education of Young Children.

Diaz-Rico, L. T. (2013). *Strategies for teaching English learners* (3rd ed.). Boston: Pearson.

Diffily, D., & Sassman, C. (2006). *Positive teacher talk for better classroom management.* New York: Scholastic.

Dillon, J. (2012). *No place for bullying: Leadership for schools that care for every student.* Thousand Oaks, CA: Corwin Press.

Dillon, J. (2015). *Reframing bullying prevention to build stronger school communities.* Thousand Oaks, CA: Corwin Press.

Doyle, M. B. (2008). *The paraeducator's guide to the inclusive classroom* (3rd ed.). Baltimore, MD: Paul H. Brookes Publishing.

Dreikurs, R., Cassel, P., & Ferguson, E. D. (2004). *Discipline without tears: How to reduce conflict and establish cooperation in the classroom* (Rev. ed.). New York: Wiley & Sons.

Dreikurs, R., Grunwald, B. B., & Pepper, F. C. (1998). *Maintaining sanity in the classroom: Classroom management techniques* (2nd ed.). Philadelphia: Taylor & Francis.

Drew, N. (2010). *No kidding about bullying.* Minneapolis, MN: Free Spirit.

Dwyer, K., & Osher, D. (2000). *Safeguarding our children: An action guide.* Washington, DC: U.S. Departments of Education and Justice, American Institute for Research. Retrieved from http://cecp.air.org/guide/actionguide.asp.

Dwyer, K., Osher, D., & Warger, C. (1998). *Early warning, timely response: A guide to safe schools.* Washington, DC: U.S. Department of Education.

Edwards, J. (2010). *Inviting students to learn: 100 tips for talking effectively with your students.* Alexandria, VA: Association for Supervision and Curriculum Development.

Edwards, C. H. (2008). *Classroom discipline and management* (5th ed.). Hoboken, NJ: John Wiley & Sons.

Elias, M. J., & Schwab, Y. (2006). From compliance to responsibility: Social and emotional learning and classroom management. In C. M. Evertson & C. S. Weinstein (Eds.), *Handbook of classroom management: Research, practice, and contemporary issues* (pp. 309–341). Mahwah, NJ: Lawrence Erlbaum Associates.

Emmer, E. T., & Evertson, C. M., (2017). *Classroom management for middle and high school teachers* (10th ed.). Boston: Pearson.

Emmer, E. T., & Gerwels, M. C. (2006). Classroom management in high school classrooms. In C. M. Evertson & C. S. Weinstein (Eds.), *Handbook of classroom management: Research, practice, and contemporary issues* (pp. 407–437). Mahwah, NJ: Lawrence Erlbaum Associates.

Evertson, C. M., & Emmer, E. T. (2017). *Classroom management for elementary teachers* (10th ed.). Boston: Pearson.

Evertson, C. M., & Weinstein, C. S. (Eds.). (2006). *Handbook of classroom management: Research,* *practice, and contemporary issues.* Mahwah, NJ: Lawrence Erlbaum Associates.

Farrell, T. S. (2009). *Talking, listening and teaching: A guide to classroom communication.* Thousand Oaks, CA: Corwin Press.

Fast, J. (2008). *Ceremonial violence: A psychological explanation of school shootings.* New York: Overlook Press.

Fay, J., & Funk, D. (1995). *Teaching with love and logic.* Golden, CO: The Love and Logic Press.

Feldman, R. S. (2016). *Child development* (7th ed.). Boston: Pearson.

Fisher, D., & Frey, N. (2010). *Enhancing RTI: How to ensure success with effective classroom instruction and intervention.* Alexandria, VA: Association for Supervision and Curriculum Development.

Fogarty, R.J. (2009). *Brain-compatible classrooms* (3rd ed.). Thousand Oaks, CA: Corwin Press.

Fogarty, R. J., & Stoehr, J. (2008). *Integrating curricula with multiple intelligences* (2nd ed.). Thousand Oaks, CA: Corwin Press.

Foley, D. (2012). *Ultimate classroom management handbook* (2nd ed.). Indianapolis, IN: JIST Publishing.

Friend, M. D., & Cook, L. (2017). *Interactions: Collaboration skills for school professionals* (8th ed.). Boston: Pearson.

Gaitan, C. D. (2005). *Involving Latino families in schools: Raising student achievement through home–school partnerships.* Thousand Oaks, CA: Corwin Press.

Gaitan, C. D. (2006). *Building culturally responsive classrooms: A guide for K–6 teachers.* Thousand Oaks, CA: Corwin Press.

Gallavan, N. P. (2011a). *Navigating cultural competence in Grades K-5.* Thousand Oaks, CA: Corwin Press.

Gallavan, N. P. (2011b). *Navigating cultural competence in Grades 6-12.* Thousand Oaks, CA: Corwin Press.

Gardner, H. E. (2006). *Multiple intelligences: New horizons* (Rev. ed.). New York: Basic Books.

Gardner, H. E. (2011). *Frames of mind: The theory of multiple intelligences* (3rd ed.) New York: Basic Books.

Garrett, T. (2014). *Effective classroom management: The essentials.* New York: Teachers College Press.

Gay, G. (2005). Politics of multicultural teacher education. *Journal of Teacher Education*, 56(3), 221–228.

Gay, G. (2010). *Culturally responsive teaching* (2nd ed.). New York: Teachers College Press.

Gettinger, M., & Kohler, K. M. (2006). Process-outcome approaches to classroom management and effective teaching. In C. M. Evertson & C. S. Weinstein (Eds.), *Handbook of classroom management: Research, practice, and contemporary issues* (pp. 73–95). Mahwah, NJ: Lawrence Erlbaum Associates.

Gillies, R. M. (2007). *Cooperative learning: Integrating theory into practice.* Thousand Oaks, CA: Sage.

Ginott, H. G. (1972). *Teacher and child*. New York: Macmillan.

Ginott, H. G. (1988). *Between parent and teenager*. New York: Avon Books.

Ginott, H. G. (2003). *Between parent and child* (revised and updated by A. Ginott & H. W. Goddard). New York: Three Rivers Press.

Glaser, J. (2005). *Leading through collaboration: Guiding groups to productive solutions*. Thousand Oaks, CA: Corwin Press.

Glasser, W. (1965). *Reality therapy*. New York: Harper & Row.

Glasser, W. (1969). *Schools without failure*. New York: Harper & Row.

Glasser, W. (1985). *Control theory: A new explanation of how we control our lives*. New York: Harper & Row.

Glasser, W. (1986). *Control theory in the classroom*. New York: Harper & Row.

Glasser, W. (1998a). *The quality school: Managing students without coercion* (Rev. ed.). New York: HarperPerennial.

Glasser, W. (1998b). *The quality school teacher* (Rev. ed.). New York: HarperPerennial.

Glasser, W. (2000). *Every student can succeed*. Chatsworth, CA: Black Forest Press.

Gollnick, D. M., & Chinn, P. C. (2017). *Multicultural education in a pluralistic society* (10th ed.). Boston: Pearson.

Good, T. L., & Brophy, J. E. (2008). *Looking into classrooms* (10th ed.). Boston: Pearson.

Gootman, M. E. (2008). *The caring teacher's guide to discipline: Helping young students learn self-control, responsibility, and respect* (3rd ed.). Thousand Oaks, CA: Corwin Press.

Gordon, T. (1991). *Discipline that works: Promoting self-discipline in children*. New York: Plume (a division of Penguin).

Gordon, T. (2003). *Teacher effectiveness training*. New York: Three Rivers Press.

Gorski, P. C. (2013). *Reaching and teaching students in poverty: Strategies for erasing the achievement gap*. New York: Teachers College Press.

Grant, K. B., & Ray, J. A. (2015). *Home, school, and community collaboration: Culturally responsive family engagement* (3rd ed.). Thousand Oaks, CA: Sage Publications.

Gregory, G. H., & Chapman, C. (2012). *Differentiated instructional strategies: One size doesn't fit all* (3rd ed.). Thousand Oaks, CA: Corwin Press.

Gregory G. H., & Kaufeldt, M. (2015). *The motivated brain: Improving student attention, engagement, and perseverance*. Alexandria, VA: Association for Supervision and Curriculum Development.

Gregory, G. H., & Parry, T. (2006). *Designing brain-compatible learning* (3rd ed.). Thousand Oaks, CA: Corwin Press.

Greytak, E. A., Kosciw, F. G., & Diaz, E. M. (2009). *Harsh realities: The experiences of transgender youth in our nation's schools*. New York: Gay, Lesbian and Straight Education Network.

Guillaume, A. M. (2016). *K–12 classroom teaching: A primer for new professionals* (5th ed.). Boston: Pearson.

Gurian, M., & Stevens, K. (2007). *The minds of boys: Saving our sons from falling behind in school and life*. San Francisco: Jossey-Bass.

Gurian, M., & Stevens, K. (2010). *Boys and girls learn differently: A guide for teachers and parents* (Rev. ed.). San Francisco: Jossey-Bass.

Gurian, M., Stevens, K., & King, K. (2008). *Strategies for teaching boys and girls: Elementary level*. San Francisco: Jossey-Bass.

Hammeken, P. A. (2008). *The paraprofessional's essential guide to inclusive education* (3rd ed.). Thousand Oaks, CA: Corwin Press.

Hanson, M. J., & Lynch, E. W. (2013). *Understanding families: Supportive approaches to diversity, disability, and risk* (2nd ed.). Baltimore, MD: Paul H. Brookes Publishing.

Hardin, C. J. (2012). *Effective classroom management: Models and strategies for today's classroom* (3rd ed.). Boston: Pearson.

Hargis, C. H. (2006). *Teaching low achieving and disadvantaged students* (3rd ed.). Springfield, IL: Charles C Thomas Publishers.

Harlacher, J. E. (2015). *Designing effective classroom management*. Bloomington, IN: Marzano Research.

Henley, M. (2003). *Teaching self-control: A curriculum for responsible behavior* (2nd ed.). Bloomington, IN: Solution Tree.

Hoglund, W. L. G. (2007). School functioning in early adolescence: Gender-linked responses to peer victimization. *Journal of Educational Psychology, 99*, 683–699.

Holloman, H., & Yates, P. H. (2010). *What do you say when. . .? Best practice language for improving student behavior*. Larchmont, NY: Eye on Education.

Hoover, J. H., & Oliver, R. L. (2008). *The bullying prevention handbook* (2nd ed.). Bloomington, IN: Solution Tree.

Howard, M. (2009). *RTI from all sides: What every teacher needs to know*. Portsmouth, NH: Heinemann.

Hoy, A. W., & Weinstein, C. S. (2006). Student and teacher perspectives on classroom management. In C. M. Evertson & C. S. Weinstein (Eds.), *Handbook of classroom management: Research, practice, and contemporary issues* (pp. 181–219). Mahwah, NJ: Lawrence Erlbaum Associates.

Hunter, M. (1994). *Enhancing teaching*. New York: Macmillan.

Hyman, I.A. (1997). *School discipline and school violence*. Boston: Pearson.

Hyman, I.A., Kay, B., Tabori, A., Weber, M., Mahon, M., & Cohen, I. (2006). Bullying: Theory, research, and interventions. In C. M. Evertson & C. S. Weinstein (Eds.), *Handbook of classroom management: Research, practice, and contemporary issues* (pp. 855–884). Mahwah, NJ: Lawrence Erlbaum Associates.

Individuals with Disabilities Education Act. (1997 amendments). Washington, DC: U.S. Government Printing Office.

Jackson, R. R., & Lambert, C. (2010). *How to support struggling students.* Alexandria, VA: Association for Supervision and Curriculum Development.

Jacobs, G. M., Power, M. P., & Inn, L. W. (2003). *The teacher's sourcebook for cooperative learning.* Thousand Oaks, CA: Corwin Press.

James, A. N. (2009). *Teaching the female brain: How girls learn math and science.* Thousand Oaks, CA: Corwin Press.

James, A. N. (2015). *Teaching the male brain: How boys, think, feel, and learn in school* (2nd ed.). Thousand Oaks, CA: Corwin Press.

Jenson, W. R., Rhode, G., & Reavis, H. K. (2009). *The tough kid tool box* (2nd ed.). Eugene, OR: Pacific Northwest Publishing.

Jensen, E. (2009). *Teaching with poverty in mind.* Alexandria, VA: Association for Supervision and Curriculum Development.

Jensen, E. (2013). *Engaging students with poverty in mind: Practical strategies for raising achievement.* Alexandria, VA: Association for Supervision and Curriculum Development.

Jimerson, S. R., Nickerson, A., Mayer, M. J., & Furlong, M. J. (2012). *Handbook of school violence and school safety* (2nd ed.). New York: Taylor & Francis.

Johnson, D. W., & Johnson, F. P. (2013). *Joining together: Group theory and group skills* (11th ed.). Boston: Pearson.

Johnson, D. W., & Johnson, R. T. (2005). *Teaching students to be peacemakers* (4th ed.). Edina, MN: Interaction Book Company.

Johnson, D. W., Johnson, R. T., & Holubec, E. J. (2007). *The nuts and bolts of cooperative learning* (2nd ed.). Edina, MN: Interaction Book Company.

Johnson, D. W., Johnson, R. T., & Holubec, E. J. (2009). *Circles of learning: Cooperation in the classroom.* Edina, MN: Interaction Book Company.

Johnston, P. H. (2004). *Choice words: How our language affects children's learning.* Portland, ME: Stenhouse Publishers.

Jolliffe, W. (2007). *Cooperative learning in the classroom: Putting it into practice.* Thousand Oaks, CA: Sage Publications.

Jones, F. H. (1987). *Positive classroom discipline.* New York: McGraw-Hill.

Jones, F. H. (2013). *Tools for teaching* (3rd ed.). Santa Cruz, CA: Frederic H. Jones & Associates.

Jones, T. G., & Fuller, M. L. (2003). *Teaching Hispanic children.* Boston: Pearson.

Jones, V. F. (2011). *Practical classroom management.* Boston: Pearson.

Jones, V. F., & Jones, L. S. (2016). *Comprehensive classroom management: Creating communities of support and solving problems* (11th ed.). Boston: Pearson.

Jonson, K. F. (2010). *The new elementary teacher's handbook: Flourishing in your first year* (3rd ed.). Thousand Oaks, CA: Corwin Press.

Kagan, S., Kyle, P., & Scott, S. (2004). *Win–win discipline.* San Clemente, CA: Kagan Publishing.

Kaiser, B., & Rasminsky, J. S. (2017). *Challenging behavior in young children: Understanding, preventing, and responding effectively* (4th ed.). Boston: Pearson.

Kapalka, G. (2009). *8 steps to classroom management success: A guide for teachers of challenging students.* Thousand Oaks, CA: Corwin Press.

Karnes, F. A., & Stephens, K. R. (2008). *Achieving excellence: Educating the gifted and talented.* Boston: Pearson.

Kelly, M. (2010). *The everything new teacher book* (2nd ed.). Avon, MA: Adams Media.

Kerr, M. M., & Nelson, C. M. (2010). *Strategies for addressing behavior problems in the classroom* (6th ed.). Boston: Pearson.

Khalsa, S. S. (2007a). *Break the bully cycle: Intervention techniques and activities to create a respectful school community.* Tucson, AZ: Good Year Books.

Khalsa, S. S. (2007b). *Teaching discipline and self-respect.* Thousand Oaks, CA: Corwin Press.

Knapp, M. L., & Hall, J. A. (2014). *Nonverbal communication in human interaction* (8th ed.). Boston: Cengage.

Kochhar-Bryant, C. A., & Heishman, A. (2010). *Effective collaboration for educating the whole child.* Thousand Oaks, CA: Corwin Press.

Kohn, A. (1999). *Punished by rewards* (Rev. ed.). Boston: Houghton Mifflin.

Kohn, A. (2006). *Beyond discipline: From compliance to community* (10th anniversary ed.). Alexandria, VA: Association for Supervision and Curriculum Development.

Korb, R. (2012). *Motivating defiant and disruptive students to learn: Positive classroom management strategies.* Thousand Oaks, CA: Corwin Press.

Kottler, E., Kottler, J. A., & Street, C. (2008). *English language learners in your classroom* (3rd ed.). Thousand Oaks, CA: Corwin Press.

Kottler, J. A., & Kottler, E. (2007). *Counseling skills for teachers* (2nd ed.). Thousand Oaks, CA: Corwin Press.

Kounin, J. S. (1970). *Discipline and group management in classrooms.* New York: Holt, Rinehart & Winston.

Kronowitz, E. L. (2012). *The teacher's guide to success* (2nd ed.). Boston: Pearson.

Ladson-Billings, G. (2009). *The dreamkeepers: Successful teachers of African American children* (2nd ed.). San Francisco: Jossey-Bass.

Larmer, J., Mergendoller, J., & Boss, S. (2015). *Setting the standard for project based learning*. Alexandria, VA: Association for Supervision and Curriculum Development.

Larrivee, B. (2009). *Authentic classroom management: Creating a learning community and building reflective practice* (3rd ed.). Boston: Pearson.

Lassonde, C. A., Israel, S. E., & Almasi, J. F. (2009). *Teacher collaboration for professional learning: Facilitating study, research, and inquiry communities*. San Francisco: Jossey-Bass.

Leathers, D., & Eaves, M. H. (2008). *Successful nonverbal communication: Principles and applications* (4th ed.). Boston: Pearson.

Lee, J. S., & Bowen, N. K. (2006). Parent involvement, cultural capital, and the achievement gap among elementary school children. *American Educational Research Journal*, 43, 193–218.

Levin, J., & Nolan, J. F. (2014). *Principles of classroom management* (7th ed.). Boston: Pearson.

Levine, D. A. (2003). *Building classroom communities: Strategies for developing a culture of caring*. Bloomington, IN: Solution Tree.

Lindberg, J. A., & Swick, A. M. (2006). *Common-sense classroom management for elementary school teachers* (2nd ed.). Thousand Oaks, CA: Corwin Press.

Lundy, K. G., & Swartz, L. (2011). *Creating caring classrooms: How to encourage students to communicate, create, and be compassionate of others*. Markham, Ontario, Canada: Pembroke Publishers. (Distributed in the U.S. by Stenhouse Publishers).

Lynch, E. W., & Hanson, M. J. (Eds.). (2011). *Developing cross-cultural competence: A guide for working with children and their families* (4th ed.). Baltimore, MD: Paul H. Brookes Publishing.

MacKenzie, R. J., & Stanzione, L. E. (2010). *Setting limits in the classroom: A complete guide to effective classroom management with a school-wide discipline plan* (3rd ed.). New York: Three Rivers Press.

Manning, M. L., & Bucher, K. T. (2013). *Classroom management: Models, applications, and cases* (3rd ed.). Boston: Pearson.

Marlowe, M. J., & Hayden, T. (2013). *Teaching children who are hard to reach: Relationship-driven classroom practice*. Thousand Oaks, CA: Corwin Press.

Marshall, M. L. (2012). *Discipline without stress, punishments, or rewards: How teachers and parents promote responsibility and learning* (2nd ed. revised). Los Alamitos, CA: Piper Press.

Marzano, R. J. (2007). *The art and science of teaching: A comprehensive framework for effective instruction*. Alexandria, VA: Association for Supervision and Curriculum Development.

Marzano, R. J., Gaddy, B. B., Foseid, M. C., Foseid, M. P., & Marzano, J. S. (2009). *A handbook for classroom management that works*. Boston: Pearson.

Marzano, R. J., Marzano, J. S., & Pickering, D. J. (2003). *Classroom management that works: Research-based strategies for every teacher*. Alexandria, VA: Association for Supervision and Curriculum Development.

Mazur, A. J., & Doran, P. R. (2010). *Teaching diverse learners: Principles for best practice*. Thousand Oaks, CA: Corwin Press.

McEwan, E. K. (2005). *How to deal with parents who are angry, troubled, afraid, or just plain crazy* (2nd ed.). Thousand Oaks, CA: Corwin Press.

McEwan, E. K. (2006). *How to survive and thrive in the first three weeks of school*. Thousand Oaks, CA: Corwin Press.

McEwan, E. K. (2007). *40 ways to support struggling readers in content classrooms, grades 6–12*. Thousand Oaks, CA: Corwin Press.

Mendler, A. N., & Curwin, R. L. (2007). *Discipline with dignity for challenging youth* (Rev. ed.). Bloomington, IN: Solution Tree.

Mendler, B. D., Curwin, R. L., & Mendler, A. N. (2008). *Strategies for successful classroom management*. Thousand Oaks, CA: Corwin Press.

Mertler, C. A. (2014). *Action research: Improving schools and empowering educators* (4th ed.). Thousand Oaks, CA: Sage.

Middleton, M., & Perks, K. (2014). *Motivation to learn: Transforming classroom culture to support student achievement*. Thousand Oaks, CA: Corwin Press.

Mierzwik, D. (2005). *Classroom record keeping made simple*. Thousand Oaks, CA: Corwin Press.

Miller, M. D., Linn, R. L., & Gronlund, N. E. (2013). *Measurement and assessment in teaching* (11th ed.). Boston: Pearson.

Miller, P. W. (2005). *Body language: An illustrated introduction for teachers*. Munster, IN: Patrick W. Miller & Associates.

Miltenberger, R. G. (2016). *Behavior modification* (6th ed.). Belmont, CA: Wadsworth, Cengage Learning.

Mooney, C. G. (2005). *Use your words: How teacher talk helps children learn*. St. Paul, MN: Redleaf Press.

Moran, C., Stobbe, J., Baron, W., Miller, J., & Moir, E. (2009). *Keys to the elementary classroom: A new teacher's guide to the first month of school* (3rd ed.). Thousand Oaks, CA: Corwin Press.

Morgan, D. P., Young, K. R., West, R. P., & Smith, D. J. (2012). *Teaching self-management strategies to adolescents* (2nd ed.). Frederick, CO: Cambium Learning Group/Sopris.

Murawski, W. W. (2009). *Collaborative teaching in secondary schools*. Thousand Oaks, CA: Corwin Press.

Murawski, W. W., & Spencer, S. (2011). *Collaborate, communicate, and differentiate! How to increase student learning in today's diverse schools.* Thousand Oaks, CA: Corwin Press.

National Center for Education Statistics (NCES). (2007). Crime, *violence, discipline, and safety in U.S. public schools: Findings from the school survey on crime and safety—2005–06.* Washington, DC: Author. Available at http://nces.ed.gov/pubs2007/2007361.pdf.

National Center for Education Statistics (NCES). (2010). *Indicators of school crime and safety: 2010.* Washington, DC: Author. Retrieved from http://nces.ed.gov/programs/crimeindicators/crimeindicators2010/key.asp.

National Clearinghouse for English Language Acquisition (NCELA). (2008). *Title III Biennial Report 2004–2006.* Washington, DC: Author. Retrieved from www.ncela.gwu.edu/accountability.

National Clearinghouse for English Language Acquisition (NCELA). (2009). *The growing numbers of limited English proficient students.* Washington, DC: Author. Retrieved from www.ncela.gwu.edu/faqs/view/4.

National Institute of Mental Health. (2013). *Attention deficit hyperactivity disorder.* Washington, DC: Author. Retrieved from http://www.nimh.nih.gov/health/publications/attention-deficit-hyperactivity-disorder-easy-to-read/index.shtml.

National PTA. (2000). *Building successful partnerships: A guide for developing parent and family involvement programs.* Bloomington, IN: Solution Tree.

Nelsen, J. (2006). *Positive discipline* (Rev. ed.). New York: Ballantine Books.

Nelsen, J., Lott, L., & Glenn, H. S. (2013). *Positive discipline in the classroom: Developing mutual respect, cooperation, and responsibility in your classroom* (4th ed. revised). New York: Three Rivers Press/Crown Publishing Group.

Nevin, A. I., Villa, R. A., & Thousand, J. S. (2008). *A guide to co-teaching with paraeducators: Practical tips for K–12 educators.* Thousand Oaks, CA: Corwin Press.

Newman, R. (2008). Adaptive and nonadaptive help seeking with peer harassment: An integrative perspective of coping and self-regulation. *Educational Psychologist, 42*(1), 1–15.

Nieto, S., & Bode, P. (2012). *Affirming diversity: The sociopolitical context of multicultural education* (6th ed.). Boston: Pearson.

No Child Left Behind (2002). U.S. Department of Education. www.ed.gov/nclb/landing.jhtml.

Nuri-Robins, K., Lindsey, D. B., Lindsey, R. B., & Terrell, R. D. (2011). *Culturally proficient instruction: A guide for people who teach* (3rd ed.). Thousand Oaks, CA: Corwin Press.

Oakes, J. (2005). *Keeping track: How schools structure inequality* (2nd ed.). New Haven, CT: Yale University Press.

Olender, R. A., Elias, J., & Mastroleo, R. D. (2010). *The school-home connection: Forging positive relationships with parents.* Thousand Oaks, CA: Corwin Press.

Olsen, G. W., & Fuller, M. L. (2012). *Home–school relations: Working successfully with parents and families* (4th ed.). Boston: Pearson.

Ormrod, J. E., Anderman, E. M., & Anderman, L. (2017). *Educational psychology: Developing learners* (9th ed.). Boston: Pearson.

Ost, L., & Gates, G. J. (2004). *The gay and lesbian atlas.* Washington, DC: Urban Institute.

Partin, R. L. (2009). *The classroom teacher's survival guide* (3rd ed.). San Francisco: Jossey-Bass.

Payne, R. K. (2005). *A framework for understanding poverty* (Rev. ed.). Highlands, TX: aha! Process, Inc.

Powell, R. G., & Powell, D. L. (2015). *Classroom communication and diversity: Enhancing instructional practice* (3rd ed.). New York: Routledge.

Protheroe, N., Shellard, E., & Turner, J. (2004). *Helping struggling learners in the elementary and middle grades.* Bethesda, MD: Educational Research Service.

Purkey, W. W., & Novak, J. M. (1996). *Inviting school success: A self-concept approach to teaching, learning, and democratic practice* (3rd ed.). Belmont, CA: Wadsworth.

Purkey, W. W., & Strahan, D. B. (2002). *Inviting positive classroom discipline.* Westerville, OH: National Middle School Association.

Quate, S., & McDermott, J. (2009). *Clock watchers: Six steps to motivating and engaging disengaged students across content areas.* Portsmouth, NH: Heinemann.

Raskauskas, J., & Stoltz, A. (2007). Involvement in traditional and electronic bullying among adolescents, *Developmental Psychology, 43*(3) 564–575.

Reeve, J. (2006). Extrinsic rewards and inner motivation. In C. M. Evertson & C. S. Weinstein (Eds.), *Handbook of classroom management: Research, practice, and contemporary issues* (pp. 645–664). Mahwah, NJ: Lawrence Erlbaum Associates.

Responsive Classroom. (2015). *First six weeks of school* (2nd ed.). Turners Falls, MA: Center for Responsive Schools.

Rhode, G., Jenson, W. R., & Reavis, H. K. (2010). *The tough kid book: Practical classroom management strategies* (2nd ed.) Eugene, OR: Pacific Northwest Publishing.

Richmond, V. P., McCroskey, J. C., & Hickson, M. L. (2012). *Nonverbal behavior in interpersonal relations* (7th ed.). Boston: Pearson.

Roberts, W. B. (2006). *Bullying from both sides.* Thousand Oaks, CA: Corwin Press.

Roberts, W. B. (2008). *Working with parents of bullies and victims*. Thousand Oaks, CA: Corwin Press.

Rominger, L., Hesisinger, K., & Elkin, N. (2001). *Your first year as an elementary school teacher*. New York: Three Rivers Press.

Rong, S. L., & Preissle, J. (2009). *Educating immigrant students in the 21st century: What educators need to know* (2nd ed.). Thousand Oaks, CA: Corwin Press.

Rothstein-Fisch, C., & Trumbull, E. (2008). *Managing diverse classrooms: How to build on students' cultural strengths*. Alexandria, VA: Association for Supervision and Curriculum Development.

Sadker, D. M., & Silber, E. S. (2007). *Gender in the classroom: Foundations, skills, methods, and strategies across the curriculum*. Mahwah, NJ: Lawrence Erlbaum Associates.

Salend, S. J. (2016). *Creating inclusive classrooms: Effective, differentiated, and reflective practices* (8th ed.). Boston: Pearson.

Sanders, M. G. (2006). *Building school-community partnerships: Collaboration for student success*. Thousand Oaks, CA: Corwin Press.

Sapon-Shevin, M. (2007). *Widening the circle: The power of inclusive classrooms*. Boston: Beacon Press.

Sapon-Shevin, M. (2010). *Because we can change the world: A practical guide to building cooperative, inclusive classroom communities* (2nd ed.) Thousand Oaks, CA: Corwin Press.

Schell, L. M., & Burden, P. R. (2006). *Countdown to the first day of school* (3rd ed.). Washington, DC: National Education Association.

Schunk, D. H., Meece, J. R., & Pintrich, P. R. (2014). *Motivation in education: Theory, research, and applications* (4th ed.). Boston: Pearson.

Shae, T. M., & Bauer, A. (2012). *Behavior management: A practical approach for educators* (10th ed.). Boston: Pearson.

Shostak, R. (2014). *Involving students in learning*. In J. M. Cooper (Ed.), Classroom teaching skills (10th ed.). Belmont, CA: Wadsworth, Cengage Learning.

Silver, H. F., Strong, R. W., & Perini, M. J. (2000). *So each may learn: Integrating learning styles and multiple intelligences*. Alexandria, VA: Association for Supervision and Curriculum Development.

Siris, K., & Osterman, K. (2004). Interrupting the cycle of bullying and victimization in the elementary classroom. *Phi Delta Kappan*, 86(4), 288–291.

Skinner, B. F. (1971). *Beyond freedom and dignity*. New York: Knopf.

Slavin, R. E. (2015). *Educational psychology: Theory and practice* (11th ed.). Boston: Pearson.

Smith, D., Fisher, D., & Frey, N. (2015). *Better than carrots or sticks: Restorative practices for positive classroom management*. Alexandria, VA: Association for Supervision and Curriculum Development.

Smith, T. E., Polloway, E. A., Patton, J. R., Dowdy, C. A., & Doughty, T. T. (2016). *Teaching students with special needs in inclusive settings* (7th ed.). Boston: Pearson.

Smutny, J. F., & von Fremd, S. (2009). *Igniting creativity in gifted learners, K–6*. Thousand Oaks, CA: Corwin Press.

Smutny, J. F., & von Fremd, S. (2011). *Teaching advanced learners in the general education classroom*. Thousand Oaks, CA: Corwin Press.

Sousa, D. A. (2009). *How the gifted brain learns* (2nd ed.). Thousand Oaks, CA: Corwin Press.

Sousa, D. A. (2011). *How the brain learns* (4th ed.). Thousand Oaks, CA: Corwin Press.

Sprick, R. S. (2013). *Discipline in the secondary classroom: A positive approach to behavior management* (3rd ed.). San Francisco: Jossey-Bass.

Stein, J., Meltzer, L., Krishnan, K., Pollica, L. S., Papadopoulos, I., & Roditi, B. (2007). *Parent guide to hassle-free homework*. New York: Scholastic.

Steinberg, L. (2014). *Adolescence* (10th ed.). New York: McGraw-Hill.

Stepanek, J., Appel, G., Leong, M., Mangan, M.T., & Mitchell, M. (2007). *Leading lesson study: A practical guide for teachers and facilitators*. Thousand Oaks, CA: Corwin Press.

Stobbe, M. (2007, December 4). *Studies suggest online harassment of children is on the rise*. Salt Lake Tribune, p. E4.

Sullo, B. (2009). *The motivated student: Unlocking the enthusiasm for learning*. Alexandria, VA: Association for Supervision and Curriculum Development.

Swearer, S. M., Espelage, D. L., & Napolitano, S. A. (2009). *Bullying prevention and intervention: Realistic strategies for schools*. New York: Guilford Press.

Thompson, G. L. (2007a). *Through ebony eyes: What teachers need to know but are afraid to ask about African American students*. San Francisco: Jossey-Bass.

Thompson, G. L. (2007b). *Up where we belong: Helping African American and Latino students rise in school and life*. San Francisco: Jossey-Bass.

Thompson, G. L., & Thompson, R. (2014). *Yes, you can! Advice for teachers who want a great start and a great finish with their students of color*. Thousand Oaks, CA: Corwin Press.

Thompson, J. G. (2009). *The first-year teacher's checklist*. San Francisco: Jossey-Bass.

Thompson, J. G. (2011). *Discipline survival guide for the secondary teacher* (2nd ed.). San Francisco: Jossey-Bass.

Thompson, J. G. (2013). *First-year teacher's survival guide* (3rd ed.). San Francisco: Jossey-Bass.

Tileston, D. W., & Darling, S. K. (2008). *Why culture counts: Teaching children of poverty*. Bloomington, IN: Solution Tree.

Tomlinson, C. A. (2014). *The differentiated classroom: Responding to the needs of all learners* (2nd ed.). Alexandria, VA: Association for Supervision and Curriculum Development.

Tomlinson, C. A., & Imbeau, M. B. (2010). *Leading and managing a differentiated classroom*. Alexandria, VA: Association for Supervision and Curriculum Development.

Turnbull, A. A., Turnbull, H. R., Erwin, E. J., Soodak, L. C., & Shogren, K. A. (2015). *Families, professionals, and exceptionality* (7th ed.). Boston: Pearson.

Turnbull, A. A., Turnbull, H. R., Wehmeyer, M. L., & Shogren, K. A. (2016). *Exceptional lives: Special education in today's schools* (8th ed.). Boston: Pearson.

Udvari-Solner, A., & Kluth, P. (2008). *Joyful learning: Active and collaborative learning in inclusive classrooms*. Thousand Oaks, CA: Corwin Press.

U.S. Department of Education. (2011a). *Effects of bullying*. Retrieved from http://www.stopbullying.gov/topics/risk_factors.html.

U.S. Department of Education. (2011b). *Know the risk factors before bullying begins*. Retrieved from http://www.stopbullying.gov/topics/risk_factors.html

Vaughn, S., & Bos, C. S. (2015). *Strategies for teaching students with learning and behavior problems* (9th ed.). Boston: Pearson.

Vaughn, S., Bos, C. S., & Schumm, J. S. (2014). *Teaching students who are exceptional, diverse, and at-risk in the general education classroom* (6th ed.). Boston: Pearson.

Venables, D. R. (2011). *The practice of authentic PLCs: A guide to effective teacher teams*. Thousand Oaks, CA: Corwin Press.

Viadero, D. (2003). Two studies highlight links between violence, bullying by student. *Education Week, 22*(36), 6.

Villa, R. A., Thousand, J. S., & Nevin, A. I. (2010). *Collaborating with students in instruction and decision making*. Thousand Oaks, CA: Corwin Press.

Villa, R. A., Thousand, J. S., & Nevin, A. I. (2013). *A guide to co-teaching: Practical tips for facilitating student learning* (3rd ed.). Thousand Oaks, CA: Corwin Press.

Weinstein, C. S., & Novodvorsky, I. (2015). *Middle and secondary classroom management: Lessons from research and practice* (5th ed.). New York: McGraw-Hill.

Weinstein, C. S., & Romano, M. E. (2015). *Elementary classroom management: Lessons from research and practice* (6th ed.). New York: McGraw-Hill.

Wentzel, K. R., & Brophy, J. E. (2014). *Motivating students to learn* (4th ed.). New York: Routledge.

Willard, N. (2006). *Cyberbullying and cyberthreats: Responding to the challenge of online social cruelty, threats, and distress*. Eugene, OR: Center for Safe and Responsible Internet Use.

Winslade, J., & Williams, M. (2011). *Safe and peaceful schools: Addressing conflict and eliminating violence*. Thousand Oaks, CA: Corwin Press.

Wolfgang, C. H. (2009). *Solving discipline and classroom management problems* (7th ed.). Hoboken, NJ: John Wiley & Sons.

Wong, H. K., & Wong, R. T. (2009). *The first days of school: How to be an effective teacher* (4th ed.). Mountain View, CA: Harry Wong Publications.

Wong, H. K., & Wong, R. T. (2014). *The classroom management book*. Mountain View, CA: Harry Wong Publications.

Wood, C. (2007). *Yardsticks: Children in the classroom, ages 4–14* (3rd ed.). Turners Falls, MA: Center for Responsive Schools.

Woolfolk, A. (2016). *Educational psychology* (13th ed.). Boston: Pearson.

Wyatt, R. L., & White, J. E. (2007). *Making your first year a success: A classroom survival guide for middle and high school teachers* (2nd ed.). Thousand Oaks, CA: Corwin Press.

Name Index

Subject Index